D1707643

Antifraternalism and Anticlericalism in the German Reformation

St Andrews Studies in Reformation History

Editorial Board:

Andrew Pettegree, Bruce Gordon and John Guy

Titles in this series include:

The Shaping of a Community: The Rise and Reformation of the English Parish c. 1400–1560
Beat Kümin

Seminary or University? The Genevan Academy and Reformed Higher Education, 1560–1620
Karin Maag

Protestant History and Identity in Sixteenth-Century Europe
(2 volumes)
edited by Bruce Gordon

Marian Protestantism: Six Studies
Andrew Pettegree

Forthcoming:

Reformations Old and New: Essays on the Socio-Economic Impact of Religious Change c. 1470–1630
Beat Kümin

Piety and the People: Religious Printing in French, 1511–51
Francis Higman

Antifraternalism and Anticlericalism in the German Reformation

Johann Eberlin von Günzburg and the Campaign against the Friars

GEOFFREY DIPPLE

SCOLAR PRESS

WITHDRAWN
HIEBERT LIBRARY
FRESNO PACIFIC UNIV.-M. B. SEMINARY
FRESNO, CA 93702

© Geoffrey Dipple, 1996

All rights reserved. No part of this publication may be reproduced, stored in a retrieval system, or transmitted in any form or by any means, electronic, mechanical, photocopying, recording, or otherwise without the prior permission of the publisher.

Published by
SCOLAR PRESS
Gower House
Croft Road
Aldershot
Hants GU11 3HR
England

Ashgate Publishing Company
Old Post Road
Brookfield
Vermont 05036–9704
USA

British Library Cataloguing in Publication Data

Dipple, Geoffrey
  Antifraternalism and Anticlericalism in the German Reformation : Johann Eberlin
  von Günzburg and the Campaign against the Friars.
  (St Andrews Studies in Reformation History)
  1. Friars — Germany — History — 16th century. 2. Reformation — Germany —
  History. 3. Germany — History — 1517–1648.
  I. Title
  274.3'06

  ISBN 1–85928–267–9

Library of Congress Cataloging-in-Publication Data

Dipple, Geoffrey
  Antifraternalism and Anticlericalism in the German Reformation :
  Johann Eberlin von Günzburg and the Campaign against the Friars / Geoffrey
  Dipple.
      p.   cm. (St Andrews Studies in Reformation History)
  Includes bibliographical references and index.
  ISBN 1–85928–267–9 (cloth)
    1. Eberlin von Günzburg, Johann, ca. 1470–1533. 2. Reformation — Germany.
  3. Reformation — Switzerland, German-speaking. 4. Friars — Germany — History
  — 16th century. 5. Friars — Switzerland, German-speaking — History — 16th
  century. 6. Anticlericalism — Germany — History — 16th century.
  7. Anticlericalism — Switzerland — History — 16th century. 8. Germany —
  Church history — 16th century. 9. Switzerland, German-speaking — Church
  history — 16th century.
  I. Title. II. Series.
  BR350. E24D57   1996
  274.3'06 — dc20   95–53936
                                                                        CIP
  ISBN 1 85928 267 9

Typeset in Sabon by Photoprint, Torquay, Devon
and printed in Great Britain by The University Press, Cambridge

Contents

For Joseph and Benjamin

Acknowledgements

This study began as a doctoral dissertation at Queen's University at Kingston (Canada). Queen's generously provided the financial support which made graduate study possible. This was supplemented by a fellowship from the Social Sciences and Humanities Research Council of Canada. A fellowship from the German Academic Exchange Service (DAAD) made possible a year of study and research in Germany which was crucial for a proper investigation of this topic. Much of that year was spent in tracking down a large number of sources not generally available to North American students of the Reformation. Special thanks are due to the staff of the Ulm Stadtarchiv, without whose help this task would have verged on the impossible. I have also relied heavily on the resources of the Hamburg Universitätsbibliothek and, after my return to Canada, the Centre for Reformation and Renaissance Studies at Victoria University, in the University of Toronto. Elements of chapter seven were published in *Mennonitische Geschichtsblätter* in 1993, and a version of chapter six is appearing in *Franciscan Studies* in 1996. Thanks are due to the publishers of these journals for permission to use this material here.

The debts which I have accrued to individuals far outweigh those to institutions. Professor Hans-Jürgen Goertz provided much-needed encouragement and opened many doors during my year in Hamburg. Since then his encouragement and stimulating responses to my queries have been invaluable in my attempts to understand Reformation anticlericalism and its place in the events of the early sixteenth century. Professor Werner Packull first called my attention to the relationship between Eberlin, Kettenbach and Rot-Locher and hence set the whole process in motion. Professors Christopher Crowder and Catherine Brown read parts of the manuscript and offered valuable comments as general readers and experienced medievalists. Professor Bruce Gordon at St Andrews and Caroline Cornish at Scolar Press have gone above and beyond the call of duty in helping to transform the dissertation into a book. A special thanks is owed to my dissertation supervisor, Professor James M. Stayer, who provided patient, careful supervision during the writing of the dissertation, and more recently has been no less generous in offering editorial advice. Finally, I wish to express my thanks to my family. My wife, Sharon Judd, has not only been a constant source of support and encouragement, but also has been involved in the development of this project at every stage as an editor, typist and technical adviser. Our sons, Joseph and Benjamin, have been at least tolerant of the demands placed on the family by this book.

List of abbreviations

ADB	Allgemeine Deutsche Biographie
ARG	Archiv für Reformationsgeschichte
BbKG	Beiträge zur bayerischen Kirchengeschichte
Berger	Arnold E. Berger (ed.), *Sturmtruppen der Reformation. Ausgewählte Schriften der Jahre 1520–1525* (Leipzig: Phillip Reclam jun. Verlag, 1931)
Böcking	Eduard Böcking (ed.), *Vlrichi Hvtteni Equitis Germani Opera Quae Reperiri Potuerunt Omnia* (7 vols, Leipzig: B.G. Teubner, 1859–1861; reprint edn, Aalen: Otto Zeller Verlagsbuchhandlung, 1963)
Clemen	Otto Clemen (ed.), *Die Schriften Heinrichs von Kettenbach*. Flugschriften aus den ersten Jahren der Reformation, vol. 2, Book 1 (Halle: Rudolf Haupt Verlag, 1907)
Dykema and Oberman	Peter Dykema and Heiko Oberman (eds), *Anticlericalism in Late Medieval and Early Modern Europe* (Leiden: E.J. Brill, 1993)
Enders	Ludwig Enders (ed.), *Johann Eberlin von Günzburg, Ausgewählte Schriften*, vol. 1. Flugschriften aus der Reformationszeit, vol. 11 (Halle: Max Niemeyer, 1896); *Johann Eberlin von Günzburg, Sämtliche Schriften*, vol. 2. Flugschriften aus der Reformationszeit, vol. 15 (1900); *Johann Eberlin von Günzburg, Sämtliche Schriften*, vol. 3, Flugschriften aus der Reformationszeit, vol. 18 (1902)
Köhler *et al.*	Hans-Joachim Köhler *et al.*, *Early Modern Pamphlets: Sixteenth-Century German and Latin, 1501–1530* (Zug, Switzerland: Interdocumentation Co.), 1980ff.
Laube	Adolf Laube *et al.* (eds), *Flugschriften der frühen Reformationsbewegung (1518–1524)* (2 vols, Berlin Akademie-Verlag, 1983)
NDB	Neue Deutsche Biographie
WA	*D. Martin Luthers Werke. Kritische Gesamtausgabe* (64 vols, Weimar: Hermann Böhlau, 1883ff.)
WABr	*D. Martin Luthers Werke. Kritische Gesamtausgabe.*

Briefwechsel (11 vols, Weimar: Hermann Böhlau, 1930–1948)

ZbKG	Zeitschrift für bayerische Kirchengeschichte
ZKG	Zeitschrift für Kirchengeschichte

Introduction

In the pamphlet 'Against the False Religious known as the Barefoot Friars or Franciscans,' penned in the spring of 1523, an apostate Franciscan from Ulm, Johann Eberlin von Günzburg, wrote of St Francis:

> If its founder was so foolish to think that this Rule is the Gospel and was thereby deceived and deceived others, then he is indeed a great and harmful fool, . . . If, however, he knew that this rule is not the Gospel and, nonetheless, introduced this deceit into the world, then he is an arch-rogue, . . .[1]

Although the sharpest in his criticism, Eberlin was not the only former Franciscan to turn his pen on the order in the first half of 1523. On 27 February, Johannes Schwan completed 'An Epistle, in Which He Shows from the Bible and Scripture Why He Left the Franciscan Order in Whose Cloister at Basel He Formerly Was.'[2] Also in February, Francis Lambert of Avignon wrote 'The Reasons why He Rejects the Status of and Association with the Minors,' and in March, he began writing 'An Evangelical Description of the Franciscan Rule.'[3] During the same month a response by Johannes Briesmann to Caspar Schatzgeyer, the south German provincial of the Franciscan Observants who had written against Luther's 'Judgement on Monastic Vows,' was printed in Wittenberg.[4] Thereafter, the polemics became more virulent and more

---

[1] Eberlin, 'Wider die falschen Geistlichen, genannt die Barfüsser und Franziskaner,' Enders, vol. 3, p. 65.

[2] 'Ein Sendbriff Johannis Schwan. Darinne er anzeigt ausz der Bibel und Schryfft warüb er Barfusser orden des er etwan ym kloster zů Bassell gewest verlassen,' in Köhler et al., F 1186, #2980, Biii(c).

[3] Roy L. Winters, *Francis Lambert of Avignon (1487–1530): A Study in Reformation Origins* (Philadelphia, 1938), p. 45; Lambert, 'Rationes, propter quas Minoritarum conversationem habitumque reiecit,' Köhler et al., F 779, #1959. Edmund Kurten, *Franz Lambert von Avignon und Nikolaus Herborn in ihrer Stellung zum Ordensgedanken und zum Franziskanertum im Besonderen* (Münster, 1950), pp. 61–2; Lambert, 'Ein Evangelische beschreibung über der Barfüsser Regel,' Köhler et al., F 378, #1050; Christian Peters, *Johann Eberlin von Günzburg ca. 1465–1533. Fanziskanischer Reformer, Humanist und konservativer Reformator.* Quellen und Forschungen zur Reformationsgeschichte 60 (Gütersloh, 1994), pp. 156–7; WA, 11:457.

[4] Briesmann, 'Ad Gasparis Schatzgeyri plicas responsio pro Lutherano libello de Missis et Votis Monasticis,' Köhler et al., F 374, #1042, p. 42. See also WA, 11: 282; Peters, p. 125.

detailed, and the object of attack was expanded to include the mendicants and, in some cases, the cloistered in general. Eberlin's 'A Second True Admonition to the Council of Ulm,' written between 16 April and 23 May, identifies the Franciscans and Dominicans as the chief opponents of reform in the imperial city, and develops several themes which foreshadow the contents of his 'Against the False Religious.'[5] Shortly thereafter, Heinrich Spelt completed 'A True Declaration or Explanation of the Profession, Vows and Life which the Coloured, False Religious Pursue Against Evangelical Freedom and Christian Love.'[6] Sometime during this period Johannes Schwan returned to the fray with 'A Brief Explanation of the Frightful Estate of the Monks;'[7] and Eberlin's 'Against the False Religious,' although not published until early 1524, was written between May and July 1523.[8] Closely related to this group of pamphlets is 'A Sermon on the Eighth Sunday after Pentecost' by Heinrich von Kettenbach.[9]

Besides their temporal proximity, there are good reasons to treat these pamphlets as a unity and clear indications that they constitute a concerted assault by adherents of the Reformation on the Franciscans, and ultimately, on the regular clergy as a whole. Schwan, Lambert, Briesmann and Eberlin were all living and writing in Wittenberg in the spring of 1523. Eberlin and Kettenbach may have been acquainted as members of the Franciscan Observant cloister in Ulm and, after he left the imperial city, Eberlin continued to refer to the activities of Kettenbach on behalf of the Gospel there.[10] At the end of his defence for leaving the order, Lambert informed his readers that 'our commentaries on their Rule' would be available shortly.[11] Spelt claimed that he and others had been commissioned by God to write against the evils of monasticism.[12] And Eberlin prayed that his and the other works would open the eyes of those led astray among the Franciscans.[13] Certainly,

---

[5] Eberlin, 'Die andere getreue Vermahnung an den Rath von Ulm,' Enders, vol. 3, pp. 3 and 40.

[6] Enders, vol. 3, p. xx; Spelt, 'Ain ware Declaration oder Erklärung der Profession / Gelübten uñ leben / So die gemalten / Falschen / Gaystlichenn / wider alle Ewangelische freyhayt Und Christliche lyeb / thůn /,' Köhler et al., F 47, #131.

[7] Schwan, 'Ein kurtzer begriff des Erschrocklichē stands der munch / . . .' Köhler et al., F 208, #593.

[8] 'Wider die falschen Geistlichen,' Enders, vol. 3, pp. 70, 88; Peters, pp. 160, 170.

[9] Kettenbach, 'Eine Predigt auf den achten Sonntag nach dem Pfingsttag,' Clemen, pp. 214–24. Although not printed until 1525, the contents of this sermon suggest that it was written to supplement the other attacks on the Franciscans. See below, pp. 181–2.

[10] Eberlin, 'Die andere getreue Vermahnung an den Rath von Ulm,' p. 38.

[11] 'Rationes propter quas,' Köhler et al., F 779, #1959, A4(c)–A4(d).

[12] Spelt, 'Ain ware Declaration oder Erklärung', Aii.

[13] 'Wider die falschen Geistlichen,' Enders, vol. 3, p. 49; Peters, p. 162.

Caspar Schatzgeyer saw these works as a unity. In late 1523 he responded to Briesmann and in March 1524 he answered Spelt, Lambert and Eberlin as a group.[14] Luther had specifically commissioned Briesmann to respond to Schatzgeyer. Schwan indicates the proximity of the other pamphlets to Briesmann's when he cites Schatzgeyer's response to Luther as an indication that the provincial minister is an 'unlettered papist.'[15]

It was, therefore, Schatzgeyer's defence of the monastic life, and the hardening of lines between the Evangelicals and Franciscans which it heralded, that called forth these polemics.[16] The occurrence of a showdown between the Reformers and the Franciscans in 1523 is hardly surprising. As a prominent and powerful corporation within the old church, the Franciscans were a natural target for the barbs of the Reformers. And examples of such conflict come readily to mind: for example, Luther's exchanges with Alveld or Müntzer's with the Franciscans in Jüterbog and Zwickau. Yet, the 1523 campaign against the order deserves special attention. Although only a few of the participants in it ever made it into the circle of Luther's closest intimates, all were well versed in his writings and considered themselves adherents of the movement he led. Furthermore, as responses to Schatzgeyer's answer to Luther's 'Judgement on Monastic Vows,' their writings deal necessarily with the Reformer's critique of the cloistered life. We have here, then, an early attempt to apply Luther's teaching to a concrete situation, and a valuable opportunity to study the dissemination and reception of that teaching.

To date, historians have tended to ignore this broadside against the Franciscans. Investigations of the works of individual authors involved in it have pointed to similarities between their writings.[17] However, no synthetic analysis of these polemics as a group has been forthcoming.

---

[14] Max Radlkofer, *Johann Eberlin von Günzburg und sein Vetter Hans Jakob Wehe von Leipheim* (Nördlingen, 1887), p. 117; Nikolaus Paulus, *Kaspar Schatzgeyer, ein Vorkämpfer der katholischen Kirche gegen Luther in Süddeutschland* (Strasbourg, 1898), pp. 66–7.

[15] 'Ein Sendbriff Johannis Schwan,' Aiii(c). On Luther's relationship to the campaign of 1523, see below, pp. 132–4.

[16] On the developing response of the Franciscans to Luther, especially within the south German province, see below, pp. 133–4.

[17] Enders, vol. 3, pp. xix–xxiii suggested a relationship between these pamphlets and linked them to Schatzgeyer's responses to Luther. Referring to a special campaign of the Reformers against Franciscanism, Edmund Kurten, pp. viii and 39, has suggested similarities between the writings of Lambert, Eberlin and Schwan. Most recently Peters, pp. 154–72, has noted the temporal convergence of, and the similarities of content between, the writings of Eberlin, Lambert, Schwann, Briesmann and Spelt, which he classifies together as a literary event.

This oversight mirrors a broader neglect of the place of the Franciscans and other mendicant orders in the history of the Reformation. Although individual friars who played prominent roles in the Reformation have been the subject of numerous books and articles, the orders as a whole continue to receive only passing attention. Ulrich von Hutten's initial judgement of the controversy surrounding Luther as a 'monkish squabble' between orders of friars appears, however, to have borne some fruit. The initial prominence of the Dominicans among Luther's opponents has won them a place of honour in the annals of the Counter-Reformation, while Luther's own allegiance has fuelled an ongoing debate about the existence of a school of late medieval Augustinianism both within and outside of the Augustinian order.[18] On the other hand, the Carmelites are conspicuous by their absence from Reformation studies and the Franciscans as a whole fare little better. Ranke noted that a number of Franciscans turned to the new teaching but, unlike the Augustinians, were unsupported by their order.[19] Beyond these scattered references, the mendicant orders remain on the periphery of Reformation studies. On the other side of the fence, until recently studies of the friars in the later Middle Ages have refused to bridge the gap to the history of the Reformation.[20]

In the absence of detailed research into the mendicant orders on the eve of the Reformation, analysis of the criticism of the friars has traditionally taken the claims of the Reformers at face value. Charges of immorality and relaxed discipline within the mendicant cloisters have been seen as yet another example of the decadence of the late medieval church. However, subsequent research now makes such conclusions

---

[18] Nikolaus Paulus, *Die deutschen Dominikaner im Kampf gegen Luther* (Freiburg, 1903). For a summary of the debate on late medieval Augustinianism, see David Steinmetz, *Luther and Staupitz: An Essay in the Intellectual Origins of the Protestant Reformation* (Durham, NC, 1980), pp. 13–27.

[19] Leopold von Ranke, *History of the Reformation in Germany*, trans. Sarah Austin (London, 1905), p. 278.

[20] Historians of the Franciscan order in particular have avoided dealing with the response to Luther. The recognition by Leo X of the Observance as the true sons of Francis in 1517 has provided a natural place to end accounts of the medieval history of the order. See John Moorman, *A History of the Franciscan Order from its Origins to the Year 1517* (Oxford, 1968) and Raphael Huber, *A Documented History of the Franciscan Order 1182–1517* (Milwaukee, 1944). An exception to this rule is Heribert Holzapfel, *Handbuch der Geschichte des Franziskanerordens* (Freiburg, 1909). Despite the recent interest in the fifteenth- and sixteenth-century history of the order, its response to Luther continues to be ignored. The most recent survey of reform within late medieval Franciscanism, although extending its scope to the official recognition of the Capuchins in 1528, limits itself exclusively to concern with reform of the order. See Duncan Nimmo, *Reform and Division in the Medieval Franciscan Order from St Francis to the Foundation of the Capuchins* (Rome, 1987).

untenable. Studies of the fifteenth-century reforming movements within the orders and of the friars' popularity among the laity suggest that their lives were hardly as depicted by their foes.[21] These revisions in turn call for a reassessment of the nature and effectiveness of the Reformation's campaign against the friars. Paul Nyhus has made an important start to such a reassessment with his research into the history of the south German Franciscans in the fifteenth and early sixteenth centuries. His stated purpose is to indicate 'the process by which the spiritual leaders of the thirteenth century became prime targets of criticism from the new spiritual leaders of the sixteenth century.'[22] Nyhus goes beyond the fifteenth-century efforts to reform the order and examines the responses among the Franciscans to movements aimed at reforming the church from humanist and reforming quarters. Discussions of the careers of Caspar Schatzgeyer, Thomas Murner, Conrad Pellican and Johann Eberlin von Günzburg indicate clearly the ambiguity of the term 'reform' and the fluidity of reform programmes among the Franciscans in the late fifteenth and early sixteenth centuries.[23] In this sense, Nyhus outlines clearly the appeal of the Reformation for apostate Franciscans – and I believe that we can apply his conclusions to apostates from other mendicant orders – but there remains the question of the virulence and effectiveness of the Reformation's attack on the friars. On this issue, Edmund Kurten, in his biography of Lambert, has suggested a direction for fruitful research. Alluding to the 1523 attack on the Franciscans, he suggested that the polemics in question appeared to revive themes from the conflicts between the mendicants and secular masters at the University of Paris from the middle of the thirteenth century. At stake were issues of mendicant privileges and their roles in the cure of souls, and the questions of mendicancy, of the substance of perfection and the proper imitation of Christ.[24] To be properly understood, then, these polemics require as much an analysis of relations between the friars and the secular clergy in the later Middle Ages as of the level of observance on the eve of the Reformation. Inter-clerical rivalries within the medieval church need to be weighed in the balance along with relations between the friars and the laity.

The results of investigations into criticisms of the friars in Middle

---

[21] For a discussion of the traditional perception of the level of observance among the mendicants and the revision of that perception, see below, pp. 18–25.

[22] Paul Nyhus, 'The Franciscans in South Germany, 1400–1530: Reform and Revolution,' *Transactions of the American Philosophical Society*, n.s. 65(8) (1975), p. 5.

[23] Ibid., pp. 11–43; id., 'Caspar Schatzgeyer and Conrad Pellican: The Triumph of Dissension in the Early Sixteenth Century,' ARG, 61 (1970), pp. 179–204.

[24] Kurten, pp. 138–9.

English literature may be enlightening on this issue. As late as 1955 David Knowles wrote of the medieval English antifraternal tradition:

> The close agreement, however, between Langland, Wyclif and Chaucer as to the worldliness of the monks and the rascality of the friars is too remarkable to be dismissed. It is, we may feel, only a partial picture. . . . Nevertheless, it is hard to escape the conviction that the three writers we have just reviewed are in their different ways witnesses to a corruption among the mendicants, and a worldliness among the black monks, which were only too real, whatever the limits we may put upon their extent and the severity of their incidence.[25]

However, research by scholars of several disciplines, and particularly that of Arnold Williams, has seriously challenged the assessment that this criticism reflected the contemporary corruption of the mendicant orders. Williams has indicated that Chaucer's treatment of the friars is paralleled by the picture developed of the mendicants during their conflict with the secular clergy at the University of Paris in the middle of the thirteenth century, and particularly in the writings of William of St Amour.[26] Penn Szittya has proceeded further in the investigation of such conventions in the English antifraternal traditions: 'Antifraternalism is not a straightforward tradition of political criticism as is usually thought, but a tradition of political theology, a tradition whose conventions are governed as much by eschatology, salvation history and the Bible as by political conditions in the real world of the friars.'[27] Because the friars were defined by unchanging biblical analogues, the charges brought against them continued to appear centuries later despite changed environments and contexts.[28] Medieval antifraternalism has excited much less interest outside of the English context. However, Jill Mann has indicated its importance in medieval estates satire on the Continent as well, and Hellmut Rosenfeld has called attention to this phenomenon in Middle High German literature.[29] As I shall indicate, Reformation conflicts, too, belong in this tradition of antifraternalism. This perspective on the clash with the mendicants is particularly useful

---

[25] David Knowles, *The Religious Orders in England*, vol. 2: *The End of the Middle Ages* (reprint edn, Cambridge, 1961), p. 114.

[26] Arnold Williams, 'Chaucer and the Friars,' *Speculum*, 28 (1953), pp. 499–513.

[27] Penn Szittya, 'The Antifraternal Tradition in Middle English Literature,' *Speculum*, 52 (1977), p. 288.

[28] Ibid., pp. 293–4; id., *The Antifraternal Tradition in Medieval Literature* (Princeton, NJ, 1986), pp. 184 and 200–1.

[29] Jill Mann, *Chaucer and Medieval Estates Satire: The Literature of Social Classes and the General Prologue to the Canterbury Tales* (Cambridge, 1973); Hellmut Rosenfeld, 'Die Entwicklung der Ständesatire im Mittelalter,' *Zeitschrift für Deutsche Philologie*, 71 (1951/52), pp. 196–207.

for understanding the nature of the criticism levelled at them, and the effectiveness of that criticism.

But the attack of the Reformers on the mendicant orders amounted to more than just a rehashing of old polemics. On the one hand, the charges of the Reformers are of unprecedented radicalism – unlike most of their medieval predecessors among the critics of the friars, they were willing to openly denounce the papacy and the entire ecclesiastical organization along with the friars. On the other hand, as I have indicated, their attack also developed out of Luther's theology and his criticisms of monasticism and the Catholic clergy more generally. Reformation antifraternalism, then, must be analysed in the context of Reformation antimonasticism and Reformation anticlericalism. Furthermore, as criticism of a central institution in the ecclesiastical hierarchy, the antifraternalism of the Reformation will highlight and clarify elements of the more general anticlericalism of the age.

Surprisingly little work has been done on the response to monasticism by the first-generation Reformers. Bernhard Lohse has investigated Luther's criticism of monasticism – and to a lesser extent the criticism of Melanchthon and Karlstadt – within the context of its medieval ideal. He argues for the theological novelty of Luther's attack on the institution. Robert Bast concurs, although Bast emphasizes much more than Lohse does the importance of Luther's teaching on the Law in this process. Lohse, Bast and Heinz-Meinolf Stamm agree that in his 'Judgement on Monastic Vows' Luther had not yet fully repudiated the institution of monasticism. Nonetheless, they all see in this work a significant development in Luther's criticism of vows.[30] On the other hand, Robert Scribner has called attention to the prominence of antimonasticism in propaganda for the early Reformation from its beginnings and its relationship to criticisms of the monks in popular tradition and the writings of the humanists.[31]

No less controversial, but more intensively studied, is the theme of anticlericalism in the Reformation. At the centre of current discussions of this topic remains Hans-Jürgen Goertz's *Pfaffenhaß und groß Geschrei*. In Goertz's analysis, anticlericalism and the Reformation are

---

[30] Bernhard Lohse, 'Die Kritik am Mönchtum bei Luther und Melanchthon,' in *Luther und Melanchthon*, ed. Vilmos Vatja (Göttingen, 1961), pp. 129–145 and *Mönchtum und Reformation. Luthers Auseinandersetzung mit dem Monchsideal des Mittelalters* (Göttingen, 1963). See especially p. 200 of *Mönchtum und Reformation*; Robert Bast, ' "*Je geistlicher . . . je blinder:*" Anticlericalism, the Law, and Social Ethics in Luther's Sermons on Matthew 22: 34–41,' in Dykema and Oberman, pp. 367–78; Heinz-Meinolf Stamm, *Luthers Stellung zum Ordensleben* (Wiesbaden, 1980).

[31] Robert Scribner, *For the Sake of Simple Folk: Popular Propaganda for the German Reformation* (Cambridge, 1981), p. 37.

closely intertwined. On the one hand, this concept helps to explain the popularity of Luther's message, and the heterogeneity and vitality of the early Reformation movements. According to this interpretation, Luther was able to tap into a well of anticlerical feeling, and the various movements of the early Reformation were united by a common hatred of the priests: 'The "revolt against the priests" was the beginning of the Reformation in Germany.' Furthermore, anticlericalism served as the catalyst for the mobilization of these movements; it was the bridge between 'Reformation word' and 'Reformation action.' On the other hand, Luther did not just exploit existing anticlerical sentiment in the early years of the Reformation. Rather, his anticlericalism grew out of the centre of his Reformation theology; his teaching on forensic justification rendered superfluous any priestly mediation of salvation. From the attack on indulgences through to the rejection of confession and the repudiation of orthodox theology of the mass, Luther undermined the sacramental system of the papal church and the mediatory role of the clergy in it. The distinctive ontological and social status of the first estate was thereby eroded, and traditional calls for its reform were replaced by demands for its abolition. The fully developed justification for the abolition of the priestly estate was set forth in the doctrine of the priesthood of all believers, as expounded already in Luther's famous works of 1520, 'Address to the Christian Nobility,' 'The Babylonian Captivity of the Church,' and 'On the Freedom of a Christian.'[32]

While the validity of applying the concept of anticlericalism to analysis of the Reformation has been generally accepted, Goertz's thesis has not been without its critics. Many of these have concentrated on questioning the extent to which Luther's writings can be characterized as anticlerical and what the relationship is between this anticlericalism and Luther's theology. Martin Brecht has analysed Luther's earliest reforming writings and discovered in them little that qualifies as truly anticlerical invective. Rather, Luther's statements here look much more to the reform of the first estate than its removal.[33] Similar conclusions have been reached in Bernd Moeller's analysis of Luther's 'Address to the Christian Nobility.' Moeller notes that Luther employs the doctrine of the priesthood of all believers at the outset of this pamphlet, but its purpose here is not to damn the clergy as a whole, but merely to justify

---

[32] Hans-Jürgen Goertz, *Pfaffenhaß und groß Geschrei. Die reformatorischen Bewegungen in Deutschland 1517–1529* (Munich, 1987); id., ' "What a tangled and tenuous mess the clergy is!" Clerical Anticlericalism in the Reformation Period,' in Dykema and Oberman, pp. 499–519.

[33] Martin Brecht, 'Antiklerikalismus beim jungen Luther?' in Dykema and Oberman, pp. 343–51.

Luther's call for a reform of the first estate by the second. In this sense, the 'Address to the Christian Nobility' is more antipapal and anticurial than anticlerical, and its vision of reform centres on the creation of a German national church which would strengthen episcopal and parochial authority at the expense of papal jurisdiction.[34]

Despite their criticisms of Goertz's thesis, Brecht and Moeller do not deny that Luther made statements which sound clearly anticlerical, or that anticlerical agitation played a role in the dissemination of Reformation ideas. Rather, they question the extent to which anticlericalism was integral to Luther's theology. Brecht argues that Luther's attack on the ecclesiastical hierarchy was only one element in the '95 Theses,' and, at best, only tangentially related to the more positive aspects of his theological breakthrough. It was the response of Luther's opponents which concentrated subsequent attention on the question of papal authority raised in the theses.[35] Moeller's conclusions about the 'Address to the Christian Nobility' continue to ride in tandem with Brecht's. Again, blame for the integration of Reformation theology with anticlericalism rests as much on the shoulders of Luther's Catholic opponents as on those of the Reformer himself. In their responses to the 'Address to the Christian Nobility,' Eck, Murner, Emser and Wulffer concentrated on the wider anticlerical implications of the priesthood of all believers rather than the explicit antipapalism of Luther's pamphlet. This response highlighted and drew out the most radical and sensational aspect of Luther's teaching.[36] In Brecht's and Moeller's eyes, then, Luther's Reformation theology contained only potentially anticlerical elements and only in the midst of heated controversy were these made explicit.

Similar conclusions have been reached, although with significantly different nuances, by Hans-Christoph Rublack. Rublack takes seriously Luther's criticism of the ecclesiastical hierarchy in the 'Address to the Christian Nobility,' but stresses the differences between this work and Luther's more theological writings. He admits that this work did provide the basis for an appeal to and exploitation of popular anticlericalism, but suggests that all of this was peripheral to Luther's theological message. Implicit in this argument is the perception that

---

[34] Bernd Moeller, 'Klerus und Antiklerikalismus in Luthers Schrift *An Den Christlichen Adel Deutscher Nation* von 1520,' in Dykema and Oberman, pp. 353–65. On Luther's use of the priesthood of all believers in the 'Address to the Christian Nobility,' see also David Bagchi, ' "Eyn merklich underscheyd": Catholic Reactions to Luther's Doctrine of the Priesthood of All Believers,' in W.J. Scheils and Diana Wood (eds), *The Ministry: Clerical and Lay. Studies in Church History*, 26 (Oxford, 1989), p. 155.

[35] Brecht, pp. 349–51.

[36] Moeller, 'Klerus und Antiklerikalismus,' pp. 363–5.

Luther was, indeed, not pushed to realize the radical anticlerical implications of his teaching, but that he consciously and effectively exploited existing anticlerical sentiment to suit his own purposes. Rublack concludes, therefore, that anticlericalism provided a 'certain impetus' for the Reformation and a link to its medieval past, but that it was not the primary agent in effecting the spread of the Reformation.[37]

Despite these criticisms, I believe that Goertz's thesis remains the best model for understanding Reformation anticlericalism in all of its manifestations. I have argued elsewhere that Luther did turn the doctrine of the priesthood of all believers against the clergy as a whole, but that this has been obscured by concentration on the wrong sources. Here Moeller's suggestion that the full implications of the priesthood of all believers were first drawn out by the responses to the 'Address to the Christian Nobility' has been fruitful. Particularly in the controversial exchange with Jerome Emser we can trace the evolution of Luther's polemics from attacks on specific groups of clergy, the papacy, curia and those who support them, to a general denunciation of the first estate. However, the complete explication of this new stance did not appear until shortly after Luther allowed the conflict with Emser to drop, in 'On the Misuse of the Mass,' in a context directly related to the central themes of the Reformation theology, as Goertz has suggested.[38] With the rejection of the orthodox theology of the mass went necessarily a repudiation of the priesthood performing the mass.[39] David Bagchi has argued for the use of a 'disputation model' to understand Luther's exchanges with his earliest opponents, and the importance of these exchanges for the development of his theology.[40] This concept seems to provide the basis for a reconciliation of Goertz's observations with those of Brecht and Moeller. Luther's anticlericalism does develop out of the central tenets of his Reformation theology, but this development, like so many other elements of the Reformer's thought, only became clear in the course of polemical exchange.

Goertz argues further that the tumult which greeted the spread of Luther's anticlerical polemics quickly opened his eyes to the dangerous consequences of such diatribes against the clergy. And, with 'A Sincere Admonition by Martin Luther to All Christians to Guard Against

---

[37] Hans-Christoph Rublack, 'Anticlericalism in German Reformation Pamphlets,' in Dykema and Oberman, pp. 461–89, especially 468 and 481–2.

[38] Goertz, *Pfaffenhaß* pp. 64–5, indicates how intimate the link was between the distinctiveness of the clerical estate and the orthodox theology of the mass.

[39] See my 'Luther, Emser and the Development of Reformation Anticlericalism,' *ARG* (forthcoming, 1996).

[40] David Bagchi, *Luther's Earliest Opponents: Catholic Controversialists, 1518–1525* (Minneapolis, 1991), pp. 256–63.

Insurrection and Rebellion,' he attempted to retreat from direct anticlerical agitation, although not from an anticlerical standpoint.[41] I argue further that shortly thereafter, in 'Against the Spiritual Estate of the Pope and Bishops, Falsely So Called,' Luther effected a fundamental transformation in the nature of his anticlericalism. Where earlier he had contrasted the false, papal clergy directly with the true priesthood of all believers, he now juxtaposed to it a reformed evangelical clergy derived from scriptural descriptions of the primitive church.[42]

Two further aspects of Luther's anticlerical episode are relevant to the present topic. On the one hand, although Luther's direct anticlerical agitation was of a brief duration – 'On the Misuse of the Mass' was completed in November 1521, 'A Sincere Admonition' by mid-December 1521 and 'Against the Spiritual Estate' in the first half of 1522 – it had wider reverberations beyond the walls of Wittenberg. Furthermore, as Goertz suggests, even after 1522 Luther was willing to adopt an anticlerical standpoint when this appeared to suit his needs.

To this point I have not yet ventured an explicit definition of Reformation anticlericalism. Most analysts of Reformation anticlericalism note that the term was not in use in the sixteenth century; rather it was borrowed from the laicist language of the nineteenth century. An implied element in the subsequent definitions of anticlericalism, which is only occasionally made explicit, is the assumption that true anticlericalism must involve a repudiation of the clergy as any sort of intermediary between God and humanity, including its role as a mediator of the divine Word. As Goertz notes, such a definition is largely impossible prior to the Enlightenment. Consequently, if the concept of anticlericalism is to have any validity in an analysis of the Reformation, it must be redefined. Goertz has attempted such a redefinition, arguing for the use of the term as a 'generic concept,' thereby allowing for the characterization of a whole range of actions and statements as anticlerical.[43]

The breadth of Goertz's definition raises the question of the novelty of Reformation anticlericalism and its relationship to its medieval pre-decessors. Goertz sees as the distinction between pre-Reformation and Reformation anticlericalism the move from an ethically based criticism of the sins of specific clerics and groups of clergy to a theologically based rejection of the intermediary role of the clergy in the process of salvation, and consequently of their distinctive place in the metaphysical and social hierarchy.[44] This led, as we have already noted, to calls for

---

[41] Goertz, *Pfaffenhaß*, p. 90 and 'Tangled Mess,' p. 500.
[42] Dipple, 'Luther and Emser'.
[43] Goertz, 'Tangled Mess,' pp. 518–19.
[44] Goertz, *Pfaffenhaß*, pp. 84–90.

the abolition of the clerical order, rather than just its reform. For the most part, this aspect of Goertz's thesis has enjoyed wide support. Thomas Brady agrees that the attack on the sacramental view of the church deepened and fortified existing anticlericalism.[45] Susan Karant-Nunn argues that the novelty of Evangelical criticisms of the clergy lay in the willingness to call for the eradication, not just the correction, of groups of clerics considered detrimental to the common weal.[46]

Research into the nature of medieval anticlericalism, too, indicates the validity of Goertz's thesis, although with some qualifications. In general, late medieval criticism of the clergy was directed toward the reform of the first estate rather than its eradication. It usually proceeded from the teachings of the church and can be best characterized as interior criticism which functioned as a safety valve capable of disarming more threatening criticism.[47] This characterization is valid even for the phenomenon defined as the 'new anticlericalism' expressed among heretical groups such as the Lollards and Hussites. Here, too, the aim was not to desacralize the priesthood in the sense that Luther did, but to elevate it to a higher spiritual plane and dignity. The criticism was not of the priesthood *per se*, but of bad priests.[48]

However, among these groups there did develop on occasion explicit criticism of the clergy which denied specific roles exercised by them as intermediaries between God and humanity, but these appear to be the exception rather than the rule.[49] What, then, was novel in Luther's

---

[45] Thomas A. Brady, Jr, ' "You hate us priests": Anticlericalism, Communalism and the Control of Women at Strasbourg in the Age of Reformation,' in Dykema and Oberman, p. 204.

[46] Susan Karant-Nunn, 'Clerical Anticlericalism in the Early German Reformation: An Oxymoron?' in Dykema and Oberman, pp. 529–30.

[47] Kaspar Elm, 'Antiklerikalismus im Deutschen Mittelalter,' in Dykema and Oberman, pp. 3–18; Frantisek Graus, 'The Church and its Critics in Time of Crisis,' in Dykema and Oberman, pp. 66–73; John Van Engen, 'Late Medieval Anticlericalism: The Case of the Devout,' in Dykema and Oberman, pp. 19–52.

[48] John Van Engen, 'Anticlericalism among the Lollards,' in Dykema and Oberman, pp. 53–63; Wendy Scase, *Piers Plowman and the New Anticlericalism* (Cambridge, 1989); Frantisek Smahel, 'The Hussite Critique of the Clergy's Civil Dominion,' in Dykema and Oberman, pp. 83–90; Geoffrey Dipple, 'Uthred and the Friars: Apostolic Poverty and Clerical Dominion between FitzRalph and Wyclif,' *Traditio*, 49 (1994), pp. 235–58.

[49] For example, among the Lollards there appears to have been a rejection of priestly confession and absolution. See Van Engen, 'Anticlericalism among the Lollards,' pp. 56–9 and Anne Hudson (ed.), *Selections From English Wycliffite Writings* (Cambridge, 1978), pp. 19, 22, 25. Similarly, radicals among the Taborites rejected the role of the priesthood in the orthodox interpretation of the mass. See Smahel, 'The Hussite Critique,' pp. 86–7 and Howard Kaminsky, *A History of the Hussite Revolution* (Berkeley and Los Angeles, 1967), pp. 384–433.

attack on the clergy? At the heart of this matter remains Luther's general rejection of the intermediary role of the clergy and, consequently, their very *raison d'être* in the sacramental church. This stance was novel in that it was being made by a learned theologian at the centre of a reforming movement and not by the disaffected on its fringes. With this came an alternative theology and, ultimately, an alternative vision of a distinct clerical order. Reformation anticlericalism, then, does not need to include a complete rejection of a clerical intermediary between God and man, but the rejection of the existing priesthood and its specific mediatory role in the late medieval church.

The preceding may appear to re-enshrine Luther's theology at the centre of all reforming movements. However, this is not necessarily the case. The starting point for Luther's attack on the clergy may have been his soteriology and the doctrine of the priesthood of all believers. But for many of his contemporaries this was the endpoint; only gradually did they come to realize the full anticlerical implications of his teachings. And they were brought to this realization as much by more traditional anticlerical forms as by the inner logic of Luther's theology. Here the study of medieval antifraternalism and the 1523 attack on the Franciscans can aid in understanding the nature and effectiveness of Reformation anticlericalism more generally. At the centre of medieval polemics against the friars lies the exploitation of biblical metaphors and images of the opponents of God and the Gospel. Penn Szittya refers to this theological and symbolic treatment of the friars in medieval antifraternal literature as 'an emphatically medieval mode of perceiving the friars.'[50] Jan Huizinga's argument about the fundamental philosophical realism of medieval ways of thinking, and the need of the medieval mind to concretize all images, suggests that Szittya's comment is useful also in understanding criticism of other elements of the first estate.[51] Robert Scribner describes as a crucial moment in the development of Reformation propaganda the transition from implying that the clergy of the old church were unchristian to forthrightly identifying them as antichristian.[52] The use of traditional literary devices to pillory the clergy was crucial in effecting this transition. However revolutionary Luther's theologically grounded repudiation of the first estate was, the dissemination of that message was much more evolutionary. As Goertz notes, pre-Reformation and Reformation anticlerical themes are regu-

---

[50] Penn Szittya, 'Antifraternal Tradition,' p. 313.
[51] Jan Huizinga, *The Waning of the Middle Ages* (New York, 1989), pp. 214–20.
[52] Scribner, *Simple Folk*, p. 48.

larly present alongside one another in the same pamphlet.[53] This is nowhere more apparent than in the 1523 campaign against the friars.

At the centre of the Reformation attack on the Franciscans, and consequently at the centre of this study, looms the figure of Eberlin von Günzburg. Eberlin is unique among the critics of the order in that he was a primary foe of the friars throughout much of his reforming career. Consequently, an analysis of the entire corpus of his writings provides interesting insights into the development of a central element of Reformation anticlericalism during the crucial years from 1521 to 1526. The importance of Eberlin's writings is further highlighted by his stature both as a polemicist for the Reformation and in subsequent historical writing on this topic. Commenting on the profusion and popularity of Eberlin's writings in the sixteenth century, Steven Ozment has labelled him 'after Luther the most prolific Protestant pamphleteer.'[54] This popularity has been reflected in subsequent historical writing. Biographies of him and articles on various aspects of his reforming thought and career are plentiful in the German literature on the Reformation.[55] Even more than among established historians, Eberlin has been a perennial favourite of German graduate students, and unpublished dissertations on various aspects of his thought abound.[56]

Eberlin's popularity has been only marginally less pronounced among English-speaking historians in recent years. In his first published work, a collection of *Flugschriften* entitled 'The Fifteen Confederates,' Eberlin included a series of 'statutes' outlining the structure of an imaginary society known as Wolfaria. These statutes enjoyed a vogue among English-speaking historians in the late 1960s and early 1970s as 'the

---

[53] Goertz, *Pfaffenhaß*, p. 89.

[54] Steven Ozment, 'The Social History of the Reformation: What Can We Learn from Pamphlets?' in *Flugschriften als Massenmedium der Reformationszeit. Beiträge zum Tübinger Symposion 1980*, ed. H.J. Köhler (Stuttgart, 1981), p. 189.

[55] Peters's biography is the most comprehensive and recent. For a full catalogue of monographs and articles on Eberlin, please see the bibliography.

[56] Roberta Adamczyck, *Die Flugschriften des Johann Eberlin von Günzburg*, Phil. Diss. (Vienna, 1981); Hans-Herbert Ahrens, *Die religiösen, nationalen und sozialen Gedanken Johann Eberlin von Günzburgs mit besonderer Berücksichtigung seiner anonym Flugschriften*, Phil. Diss. (Universität Hamburg, 1939); Wilhelm Lucke, *Die Entstehung der '15 Bundesgenossen' des Johann Eberlins von Günzburg*, Phil. Diss. (Halle, 1902); Johann Heinrich Schmidt, *'Die 15 Bundesgenossen' des Johann Eberlin von Günzburg*, Phil. Diss. (Leipzig, 1900); Kurt Stöckl, *Untersuchungen zu Johann Eberlin von Günzburg*, Phil. Diss. (Munich, 1952); Helmut Weidhase, *Kunst und Sprache im Spiegel der reformatorischen und humanistischen Schriften Eberlins von Günzburg*, Phil. Diss. (Tübingen, 1967); Curt Wulkau, *Das kirchliche Ideal des Johann Eberlin von Günzburg*, Phil. Diss. (Halle-Wittenberg, 1922).

first Protestant utopia.'[57] More recently Eberlin's writings have come back into fashion again, not surprisingly, among historians interested in the theme of Reformation anticlericalism.[58] Unfortunately, largely because so much of the work on Eberlin in German remains unpublished, English-speaking scholars have not had the full benefits of the results of research carried on in Eberlin's homeland. For this reason alone, a reassessment of Eberlin's corpus in English is called for.

In an analysis of his earliest writings, Gottfried Geiger labelled Eberlin 'an eclectic and elementary student' of the Reformation.[59] Eberlin's eclecticism has been reflected in the analyses of his writings; he has been characterized as a mediator of Luther's message to the common people, a biblical humanist and admirer of More and Erasmus, a radical Karlstadtian and a spokesman for the common man. All of these streams do, in fact, surface in his thought at various stages of his reforming career. Consequently, an analysis of the development of his anticlerical polemics provides valuable insights into the reception and refraction of Luther's statements in the reforming turbulence of the early Reformation.

Eberlin began agitating for reform while still a member of the Observant priory in Ulm, before the Luther issue had been decided at the political level at the Diet of Worms in 1521. However, by this time he had already imbibed as well a good measure of the reforming thought of the humanist Christian renaissance. His earliest writings reveal the response of a committed member of the Franciscan Observance to the goings on in Wittenberg and elsewhere in the empire. The vision of reform presented here suggests not only that Luther's earliest pamphlets could be regarded as compatible with calls for reform from humanist quarters, but also that both of these movements could be reconciled with ongoing reform sentiment within the Franciscan order.

Eberlin's brethren and superiors in Ulm did not share his perception of the compatibility of the visions of Luther and Francis, and he was soon driven from the order. In the pamphlets written during and shortly

---

[57] Susan Groag Bell, 'Johann Eberlin von Günzburg's "Wolfaria": The First Protestant Utopia?' *Church History* – 36 (1967), pp. 122–39; Richard G. Cole, *Eberlin von Günzburg and the German Reformation*, PhD dissertation (Ohio State, 1963); id., 'The Pamphlet and Social Forces in the Reformation,' *Lutheran Quarterly*, 18 (1965), pp. 195–205; id., 'Law and Order in the Sixteenth Century: Eberlin von Günzburg and the Problem of Political Authority,' *Lutheran Quarterly*, 23 (1971), pp. 251–56; William R. Hitchcock, *The Background of the Knights' Revolt 1522–1523* (Berkeley and Los Angeles, 1958); Steven Ozment, *The Reformation in the Cities: The Appeal of Protestantism to Sixteenth-Century Germany and Switzerland* (New Haven, 1975).

[58] See especially the articles by Scott Hendrix, Hans-Christoph Rublack, R. Po-Chia Hsia, Hans-Jürgen Goertz and Susan Karant-Nunn in Dykema and Oberman.

[59] Geiger, 'Die reformatorischen Initia Eberlins,' pp. 185–95.

after the conflict which led to Eberlin's departure, his perception of the possibility of reform within the order gives way to a bitter denunciation of the Franciscans in particular, and the mendicants in general, as the chief opponents of the Gospel. This attack on the friars bears marked similarities to the medieval antifraternal polemics and suggests that elements of this tradition still had currency in the period of the Renaissance and Reformation. Although Eberlin no longer saw reform as possible within the Franciscan context, he did continue to regard the humanists and Luther as members of the same camp, and he drew a direct line from the activities of Reuchlin to those of Luther.

After completing 'The Fifteen Confederates,' Eberlin travelled to Wittenberg. His works written there indicate that Eberlin quickly came to accept Luther's utterances as the standard for reform. On the one hand, his writings came to concentrate more and more on the central themes of Reformation theology, and an analysis of them indicates how anticlericalism served as a bridge to Reformation thought. On the other hand, he began to tone down his anticlerical diatribes and to repent some of his earlier, more forceful statements against the clergy. In their place Eberlin concentrated on defining new, scripturally based clerical offices, echoing Luther's concerns in 'Against the Spiritual Estate.'

In these writings from 1522 and early 1523, Eberlin's attacks specifically on the mendicants all but disappear. They return, however, with renewed virulence in his and others' polemics against the Franciscans in the second half of 1523. It seems reasonably clear that Luther himself had called forth this response by former members of the order to Schatzgeyer's attacks on him. This indicates that, as Goertz argues, Luther had not withdrawn entirely from an anticlerical stance in 1522. Furthermore, it suggests that by 1523 Luther had come to appreciate the value of anticlericalism as a polemical tool, and that he was willing to exploit it when this seemed necessary. In addition, these pamphlets provide an interesting case study in how anticlerical themes derived from Reformation theology could be integrated effectively with more traditional criticism of the friars.

After 1523 Eberlin alone continued to write against the friars, although another former Franciscan from Ulm, Johann Rot-Locher, produced a collection of disputation articles denouncing the Franciscans in mid-1524, probably with the assistance of Eberlin. However, eventually even Eberlin began to back away from his attacks on the mendicants. In his later writings the denunciations of the friars gradually give way to criticism of the enthusiasts, who, in the last writings, replace the mendicants as the chief opponents of the Gospel. At the same time, Eberlin begins to portray himself as the defender of the clergy against the excesses of the *Schwärmer*. These final works, then, suggest the point at which anticlericalism ceased to be a viable plank in the Wittenberg platform.

However, the later writings of Rot-Locher and Kettenbach question the extent to which this message was effectual beyond the walls of Wittenberg. Unlike Eberlin, neither of these men actually studied in Wittenberg, although both regarded themselves as adherents of Luther's movement. Their later writings reflect Luther's retreat from direct anticlerical agitation. Yet, within this context, Kettenbach thought it still possible to reconcile Luther with Hutten, and he actively campaigned for the cause of Franz von Sickingen. Rot-Locher, long considered the most radical of the three apostates from Ulm, specifically distanced himself from the *Schwärmer* in his final *Flugschriften* while nevertheless denouncing the powerful at all levels of society and agitating for a 'reformation of the common man.' This suggests that by early 1524 there was a delineation of an orthodoxy for the adherents of Luther's movement, but that this was sufficiently vague to allow self-proclaimed Lutherans to continue to expect significant social and political reform from the Gospel. The peasants, then, were not alone in their 'misunderstanding' of Luther's message.

CHAPTER ONE

The friars and their critics on the eve of the Reformation

Any analysis of antifraternal polemics in the Reformation necessarily must begin with Paul Nyhus's question of what happened to the vitality of the mendicant orders between the fourteenth and sixteenth centuries. The obvious explanation for the apparent eclipse of the friars as the intellectual and spiritual leaders of Christendom rests on the assumption that the mendicant orders of the later Middle Ages were unable to maintain the high standards established by their founders and early adherents. Such an explanation assumes that religious orders follow an organic life cycle: as they age the strength of adherence to their original ideals is sapped until replaced by a new vitality in the form of a reform movement. In the fifteenth and sixteenth centuries, then, the friars gradually fell away from the ideals of Francis and Dominic. As a result, discipline within the orders was relaxed, the friars became more worldly, the contrast between their lives and their ideals became more obvious, and the early enthusiasm of the laity for the friars and their vision of the apostolic ideal was eroded. When the Christian Renaissance of the humanists and the Reformation arrived on the stage, the mendicant orders were only a shadow of their former greatness, and they amounted to little more than houses of cards which were easily toppled by the telling and accurate criticisms of the humanists and Reformers.

The popularity of this scenario is easy to account for. It accords well with the picture presented of the friars in much of the literary evidence left by their contemporaries, the bulk of which was written by the opponents of the friars among the humanists and Reformers. Furthermore, it reinforces the traditional perception of the later Middle Ages as an age of decline preceding the Renaissance and Reformation. The deterioration of the mendicant orders was, then, part of the general decline of the church in the fifteenth century. As central institutions of the 'fallen' church, the mendicant orders were, of course, incapable of putting their own houses in order. True reform had to come from outside.[1]

Rounding out this picture, there has developed the perception that the particular virulence with which the friars were attacked during the later

---

[1] Kaspar Elm, 'Reform- und Observanzbestrebungen im spätmittelalterlichen Ordenswesen. Ein Überblick,' in Kaspar Elm (ed.), *Reformbemühungen und Observanzbestrebungen in spätmittelalterlichen Ordenswesen* (Berlin, 1989), pp. 3–4.

Middle Ages derives from the anachronism of their ideals. They were, at a fundamental level, out of step with their times and represented the ideals of a bygone age on the eve of the Renaissance. Jan Huizinga noted that within the context of a general contempt for the clergy, special hatred was reserved for the mendicants. This point he illustrated with a particularly brutal passage from *Cent Nouvelles Nouvelles*:

> Let us pray to God that the Jacobins
> May eat the Augustinians
> And that the Carmelites may be hanged
> With the cords of the Minorites.

Huizinga explained that the mendicant idealization of poverty was in decline, replaced by the growing sentiment that poverty was a social evil rather than an apostolic virtue.[2]

This picture of the friars has been given new life and provided with empirical grounding by Francis Rapp's research in Strasbourg. In an attempt to understand the speed and ease with which the mendicant orders in Strasbourg disappeared after the arrival of the Reformation, Rapp set out to chart the evolution of relations between the friars and the populace of the city from the thirteenth to the sixteenth century. An exhaustive analysis of bequests and professions to the mendicant orders indicated that by the middle of the fifteenth century the friars had squandered the good will of their hosts: gifts to the cloisters were down remarkably, the total number of friars had dropped off considerably and novices now tended to come from outside the city walls. Furthermore, the real wealth of the cloisters had increased markedly, due largely to more careful exploitation of the cloisters' financial resources, greater wealth both of novices and members and the sale of spiritual services to the laity. Rapp's explanation for the declining popularity of the friars follows a familiar pattern. Through their betrayal of the poverty ideal and constant infighting, the mendicants had undermined their own positions in the city. Added to this was the rejection by urban society of the ideal of apostolic poverty and criticisms of the friars by their opponents among the secular clergy and the humanists. Particularly damaging for the friars were the questions raised by humanists about their social utility.[3]

In the picture of the Strasbourg friaries painted by Rapp, their rapid

---

[2] Jan Huizinga, *The Waning of the Middle Ages* (New York, 1989), p. 179.

[3] Francis Rapp, 'Die Mendikanten und die Strassburger Gesellschaft am Ende des Mittelalters,' in Kaspar Elm (ed.), *Stellung und Wirksamkeit der Bettelorden in der städtischen Gesellschaft* (Berlin, 1981), pp. 85–102. A similar scenario is chronicled for the Zurich friars by Martina Wehrli-Johns, 'Stellung und Wirksamkeit der Bettelorden in Zürich,' in Elm, *Stellung und Wirksamkeit der Bettelorden*, pp. 77–84.

demise during the Reformation comes as no surprise. The friaries here appear as the urban counterparts of the exploitive, parasitic endowed monasteries on the land which, according to Henry Cohn, played such a prominent role in raising lay resentment of clerical privilege leading to the outbreak of the Peasants' War.[4] Anticlericalism, or more specifically antimonasticism, appears in this context as an easily understandable economic phenomenon. But how complete is this picture? Much of Rapp's evidence comes from the Dominican and Franciscan cloisters in Strasbourg, neither of which were reformed during the fifteenth-century movements aimed at the strict observance of the Rules of the mendicant orders. A much different picture to that presented by Rapp has been produced by Bernhard Neidiger's research into the reformed Franciscan and Dominican cloisters in Basel. Neidiger suggests that friars of the Observance remained a vital force in the religious life of the city into the sixteenth century. He notes a deterioration of discipline and loss of focus on the original ideals of the mendicant orders in the Basel cloisters in the early fifteenth century, but suggests that this led to the introduction of the Observant reform which revitalized the mendicant cloisters. Thereafter the popularity of the friars again soared and numbers grew, as did bequests from the populace.[5]

The importance of Neidiger's findings is indicated by the strength of the Observant reform movements which swept through the mendicant orders throughout the fifteenth century and into the sixteenth. Of these the most spectacular and best known is that of the Franciscans. From its very humble beginnings in the second half of the fourteenth century in Umbria, the Franciscan Observance spread rapidly, and by the middle of the fifteenth century controlled over 600 cloisters in Italy and could boast among its members such luminaries as Bernardino of Siena, John of Capistrano, Albert of Sarteano and James of the March. Transposed beyond the Alps, the movement not only continued to grow rapidly, but also ran into independently developing indigenous movements aimed at strict observance of the Rule of St Francis. By the beginning of the sixteenth century 16 of the 57 priories in the south German province of the Franciscan order were controlled by the Observants. And in 1517 the Observance was recognized by the pope as the true order of Francis.

---

[4] Henry J. Cohn, 'Anticlericalism in the German Peasants' War of 1525,' *Past and Present, 83 (1979), pp. 3–31.*

[5] Bernhard Neidiger, 'Liegenschaftsbesitz und Eigentumsrecht der Basler Bettelsorden-konvente,' in Elm, *Stellung und Wirksamkeit der Bettelorden*, pp. 103–17; id. *Mendikanten zwischen Ordensideal und städtischer Realität. Untersuchungen zum wirtschaftlichen Verhalten der Bettelorden in Basel* (Berlin, 1981); id. 'Stadtregiment und Klosterreform in Basel,' in Elm, *Reformbemühungen und Observanzbestrebungen*, pp. 539–67.

The strength and vitality of this movement has led to its characterization as one of 'the religious wonders of the late Middle Ages.'[6]

Although not nearly as spectacular, the reform movements in the Dominican, Augustinian and Carmelite orders were no less real than the Franciscan Observance. The Dominican Observance is usually dated from the last quarter of the fourteenth century in Italy. It quickly spread into the German province of the order, where it is considered to have achieved a major breakthrough with the election of an Observant as Provincial Minister in 1475.[7] The reform movement among the Augustinian Hermits, too, began in the late fourteenth century in Italy. It also spread rapidly through Italy and by the early fifteenth century had entered south Germany. By the middle of the fifteenth century the Observants had captured control of the order's hierarchy and by 1459 a distinct German congregation of the Observance was established, the Saxon Congregation to which Luther later belonged.[8]

Finally, the Carmelite Observance movement began early in the

---

[6] Elm, 'Reform- und Observanzbestrebungen,' p. 9. The most detailed account of the history of the Observance and its growth against the background of relaxed Conventualism is Duncan Nimmo's *Reform and Division in the Medieval Franciscan Order, From St Francis to the Foundation of the Capuchins* (Rome, 1987), pp. 205–658. See also John Moorman, *A History of the Franciscan Order From its Origins to the Year 1517* (Oxford, 1968), pp. 369–83, 441–56, 479–500, 569–85; Heribert Holzapfel, *Handbuch der Geschichte des Franziskanerordens* (Freiburg, 1909), pp. 80–157; Raphael Huber, *A Documented History of the Franciscan Order* (Milwaukee, 1944), pp. 255–502; Duncan Nimmo, 'Reform at the Council of Constance: The Franciscan Case,' in Derek Baker (ed.), *Renaissance and Renewal in Christian History*, Studies in Church History, vol. 14 (Oxford, 1977), pp. 159–73; Paul Nyhus, 'The Observant Reform Movement in Southern Germany, *Franciscan Studies*, 32 (1972), pp. 154–67; id., 'The Franciscans in South Germany, 1400–1530: Reform and Revolution,' *Transactions of the American Philosophical Society*, 65(8) (1975), pp. 10–17; Brigitte Degler-Spengler, 'Observanten außerhalb der Observanz. Die franziskanischen Reformen "sub ministris"', *ZKG*, 89 (1978), pp. 354–71; Duncan Nimmo 'The Franciscan Regular Observance. The Culmination of Medieval Franciscan Reform,' in Elm, *Reformbemühungen und Observanzbestrebungen*, pp. 189–205 and Paul Nyhus, 'The Franciscan Observant Reform in Germany,' in Elm, *Reformbemühungen und Observanzbestrebungen*, pp. 207–17.

[7] The most recent survey of the history of the Dominican Observance in Germany is Eugen Hillenbrand, 'Die Observantenbewegung in der deutschen Ordensprovinz der Dominikaner,' in Elm, *Reformbemühungen und Observanzbestrebungen*, pp. 219–71. See also Servatius Petrus Wolfs, 'Dominikanische Observanzbestrebungen: Die Congregatio Hollandiae (1464–1517),' in Elm, *Reformbemühungen und Observanzbestrebungen*, pp. 273–92, Annette Barthelemé, *La Réforme Dominicaine au XVe Siecle, en Alsace et dans L'Ensemble de la Province de Teutonie* (Strasbourg, 1931).

[8] For a general account of the growth of the Augustinian Observance see Francis Xavier Martin, 'The Augustinian Observant Movement,' in Elm, *Reformbemühungen und Observanzbestrebungen*, pp. 325–45. See also id., 'The Augustinian Order on the Eve of the Reformation,' in *Miscellanea Historiae Ecclesiasticae*, II (Louvain, 1967), pp. 71–104; Th. Kolde, *Die deutsche Augustiner-Congregation und Johann von Staupitz* (Gotha,

fifteenth century in Italy, and had spread to Germany by the middle of the century. It also was undergoing a period of particularly vigorous growth at the time of the outbreak of the Reformation in the 1510s and 1520s.[9] Of particular interest for the present study is the timing of the arrival of the Observant reform movements in Germany. All entered their most vigorous phases there in the second half of the fifteenth century or the beginning of the sixteenth.

The vibrancy of these reforming movements on the eve of the Reformation means that it is necessary to rethink significantly the place of the friars in the history of the Reformation. On the one hand, historians of the mendicant orders have demanded that the motifs of reform and regeneration take their place beside that of degeneration in characterizing the late medieval church and religious orders. The Reformation needs to be reconceptualized as an extension of, rather than just a reaction to, the conditions in the fifteenth-century church. With reference to the specific topic at hand, this means that the activities of Luther and the former friars who joined him need to be understood in the light of the reform movements within the mendicant orders. It also suggests that the prominence of friars among Luther's opponents be seen, as well, as a further sign of the vitality of these movements.[10]

On the other hand, historians of the mendicant orders point to the need to reassess the popularity of the friars on the eve of the Reformation. The congruence of the beginnings of the mendicant orders and growing urbanization of the high Middle Ages has often been noted. As products of the 'medieval renaissance,' the friars have been seen as fundamentally urban phenomena, especially when contrasted with the older, endowed orders. Unlike their cloistered predecessors, their *raison d'être* involved ministering to the laity, especially the growing class of educated laymen of the towns. Furthermore, the friars' reliance on alms ensured that they were dependent on a sufficient concentration of laymen to ensure their survival. And it appears that this natural alliance between the friars and townspeople encouraged the development of

---

1879); Adalbero Kunzelmann, *Geschichte der Deutschen Augustiner-Eremiten*, vol. 5: *Die sächsisch-thüringische Provinz und die sächsische Reformkongregation bis zum Untergang der Beiden* (Würzburg, 1974).

[9] Joachim Smet, 'Pre-Tridentine Reform in the Carmelite Order,' in Elm, *Reformbemühungen und Observanzbestrebungen*, pp. 293–323.

[10] Walter Ziegler, 'Reformation und Klosterauflösung. Ein ordensgeschichtlicher Vergleich,' in Elm, *Reformbemühungen und Observanzbestrebungen*, pp. 590–2; Lothar Graf zu Dohna, 'Von der Ordensreform zur Reformation,' in Elm, *Reformbemühungen und Observanzbestrebungen*, pp. 571–84, sees the reforming activities of Staupitz as an important backdrop for those of Luther. Martin, 'Augustinian Observant Movement,' pp. 342–5, emphasizes instead the reforming activities of the minister general of the order, Giles of Viterbo.

further bonds between them. According to Bernd Moeller, crucial to the development of an independent urban communal ethos in the late medieval imperial cities was the successful resolution of a city's conflict with independent ecclesiastical institutions within its walls. This was particularly true of any city which served as an episcopal residence.[11] Examples abound of mendicants siding with cities and defying interdicts of the latter's ecclesiastical opponents, even into the fifteenth century. The autonomy of the friars from local ecclesiastical authorities, and their conflicts with local representatives of the secular clergy, predisposed them to adopt a position favourable to the interests of the civic community.[12]

The thesis emphasizing the deterioration of the mendicant orders in the later Middle Ages, and the evidence presented by Rapp for Strasbourg, suggests that this natural alliance had eroded during the course of the fifteenth century. Bernd Moeller has described how the late medieval imperial cities sought from the fourteenth century onward to incorporate the local clergy into the 'sacred society' of the urban commune and create a 'private church.'[13] In Strasbourg, argues Rapp, the civic authorities regarded the friars as foreign bodies within the city from the thirteenth century on. While the fundamental distrust of the authorities did not change, their relations with the mendicants worsened with the latter's deterioration in the fifteenth century.[14]

Again, Neidiger's research into the Basel cloisters has yielded drastically different results, due largely to the success of the Observant reform there. Neidiger argues that the ruling authorities of Basel actively encouraged the introduction of the Observant reform to the Dominican and Franciscan cloisters, and to the female cloisters associated with them. As a result of this intervention, the secular authorities not only gained considerable control over the financial transactions of the

---

[11] Bernd Moeller, 'Imperial Cities and the Reformation,' in Bernd Moeller, *Imperial Cities and the Reformation. Three Essays*, trans. H.C. Erik Midelfort and Mark U. Edwards, Jr (Durham, NC, 1982), p. 48.

[12] This thesis is most fully developed by Norbert Hecker, *Bettelorden und Bürgertum: Konflikt und Kooperation in deutschen Städten des Spätmittelalters* (Frankfurt, 1981), see especially pp. 95–8. See also Wehrli-Johns, pp. 77–81, on the role of the mendicant orders in the growth and development of Zurich and Ingo Ulpts, 'Zur Rolle der Mendikanten in städtischen Konflikten des Mittelalters. Ausgewählte Beispiele aus Bremen, Hamburg und Lübeck,' in Dieter Berg (ed.), *Bettelorden und Stadt. Bettelorden und städtischer Leben im Mittelalter und in der Neuzeit* (Werl, 1992), pp. 131–51.

[13] Moeller, 'Imperial Cities,' pp. 47–9.

[14] Rapp, 'Mendikanten und Strassburger Gesellschaft,' pp. 99–100. Rapp notes, as part of the deteriorating relations between the friars and local authorities, the decline in numbers of novices in the mendicant orders from notable Strasbourg families. Neidiger, *Mendikanten*, pp. 186–7, suggests that a similar process in Basel resulted from efforts at centralization within the orders and the undermining of local influence on the cloisters.

cloisters, but also by the end of the fifteenth century the mendicants were firmly integrated into the urban community.[15] In Basel, then, the mendicants became an important part of Moeller's 'private church' of the late medieval urban commune. Granted, as Neidiger himself indicates, relations between the mendicants and city council in Basel were particularly harmonious. But in numerous cities and territories the Observance was introduced to mendicant cloisters on the initiative of local secular authorities.[16]

The role of secular authorities in the introduction of reform to local cloisters raises the question of the motivation behind this activity. Integral to the process of reform was the extension of control over the cloisters by those local authorities. But this was hardly a cynical grab for wealth and power. Neidiger's research into the reform of cloisters in Basel suggests that the city council encouraged the reform movements despite the costs and perceived threats to civic unity. Contrary to the established policy of the council to limit the flow of money into the dead hand of the church, the council consistently encouraged reform despite the increased popularity of the Observant cloisters among the city's donors. Furthermore, on several occasions, the process of reform actually called for capital expenditure on the part of the city. In return the city received no immediate windfall; property taken over from the reformed monasteries was applied to other pious purposes rather than flowing into city coffers. Neidiger concludes, therefore, that city councillors were not motivated by the perceived material gains of reform.[17] Rather, they looked to social and spiritual benefits to be expected from the prayers, masses and preaching of the Observant friars. In Moeller's terms, they were concerned as much for the spiritual as the material welfare of the urban 'sacred society.'

Indications are that the general populace of the cities shared the enthusiasm of their governments for the Observant reform movements. In Basel the reformed cloisters witnessed a growth in vocations, endowments and confraternities, all of which suggest that their popularity

---

[15] Neidiger, *Mendikanten*, pp. 211–28 and 'Stadtregiment und Klosterreform,' pp. 539–67.

[16] For details of the role of secular authorities as sponsors of the Observant reform movements, see Nyhus, 'Observant Reform Movement,' pp. 163–7; Hillenbrand, pp. 239–62; Hecker, pp. 130–1; Susanne Drexhage-Leisebein, 'Reformerisches Engagement städtischer Obrigkeit in der zweiten Hälfte des 15. Jahrhunderts. Die franziskanischen Reformbewegung in der städtischen Kirchen- und Klosterpolitik am Beispiel ausgewählter Städte im Gebiet der Sächsischen Ordensprovinz,' in Berg (ed.), *Bettelorden und Stadt*, pp. 209–34.

[17] Neidiger, 'Stadtregiment und Klosterreform,' pp. 562–4. Martina Wehrli-Johns, p. 83, indicates that in Zurich the city council actually opposed the introduction of the reform movements because of the perceived costs involved.

was restored. Furthermore, architectural changes to their churches suggest that this new popularity was reflected directly in their roles in the spiritual life of the city.[18] Evidence from Dominican cloisters elsewhere in the German province indicates that Basel was not an isolated case, and generally endowments to the priories and confraternities associated with them increased significantly in the wake of the introduction of the Observance.[19]

If Neidiger's assessment of the situation is accurate, the improved relations between the friars and the laity was directly related to the success of the friars' pastoral activity. In particular, the role of the Observants as preachers was especially important. Preaching was an integral component of the Observant reform movements, and many of the most popular preachers of the fifteenth century came from the ranks of the Observant friars.[20] This popularity has important implications for understanding the place of the friars in the Reformation. On the one hand, it drives home the point that the mendicant orders were still vibrant institutions in the later Middle Ages. This in turn casts the Reformers' attacks on them in an entirely different light. The friars were not singled out for abuse by the Reformers because they epitomized the decadence of the fallen church. Rather, as the chief competitors to the Reformers, they necessarily had to be discredited. It was the strength, not the weakness, of the friars' position that most recommended them as targets for the Reformers' slings.[21]

On the other hand, the popularity of the friars' preaching also provides important insights into the context in which the Reformation campaign against the friars occurred. As an increasingly important element in the spiritual life of the later Middle Ages, preaching remained a central issue of contention in the endemic conflicts between the friars and the secular clergy. Almost from their inception, the mendicant orders became embroiled in bitter conflicts with the secular clergy. The spread of heresy in the twelfth and early thirteenth centuries has been regularly attributed to the ignorance and worldliness of the secular clergy, and the institution of the mendicants as preachers, a role adopted immediately by the Dominicans and shortly thereafter by the Franciscans, was regarded as a blessing by the ecclesiastical hierarchy. The

---

[18] Neidiger, *Mendikanten*, pp. 162–6 and 195–6.

[19] Hillenbrand, pp. 265–6.

[20] Martin, 'Augustinian Observant Movement,' pp. 338–40; Moorman, pp. 517–32; Holzapfel, pp. 219–24.

[21] Ziegler, pp. 598–608, indicates the importance of the friars, especially the members of the Observance, in opposing the introduction of the Reformation at the local level.

superior training of the friars led to their general popularity with the laity and, consequently, a diminution of the status and influence of the parochial clergy. As their reputation spread, the friars were increasingly chosen as confessors by the laity, and burial in their churchyards came to be viewed as both honourable and desirable. Hence, the parish priest not only saw his perogative infringed and a strong element of his control over and contact with his parishioners lost, but he was also deprived of benefactions and burial dues, both essential sources of income. Of course, the result was a state of almost constant bickering between the mendicants and the parochial clergy.

The first general conflagration in the conflict between the mendicants and the secular clergy occurred at the University of Paris in 1253. In addition to the normal sources of friction in the pastoral realm, the arrival of the friars at the universities led to a defection of some of the better minds of the age to the mendicant camp and a loss of prestige and intellectual leadership by the secular masters. Faced with a very real threat of domination of the university government by the friars, a delegation of secular masters led by William of St Amour in March 1254 initiated an attack on the friars at the papal curia. In addition to the inherent importance of a direct confrontation at Christendom's most influential university, the Parisian conflict is of note for the role played in it by William of St Amour. St Amour's *De periculis novissimorum temporum* not only dominated the attack on the friars at Paris, but it also provided the pattern and much of the polemical language for subsequent denunciations of the friars.[22]

The subsequent history of secular–mendicant relations in the Middle Ages is one of failed compromises and dashed hopes. The respective fortunes of the contestants rose and fell as successive popes passed legislation favouring one side and then the other. Boniface VIII came closest to establishing a workable compromise with the Bull *Super cathedram*, issued in February 1300. The frequent confirmations of this Bull throughout the fourteenth century indicate the faith administrators had in it as a workable compromise, but also that conflict between the mendicants and seculars continued unabated.[23]

---

[22] See below, pp. 73–83.

[23] On the fourteenth-century conflicts between the friars and the secular clergy, see Decima Douie, *The Conflict Between the Seculars and Mendicants at the University of Paris in the Thirteenth Century* (London, 1954); J.G. Sikes, 'Jean de Pouilli and Peter de la Palu,' *English Historical Review*, 49 (1934), pp. 219–40; Richard W. Emery, 'The Second Council of Lyons and the Mendicant Orders', *The Catholic Historical Review*, 39 (1953), pp. 257–71; Hugolin Lippens, 'Le Droit Nouveau des Mendiants en conflit avec le Droit Coutumier du Clergé Séculier, du Concile de Vienne à celui de Trente,' *Archivum Franciscanum Historicum*, 47 (1954), pp. 241–92.

It seems that tensions between the friars and the parochial clergy remained high throughout the fifteenth century, especially in Germany. They escalated even further in the last quarter of the century when Pope Sixtus IV, the former minister general of the Franciscans, modified *Super cathedram* in favour of the mendicants. In 1516 the Fifth Lateran Council sought to re-establish an acceptable compromise, but already in 1517 Leo X modified its decisions in favour of the friars.[24] These changes both reflected and initiated local conflicts, which seem to have been particularly virulent in Germany. In 1478 Sixtus IV had to intervene in German affairs to settle a particularly bitter contest between the mendicants and seculars.[25] But papal intervention appears not to have had the desired effect. In 1490 an agreement was reached in Munich aimed at quashing a developing controversy over preaching privileges between the friars and the secular clergy. As well, the law faculty at the University of Ingolstadt was asked to decide whether the attendance at mass in the churches of the friars fulfilled canonical requirements or whether worshippers were required in addition to attend their parish church.[26] And in 1517 a bitter controversy erupted between the mendicants and secular clergy in Strasbourg over the activities of the friars as confessors for the laity.[27]

It appears further that along with the revived conflicts between the mendicants and seculars there was renewed interest in the history of secular–mendicant relations and the literature associated with that history. In Lent 1507 a 'Defense of the Mendicant Friars against those Curates who unjustly Assail the Privileges of the Friars' appeared from the pen of Jakob von Hochstraten, the Dominican inquisitor of Cologne.[28] Hochstraten concentrates his attention on developing a legal defence of the mendicants' pastoral activity, and particularly their role in the confessional, in terms of *Super Cathedram*; however, he introduces this discussion with reference to the most prominent medieval opponents of the friars including William of St Amour and Richard FitzRalph, the Archbishop of Armagh, who inaugurated a particularly virulent controversy between the mendicants and secular clergy in the middle of the fourteenth century and whose activities are

---

[24] Holzapfel, p. 240; Moorman, pp. 511–13.

[25] Moorman, p. 513.

[26] Nikolaus Paulus, *Kaspar Schatzgeyer, ein Vorkämpfer der katholischen Kirche gegen Luther in Süddeutschland* (Strasbourg, 1898), pp. 17, 22.

[27] Rapp, 'Mendikanten und Strassburger Gesellschaft,' p. 90.

[28] Paulus, *Kaspar Schatzgeyer*, pp. 17, 22; id., *Die deutschen Dominikaner im Kampfe gegen Luther (1518–1563)* (Freiburg, 1903), p. 88.

regarded as the backdrop for Wyclif's reforming activities.[29] A survey of library holdings indicates that the works of St Amour and FitzRalph, as well as other prominent opponents of the friars such as Wyclif, were disseminated widely in the German-speaking lands.[30]

The significance of ongoing conflicts between the mendicants and the secular clergy becomes apparent when one looks into the charges directed against the friars by their new opponents in the fifteenth and sixteenth centuries, the humanists and Reformers. It is generally assumed that the late medieval friars, as the institutional heirs of the great scholastics of the high Middle Ages, were the natural opponents of the new humanist learning. This picture is, however, in need of revision. James Overfield has questioned the extent to which a fundamental opposition existed between humanism and scholasticism in Germany, at least before the Reuchlin Affair.[31] More importantly, despite their importance in the history of late medieval scholasticism, the friars were not generally averse to the new learning, as has been thought.

Historians of the Augustinian Hermits have long noted the close relationship which existed between members of the order and Petrarch and Boccaccio, and the close connection between the early years of the Observance in Florence and the humanist culture of the city.[32] This relationship did not pass away with the fifteenth century. Giles of Viterbo, Minister General of the order from 1506 to 1518, has been

---

[29] 'Defensorium fratrum mendicantium contra curatos illos qui privilegia fratrum iniuste impugnant,' Köhler *et al.*, F 1085, # 2751, Aii. On FitzRalph, see Katherine Walsh, 'Archbishop FitzRalph and the Friars at the Papal Curia in Avignon 1357–60,' *Traditio*, 31 (1975), pp. 233–75; id., *A Fourteenth-Century Scholar and Primate: Richard FitzRalph in Oxford, Avignon and Armagh* (Oxford, 1981); James Doyne Dawson, 'Richard FitzRalph and the Fourteenth-Century Poverty Controversies,' *Journal of Ecclesiastical History*, 34 (1983), pp. 315–44; Janet Coleman, 'FitzRalph's Antimendicant "proposicio" (1350) and the Politics of the Papal Curia at Avignon,' *JEH*, 35 (1984), pp. 376–90; Geoffrey L. Dipple, 'Uthred and the Friars: Apostolic Poverty and Clerical Dominion Between FitzRalph and Wyclif,' *Traditio*, 49 (1994), pp. 235–58.

[30] On the popularity especially of FitzRalph's works in the German-speaking lands, see Jean Phillipe Genet, 'The Dissemination of Manuscripts Relating to English Political Thought in the Fourteenth Century,' in Michael Jones and Malcolm Vale (eds), *England and Her Neighbours, 1066–1453: Essays in Honour of Pierre Chaplais* (London, 1989), pp. 217–37. St Amour's works also seem to have enjoyed considerable popularity in Central Europe. M.M. Dufeil, *Guillaume de St Amour et la Polemique Universitaire 1250–1259* (Paris, 1972), discusses the dissemination of manuscripts of St Amour's works.

[31] See James Overfield, 'A New Look at the Reuchlin Affair,' *Studies in Medieval and Renaissance History*, 8 (1971), pp. 167–207; id., *Humanism and Scholasticism in Late Medieval Germany* (Princeton, 1984). Overfield's thesis has not been without its critics, however; see Erika Rummel, '*Et cum theologo bella poeta gerit*. The Conflict between Humanists and Scholastics Revisited,' *Sixteenth Century Journal*, 23 (1992), pp. 713–26.

[32] Martin, 'Augustinian Observant Movement,' p. 341; Rudolph Arbesmann, *Der Augustinereremitenorden und der Beginn der humanistischen Bewegung* (Würzburg, 1965).

characterized as an embodiment of the meeting of the ideals of the Observant reform movement with those of Renaissance humanism.[33] Similarly, Paul Nyhus sees the activities of Paul Scriptoris and Conrad Pellikan as indicative of the vibrancy of a pre-Lutheran humanist reform programme among the south German Franciscan Observants. In Pellikan's close relationship with the Provincial Minister, Kaspar Schatzgeyer, he sees a similar meeting of the Observance with humanism.[34] The humanists for their part tended not to assume a direct identification of the friars with the scholastics. For example, in *Praise of Folly* Erasmus's attack on the friars is distinct from that on the doctors. Of course, this approach spelled double jeopardy for those friars who were also scholastic theologians.[35]

Francis Rapp claims that of the accusations levelled against the Strasbourg mendicants during the course of the fifteenth century the most effective was the charge, emanating from the humanist corner, that the friars served no useful social purpose.[36] This charge strikes at the very *raison d'être* of the mendicant orders and revives the perception that their ideals were not consonant with those of the dawning age. But how common was this attack? By far the most novel humanist criticism of the friars came from the pen of Lorenzo Valla. Valla's *Profession of the Religious*, completed c. 1439–42, stands out amongst the anticlerical literature of quattrocento Italy in that Valla moves beyond the commonplace attacks on the friars which were content merely to vilify them as hypocritical, lazy and greedy. Instead he goes to the heart of the matter and challenges the claim, likely made by Aquinas, that actions of the religious performed under vows are more meritorious than similar actions performed by the laity. He goes on to argue that the vows of the religious are redundant as all Christians promise at baptism to observe God's commandments.[37] This juxtaposition of baptism with monastic vows appears to anticipate Luther's criticism of the cloistered life and

---

[33] Martin, 'Augustinian Observant Movement,' pp. 342–5.

[34] Nyhus, 'Schatzgeyer and Pellican,' pp. 179–90. For a more general assessment of the compatibility of the Observant and humanist movements, see Kaspar Elm, 'Die Franziskanerobservanz als Bildungsreform,' in Hartmut Boockmann, Bernd Moeller and Karl Stackmann (eds), *Lebenslehren und Weltentwürfe im übergang vom Mittelalter zur Neuzeit* (Göttingen, 1989), pp. 201–13.

[35] *The Collected Works of Erasmus*, vol. 27: *Literary and Educational Writings*, vol. 5, ed. A.H.T. Levy, trans. and annotated by Betty Radice (Toronto, 1986), pp. 126–35. The friars do come under attack briefly as theologians when Erasmus describes their preaching, see pp. 133–4.

[36] Rapp, 'Mendikanten und Strassburger Gesellschaft,' p. 101.

[37] Lorenzo Valla, *The Profession of the Religious*, in Olga Zorzi Pugliese (trans. and ed.), *The Profession of the Religious and the principal arguments from The Falsely-Believed and Forged Donation of Constantine* (Toronto, 1985), pp. 17–55.

one sees in Valla's line of attack a revaluation of the secular life similar to the one which underlies Luther's criticism of monasticism.[38] Valla further attacked the individual vows of the friars and his statements on the vow of poverty are interesting in light of Huizinga's and Rapp's analyses of the poverty ideal in late medieval Europe. Valla charges that poverty is not essential and, citing Aristotle, claims that it is better to provide for oneself and to avoid extremes.[39] We have here a clear statement of the novel, secular ethics which lie at the centre of Hans Baron's definition of civic humanism as the antithesis of the medieval social ethic.[40] The distinguishing feature of Valla's attack on the religious is, however, its uniqueness. Of particular note is the fact that unlike Valla's denunciation of the Donation of Constantine, which Ulrich von Hutten popularized in Reformation Germany, *Profession of the Religious* remained unknown north of the Alps in the sixteenth century.[41]

Rather, as I will indicate, the charges levelled against the friars by Northern humanists remained much more conventional and, in fact, leaned heavily on the conventions of the medieval antifraternal tradition. A clear example of the humanist critique is provided by Erasmus's 1523 colloquy *Funus*, in which a parish priest voices a stinging indictment of the friars:

> 'I could make much better bachelors than you out of beanstalks,' says he. 'Where did Dominic and Francis, the founders and heads of your orders, learn the Aristotelian philosophy, or the reasonings of Thomas, or the speculations of Scotus? Or where were they granted their bachelor's degrees? You crept into a world still credulous, but you were few, humble, and some of you even learned and holy. You nested in fields and villages. Soon you migrated to some of the wealthiest cities and to the best part of town. You used to work in whatever fields could not support a shepherd; nowadays you're not anywhere but in rich men's houses. . . . If I lack any learning, I won't seek it from you. Or do you believe the world is still so stupid that whenever it sees the garb of Dominic or Francis it thinks their sanctity is present too? Is it any of your business what I do at my own home? What you do in your retreats, how you behave with the nuns, even the public knows. How far from good or decent are the homes of the wealthy that you frequent 'is known to every blear-eyed man and barber.'[42]

---

[38] See below, pp. 135–42.

[39] Valla, *The Profession of the Religious*, pp. 43–7.

[40] Hans Baron, 'Cicero and the Roman Spirit in the Middle Ages and Early Renaissance,' *Bulletin of the John Rylands Library*, 22 (1938), pp. 73–97; id., 'Franciscan Poverty and Civic Wealth in Humanistic Thought,' *Speculum*, 13 (1938), pp. 1–37.

[41] Pugliese, p. 1.

[42] Craig R. Thompson (trans.), *The Colloquies of Erasmus* (Chicago and London, 1965), p. 362.

Erasmus's references to the reasonings of Thomas and the speculations of Scotus indicate clearly his point of departure. But to drive home his criticism of the friars, he relies not on a sophisticated critique of scholastic theology, but much more on base denigration of the characters of the friars.

Central to Erasmus's enterprise is the attempt to highlight the hypocrisy of the mendicants who feign the sanctity of Francis and Dominic, while hungering after the spoils of the wealthy and casting a lecherous eye at the nuns under their care. Here we have, I believe, the basis for arguments that deterioration of the mendicant orders in the fifteenth century led to their eclipse in the Renaissance and Reformation. But Erasmus's claims may not be so accurate or insightful as they appear. According to Penn Szittya's analysis, the charges levelled against the friars in the Middle Ages were determined more by the biblical types with which they were identified than by conditions in the 'real world.' A key text in William of St Amour's exegesis was Matthew 23 and its repeated chorus: 'Woe unto you scribes and Pharisees, hypocrites.' On the basis of this identification the characterization of the friars as hypocritical became a commonplace in the medieval antifraternal tradition.[43] One need only think of such characters as the friars Ipocresie and Flaterie in Gower's *Mirour de l'Omme*, frère Flaterere in *Piers Plowman* or Faus Semblant in the *Roman de la Rose* to recognize how pervasive this identification was.[44] G. R. Owst has discovered similar sentiments in even strongly anti-Lollard sermons of late medieval England. A common theme of sermon allegory was the description of vices personified as daughters of the devil who marry into various social classes: 'The feend hath maryed Wast to ryotours, and Raveyn to knyztes and to men of lawe, and Symonye to byschopys and prelatys and clerkys, and Ypocrysie to frerys, and Leccherye to alle astatys.'[45] In the German-speaking lands the identification appears to have been equally well established. An anonymous late fifteenth-century poem, 'The Devil's Net,' similarly identifies hypocrisy as the particular vice of the friars.[46]

---

[43] Penn Szittya, 'The Antifraternal Tradition in Middle English Literature,' *Speculum*, 52 (1977), pp. 293–301; id., *The Antifraternal Tradition in Medieval Literature* (Princeton, 1986), pp. 34–41.

[44] Jill Mann, *Chaucer and Medieval Estates Satire: The Literature of Social Classes and the General Prologue to the Canterbury Tales* (Cambridge, 1973), p. 38; Douie, *Conflict*, p. 12.

[45] G.R. Owst, *Literature and Pulpit in Medieval England* (Oxford, 1961), p. 96.

[46] K.A. Barack (ed.), *Des Teufels Netz. Satirisch-didaktisches Gedicht aus der ersten Hälfte des fünfzehnten Jahrhunderts* (Stuttgart, 1863; reprint edn, Amsterdam, 1968), p. 176: 'Sie sind all glichsner von der art, / Wie vil bücher sie hand gelart / Und biegends hin und wider.' On the importance of this poem in the development of medieval estates satire in Middle German literature, see Hellmut Rosenfeld, 'Die Entwicklung der Ständesatire im Mittelalter,' *Zeitschrift für deutsche Philologie*, 71 (1951/52), p. 200.

Similarly, criticism of the mendicancy of the friars, although not necessarily the poverty ideal, was firmly established in the medieval tradition and reappeared virtually unchanged in the criticisms of the friars by the humanists. William of St Amour had charged the friars with living illegitimately from the Gospel and contrasted their begging with Paul's claim that the apostles had worked with their hands to feed themselves [2 Thessalonians 3:6–12].[47] The mendicancy of the friars remained a crucial element in subsequent attacks on them by the secular clergy.[48] It was also carried over into the literary attack on the friars. Chaucer's friar Huberd

> . . . was the beste beggere in his hous.
> And yaf a certain ferme for the graunt:
> Noon of his brethreren cam there in his haunt.
> For though a widwe hadde nought a sho,
> So pleasant was his *In principio*
> Yit wolde have a ferthing er he wente;[49]

'The Devil's Net' makes the same point much more forcefully:

> So the collectors of alms go out,
> Then they sell the truth
> to peasant women and maids
> For cheese, fat and eggs.
> Throughout the land
> Here cultivating the greatest dishonour
> Which everywhere is a blemish.
> There bringing such evil, false sorcery,
> As they fleece the people
> With their false prattle.[50]

Erasmus revived this charge in *Praise of Folly*, sharpening the accusation that the friars were depriving the more deserving poor of their sustenance: 'Many of them too make a good living of their squalor and beggary, bellowing for bread from door to door, and indeed making a nuisance of themselves in every inn, carriage or boat to the great loss of all other beggars.'[51]

Most of the humanists, then, did little more than take over established

---

[47] Szittya, 'Antifraternal Tradition,' p. 304; id., *Antifraternal Tradition in Medieval Literature*, pp. 47–51; 'De periculis Ecclesiae,' in Ortwin Gratius, *Fasciculum rerum expetendarum*, ed. Edward Brown (London, 1690; reprint edn, Tucson, 1967), pp. 36 and 39–40.

[48] For specific examples, see Walsh, *Richard FitzRalph*, pp. 349–451 and Arnold Williams, 'Chaucer and the Friars,' *Speculum*, 28 (1953), pp. 505–6.

[49] Geoffrey Chaucer, *Canterbury Tales*, ed. John Manly (New York, 1928), pp. 155–6. See also the description of the friar's begging in the summoner's tale, pp. 320–1.

[50] *Des Teufels Netz*, pp. 170–1.

[51] *Collected Works of Erasmus*, vol. 27, p. 131.

criticisms of the friars and incorporate them into their own satires. As we will see, the critics of the friars from among the ranks of the Reformers also adopted many of the traditional charges against the friars. The advantages of this tactic are significant. If, as Penn Szittya has argued, the friars were identified directly with these biblical types in the later Middle Ages, both humanists and Reformers could play on established traditions to drive home their own messages. Robert Scribner has argued that a basic technique of Reformation propaganda was the gradual shift from one 'symbolic universe' to another through the transformation of images and symbols familiar to the audience.[52] This transformation the opponents of the friars achieved by coupling their criticisms of the friars to the traditional commonplace characterizations of them. They sought thereby to undermine the security of the friars' place in the 'private church' of the late medieval urban commune.

This tactic was supplemented during the early years of the Reformation by another equally important attempt to undercut the local legitimacy of the friars. In the second decade of the sixteenth century, the opponents of the friars began playing up their ties to the papacy and their role in the extension of papal power. This strategy is clearly apparent in the writings of Ulrich von Hutten, where the ties of the friars to the papacy serve to fuel a patriotic outrage at how the papacy, and Italians generally, have treated Germany.

However, this tactic develops only gradually in Hutten's polemics. His earliest attacks on scholastic theology, much like Erasmus's satires, do not specifically identify the friars with scholastic theology. Rather he treats the scholastics as a distinct category. In the second part of the *Letters of Obscure Men* his denunciation remains in general terms. He derides the 'impoverished, obscure theology of the last few centuries,' which has turned from 'the old, learned theology developed from the light of Scripture.'[53] This tactic is arresting in light of the identity of Hutten's chief opponents, the Dominican theologians of Cologne. But even when referring specifically to these opponents, he calls them philosophers, that is Sophists, or Turks, 'by whom true studies have perished, letters have been trampled, and divine theology reduced to loquacity, unadulterated jests, silly trifles,'[54] but does not exploit their identification as friars.

However, in 1517 Hutten returned to Germany from his second visit to Rome intent on investigating the history of papal–imperial relations

---

[52] Robert Scribner, *For the Sake of Simple Folk. Popular Propaganda for the German Reformation* (Cambridge, 1981), p. 9.

[53] Böcking, vol. 6, pp. 264–65.

[54] Böcking, vol. 1, p. 237.

and the relations between Italy and Germany. In a letter dated 3 August 1518 he indicates that he has begun work on *Vadiscus*, a dialogue which linked his humanistically oriented criticism of scholasticism with his nationalist, political attack on the papacy.[55] Thereafter his historical investigations fed a flood of polemics against the papacy. In March 1520 he sent to Ferdinand of Austria a document which he had discovered from the conflict between Henry IV and Gregory VII.[56] In late May of that year he sent to the printer a collection of documents from the schism.[57] Later that same year he produced several pamphlets outlining the fruits of his research into the history of papal–imperial relations. Of particular significance for the topic at hand is the new avenue developed by Hutten in these writings for attacking the friars. No longer are they only the implied purveyors of false, scholastic teachings. Now they are also cast as the chief agents in the extension of papal power. In 'A Remonstrance and Warning against the Presumptuous Unchristian Power of the Bishop of Rome and the Unspiritual Spiritual Estate,' Hutten openly denounces the activities of the mendicants in the service of the papacy:

> I say, they are completely without decency,
> and they are motivated by greed alone.
> For every order brings something
> they have begged in all lands,
> and have proclaimed the power of the pope.[58]

According to Lohse's analysis Luther's criticism of monastic vows amounted to a novel attack on the institution of monasticism, distinct from that of his predecessors. However, Luther's earliest treatment of the mendicants was not that different from Hutten's. Many of Luther's earliest opponents, as defenders of scholastic theology, naturally came from among the friars. Although Luther's 'Reformation breakthrough' is often cast as something distinct from the intellectual world of the humanists, he did couch his earliest reforming claims in terms remarkably similar to theirs. In his earliest reforming works Luther's chief academic concern was to reform theology and purge from it the Aristotelian accretions of the preceding three to four hundred years.[59] In a letter to Johannes Lang dated 18 May 1517, Luther reported on the

---

[55] Hajo Holborn, *Ulrich von Hutten and the German Reformation* (New Haven, 1937; reprint edn, New York, 1966), p. 113.

[56] Holborn, pp. 110–11; see Böcking, vol. 1, pp. 325–34.

[57] Holborn, p. 112; Böcking, vol. 1, pp. 371–83.

[58] Böcking, vol. 3, pp. 487–8.

[59] Scott H. Hendrix, *Luther and the Papacy: Stages in a Reformation Conflict* (Philadelphia, 1981), pp. 37 and 167–8.

advance of 'our theology and St Augustine' and the parallel decline of Aristotle at Wittenberg.[60] In August or early September of that year he wrote a 'Disputation against Scholastic Theology.'[61]

Interestingly, like the humanists, Luther avoided in his early works identifying his opponents among the scholastics as friars. But this fact is not so surprising when one remembers that Luther himself was a member of an Observant order and that for some time after his break with Rome he continued to wear his cowl and live in the cloister of the Wittenberg Augustinian Hermits. Furthermore it appears that Luther remained on good terms not only with members of his own order, but also with the local Franciscans through 1520.[62]

1520, however, marks a turning point in Luther's relationship with the mendicant orders. This is most clearly manifest in his treatment of them in the 'Address to the Christian Nobility':

> And they [the mendicants] should also be relieved of preaching and hearing confession, unless they are called to do this by the bishops, parishes, congregations, or civil authorities. Nothing but hatred and envy between priests and monks has come out of this kind of preaching and confessing, and great offense and hindrance to the common people has grown out of it. It ought to stop because it can well be dispensed with. It looks suspiciously as though the Holy Roman See has purposely increased this army lest the priests and bishops, unable to stand the pope's tyranny any longer, some day become too powerful for him and start a reformation. That would be unbearable to his holiness.[63]

Luther goes on to warn against the infighting between orders and the dangers of reliance on works righteousness in them.[64] In the above quotation, Luther identifies clearly the primary issues of contention between the mendicants and the secular clergy and comes down firmly on the side of the latter in the age-old conflict between them. Bernd Moeller has suggested that Luther's strategy in the 'Address to the Christian Nobility' is to drum up support and create a reforming bloc by inventing a 'We' party among the clergy and laity against the 'They'

---

[60] WABr, 1:99: 'Theologia nostra et S Augustinus prospere proscedunt et regnant in nostra universitate Deo operante. Aristoteles descendit paulatim inclinatus ad ruinam prope futuram sempiternam.'

[61] WA, 1:221.

[62] Gerhard Hammer, 'Militia Franciscana seu militia Christi. Das neugefundene Protokoll einer Disputation der sächsischen Franziskaner mit Vertretern der Wittenberger theologischen Fakultät am 3. und 4. Oktober 1519,' ARG, 69 (1978), pp. 51–81 and ARG, 70 (1979), pp. 59–105.

[63] WA, 6:438.

[64] Ibid., pp. 438–40.

party of Rome.[65] Here Luther accurately identifies the role of the mendicants in the extension of papal power and, in the spirit of Hutten, lays the blame for the deterioration of the church on this alliance. Obviously, in denouncing the alliance of the papacy and mendicants, Luther is reaching out to the parochial clergy as the allies for his cause.

---

[65] Bernd Moeller, 'Klerus und Antiklerikalismus in Luthers Schrift *An den Christlichen Adel Deutscher Nation* von 1520,' in Dykema and Oberman, pp. 353–65.

CHAPTER TWO

'Foolish little monks and priests'

At the centre of the Reformation campaign against the friars looms the figure of Johann Eberlin von Günzburg. More than any of his fellows among the former Franciscans who opted for the Evangelicals, Eberlin was an implacable foe of the friars throughout much of his reforming career. Already in his early writings, which were published collectively under the title 'The Fifteen Confederates,' he devoted considerable attention specifically to the crimes perpetrated on Christendom by the mendicant orders. Many of the themes developed in this cycle of pamphlets reappear later, albeit often in noticeably modified forms, in the 1523 campaign against the friars. Therefore, Eberlin's early writings form a necessary backdrop for the evolution of Reformation antifraternalism.

Gottfried Geiger, in a recent analysis of Eberlin's early reforming pamphlets, labelled Eberlin 'an eclectic and elementary student' of the Reformation.[1] Even Eberlin's earliest writings have been characterized at various times as the work of a Franciscan Observant, a biblical humanist or a Protestant Reformer. In each case convincing evidence has been marshalled to support the characterization applied. This apparent ambiguity points to the shared concern with the reform of the church in all of these movements and to the fluid nature of the boundaries between them. Eberlin's eclecticism, then, is indicative of the ease with which would-be reformers in the early sixteenth century could migrate in and out of the various reforming camps in the initial years of the Reformation. Hans-Jürgen Goertz has described anticlericalism as something of a meta-theme in Reformation polemics: it provided form and direction for other themes developed in reforming *Flugschriften*.[2] An analysis of the role of anticlerical themes in Eberlin's early pamphlets will provide valuable insights not only into the evolution of Reformation anticlericalism, but also into the role of anticlericalism in the dissemination of reforming thought.

Eberlin's early writings concentrate on social and political issues to an extent traditionally regarded as antithetical to the concerns of the

---

[1] Gottfried Geiger, 'Die reformatorischen Initia Johann Eberlins von Günzburg nach seinem Flugschriften,' in *Festgabe für Ernst Walter Zeeden zum 60. Geburtstag am 14. Mai 1976*, ed. Horst Rabe *et al.* (Münster, 1976), pp. 185–95.

[2] Hans-Jürgen Goertz, *Pfaffenhaß und groß Geschrei. Die reformatorischen Bewegungen in Deutschland 1517–1529* (Munich, 1987), pp. 117–18.

Wittenberg Reformation. These social and political concerns initially drew to the study of Eberlin's works disaffected members of both confessional camps of modern Germany, as well as reformers of various stripes. In Eberlin they thought they found an independently minded Reformer who was a friend neither of the Protestant state church nor of the papacy.[3] Recent research has tended to discredit this interpretation and emphasizes instead the distance between Eberlin's early social activism and the more Lutheran apoliticism of his later writings, as well as highlighting the importance of observing the chronology of Eberlin's writings and the evolution of his reforming thought.[4] The starting point for Eberlin's reforming vision is now thought to consist of an essentially Erasmian stance supplemented with specific Lutheran accretions.[5] In the integration of these two reforming traditions Eberlin was likely not unique. Cornelis Augustijn has challenged the established interpretation that in the 1520s the humanist movement was split by the Luther issue and its members absorbed into one or the other of two distinct confessional camps. He suggests instead that this decade witnessed a further development of humanists' theological programme, and that

---

[3] G. Strobel, 'Nachricht von Johann Eberlins von Günzburg Leben und Schriften,' *Literarisches Museum* I (Altdorf, 1778), pp. 363–85, enlisted Eberlin as an ally in defence of Phillipist pietism against Lutheran orthodoxy. Bernhard Riggenbach, *Johann Eberlin von Günzburg und sein Reformprogramm. Ein Beitrag zur Geschichte des sechzehnten Jahrhunderts* (Tübingen, 1874), saw in him an independently minded forerunner of the Old Catholic party. Julius Werner, *Johann Eberlin von Günzburg. Ein reformatorisches Charakterbild aus Luthers Zeit*, 2nd edn (Heidelberg, 1905), regarded Eberlin's reforming vision as a model for Christian socialists at the turn of the century.

[4] The first thorough analysis of the development of Eberlin's reforming thought was produced by Max Radlkofer, *Johann Eberlin von Günzburg und sein Vetter Hans Jakob Wehe von Leipheim* (Nördlingen, 1887).

[5] German-speaking historians emphasize Eberlin's ties to the humanists. Their English-speaking counterparts, while not neglecting this aspect of Eberlin's thought, play up more the influences of Luther on his reforming vision. See Helmut Weidhase, *Kunst und Sprache im Spiegel der reformatorischen und humanistischen Schriften Johann Eberlins von Günzburg,* Phil. Diss. (Tübingen, 1967); Geiger, 'Die reformatorischen Initia Eberlins'; Christian Peters, *Johann Eberlin von Günzburg ca. 1465–1533. Franziskanische Reformer, Humanist und konservativer Reformator* (Gütersloh, 1994); Susan Groag Bell, 'Johann Eberlin von Günzburg's Wolfaria: The First Protestant Utopia,' *Church History*, 36 (1967), pp. 122–39; Richard G. Cole, *Eberlin von Günzburg and the German Reformation*, PhD dissertation (Ohio State University, 1963); id., 'The Pamphlet and Social Forces in the Reformation,' *Lutheran Quarterly*, 18 (1965), pp. 195–205; id., 'Law and Order in the Sixteenth Century: Johann Eberlin von Günzburg and the Problem of Political Authority,' *Lutheran Quarterly*, 23 (1971), pp. 251–6; id., 'The Dynamics of Printing in the Sixteenth Century,' in Lawrence P. Buck and Jonathan Zophy (eds), *The Social History of the Reformation* (Columbus, 1972), pp. 93–105; Steven Ozment, *The Reformation in the Cities* (New Haven, 1975), pp. 91–108.

initially the boundaries between proto-confessional camps were not as clearly defined for their contemporaries as they appear to later observers.[6] Like many of his contemporaries, Eberlin shared much of the humanist ideal of the church, but drew particulars from the visions of both Luther and Erasmus with no awareness of contradiction between them.

However, current research, although not specifically denying its importance, has tended to play down the significance of a third recognized influence on Eberlin's reforming vision, his background as a member of the Franciscan Observance. While attempts have been made to illuminate the medieval background to Eberlin's thought, these have concentrated usually on comparing his utterances with select examples of late medieval reforming sentiment in the most general terms.[7] A notable exception to this trend is to be found in the 1902 dissertation of Wilhelm Lucke. Lucke argued that apparent inconsistencies within 'The Fifteen Confederates' largely disappear when one realizes that the individual confederates were written in an order different from that in which they appear in the collection.[8] He suggested an alternate chronological order for the confederates and, integrating the known biographical data from Eberlin's life, proposed an intellectual development from a committed Franciscan piety via Erasmian humanism to the Wittenberg reform movement. Although strongly critical of ecclesiastical abuse, Eberlin's statements in the earliest confederates could have been made by any member of the Franciscan Observance.[9] Lucke's analysis of Eberlin's debt to the ideals of the Franciscan Observance

[6] Cornelis Augustijn, 'Die Stellung der Humanisten zur Glaubensspaltung 1518 1530,' in Erwin Iserloh (ed.), *Confessio Augustana und Confutatio. Der Augsburger Reichstag 1530 und die Einheit der Kirche* (Münster, 1980), pp. 37–8.

[7] Johann Heinrich Schmidt, *'Die 15 Bundesgenossen' des Johann Eberlin von Günzburg*, Phil. Diss. (Leipzig, 1900), pp. 29–33, saw in Eberlin's thought echoes of the teachings of the great late medieval mystics and reform preachers. Hans-Herbert Ahrens, *Die religiosen, nationalen und sozialen Gedanken Johann Eberlin von Günzburgs mit besonderer Berücksichtigung seiner anonymen Flugschriften*, Phil. Diss. (Hamburg, 1939), pp. 10 and 21–35, suggested that Eberlin's early writings reveal the evolution of his reforming thought from Catholic orthodoxy to Lutheran orthodoxy via a return to the original vision of St Francis. More recently, Kurt Stöckl, *Untersuchungen zu Johann Eberlin von Günzburg*, Phil. Diss. (Munich, 1952), pp. 69–70, has argued that the style of Eberlin's early pamphlets places him in the tradition of the great medieval penance preachers like Geiler von Kaisersberg.

[8] Wilhelm Lucke, *Die Enstehung der '15 Bundesgenossen' des Johann Eberlins von Günzburg*, Phil. Diss. (Hall, 1902), pp. 32–9.

[9] Ibid., pp. 41–8.

does not go much beyond this and subsequent interpreters have failed to take up his line of investigation. The most recent biography of Eberlin, Christian Peters's *Johann Eberlin von Günzburg ca. 1465–1533. Franziskanische Reformer, Humanist und konservativer Reformator*, continues to characterize the earliest stages of Eberlin's reforming thought as a mixture of late medieval reform sentiment and the programme of the Christian humanists. Yet, despite the title of his book, Peters's analysis of Eberlin as a Franciscan reformer amounts to little more than suggesting the influences on his thought of such general reform programmes as the *Gravamina Germanicae Nationis* and the *Reformatio Sigismundi*.[10]

Yet, the integration of humanist and Observant reforming themes appears the best way to characterize Eberlin's earliest reform proposals. It appears that Eberlin regarded the humanist reform programme as fully compatible with his membership in the Franciscan order. Hans-Jürgen Goertz has distinguished medieval from Reformation anticlericalism on the basis that the former aimed only at resolving particular grievances against the clergy, while the latter sought to 'break the domination of the Catholic clergy and to dissolve the estate entirely.'[11] Initially, Eberlin's anticlericalism was of the former variety. He aimed at a correction of perceived abuses within the first estate, but behind this lay a continued respect for and veneration of the status and role of the clergy. This becomes especially clear when one looks into his suggestions for the reform of the regular clergy, which, while indebted to the reform programmes of Luther and Erasmus on specific details, proceed from the standpoint of the fifteenth-century Observant reform movement within the Franciscan order.

Describing himself, Eberlin indicated his own earlier zeal for the ideals of the Franciscan order: 'Eberlin also praised the Poor Clares in Horb so much, when he preached the Rule in Advent – God forgive him that he preached Franciscan fables for Christ's teaching – that afterwards the imperial official was unable to demand the general taxes from them . . .'[12] The uniqueness of Eberlin's conversion to the Lutheran movement as a mature man has often been noted. Max Radlkofer has remarked as well that Eberlin was no child novice to the Franciscan order and that his decision to enter it reflects a mature

---

[10] Peters, p. 51.

[11] Hans-Jürgen Goertz, ' "What a Tangled and Tenuous Mess the Clergy is!" Clerical Anticlericalism in the Reformation Period,' in Dykema and Oberman, p. 517.

[12] 'Klage der sieben frommen Pfaffen,' Enders, vol. 2, p. 70.

identification with its ideals.[13] Born sometime around 1465 in Klein-kötz, a small village six kilometres south of Günzburg, Eberlin would have been in his mid-fifties when he joined the Reformers and his mid-thirties when he became a Franciscan, probably sometime around 1500.[14] Prior to his profession, he had attended several universities, attaining at least the degree of *Magister*. The university matriculations indicate, in addition, that he took orders and served for some time as a priest in the diocese of Augsburg.[15]

Eberlin does not specifically state where or when he entered the Franciscan order, although this may have occurred in Heilbronn sometime around 1501.[16] Christian Peters argues that in Heilbronn Eberlin may have first come into contact with the humanist movement under the tutelage of Johann Kröner von Scherdüng, who Eberlin himself claims encouraged him to join the Observant Franciscans.[17] Of his early years in the order we are also inadequately informed, although there has been a suggestion that he came to know Conrad Pellican, the reform-minded prior of the Observant cloister in Basel, and other members of the Alsatian humanist circle during this period. Throughout his writings Eberlin makes detailed references to people and places in Alsace. On the basis of these, Wilhelm Lucke has suggested convincingly that he was a member of the Observant priory in the town of Barr in Upper Alsace. Here he came to know the Schlettstätter humanists,

---

[13] Radlkofer, p. 571.

[14] Ernst Deuerlein first suggested, on the basis of Eberlin's matriculation record at Freiburg University, that he was born in Kleinkötz instead of Günzburg. See Ernst Duerlein, 'Nachtrag zu Johann Eberlin von Günzburg' in Götz, Freiherrn von Pölnitz (ed.), *Lebensbilder aus dem bayerischen Schwaben*, 6 (Munich, 1958), p. 495. Bcll, p. 123, argued that Eberlin was born around 1460. This interpretation has been challenged and a date of 1465 or later assigned. See, Hermann Ehmer, 'Johann Eberlin von Günzburg in Wertheim,' *Wertheimer Jahrbuch*, 1983 (1985): 67 n. 48; Peters pp. 17–18.

[15] Götz, Freiherrn von Pölintz, *Die Matrikel der Ludwig-Maximillians-Universität Ingolstadt-Landshut-München*, vol. 1 (Munich, 1937), pp. 43 and 1405; Hans Georg Wackernagel (ed.), *Die Matrikel der Universität Basel*, vol. 1 1460–1529 (Basel, 1951), p. 209; Herman Mayer (ed.), *Die Matrikel der Universität Freiburg in Breisgau*, vol. 1 1460–1656 (Freiburg i Br, 1907), p. 110. The Ingolstadt matriculation may apply to a different Eberlin, see Ehmer, p. 67, n. 48; Erich Langguth, 'Einmütig in der neuen Lehre: Dr Johann Eberlin von Günzburg – Graf Micheal II. – Dr Andreas Hoffrichter. Der Wechsel im Wertheimer Pfarramt 1530,' *Wertheimer Jahrbuch*, 1983 (1985), p. 76, n. 18; Peters, p. 17, n. 13.

[16] Radlkofer, p. 3. See 'Wider die falschen Geistlichen, genannt Franziskaner und Barfüsser,' Enders, vol. 3, p. 46; 'Wie sich ein Diener Gottes Worts in seinem Thun halten soll,' Enders, vol. 3, p. 205.

[17] Peters, pp. 19–21.

including Beatus Rhenanus, and also Conrad Pellican who was active in nearby Rufach between 1508 and 1519.[18]

The first firm indication we have of Eberlin's life as a Franciscan comes from his own pen. 'Against the False Religious, Known as the Barefoot Friars and Franciscans,' written in 1523, is dedicated to the officials, councils and communities of Horb and Rottenburg, and to all citizens of the land of Hochburg, 'to all who have heard my sermons and recognize my name.' Eberlin reminds his readers of how well and often they received him 'four years ago when I was preacher at the Franciscan cloister in Tübingen.'[19] He may also have served as confessor for the cloisters of the Poor Clares under the spiritual care of the Tübingen Franciscans, an experience that would explain the particular concern in his writings for the plight of nuns.[20]

There is no indication of the length of Eberlin's stay in Tübingen, although, given the number of events he says occurred there, he must have held the post of preacher for some time.[21] In addition to the sermon to the Poor Clares mentioned above, Eberlin claims to have preached in Rottenburg a sermon which extolled the liberties of the clerical estate to such a degree that 'no one should demand an accounting from them; and even that next day two priests bathed openly with their concubines.'[22] He also indicates that he became involved in a theological controversy at the University of Tübingen, but provides no indication of its nature.[23] However, there has been some speculation that this involved a showdown between scholastic and humanist members of the faculty, and that Eberlin, in the tradition of Paul Scriptoris who had earlier been at the Tübingen friary, defended the new learning.[24] Shortly thereafter Eberlin was transferred out of the Tübingen cloister. The earlier perception of this as a form of punishment, imposed by his superiors under pressure from the imperial official and the theologians at the university, has been rejected on the

---

[18] Lucke, *Die Entstehung der 15 Bundesgenossen*, pp. 10–14. The relevant references are scattered throughout Eberlin's writings: 'Der erste Bundesgenosse,' Enders, vol. 1, p. 4; 'Der III. Bundesgenosse,' Enders, vol. 1, p. 30; 'Der VIII. Bundesgenosse,' Enders, vol. 1, p. 83; 'Der XIV. Bundesgenosse,' Enders, vol. 1, p. 160; 'Mich wundert, dass kein Geld im Land ist,' Enders, vol. 3, pp. 160 and 181; 'Wider die falschen Geistlichen, genannt Barfüsser und Franziskaner,' Enders, vol. 3, pp. 70–1.

[19] Enders, vol. 3, pp. 67–8.

[20] 'Wider den unvorsichtigen Ausgang vieler Klosterleute,' Enders, vol. 2, pp. 121 and 136 is dedicated to the abbesses of the nunneries at Söflingen and Eutingen. Lucke, *Die Entstehung der 15 Bundesgenossen*, pp. 11–12.

[21] Geiger, 'Die reformatorischen Initia Eberlins,' p. 180.

[22] 'Klage der sieben frommen Pfaffen,' Enders, vol. 2, p. 70.

[23] Ibid.

[24] Peters, pp. 21–8.

basis of the subsequent positions of honour held by Eberlin within the order, and the move is now explained by the standard practice of frequent transferrals within the mendicant orders.[25]

Unfortunately we are again forced to rely on conjecture for the most crucial phase of Eberlin's pre-reforming life: the point at which he came to know Luther's writings. Historians have divided themselves into two opposing camps over the issue of where and how Eberlin became acquainted with these. One line of interpretation, initiated by Bernhard Riggenbach and subsequently developed by Max Radlkofer and Günther Heger, suggests that Eberlin was transferred directly from Tübingen to Ulm, where he assumed the duties of preacher and lector in the Observant convent. Here he was introduced to the works of Luther through the reform-minded humanist and city doctor Wolfgang Rychard. Interrupting his tenure in Ulm he also served for a time as lector in the Franciscan priory in Freiburg, but his espousal of Luther's writings led to his transferral back to Ulm in early 1521.[26]

More convincing, however, is the argument suggested initially by Lucke, that Eberlin was transferred from Tübingen to Basel, although his claim that Eberlin there assumed the post of vice-guardian of the Franciscan house has been challenged successfully by Heger. In Basel Eberlin joined a humanist sodality whose members included Pellican, the Amerbach brothers, Beatus Rhenanus and the Froben brothers. He then came to know the early writings of Luther in an atmosphere of reform encouraged by the liberal bishop of Constance, Christoph von Uttenheim, and under the tutelage of Pellican, who was occupied with preparing the Wittenberger's works for the press of Adam Petris.[27] In a letter dated 5 April 1521, Zwingli makes reference to 'frater Aeberlinus minorita.' Zwingli assumed in the letter that Eberlin was still in Basel at this time. We are now certain that Eberlin was then in fact in Ulm, but Lucke took the reference as a further indication that Eberlin remained in Basel from 1519 until early 1521, when he was unexpectedly transferred

---

[25] Lucke, *Die Enstehung der 15 Bundesgenossen*, p. 12; Geiger, 'Die reformatorischen Initia Eberlins,' p. 180; Günther Heger, *Johann Eberlin von Günzburg und seine Vorstellungen über eine Reform in Reich und Kirche* (Berlin, 1985), p. 14. According to Bernhard Neidiger, *Mendikanten zwischen Ordensideal und städtischer Realität. Untersuchungen zum wirtschaftlichen Verhalten der Bettelorden in Basel* (Berlin, 1981), p. 177, well-educated friars were regularly shuffled between friaries to fill various posts in the order which required their particular talents.

[26] Riggenbach, pp. 12–15; Radlkofer, p. 8; Heger, pp. 14–15.

[27] Lucke, *Die Entstehung der 15 Bundesgenossen*, pp. 14–18. See also Curt Wulkau, *Das kirchliche Idea des Johann Eberlin von Günzburg*, Phil. Diss. (Halle-Wittenberg, 1922), p. 11; Geiger, 'Die reformatorischen Initia Johann Eberlins,' p. 180; Heger, p. 15; Peters, pp. 28–9.

to Ulm.[28] Eberlin himself makes only vague and infrequent reference to the Ulm humanists. The correspondence of Wolfgang Rychard indicates close ties to a number of humanists among the Ulm clergy, but first refers to Eberlin only in 1523 when he returned to the city.[29] By contrast, Zwingli's letter and a later reference to Eberlin by Basilius Amerbach indicate that he was well known in the humanist circle in Basel.[30] His later writings and activities also indicate more than a passing acquaintance with the city.

During this period Eberlin may have first tried his hand at publishing. In 1520 or shortly thereafter an anonymous pamphlet appeared, without indication of date or place of publication, entitled 'An Epistle to the Parson of Highsense (Hohensynn), concerning Dr Martin Luther's Teaching.' Alfred Götze, who has edited and published the pamphlet, has suggested Eberlin as its author.[31] Masquerading as a simple layman, the author satirically compares the life of the clergy to the chief characteristics of the example provided by Christ: his roles as shepherd, teacher, preacher and martyr. Naturally, the contemporary clergy fare badly in the comparison.[32] Götze characterizes this work as ironic throughout and it certainly lacks the bitterness of Eberlin's other writings.[33] However, during this period Eberlin was still somewhat detached from the Wittenberg reform movement and had not yet openly broken with the Franciscan order. As the present study is not directly concerned with establishing the authenticity of disputed works attributed to Eberlin, this pamphlet will be cited only to reinforce interpretations drawn from his other writings.

In early 1521, likely February, Eberlin was transferred by his superiors from Basel to Ulm.[34] Eberlin himself indicates that at the time of his arrival in Ulm, he was not yet openly preaching reform in the sense of the Wittenberg movement:

---

[28] Lucke, *Die Enstehung der 15 Bundesgenossen*, p. 14. Zwingli's letter has been published by Emil Egli, Georg Finsler and Walter Köhler (eds), *Huldreich Zwinglis Sämtliche Werke*, vol. 7: *Zwinglis Briefwechsel*, vol. 1 *Die Briefe von 1510–1522* (Leipzig, 1911), pp. 445–6.

[29] Rychard, Nr. 1–2: Briefwechsel Wolfgang Rychards (transcript by M. Georg Veesenmeyer, 1823) Stadtarchiv Ulm; Radlkofer, p. 7.

[30] Alfred Hartmann (ed.), *Die Amerbachkorrespondenz*, vol. 2 (Basel, 1943), p. 33.

[31] Alfred Götze, 'Ein Sendbrief Eberlins von Günzburg,' *Zeitschrift für deutsche Philologie*, 36 (1904), pp. 145, 150–3. The suspicion that Eberlin was the author of this piece is reinforced by Christian Peters's discovery that the original edition of it stems from the press of Adam Petris in Basel, rather than from Augsburg as Götze suggested. See Peters, pp. 29–30.

[32] 'Sendtbrieff an Pfarrer von Hohensynn' in Götze, pp. 145–9.

[33] Ibid., p. 154.

[34] Peters, pp. 30–1.

> When I came to you, God placed a great desire in your hearts to learn his Word through me, but I failed, in part because I did not know it and in part because I was afraid to speak the truth. But through Dr Luther's little book I became daily more learned and ready to preach the truth.[35]

The first clear evidence that Eberlin had openly declared himself for Luther's cause and, in doing so, attracted the attention of his superiors comes from Lent 1521. In a letter dated 15/16 March to the papal vice chancellor Guilio de Medici the legate Aleander refers to 'uno fratre Minorita de Observantia in Ulma' who had previously been preaching in an orthodox manner, but had recently turned to the new teaching.[36]

According to Wilhelm Lucke's revised chronology, it was during the period prior to Eberlin's emergence as an adherent to Luther's cause that the first confederates were written. Lucke suggested that the first to be written were numbers seven, two, three and four and that they form a unity, of which number seven still bears the signs of being the introduction. Critical of ecclesiastical abuses, yet written from an orthodox standpoint, they indicate a clear debt to elements of Luther's 'Address to the Christian Nobility' which would have been known in Basel by late September 1520. Based on this borrowing from Luther, Lucke holds that the four pamphlets were most likely written in Basel between October 1520 and January 1521.[37] While accepting the basic outlines of this argument, Gottfried Geiger suggests, I believe correctly, that they were actually written in Ulm in February and March 1521. Furthermore, they were first drafted as occasional writings, sermons and disputation articles, and were only later reworked into their present literary form.[38] In them the ironical tone of 'An Epistle to the Parson of Highsense' gives way to a more literal approach and a greater sense of urgency. It is, therefore, tempting to regard the 'Epistle' as an academic exercise, possibly indicative of Eberlin's vision of reform derived from his connections with the Basel humanists, and the early confederates as a product of more isolated and embittered attempts at reform in Ulm in the uncertainty immediately preceding the Diet of Worms.

The 'Seventh Confederate,' which is entitled 'The Praise of the Parson,' is an attack on the practice of endowing mortuary masses and the abuses associated with them. Eberlin suggests that the souls of the dead are better served by simple masses performed by the parish priest,

---

[35] 'Die andere getreue Vermahnung an den Rath von Ulm,' Enders, vol. 3, p. 2.

[36] The letter of Aleander has been reproduced in Th. Brieger, *Quellen und Forschungen zur Geschichte der Reformation*, vol. 1: *Aleander und Luther* (Gotha, 1884), p. 106 and Radlkofer, p. 9.

[37] Lucke, *Die Entstehung der 15 Bundesgenossen*, pp. 33–48.

[38] Geiger, 'Die reformatorischen Initia Eberlins,' pp. 181–2. See also Peters, pp. 43–7.

prayers and acts of charity than by all the nonsensical howling of mortuary masses, which are rarely performed and only contribute to the laziness and decadence of the clergy.[39] The 'Second Confederate,' 'On the Forty Day Fast before Easter and Others,' challenges the practice of mandatory fasting which has no biblical basis and is against common sense. Rarely observed by the clergy, who exempt each other from the strictures of canon law, fasting is a practice imposed on the laity, whose lives are least adaptable to its demands. A sample of the nationalism that underlies much of Eberlin's reform programme is the argument that these burdens are particularly onerous for the German peoples, who must work much harder for their daily bread than their neighbours in the more hospitable climates of France and lands south of the Alps.[40] In the next two confederates, Eberlin points his attack against the cloistered. The third, 'An Exhortation to all Christians to take Pity on the Cloistered Women' bewails the plight of nuns and exhorts parents not to send their daughters to convents. The cloisters are depicted as dens of iniquity where tyrannical superiors endanger not only the physical, but also the spiritual health of their charges.[41] In the 'Fourth Confederate,' 'On the long, disgusting Braying which the Monks, Priests and Nuns call the Canonical Hours,' Eberlin challenges the focal activity of cloistered life. He holds the corruption of early Christian prayers to be the origin of the contemporary form of canonical hours, which when observed are almost never performed in the spirit intended. They cannot compare to the hard work and honest piety of the simple layman. This lay diligence can, however, provide a model for monastic reform; the clergy must approach their offices as vocations and renounce their lives of laziness.[42]

Wilhelm Lucke characterizes these works as standing firmly within the bounds of orthodoxy and recognizing the authority of the church throughout. Written before Eberlin broke with either the church or his own order, they are concerned only with the correction of individual abuses. Although Luther is never mentioned by name, they do draw on his reform programme. In particular the 'Seventh Confederate' appears as an expansion of article the 16 of 'Address to the Christian Nobility.' Parallels between the other three confederates and the 'Address to the Christian Nobility' are noted by Lucke, especially between the second and article 19 of Luther's tract.[43] Subsequent interpreters of Eberlin's

[39] 'Der VII. Bundesgenosse,' Enders, vol. 1, pp. 67–78.

[40] 'Der andere Bundesgenosse,' Enders, vol. 1, pp. 15–22.

[41] 'Der III. Bundesgenosse,' Enders, vol. 1, pp. 23–33.

[42] 'Der IIII. Bundesgenosse,' Enders, vol. 1, pp. 35–43.

[43] Lucke, *Die Entstehung der 15 Bundesgenossen*, pp. 42–8.

writings have accepted that Eberlin derived specific *gravamina* from the 'Address to the Christian Nobility,' but argue that the basic thought of these pamphlets is primarily Erasmian.[44]

The outlines of Eberlin's reform programme certainly suggest that he belongs to the Christian Renaissance. Throughout the earliest confederates, he calls for the removal of empty ceremonies and their replacement with devout piety. The 'Seventh Confederate' identifies mortuary masses and vigils as impediments to true help for the departed soul.[45] Even if they did serve a purpose, they are seldom observed and, if they are, are performed mechanically with no thought to their purpose.[46] Similarly, the canonical hours observed by the clergy are understood neither by them nor by their hearers and consequently Eberlin regards them as useless.[47] However, he saves his sharpest barbs for the fasts imposed by the clergy on the laity, from which dispensations are calculated with mathematical exactitude and which lead to thousands of mortal sins annually.[48] All of these should be swept away and replaced with simpler ceremonies stressing the disposition of the participants. Vigils and mortuary masses should be replaced by simple remembrance services and sincere prayer.[49] The canonical hours should be replaced by simple prayer, tailored to the individual's needs, and the fast should be a voluntary abstinence, dictated by the individual's own physical and spiritual needs.[50]

Eberlin's discussion of the reform of ecclesiastical ceremonies indicates his distance from Luther. Rather than dealing with the central themes of Reformation theology, his vision of reform stresses an ethical reorientation of Christianity to the *lex christi*. In the 'Seventh Confeder-

---

[44] Geiger, 'Die reformatorischen Initia Eberlins,' pp. 191–3; Heger, p. 20.

[45] 'Der VII. Bundesgenosse,' Enders, vol. 1, p. 72: 'das solicher usserlicher gebracht zů grosser hindernüss dienet an hylff der todten . . .'

[46] Ibid., pp. 74–5.

[47] 'Der IIII. Bundesgenosse,' Enders, vol. 1, p. 42.

[48] 'Der andere Bundesgenosse,' Enders, vol. 1, p. 16: 'Das ist aber noch schimpfflicher, so sie uffzeichen in mathematischer ussrechnung welche da von entschuldiget siend, . . .'; p. 20: 'Solichs gebot bringt hundertausent todsünd jårlich, . . .'

[49] 'Der VII. Bundesgenosse,' Enders, vol. 1, pp. 70–1: 'Dar nach so man an fyrtagen zusamen kumpt in die tempell, soll man in gemein oder sunderheit erzelen dem volk die zal deren, so in vergangen tagen verscheiden sind, . . . Das man aber uff ein begrebnüss oder jars tag måss helt, und do mit das christlich volk versamelt und vermanet zů bitten für die todten, ist meins beduncken ia auch haltens behilfflich und trostlich den todten . . .'

[50] 'Der IIII. Bundesgenosse,' Enders, vol. 1, p. 39: 'Alle obgemelte prediger, beichtvätter, amptherren, krancken u. sollen got täglich fleissiglich in andåchtigem gebåt sich dar stellen nach wyss inen gemåss und nach anligender not. Aber welche stund oder wie lang und vyl ist in nit gebotten'; 'Der andere Bundesgenosse,' Enders, vol. 1, p. 19: 'Aber christlich fasten ist nicht dann ein williger bedachter abbruch so vyl und lang als dir not ist, nach diner art zu kestigung des lybs, in underthånig machen dem gůtwilligen gaist.'

ate,' he suggests that money used to endow masses for the dead would be better given to the poor, for the lives of the living affect the souls of departed relatives.[51] Eberlin's ethical interpretation of the essence of Christianity is, however, best illustrated by his contrast between the canonical hours and true service to God: love, faith, hope and help for the poor.[52] Gottfried Geiger suggests that this identification of the Gospel as the law of Christ indicates clearly Eberlin's distance from Luther and adherence to the biblical humanism of Erasmus.[53] However, Eberlin's primary concern with social and ethical questions also indicates his distance from the 'religion of the spirit' of Erasmus.[54] Geiger himself has indicated that in 'The Fifteen Confederates' Eberlin is not so concerned with developing theological issues as with providing a catalogue of abuses.[55] As well, Cornelis Augustijn has noted that there was little new in the humanist attack on ecclesiastical abuses, most of which had long been the subject of *gravamina*.[56] Concerned primarily with the correction of abuses in the church, Eberlin saw in Luther's 'Address to the Christian Nobility' and the writings of Erasmus comprehensive lists of these abuses and viable suggestions for their reform.

Eberlin expends much effort in these pamphlets identifying those responsible for the perversion of the *lex Christi*. Alfred Götze suggested that the difference in tone between the 'Epistle to the Parson of Highsense' and 'The Fifteen Confederates' derives from the fact that the former deals with the prelates instead of Eberlin's chief enemies, the monks and especially the Franciscan Observants.[57] The earliest confederates are, however, in no way particularly antimonastic or antifraternal. Rather, at this stage, Eberlin's anticlerical comments indicate a desire to eradicate abuses among the clergy at all levels and stations. The 'Seventh Confederate' opens with a denunciation of the self-serving teachings of the 'kitchen preachers' both within and outside of the religious orders.[58] The other objects of Eberlin's ire are the 'temple

---

[51] 'Der VII. Bundesgenosse,' Enders, vol. 1, p. 76: 'Geben spend den armen, hălfen den dürsstigen, . . .'; p. 71: 'Das aber ein gross (doch wenig erkant) hilff den todten sy besserung des lăbens deren die in irem geschlecht by lăben blibent, . . .'

[52] 'Der IIII. Bundesgenosse,' Enders, vol. 1, p. 36: 'unser münch, pfaffen und nunnen haben unss verwysen das wir meinen, nicht sy got angenemers dann ire vogel gsang, das sie nennen siben tag zeit, . . . und dar neben rechter christenlicher gots dienst versumpt wirt, welcher stadt in lieb, gloub und hoffnung, und in hilff der armen.'

[53] Geiger, 'Die reformatorischen Initia Eberlins,' p. 195.

[54] On the theological programme of the humanists, see Augustijn, pp. 40–2.

[55] Geiger, 'Die reformatorischen Initia Eberlins,' pp. 186–7.

[56] Augustijn, pp. 39–40.

[57] Götze, p. 154.

[58] 'Der VII. Bundesgenosse,' Enders, vol. 1, pp. 68–9.

servants,' whom he specifically identifies as the monks, priests and nuns.[59] On only one occasion does this work refer to the excessive numbers in the mendicant orders. This occurs in a paragraph which contains a reference to the other 14 confederates, identified by Lucke as a later insertion.[60] That the reference to the mendicants, too, is an interpolation is suggested by frequent later references in the pamphlet to monks and priests or monks, nuns and priests. Likewise, the chief villains in the 'Second Confederate' are not only the monks, but the priests as well. The two groups do not always appear together and Eberlin contrasts the hard-working German laity with the lazy, well-fed monks, who extol the merits of their unobserved fasts.[61] But the blame for the burdensome fast laid on the laity lies with the 'foolish little monks and priests.'[62]

By way of contrast the 'Third Confederate' attacks the monks almost to the exclusion of the priests. This can be explained to a large degree by the subject matter of the pamphlet. As an exposition on the trials and tribulations faced by cloistered women, it would naturally concentrate on the monks, to whom was usually entrusted the cure of souls for the nuns. Consequently, Eberlin's characterizations of unlearned monks serving as confessors and preachers of fables come as no surprise.[63] In addition, these statements may reflect the beginning of Eberlin's changed status within the Ulm cloister, adding further credence to Gottfried Geiger's claim that these works were written there in early 1521. Eberlin's description of the poor relations between the inhabitants of a cloister could carry an autobiographical note.[64] The work, in fact, concludes with a damning exposition of the oppression of nuns by monks. This, however, is identified by Lucke as also a later addition which, by presenting the nuns as the virtuous quarry of the monks, changes the nature of the polemic and reflects Eberlin's later personal grudge against the monks.[65]

Lucke's claim is reinforced by the 'Fourth Confederate' which returns to a denunciation of monks, priests and nuns as a group, often referring to them again as 'temple servants.' The monks were, admittedly the first to pervert simple Christian prayer into the canonical hours as a means to accumulate wealth and avoid useful labour. However, when the secular

---

[59] Ibid., p. 72.

[60] Ibid., pp. 75–6; Lucke, *Die Entstehung der 15 Bundesgenossen*, p. 40.

[61] 'Der andere Bundesgenosse,' Enders, vol. 1, p. 17.

[62] Ibid., p. 20.

[63] 'Der III. Bundesgenosse,' Enders, vol. 1, p. 29.

[64] For example, ibid., p. 27.

[65] Ibid., pp. 32–3; Lucke, *Die Enstehung der 15 Bundesgenossen*, p. 40.

priests noted the success of the monks, they quickly followed their example.[66]

That Eberlin blames the monks and priests for the burdensome fast is of further significance. As previously mentioned, Lucke has suggested significant parallels between the 'Second Confederate' and article 19 of the 'Address to the Christian Nobility.' Of particular note is Eberlin's use of Luther's discussion of the neglect of the fast in Rome.[67] However, Eberlin's purpose is very different from Luther's. While Luther is denouncing papal hypocrisy on the way to branding the pope the Antichrist, Eberlin nowhere attacks the upper echelons of the ecclesiastical hierarchy. In this, his adherence to orthodoxy avoids even the rhetorical forays against the higher clergy to which Erasmus was drawn. Rather, Eberlin doubts that such an unjust command as the mandatory Lenten fast could have come from the merciful church, although, even if it had, it would certainly not be valid.[68] He also makes reference to the argument, presumably Luther's, that the fast has been commanded by the pope's courtiers and the Romanists but, in the end, places the greatest emphasis on the activity of the superstitious monks and priests, who act without instruction from the prelates.[69]

This continued trust in the prelates contrasts with the satiric treatment of them in the 'Epistle to the Parson of Highsense,' which echoes some of Erasmus's criticism in the *Praise of Folly*.[70] This in itself does not invalidate Eberlin's authorship of the satirical epistle. Christian Peters sees its criticisms of the bishops and secular clergy as natural for a member of the Franciscan Observance.[71] The traditional conflict between the mendicants and seculars does seem a likely explanation for the choice of Eberlin's targets. However, if his satire was intended to serve a reforming goal, it would seem that this pamphlet belongs more to the humanist than the Franciscan reforming movement. In the thought of Erasmus the episcopacy was the central ecclesiastical office: it was established directly by Christ and maintained through apostolic succession.[72] The 'Epistle to the Parson of Highsense,' then, was likely a

---

[66] 'Der IIII. Bundesgenosse,' Enders, vol. 1, pp. 37–8.

[67] Lucke, *Die Entstehung der 15 Bundesgenossen*, p. 48; 'Der andere Bundesgenosse,' Enders, vol. 1, p. 20; Martin Luther, 'An den christlichen Adel deutscher Nation von des christlichen standes Besserung,' WA, 6:447.

[68] 'Der andere Bundesgenosse,' Enders, vol. 1, p. 18.

[69] Ibid., pp. 19–20.

[70] Compare Götz, p. 147 and A. H. T. Levi (ed.), *Collected Works of Erasmus* vol. 27: *Literary and Educational Writings*, vol. 5 (Toronto, 1986), p. 137.

[71] Peters, p. 30.

[72] Georg Gebhart, *Die Stellung des Erasmus von Rotterdam zur Römischen Kirche* (Marburg, 1966), pp. 263–7.

very serious appeal to the episcopacy to reform itself as a foundation for the reform of the church. Furthermore, as Helmut Weidhase has indicated, Eberlin suited the style of his writings to their contents and the task at hand.[73] It is possible that the differences in Eberlin's addresses to the episcopacy reflect his changed circumstances in the move from the humanist sodality in Basel to his reforming activity in the Ulm cloister.

In the 'Fourth Confederate,' Eberlin's position seems to have sharpened, possibly reflecting increasing hostility in the Ulm cloister to his preaching. Here he suggests that all papal and episcopal laws, holy legends and histories which contradict his counsel can be ignored as superstition, not reflecting God's commands.[74] Eberlin is not yet willing to denounce directly the authority of the papacy or the church, although he maintains that it must conform to the dictates of Scripture as the *lex Christi*. In statements reminiscent of Luther's about the priesthood of all believers, Eberlin identifies canonical hours as work no more honourable than that of the laity.[75] However, he fails to go on to attack the status of the priesthood or the meaning of consecration; nor does he delve into the theological basis or implications of his attack on canonical hours.

Instead, throughout the early confederates Eberlin's criticism of the clergy remains at the level of identifying and suggesting corrections for specific abuses. Robert Scribner has identified a popular tradition of anticlericalism which supplemented the attacks of the Reformers. Central to this tradition was the attribution, particularly to the regular clergy, of the vices of gluttony, drunkenness and sexual immorality.[76] As a *Volksprediger*, Eberlin makes surprisingly little use of these images in the earliest confederates. On one occasion in the 'Seventh Confederate' he refers to the clergy as 'studs' (*somen pfard*), but otherwise he avoids the charge of sexual immorality.[77] The 'Second Confederate' hints at the gluttony of the clergy, referring to 'bulging preachers' (*vollen, büchigen predigern*) and 'well-fed monks' (*vollen münch*).[78]

---

[73] Weidhase, p. 191.

[74] 'Der IIII. Bundesgenosse,' Enders, vol. 1, p. 40.

[75] Ibid., p. 38: 'Die syben tag zeit zů singen oder lăsen, ist ein arbeit wie andere lyblich arbeit, . . .'; p. 41: 'es ist ein grosse hoffart das sollich münch und pfaffen fürgeben, ir gots dienst sy verdienstlicher dann andere fromer layen gebăt, eben als ob nit husshalten und tagwerck der layen als wol gots dienst sy und meer dann das schrien und brummen der tempel knecht das got nie gebotten hat, aber jhenes ist gebotten.'

[76] Robert W. Scribner, *For the Sake of Simple Folk: Popular Propaganda for the German Reformation* (Cambridge, 1981), pp. 37–8.

[77] 'Der VII. Bundesgenosse,' Enders, vol. 1, p. 75.

[78] 'Der andere Bundesgenosse,' Enders, vol. 1, pp. 16–17.

These attributes appear, however, in direct contrast to the image of the hard-working laity on whom the clergy imposes an unbearable fast. Beyond this contrast, Eberlin is likewise little concerned with clerical gluttony.

Instead, throughout the earliest confederates, Eberlin concentrates primarily on clerical sloth and ignorance.[79] In the 'Seventh Confederate,' he remarks on the common complaint about the large numbers of unlearned clergy who serve no purpose but to devour the produce of the laity. The only justification for their unproductive lives is the reading of masses which are neither properly performed nor understood.[80] In the 'Fourth Confederate,' Eberlin indicates that the clergy are unwilling to fulfil even these simple duties.[81] Indeed, clerical sloth and greed constitute a vicious circle that is responsible for the deplorable situation in which Christendom finds itself. Having neglected their studies, the clergy are able to interpret Christianity only in the most simple, legalistic terms.[82]

Eberlin's choice of clerical vices on which to concentrate is an interesting one and it suggests again that his earliest reform programme consisted of an amalgamation of humanist and Observant themes and concerns. Much of Eberlin's analysis echoes that of Erasmus's *Antibarbari* which identifies sloth as most unpleasing to God and singles out the opponents of the new learning as those, 'who shunned work and used the honourable name of religion to cloak their indolence; there can be no better screen for lazy dawdling and sluggish idleness.'[83] Gottfried Geiger suggests that the terminology of Erasmus's biblical humanism pervades 'The Fifteen Confederates.' This does not necessarily mean that Eberlin knew the Erasmian sources themselves, but he would have encountered their notions and slogans at every turn through his association with the humanists in Basel.[84] Froben published the first edition of the *Antibarbari* in May 1520 when Eberlin was likely in Basel.[85]

Eberlin's vision of the loss of true learning indicates clearly his debt to the humanist reform programme. He claims that God has allowed Christendom to be engulfed in darkness for the past two hundred years,

---

[79] Lucke, *Die Enstehung der 15 Bundesgenossen*, pp. 41–2.

[80] 'Der VII. Bundesgenosse,' Enders, vol. 1, p. 72.

[81] 'Der IIII. Bundesgenosse,' Enders, vol. 1, p. 41.

[82] 'Der andere Bundesgenosse,' Enders, vol. 1, p. 19.

[83] *Collected Works of Erasmus*, vol. 23: *Literary and Educational Writings*, vol. 1, ed. Craig R. Thompson (Toronto, 1978), pp. 84 and 25.

[84] Geiger, 'Die reformatorischen Initia Eberlins,' p. 191.

[85] *The Collected Works of Erasmus*, vol. 23, p. 5.

a period which he identifies with the ascendancy of scholastic theology. There appear to be echoes of Luther's statements about scholastic theology from the 'Address to the Christian Nobility,' when Eberlin attributes this period of darkness to Thomas, but he takes a more conciliatory position, parallel to that adopted by Erasmus, continuing to honour the saint despite his errors.[86] The 'Third Confederate' goes on to reveal that the true essence of Christianity may only be retrieved through the study of the Bible and the Fathers.[87]

But in all of this there remain clues to Eberlin's Franciscan past. At the outset, it is interesting to note that three of Eberlin's first four pamphlets deal with matters of concern to the cloistered. Only the 'Second Confederate,' which concentrates primarily on the Lenten fast and was likely written during Lent, deals with matters which touched the lives of those outside the monasteries as much as those within them.

That Eberlin's first pamphlet, the 'Seventh Confederate,' deals with endowed anniversary masses is of particular importance. On the surface, Eberlin's disparaging contrast of the performance of mortuary masses by the superfluous temple servants with the sufficiency of the pastoral care of the local parson sounds strongly reminiscent of the reform programmes of both Erasmus and Luther.[88] However, behind these similarities there also lie concerns at the heart of the Observant reform movement. The Observance targeted mortuary masses with particular vigour, seeing in them an important source of illicit property and secure incomes. With the introduction of the Observance to Basel and Nuremburg, mortuary masses to be celebrated for the benefit of specific patrons were replaced with masses intended for the benefit of the

---

[86] 'Der andere Bundesgenosse,' Enders, vol. 1, p. 22· 'Lass dich nit bekümmern das etlich lerer als Thomas und sins gelichen, vyl uff diss und andere römisch oder menschlich ordnung gehalten haben, dann sy gelebt haben yn der begryfflichen finsternüss die got verhengt hat zwey hundert jar lang uber die christenheit, und ich gloub das die selbigen lerer, welche vylicht by got im hymmel sind, ein mitliden mit unss haben das wir durch irrsal also irr gond, und got fleissig bitten umb unser erleüchtung, . . .' See Luther, 'An den christlichen Adel,' WA, 6:458. Margaret Mann Phillips suggests that Erasmus's critique of modern theologians in the *Antibarbari* probably did not intend such a direct reference to Thomas, *Collected Works of Erasmus*, vol. 23, p. 67. On the dates assigned for the fall of the church by both Erasmus and Luther, see my 'Humanists, Reformers and Anabaptists on Scholasticism and the Deterioration of the Church,' *Mennonite Quarterly Review*, 68 (1994), pp. 461–8.

[87] 'Der III. Bundesgenosse,' Enders, vol. 1, p. 29.

[88] On the importance of the bishops and parochial clergy in the reforming thought of Erasmus, see Gebhardt, pp. 263–7. In the 'Address to the Christian Nobility' Luther frequently contrasted the sufficiency of bishops and parish priests with the activity of other, superfluous elements of the first estate; for example, see WA, 6:429–30, 440–1.

populace generally.[89] It is tempting to see in these reforms the prototype for Eberlin's suggestions on reforming mortuary masses. Furthermore, Eberlin's claim that mortuary masses were responsible for the inordinate numbers of clergy was an established element of Observant criticism of Conventual practice. The *Speculum Imperfectionis*, written by the Observant Johannes Brugman about 1460 to bewail the loss of ideals among the Observants themselves, similarly ties excessive numbers of ordained friars directly to the practice of endowing anniversary masses.[90] Similarly, Eberlin's criticism of the canonical hours in the 'Fourth Confederate' reflects other concerns of the Observance. His claim that they began as opportunities for thoughtful reflection and prayer, and his suggestions that they be returned to this format, is reminiscent of Observant criticisms of those who say the Hours only with their lips.[91]

Eberlin's perception of the decline of Christendom has significant implications for the nature of his anticlericalism. Wilhelm Lucke commented that Eberlin softens his critique of the clergy by blaming the current state of affairs in part on the gullibility of the laity.[92] Throughout these works Eberlin reproaches his readers with being superstitious and simple. By endowing masses and vigils, they encourage the slothful existence of the clergy and, consequently, pose a threat to their consciences.[93] In fact, the clergy begin to appear as victims of their own deception. In the 'Fourth Confederate,' he laments that they have been hoodwinked into believing that they must observe the canonical hours on the pain of committing a mortal sin.[94] As was the case with the introduction of Observant reform, significant initiative is expected from the laity.

When one turns to Eberlin's specific suggestions for reform, the perception of his continued respect for the clerical estate is reinforced. Eberlin's opening statements in the 'Seventh Confederate' lay the onus for reform on the laity, who must stop supporting useless clergy and,

---

[89] Neidiger, *Mendikanten*, pp. 85–90; Paul Nyhus, 'The Observant Reform Movement in South Germany,' *Franciscan Studies*, 32 (1972), pp. 212–13; id., 'The Franciscans in South Germany, 1400–1530: Reform and Revolution,' *Transactions of the American Philosophical Society* n.s. 65 (8) (1975), pp. 14–15. Luther also made similar suggestions for the reform of mortuary masses, see WA, 6:444–5.

[90] G. G. Coulton, *Five Centuries of Religion*, vol. IV: *The Last Days of Medieval Monachism* (Cambridge, 1950), p. 442.

[91] 'Der IIII. Bundesgenosse,' Enders, vol. 1, pp. 38–42 and Coulton, pp. 442–3.

[92] Lucke, *Die Entstehung der 15 Bundesgenossen*, p. 42.

[93] 'Der VII. Bundesgenosse,' Enders, vol. 1, p. 76.

[94] 'Der IIII. Bundesgenosse,' Enders, vol. 1, p. 36: 'Was ist aber schimpfflicheres zů hören, dann so sy selbs so thorecht sind, das sie halten, ir verbündnüss sy so gross, das auch tödtlich sünd durch unfliss in tag zyten geschäch.'

thereby, reduce their numbers.[95] He seems to adopt Luther's emphasis on the sufficiency of the local parish for the spiritual needs of the parishioners and juxtaposes the useful activity of the parish priest with the uselessness of the temple servants.[96] In the 'Second Confederate,' Eberlin indicates that the local clergy, having been properly instructed, will play a key role in the reform process.[97] The other pillar of Eberlin's reform programme, and here he again appears to follow Luther and Erasmus, is his trust in the good judgement of the prelates of the church. He envisions episcopal support for the reformation of the fast and of women's cloisters.[98]

In his perception of the regular orders, however, Eberlin diverges sharply from the position of Luther, although he seems to take the same point of departure. Bernhard Lohse argues that in the 'Address to the Christian Nobility' Luther had not yet solved the problem of monasticism. He denied that monastic vows had been recommended by Christ, but, as a freely chosen commitment, considered them binding. Consequently, his sharpest criticism of the abuses associated with monasticism is directed at the dispensation from vows as a source of revenue for Rome. On the other hand, his suggestions for reform would have significantly changed the nature of monasticism. With regard to the mendicant orders in particular, Luther went so far as to suggest the possibility of dissolution.[99]

Central to Luther's perception of monasticism is his view that monasteries and other such institutions had their origins at the time of the Apostles as free schools for the teaching of the Gospel. Therefore,

---

[95] 'Der VII. Bundesgenosse,' Enders, vol. 1, p. 75: 'O ir teüren christen in teutschem land, ziehen ab ewer hand von solichen gaben den tempel knechten, do mit ab gestelt werd ir faul unütz ergerlich laben.'

[96] Ibid: 'Der pfarrer gült ist in zů geben und wolt got das jetliche pfarr hätte ein pfarrer uss vollem gewalt, der nit allein järig oder ewig vicary wår, der auch ein güte ryliche provision hätte, und neben im zween oder dry priester auch wol versehen, die im bystendig weren zů nötiger zit'; WA, 6:448.

[97] 'Der andere Bundesgenosse,' Enders, vol. 1, p. 21: 'Die prediger und bychtvätter solten das christlich volck vermanen zů måssiger niessung liplicher noturfft, und zů hårtzlichem hass der laster uss liebe der tugendt, und zů hitzigem und ernstlichem gebåt zů gott, . . .'

[98] Ibid.: 'Aber ein solcher inbruch soll gschåhen mit geistlicher und wåltlicher prelaten rat und hilf'; 'Der III. Bundesgenosse,' Enders, vol. 1, p. 31: 'Magst du bewerlich hoffen, dein byschoff gebe dir urlob zů solichem aussgang, so bit in darumb, . . .'

[99] Bernhard Lohse, 'Die Kritik am Mönchtum bei Luther und Melanchthon,' in *Luther und Melanchthon*, ed. Vilmes Vatja (Göttingen, 1961), pp. 133–4; Bernhard Lohse, *Mönchtum und Reformation. Luthers Auseinandersetzung mit dem Monchsideal des Mittelalters* (Göttingen, 1963), p. 349. See WA, 6:426, 438–41.

they should be returned to this form and he suggests as a model for reform the nunnery at Quedlinburg.[100] Eberlin likewise sees the origins of monasteries and foundations as schools.[101] This leads to reform suggestions for the reorganization of female cloisters which echo the sentiments of the 'Address to the Christian Nobility.' Eberlin adopts a similar argument to Luther's that the vow of chastity requires a special gift of grace, given to only a few, to denounce the strictness of the cloistered life.[102] He adopts as a model for reform the noble foundation at Andlow in Alsace and provides a detailed programme for reorganization which, among other things, calls for the end of the taking of vows and the conversion of cloisters into schools to prepare young women for their roles as Christian wives.[103]

However, Eberlin applies drastically different criteria to the reform of monasteries for men. Although he does not devote a pamphlet specifically to this purpose, the discussion in the 'Fourth Confederate' provides some insight into the matter. On only one occasion does Eberlin advise a monk to act contrary to his vows: if his superiors will not allow him to substitute useful work for the canonical hours, he may flee the cloister because God's command to work overrides human statutes.[104] This raises the question of Eberlin's perception of the nature of monastic rules. Luther, although identifying these as of human origin, still defends the piety and intentions of those who instituted them.[105] Eberlin is not so quick to judge the rules; for instance, he carefully distances the canonical hours, which he identifies as coming with later statutes, from the original rules.[106]

As is the case with the nunneries, Eberlin wishes to return the monasteries to their original form.[107] However, it appears that this form differs fundamentally from that of the nunneries, due primarily to the fact that men were able to take orders. Throughout the 'Fourth Confederate,' Eberlin dispenses from canonical hours all committed to

---

[100] WA, 6:439–40, 461.

[101] 'Der III. Bundesgenosse,' Enders, vol. 1, p. 29: '. . . und anfencklich sind die frawen klöster nicht anders gesin dann schülen des gesatz gottes.'; 'Der IIII. Bundesgenosse,' Enders, vol. 1, p. 36: '. . . solich ort, die wir nännen styfft und klöster, sind angefangen worden in gestalt der schülen, . . .'

[102] 'Der III. Bundesgenosse,' Enders, vol. 1, p. 27: 'Erleücht ouch nit alle christen die es auch understond zů stygen uff die hohen räte der keuscheit und gantzer verlust zitlicher hab.'

[103] Ibid., pp. 30–1.

[104] 'Der IIII. Bundesgenosse,' Enders, vol. 1, pp. 39–40.

[105] WA, 6:438.

[106] 'Der IIII. Bundesgenosse,' Enders, vol. 1, p. 36.

[107] Ibid., p. 39.

study, teaching, preaching and hearing of confession.[108] However, within the scheme of clerical activity, the regular clergy appear to hold a special position. In the *Antibarbari*, Erasmus summed up the decline of learning:

> However, so that the life of men should not be absolutely blind, as it would be if no learning were to survive, the whole care and professional responsibility for letters was relegated to the monks, and for a time they managed the business not too badly. Later, when through some kind of swollen pride the monks turned to luxurious living, when languages were neglected and antiquity was neglected too, there grew up a confused sort of teaching, a kind of uneducated erudition, which corrupted not only humane studies but, in distressing ways, theology itself.[109]

Eberlin too praises the contributions of the early monastic schools and emphasizes their importance for civil administration and general education.[110] However, as the cloisters accumulated wealth, they gradually turned their backs on this social role.[111] Elsewhere, Eberlin describes earlier disputations between monks and priests on Scripture as the forerunners to the activities of the universities.[112]

Eberlin's nostalgia for the heyday of medieval monasticism suggests an attempt to reconcile the reform movement within the order with reforms inspired by Erasmus and Luther. Lothar Graf zu Dohna has suggested that in his approach to the Augustinian Observance, Luther's mentor, Johann von Staupitz, saw the reform of his order as only the first step in a general reform of Christendom.[113] This, I believe, provides a pattern for Eberlin's reconciliation of the Observant reform movement with the suggestions of Erasmus and Luther. And indications are that he was not alone in believing this reconciliation possible. In one of his later, most virulently antifraternal, pamphlets, Eberlin was still able to claim: 'In the cloister of the Teutonic Knights [in Ulm] there is a man who knows something.'[114] Ludwig Enders identifies this man as the Cantor and Hebraist Johann Behaim.[115] Behaim was a close associate of Conrad Pellican, who also saw no conflict between the ideals of the

---

[108] Ibid., pp. 38–39.

[109] *The Collected Works of Erasmus*, vol. 23, p. 26.

[110] 'Der IIII. Bundesgenosse,' Enders, vol. 1, p. 36.

[111] Ibid., p. 40.

[112] Ibid., p. 42.

[113] Lothar Graf zu Dohna, 'Von der Ordensreform zur Reformation: Johann von Staupitz,' in Kaspar Elm (ed.), *Reformbemühungen und Observanzbestrebungen in spätmittelalterlichen Ordenswesen* (Berlin, 1989), p. 581.

[114] 'Die andere getreue Vermahnung an den Rath von Ulm,' Enders, vol. 3, p. 38.

[115] Enders, vol. 3, pp. 334–5.

Franciscan order and the new teaching.[116] In fact, the early perception within the order of Luther's activity continued to regard it in a favourable light. Late in 1520 the Spanish provincial and later general of the order Franciscus Quinones, returning from a visitation tour of the Saxon Observants, told Pellican that, until the appearance of Luther's 'Babylonian Captivity of the Church,' he had found much of value in his writings.[117] Johannes Glapion, the Franciscan confessor to the Emperor, voiced the same sentiments on another occasion.[118] Again Conrad Pellican provides the best summary of the expectations of Luther within the Franciscan order in a letter to Luther dated 16 March 1520:

> There emerges everywhere among us the presumption of certain Erasmians, who indiscriminately kindle bitter hatred toward all monks, pronounce them superstitious, Pharisees, deceivers. In general they are the enemies of ceremonies, they howl at confession, the divine cult, ecclesiastical rituals. I do not doubt that much needs to be reformed in these things. I am known to detest many abuses. But they go to extremes, they write ill-advisedly against the Gospel, against Paul, against the Fathers, . . . I desire that, in the course of writing, you would restrain their bold endeavours, set a measure of restraint, in as much as those who have taken vows can be reformed and not destroyed. Certainly, it is better to bring our senses under the rule of Christ, to avoid the dangers of the world, to be mutually supported by fraternal association, to implore the grace of Christ joined together, and not to waver in ceremonies. I would wish that you reprimand such endeavours; they might be enchanted by lies. With all their powers, the Erasmians condemn monasticism by word, writings and deeds; as formerly the followers of Origen set up Origen, thus the Erasmians set up Erasmus.[119]

Pellican's letter suggests not only that Eberlin's vision of reform was not unique among those in orders, but also how he may have responded to being labelled an 'Erasmian.' Undoubtedly, he held both Erasmus and Luther in high regard. Like many of his *confreres* and others in orders, he saw in their writings a complement to his own reforming aspirations. However, these aspirations looked to reform in the medieval sense of the correction of abuses rather than fundamental theological change on

---

[116] Theodor Vulpinus (ed.), *Die Hauschronik Konrad Pellikans von Rufach. Ein Lebensbild aus der Reformationszeit* (Strasbourg, 1892), pp. 21 and 97–9. In 1525, long after he had been denounced by his fellow Franciscans, Pellican still felt that he was remaining true to the ideals of Francis.

[117] Ibid., p. 78.

[118] Nikolaus Paulus, *Kaspar Schatzgeyer ein Vorkämpfer der katholischen Kirche gegen Luther in Suddeutschland* (Strasbourg, 1898), p. 45; id., *Die deutschen Dominikaner im Kampfe gegen Luther (1518–1563)* (Freiburg, 1903), p. 307; Heribert Holzapfel, *Handbuch der Geschichte des Franziskanerordens* (Freiburg, 1909), p. 462.

[119] WABr, 2:66–7.

either the humanist or Lutheran model. This is particularly evident in the development of Eberlin's anticlerical polemics. He shares the concerns of Luther and Erasmus with the deplorable condition of the first estate. However, he is much more cautious than either of them in his treatment of the ecclesiastical hierarchy and monasticism. The greatest blame for the sad state of affairs in which Christendom finds itself rests on the shoulders of the 'superstitious little monks and priests,' and it is reform of these groups that will bring about the reform of the church. Throughout the earliest confederates, the tone of Eberlin's criticism sharpens and his position moves gradually toward the boundaries of orthodoxy. However, he did not overstep these boundaries until he realized that reform within the order was impossible, and either left or was expelled from it.

CHAPTER THREE

'The grey hypocrite from the superstitious Observants'

According to Wilhelm Lucke's reassessment of the chronological sequence of the constituent elements of 'The Fifteen Confederates,' the first to be written, numbers seven, two, three and four in the collected work, date from the period before Eberlin was in open conflict with the Franciscan order. The remainder of the confederates chronicle a crucial phase in his development as a Reformer, beginning with his break with the order and ending with his decision to go to Wittenberg. From the perspective of the present investigation, they may be divided into two groups. Numbers one, five and six, eight and nine, and thirteen and fourteen were written amid the conflict which led to his expulsion from the order, or shortly thereafter. In them, Eberlin develops his distinctive vision of the evils perpetrated on Christendom by the clergy and the special role of the mendicants in this process. Eberlin's conciliatory attitude to the papacy and those he perceives as its allies in the earliest confederates here gives way to a vehement denunciation of them. As his bitterness increases, he moves ever closer to a break with Rome and rejection of the medieval ecclesiastical structure. However, in this he continues to draw on medieval visions of reform as well as those emanating from Wittenberg and the humanists. Of note is his new adherence to the cause of Ulrich von Hutten. Numbers ten to twelve and fifteen are much more reflective works, written while Eberlin spent the summer with a cousin in Lauingen. Here he does not so much expand his anticlerical polemics as give them greater depth and incorporate them into his vision of reform. This deepening of his polemics betrays the unmistakable influence of a more careful study of Luther's reform proposals. Increasingly in these writings, Eberlin adopts the suggestions of Luther, and in the last begins to deal with the central theological issues of the Wittenberg movement. Nonetheless, it would be inaccurate to describe Eberlin as a Lutheran at this point in his career. He himself continued to regard reforming suggestions from Reuchlin to Luther as part of a unified process, although his attack on his former brethren indicates that he no longer saw the Franciscan Observance as part of that process. Luther had become for him a prominent symbol of the reforming movement, but was not yet *the* symbol of it.

The middle confederates

In a later *Flugschrift*, Eberlin reflected on the events which led to his expulsion from the Franciscan order and departure from Ulm: 'Then God allowed the devil to prepare a game through my hypocritical brothers, by which I was driven away from you despite the intervention on three occasions of the city council of Ulm, who earnestly – as they also found support among the common people – appealed to my superiors to keep me there.'[1] Wilhelm Lucke suggests that Eberlin's initial attack on ecclesiastical abuses was answered by movements against him within the cloister, but that these were in turn hindered by the intervention of the Ulm city council, possibly prompted by Wolfgang Rychard, and by indications that Johannes Glapion, the Franciscan confessor of the emperor, was inclined toward the reform movement.[2] The reform suggestions of these early confederates were neither particularly radical nor distinctly Lutheran. Nonetheless, it is conceivable that they could have raised the ire of Eberlin's confreres, particularly in the unsettled atmosphere of early 1521. If, as we suspect, Eberlin was preaching in this manner not only to the Franciscans, but also the general public, it is logical that the members of the order would attempt to defend themselves by silencing him. Unfortunately, the role of the city council in Eberlin's initial victory remains somewhat unclear. The *Ratsprotokolle* for this period make no mention of an intervention by the council on Eberlin's behalf.[3]

Shortly thereafter, Glapion himself appears to have taken interest in Eberlin's case, probably at the instigation of the papal legate Aleander.[4] Eberlin responded with 'A Pitiful Petition to the Christian, Roman Emperor Charles on Behalf of Doctor Luther and Ulrich von Hutten,' which now appears as the 'First Confederate.' As its title indicates, this work is one of a deluge of *Flugschriften* which appeared around the time of the Diet of Worms intent on influencing the emperor's decision there. The most notable change from the earliest confederates is Eberlin's open attack on not only Glapion, but also the Franciscan Observants in general. Eberlin encourages Charles V to follow the example of his

---

[1] 'Die andere getreue Vermahnung an den Rath von Ulm,' Enders, vol. 3, p. 2.

[2] Wilhelm Lucke, *Die Entstehung der '15 Bundesgenossen' des Johann Eberlins von Günzburg*, Phil. Diss. (Hall, 1902), pp. 53–4.

[3] Gottfried Geiger, 'Die reformatorischen Initia Johann Eberlins von Günzburg nach seinem Flugschriften,' in *Festgabe für Ernst Walter Zeeden zum 60. Geburtstag am 14. Mai, 1976*, ed. Horst Rabe *et al.* (Münster, 1976), p. 182.

[4] Lucke, *Die Enstehung der 15 Bundesgenossen*, p. 54; Th. Brieger, *Quellen und Forschungen zur Geschichte der Reformation*, vol. 1: *Aleander und Luther* (Gotha, 1884), p. 106. See above, p. 45.

grandfather, Maximilian I, and refuse to accept the counsel of his confessor in the affairs of the realm. Better yet, he should send Glapion away and take as his confessor Erasmus, Luther or Karlstadt, the true friends of the emperor and the German people. In secular affairs he should be counselled by Hutten, Sickingen, Count Friedrich of the Palatinate and the like instead of the mendicants, courtiers and 'Romanists.'[5] Lucke regards this as an attempt by Eberlin to discredit his opponents, especially Glapion who served as the plaintiff in the legal process against him. Despite the harsh words for Eberlin's own brethren, it was written before his departure from the order and before Luther's appearance at Worms, likely sometime during the first three weeks of April 1521.[6]

It is likely that Eberlin wrote two further tracts before his departure from the Ulm cloister.[7] The 'Fifth Confederate' calls on secular authorities at all levels in Germany to reform the preaching office. Eberlin argues that secular authorities have not only the right, but also the duty to do this. He further encourages such activity by arguing that good, biblically based preaching, not an excess of statutes, will encourage the virtues of good citizenship. Like the emperor, the other secular authorities are warned against the influence of the mendicants, but Eberlin does not here specifically single out the Franciscans.[8] 'Why one translates Erasmus into German. Why Ulrich von Hutten and Doctor Luther write in German,' now eighth in the cycle, defends writing in the vernacular as the only means of combatting the wiles of the church. It begins with a lengthy historical discussion of the power struggles between pope and emperor and a denunciation of papal meddling in secular affairs. Just when it appeared that imperial power had freed itself from the papal yoke, the pope co-opted the followers of Francis and Dominic – the founders themselves Eberlin still regards as pious men – for his cause. With the help of papal bulls, letters of indulgence and the office of the Inquisition, the mendicant orders have once again subverted imperial power and enslaved the German people. Now, however, the power of the mendicants and courtiers is being challenged by men like Luther and Hutten who dare to write in the vernacular. Their choice of the language of the people is a sure sign that

---

[5] 'Der erste Bundesgenosse,' Enders, vol. 1, pp. 1–14 (= Laube 2:709–17).

[6] Lucke, *Die Entstehung der 15 Bundesgenossen*, pp. 63 and 72.

[7] On the suggested dates for the composition of these two pamphlets, see Lucke, *Die Entstehung der 15 Bundesgenossen*, pp. 49–51 and 80, and Geiger, 'Die reformatorischen Initia Eberlins,' p. 183. I have opted for Geiger's dating which appears the most logical in the context of Eberlin's developing anticlericalism.

[8] 'Der V. Bundesgenosse,' Enders, vol. 1, pp. 45–53.

they speak the simple truth of the Bible, unlike their opponents who rely on the language of Rome and obscure sophistry.[9]

Closely related in subject matter to the 'Eighth Confederate' are numbers six and fourteen: both include translations of parts of Erasmus's *Praise of Folly* with commentaries by Eberlin. The sixth deals with Erasmus's criticisms of the activities of the mendicant preachers. They depart from their proper subject matter, the Bible, and instead fill their sermons with irrelevant fables and stories. Their sermons are rarely tailored for the audience and are intended merely to indicate their great subtlety and learning that they might thereby receive more alms from their listeners, particularly from women and merchants who are most susceptible to such antics. Eberlin's commentary consists primarily of a summary of his denunciation of the lack of learning in the monasteries from the earliest confederates and a discussion of the criteria to identify true and false preachers. He concludes with a discussion of the mendicants' exploitation of saints associated with their orders to extort yet more money from the laity.[10]

This theme is taken up and expanded in the 'Fourteenth Confederate' which begins with a loose translation of Erasmus's criticism of the abuses associated with the veneration of saints. In his commentary, Eberlin takes the opportunity to return to the theme of the use made by the mendicant orders of their patron saints to exploit the laity. Unlike the 'Sixth Confederate,' the fourteenth specifically criticizes the Franciscan Observance, but continues to regard St Francis as a pious man who would be horrified by the activities of those claiming to be his followers.[11]

While the specific events leading up to his departure from Ulm and the role of the city council in them must remain unclear, Eberlin himself indicates that he preached the final sermon of his residence there on the feast of Saints Peter and Paul (29 June) 1521 and departed the city straight away.[12] A character in one of his later pamphlets reports seeing Eberlin in Baden in the Swiss Aargau shortly thereafter on St Ulrich's day (4 July): 'There he preached in a completely Lutheran sense against

---

[9] 'Der VIII. Bundesgenosse,' Enders, vol. 1, pp. 79–88.

[10] 'Der VI. Bundesgenosse,' Enders, vol. 1, pp. 55–65.

[11] 'Der XIIII. Bundesgenosse,' Enders, vol. 1, pp. 153–61. Lucke, *Die Entstehung der 15 Bundesgenossen*, pp. 91 and 97, and Geiger, 'Die reformatorischen Initia Eberlins,' pp. 183–4 suggest that these two pamphlets were written in July or August 1521, although they can find no firm evidence for a specific dating of them. However, their obvious link to the 'Eighth Confederate' suggests that, if they were not written at the same time as it, they were likely conceived then.

[12] 'Ein kurzer schrifflicher Bericht des Glaubens, an die Ulmer,' Enders, vol. 2, p. 173.

priests, monks and nuns, much more earnestly than he had preached before.'[13]

It is possible that a printed version of this sermon forms the basis of the 'Thirteenth Confederate.' This work is a praise of the Swiss confederacy and a call for its help in the cause of the Gospel. Eberlin indulges in a form of popular etymology to achieve his purpose. Swiss (*Schweizer*) is derived from the verb to sweat (*schwitzen*) and refers to those who sweat blood for the cause of the Gospel. The confederacy (*Eidgenossenschaft*) takes its significance from the oath (*Eid*) of its members and indicates the commitment of the Swiss to oaths, especially the oath taken at baptism. Eberlin appeals to these attributes of his hosts to win their support for the cause of the Gospel and those oppressed for its sake. Intermingled with this appeal is a summary of Eberlin's understanding of the reforming movement, emphasizing the contrast between the self-serving teaching of the monks and priests and the Gospel as rediscovered by Erasmus, Luther and Melanchthon.[14]

Eberlin probably next wrote the 'Ninth Confederate.'[15] This work professes to be an appeal to both the ecclesiastical and secular authorities of Germany to come to the aid of the monks, nuns and priests and deliver them from their antichristian neighbours. Eberlin reiterates much of the material from his earlier pamphlets in the course of exposing the abuses of the monastic life and the tribulations of those dedicated to it. However, he soon digresses into his favourite theme from the 'Eighth Confederate': the evils perpetrated on the German people by the mendicant orders. Here the Franciscans come in for special abuse and the cursory history of the order provided in the 'Eighth Confederate' is expanded considerably.[16]

There is, unfortunately, no trace of any of Eberlin's other possible activities in Switzerland. Lucke speculates that Eberlin was *en route* to visit Zwingli in Zurich, although there is no evidence that this was the case or indication that, if this was his object, Eberlin ever reached his destination.[17] Georg Strobel suggested that Eberlin went to Basel and later Rheinfelden; however, Riggenbach and Radlkofer make no mention of this and it is likely that Strobel confused these events of 1521 with Eberlin's 1523 visit to Switzerland.[18] It is more likely that he went

---

[13] 'Klage der sieben frommen Pfaffen,' Enders, vol. 2, p. 71.

[14] 'Der XIII. Bundesgenosse,' Enders, vol. 1, pp. 143–51.

[15] Lucke, *Die Entstehung der 15 Bundesgenossen*, pp. 85–7. Geiger, 'Die reformatorischen Initia Eberlins,' p. 183, suggests that Eberlin penned this work while still in Switzerland. Peters, *Johann Eberlin von Günzburg*, p. 45, counters that he may have already gone to Lauingen.

[16] 'Der IX. Bundesgenosse,' Enders, vol. 1, pp. 89–105.

[17] Lucke, *Die Entstehung der 15 Bundesgenossen*, p. 20.

[18] Georg Theodor Strobel, 'Nachricht von Johann Eberlin von Günzburgs Leben und Schriften,' *Literarischen Museum*, I (Altdorf, 1778), p. 369.

directly to Lauingen on the Danube where he spent the summer with his cousin Mathias Sigk.[19]

Regarded from the perspective of the development of Eberlin's anticlerical polemics, the pamphlets discussed above mark a significant step beyond their predecessors. The most notable change is the end to any sort of conciliatory approach to the authority of Rome. The 'First Confederate' advises the emperor to prohibit the presence of any cardinals in Germany and to end all direct dependence of the church in Germany on the Roman see. The office of the papacy is not itself attacked, although henceforth the pope and cardinals should be confirmed by the emperor.[20] However, by the 'Eighth Confederate,' the Roman court is identified as a 'synagogue of satan' and the pope as a bishop like all others.[21] The authority exercised by the pope is to devolve onto the bishops who, however, are to be restricted henceforth in their influence on secular affairs. When he turns his attention to the clergy in general, Eberlin repeats many of the traditional complaints of abuses: non-residence, pluralism, neglect of office, and excessive numbers. In addition, he calls for the end of enforced clerical celibacy.[22] In the 'Fifth Confederate,' Eberlin takes up Luther's call for the communal election of the parochial clergy.[23]

Eberlin's suggestions for the reform of the monasteries are more extensive and radical. The 'First Confederate' urges the monitoring of monastic finances by secular authorities, free departure from the cloister of all monks and nuns who feel that their souls are endangered therein, and adopts the suggestion already made by both Luther and Erasmus that no one should take the monastic vows before the age of 30.[24] The 'Ninth Confederate' continues to counsel free departure from the monastery without requirement of dispensation for all disinclined to the cloistered life, but here the polemic is sharper. The monastic life, as currently practised, is a source of much evil and an affront to God. Consequently, all who depart the cloister are doing a service to God. Nonetheless, if returned to its true beginnings monasticism is a laudable profession.[25]

---

19 'Vom Missbrauch christlicher Freiheit,' Enders, vol. 2, p. 40. This work, printed in 1522, was dedicated to Sigk.

20 'Der erste Bundesgenosse,' Enders, vol. 1, pp. 12–13 (= Laube 2:716–17).

21 'Der VIII. Bundesgenosse,' Enders, vol. 1, p. 85.

22 'Der erste Bundesgenosse,' Enders, vol. 1, pp. 12–13 (= Laube 2:716).

23 'Der V. Bundesgenosse,' Enders, vol. 1, p. 47.

24 'Der erste Bundesgenosse,' Enders, vol. 1, p. 12 (= Laube 2:716); WA, 6:468; Georg Gebhardt, *Die Stellung des Erasmus von Rotterdam zur Römischen Kirche* (Marburg, 1966), p. 345.

25 'Der VIIII. Bundesgenosse,' Enders, vol. 1, p. 102–5.

This, however, does not apply to the mendicant orders. The 'First Confederate' calls on the emperor to place the mendicants under the imperial ban along with the courtiers and later suggests a moratorium on novices for the mendicant orders so that they will eventually die out.[26] A similar note is sounded in the 'Fifth Confederate' when Eberlin assures the local authorities that the expulsion of the mendicants is a service to God.[27] Finally, the 'Eighth Confederate' demands the extermination of the Franciscan order as the source of clerical mendicancy.[28] The above are only a few examples of a general antifraternal polemic that pervades and unifies this group of pamphlets. With the exception of numbers five and thirteen, which take a more general approach and were most likely delivered initially as sermons, these pamphlets chronicle the development of Eberlin's perception of the friars as the chief opponents of the Gospel.

While Eberlin's sharpened criticism of the clergy and new willingness to defy the canons of orthodoxy suggest a deeper immersion in the writings of Luther and stronger commitment to his cause, Eberlin continues to regard the Wittenberg reform movement as an extension of the activities of the humanists. The 'First Confederate' draws a direct line from Reuchlin, through Erasmus and the German humanists, to Luther and Hutten. All of these have played an assigned role in the reappearance of the true Gospel.[29] The 'Eighth Confederate' identifies Erasmus, Luther and Hutten as the chief representatives of the new learning and the 'Sixth Confederate' complains that the laity support any foolish ass as if he were Erasmus or Luther.[30] To this list, the 'Thirteenth Confederate' adds the names of Karlstadt and Melanchthon.[31]

Eberlin's eclecticism suggests numerous candidates as his intellectual

---

[26] 'Der erste Bundesgenosse,' Enders, vol. 1, pp. 9, 12 (= Laube 2:714, 716).

[27] 'Der V. Bundesgenosse,' Enders, vol. 1, p. 51.

[28] 'Der VIII. Bundesgenosse,' Enders, vol. 1, p. 87.

[29] 'Der erste Bundesgenosse,' Enders, vol. 1, pp. 3–4: 'Wiss auch o mächtiger kayser das Johann reüchlin aller walt bekant ain urhab ist alles nutzes in teütschen landen, der angefangen hat zů entdecken die ingeworffnen brunnen christlichs wåsens in verstand und in låben, darumb er ewigs lob wirdig ist. Dar nach ist zů grossem hail kummen Erasmus von Roterodam der mit englischem ingenium für und für mit gůtigkeit gottliche gaben gemeret hat in unss . . . Obgemelte zwen man haben die ersten stain gelegt alles hails, denen auch vyl andere neben behilfflich sind gesin, als Jacob wimpffling, doctor Johan von Kaysersperg im Elsass, doctor Ulrich Krafft von Ulm, Johan Eckolampadius in schwaben, mit iren anhangen . . . . hat got geschickt zwen sunder usserwelt kün und erleücht botten zů beraiten deinen wåg in das regiment, . . . Dise zwen gottes botten sind Martinus Luther und Ulrich von Hutten, . . .' (= Laube 2:710).

[30] 'Der VIII. Bundesgenosse,' Enders, vol. 1, p. 86; 'Der VI. Bundesgenosse,' Enders, vol. 1, p. 60.

[31] 'Der XIII. Bundesgenosse,' Enders, vol. 1, p. 148.

and spiritual mentors during this time. Although this group of confederates is still generally characterized by most students of Eberlin's writings as belonging in the reform tradition identified with the biblical humanism of Erasmus, several explanations have been advanced to account for the radicalization of Eberlin's vision and language in them. In particular, the explicit commitment to the cause of Luther and Hutten in the 'First Confederate' has raised the issue of their respective influence · on Eberlin. Wilhelm Lucke, in what has become a widely accepted position, suggests a strong dependence of this group of confederates on Luther's 'Address to the Christian Nobility,' particularly with regard to the specific *gravamina* put forth.[32] On the other hand, Hans-Herbert Ahrens has argued that the parallels between 'The Fifteen Confederates' and the 'Address to the Christian Nobility' are far too general to indicate a direct dependence and much more specific links can be made to the writings of Hutten.[33] According to Ahrens, Eberlin's initial break with the church led not directly into the Wittenberg camp, but back to the anti-hierarchical ideals of primitive Franciscanism which may be identified with the mystical piety of such medieval heretical traditions as the Waldensians, Cathars and Albigensians.[34] The Franciscan ideal of the poor church was complemented by a strongly Ghibelline stance in politics, for which Eberlin could appeal to long tradition within the Franciscan order from the glorious days of the Hohenstaufen to the polemics of the *fraticelli de opinione* at the court of Lewis the Bavarian. In this support for the emperor, one can also see the influence of Hutten, which becomes more marked as Eberlin narrows the scope for political reform from the universal empire to the German nation.[35]

Although unique in the emphasis he placed on it, Ahrens was not alone in identifying the influence of Hutten on this group of confederates, particularly with regard to the development of Eberlin's nationalism. Lucke noted statements reminiscent of Hutten's writings in the conclusion of the 'Eighth Confederate' and throughout the ninth, and suggested that the idea for the collection of works under the guise of a

---

[32] Lucke, *Die Entstehung der 15 Bundesgenossen*, p. 72. Many of these had already been noted by Max Radlkofer, *Johann Eberlin von Günzburg und sein Vetter Hans Jakob Wehe von Leipheim* (Nördlingen, 1887), pp. 17–18.

[33] Hans-Herbert Ahrens, *Die religiösen, nationalen und sozialen Gedanken Johann Eberlins von Günzburgs mit besonderer Berücksichtigung seiner anonymen Flugschriften* Phil. Diss. (Hamburg, 1939), p. 37.

[34] Ibid., pp. 22–4.

[35] Ibid., pp. 33–40. On the development of Hutten's nationalism see Hajo Holborn, *Ulrich von Hutten and the German Reformation* (New Haven, 1937; reprint edn, New York, 1966), p. 76.

sworn Confederation was likely prompted by Hutten.[36] Gottfried
Geiger agrees that the influence of Hutten is most notable in the 'Ninth
Confederate,' but goes further to trace elements of Hutten's imperial
ideal as early as the 'First Confederate.'[37]

The influence of Hutten on the writings of Eberlin from this period
may, however, be even more profound and enduring than has previously
been noted. The very title of the 'First Confederate,' 'A Pitiful Petition to
the Christian Roman Emperor Charles on behalf of Doctor Luther and
Ulrich von Hutten. Also on Account of the Courtesans and Friars, that
His Majesty not allow Them to lead Him Astray,' indicates that it is a
defence of Hutten as much as of Luther. Ahrens suggested that this
work was modelled on Hutten's 'Exhortation to Charles' and 'Complaint and Admonition.'[38] Eberlin may have taken as his literary models
at this time several 'manifestos' written by Hutten at the Ebernburg in
September 1520 and knew, among others, the 'Complaint and Admonition.'[39] After his address to the emperor, Hutten, too, had made a wider
appeal to the German authorities and people.[40] He concluded this work
with a defence of the translation of his writings into German, which is
also the theme of the 'Eighth Confederate.'[41]

The 'First Confederate' distinguishes between the roles of Luther and
Hutten in promoting reform. Luther seeks to preach the pure Gospel
while Hutten complements this by reawakening the old German
integrity.[42] Throughout the Ebernburg manifestos, Hutten claims to be
attempting the restoration of German freedoms and the reawakening of
German honour.[43] According to both Hutten and Eberlin the German

---

[36] Lucke, *Die Entstehung der 15 Bundesgenossen*, pp. 95–7.

[37] Geiger, 'Die reformatorischen Initia Eberlins,' pp. 183 and 191.

[38] Ahrens, p. 37; see also, Peters, p. 46.

[39] On the 'manifestos' see Holborn, p. 151.

[40] See 'Ein Clagschrift des Hochberůmten und Eernuestē herrn Ulrichs vō Hutten
gekrŏnten Poeten uñ Orator an alle stend Deŭtscher nation,' Böcking, vol. 1, p. 405; 'Der
V. Bundesgenosse. Ein vermanung zu aller oberkeit Teütscher Nation, das sy den Predig
stůl oder Cantzel reformieren,' Enders, vol. 1, p. 45.

[41] 'Ein Clagschrift an alle stend Deütscher nation,' Böcking, vol. 1, p. 419: 'Seitmal ich
auch verstandē hab, wie das etliche mir zů nachteil, meine bůcher und geschrifft, bey den
unverstēdigen übel ausslegē. Und anders, dañ die an jn selbs verstanden werdē mŏgen,
verteütschē, domit ich dañ bey yederman alles verdachts erledige, uñ auch gemeinen man,
wie billich oder unbillich ich gehandelt, . . .'; 'Der VIII. Bundesgenosse,' Enders, vol. 1, p.
84: 'Aber die waren prediger und lerer haben sich lang enthalten von widerzalung mit
schmochwort, biss sie sehen, das es not ist, das man dem volck den rechten grund fürhalte,
was unbillichs biss har inen sei auffgeleit worden, wider gott und eer, und schriben solichs
auss in teütscher sprach das ein jetlicher frommer christ in seim hauss mag lāsen und wol
bedencken.'

[42] 'Der erste Bundesgenosse,' pp. 4–5 (= Laube 2:710–11).

[43] 'Huttenus ad Carolum,' Böcking, vol. 1, p. 375; 'Ein Clagschrift an alle stend
Deütscher nation,' Böcking, vol. 1, p. 411.

virtues have been subverted by vices imported from south of the Alps.[44] Because of their efforts, Luther and Hutten face specific opponents: Luther the mendicants ('specifically the Observant Franciscans') and Hutten the courtiers, whom he himself designates as his chief enemies.[45] Gottfried Geiger has indicated that in 'The Fifteen Confederates' Eberlin's claims are not theologically grounded, but rest on the evidence of a catalogue of abuses, behind which lies a vision of the history of Christendom as a conflict between the Gospel and the antichristian devilish sect of Rome.[46] Like so many of his contemporaries, Eberlin interpreted the events around him in cosmic terms. The reforming movements from Reuchlin to Luther have rediscovered the Gospel; an event which Eberlin regards as no less significant than what occurred in Judea 1500 years earlier.[47]

Those espousing reform are, however, teaching nothing new, but rather returning to the true Gospel which the 'Eighth Confederate' and the 'Fifth Confederate' declare had been falsified for the preceding 300 years (hence 100 years longer than in the earlier more moderate 'Second Confederate').[48] The 'Fifth Confederate' attributes much of the perversion of the Gospel to the mendicants who, under the guise of simplicity and humility, were able to secure a place among the people until they were strong enough to show their true colours.[49] In the 'Eighth Confederate,' Eberlin develops this theme more fully and describes a conspiracy between the pope and the mendicants for the ruin of Christendom:

> Then they [the popes and the papal curia] began to make a pact with the begging monks, . . . Then the power of the bishops and parish priests began to diminish, and the universities were forcibly occupied by the friars as were all pulpits and confessionals.[50]

The 'Ninth Confederate' continues in the same vein:

> The Holy Spirit had at first sufficiently warned the heads of the Christian churches, were it wished to follow through in thwarting the plans of the friars. For almost all of the bishops and priests in the entire world as well as many of the universities set themselves against them until the papal court realized what benefits these

44 'Ein Clagschrift an alle stend Deütscher nation,' Böcking, vol. 1, p. 416; 'Der erste Bundesgenosse,' Enders, vol. 1, p. 8 (= Laube 2:713).

45 'Der erste Bundesgenosse,' Enders, vol. 1, pp. 6–7 (= Laube 2:712).

46 Geiger, 'Die reformatorischen Initia Eberlins,' pp. 186–7.

47 'Der erste Bundesgenosse,' Enders, vol. 1, p. 3 (= Laube 2:709).

48 'Der V. Bundesgenosse,' Enders, vol. 1, p. 51; 'Der VIII. Bundesgenosse,' Enders, vol. 1, p. 86.

49 'Der V. Bundesgenosse,' Enders, vol. 1, p. 49.

50 'Der VIII. Bundesgenosse,' Enders, vol. 1, p. 82.

begging people brought it. Then it bestowed on the beggars all of their means through bulls, interdicts and freedoms.[51]

The friars have also played a crucial role in the extension of papal power at the expense of secular authorities. The 'Eighth Confederate' provides a brief overview of the history of papal–imperial conflicts to indicate the role of the mendicants in the papal victory. Just when it appeared that the yoke of papal tyranny would be broken, the pope enlisted the followers of Francis and Dominic for his cause and was thereby assured of victory.[52]

Gottfried Geiger has suggested that the source of Eberlin's perception of history was Melanchthon's anonymous defence of Luther from early 1521, 'An Oration of Didymus Faventinus in Defense of Martin Luther against Thomas Placentinus.' He maintains that Eberlin adopted from Melanchthon the denunciation of scholasticism as a perversion of Christian teaching, which has held the upper hand for the last 300 years, and the term 'synagogues of Satan,' with which Melanchthon designated the universities and Eberlin the cloisters and the Roman Curia.[53] As a justification for Luther's activity aimed specifically at avoiding tension with the humanist movement, this work would have reinforced Eberlin's perception of the unity of the reforming movements and their historical context.[54]

While admitting that Eberlin's nationalist orientation derived from Hutten, Geiger suggests that his discussion of the history of papal–imperial relations, too, was influenced by Melanchthon's work.[55] However, on this issue Hutten seems the more likely candidate. Melanchthon's work deals only briefly with the conflicts between the emperors and popes in a general history of the rise of caesaro-papalism and the fall of the church, and it concentrates only on the best-known examples from the high Middle Ages.[56] Eberlin's reference, although brief, encompasses a much broader period of German history from Otto I to Lewis the Bavarian.[57] This very likely draws upon Hutten's 'Disclosure of How the Roman Bishops or Popes have Acted against the

---

[51] 'Der VIIII. Bundesgenosse,' Enders, vol. 1, p. 97.

[52] 'Der VIII. Bundesgenosse,' Enders, vol. 1, pp. 81–2.

[53] Geiger, 'Die reformatorischen Initia Eberlins,' pp. 189–90. Hutten also referred to the perversion of Christian teaching for the last 300 years. See Böcking, vol. 1, p. 182.

[54] Wilhelm Maurer, Der junge Melanchthon zwischen Humanismus und Reformation, vol. 2: Der Theologe (Göttingen, 1969), p. 132.

[55] Geiger, 'Die reformatorischen Initia Eberlins,' p. 190.

[56] 'Didymi Faventini adversus Thomam Placentinum pro Martino Luthero theologo oratio,' in Melanchthons Werke in Auswahl, ed. Robert Stupperich, vol. 1: Reformatorische Schriften (Gütersloh, 1951), pp. 119–20.

[57] 'Der VIII. Bundesgenosse,' Enders, vol. 1, p. 81.

German Emperors.' This work, produced in the late autumn of 1520, detailed papal-imperial conflict from the time of Otto I to that of Lewis the Bavarian and beyond.[58]

But the history of papal-imperial relations is only one half of Eberlin's historical vision. As indicated above, Eberlin supplements it with a discussion of the history of secular–mendicant conflicts and their relationship to the extension of papal power. In this he echoes Luther's criticisms of the friars in the 'Address to the Christian Nobility.'[59] Thus Eberlin unified the historical visions of the two men identified by the 'First Confederate' as the leaders of the Reformation.

According to Geiger, Eberlin's unique contribution to this view of historical development was the role he assigned to the mendicants and their pact with the papacy.[60] Eberlin's bitterness against Glapion and his former brethren in general has traditionally been regarded as a reflection of his own experiences during the final days in the Ulm Cloister.[61] No doubt, the venomous attacks Eberlin levels at his former brethren reflect to a large degree his anger at their rejection of his programme for the further reform of the order and Christendom. However, it appears that Eberlin's attack on the order was neither as unique nor as deeply rooted in personal experience as has been suggested. Although Eberlin's personal vendetta against Glapion may have played a role, there were also other reasons for denouncing the emperor's confessor. In February 1521 Glapion had attempted to mediate between the imperial court and the chancellor of Electoral Saxony on the Luther issue. Immediately before the Diet of Worms he made similar overtures to Hutten and Sickingen at the Ebernburg. On both occasions he gave the impression that the emperor was inclined to reform.[62] In the 'First Confederate,' Eberlin indicates that the emperor is in fact inclining away from the reforming movement. The most pointed of these references excuses disregard of imperial mandates against Luther and Hutten on the basis that the emperor is misinformed by those around him.[63] In Eberlin's analysis, a key player in turning Charles V against Luther and Hutten is Glapion, the 'grey hypocrite' from the superstitious Observants.[64]

---

[58] 'Eiñ trewe Warnung, Wie die bãpst allwegen wider die Teutschen keyser gewest,' Böcking, vol. 5, pp. 363–95. On the dating of this tract, see Holborn, p. 159.

[59] See above, p. 35–6.

[60] Geiger, 'Die reformatorischen Initia Eberlins,' p. 190. Radlkofer, p. 18, similarly noted Eberlin's emphasis on the mendicants as unique.

[61] Lucke, *Die Entstehung der 15 Bundesgenossen*, p. 63; Geiger, 'Die reformatorischen Initia Eberlins,' p. 190.

[62] Holborn, pp. 169–70.

[63] 'Der erste Bundesgenosse,' Enders, vol. 1, p. 9 (= Laube 2:714).

[64] 'Der erste Bundesgenosse,' Enders, vol. 1, pp. 5–6 (= Laube 2:711–12).

Eberlin was not alone in holding Glapion responsible for his own woes and those of the Reformers. In 'A Remonstrance and Warning against the Presumptuous Unchristian Power of the Bishop of Rome and the Unspiritual Spiritual Estate,' Hutten, too, turned his attention to the emperor's confessor:

> Also, to King Charles was sent
> a grey monk with wooden shoes.
> This same hypocrite has a mandate
> to seize me in every city,
> and where he catches me in the land.[65]

Like Eberlin, Hutten suggests that Glapion has been providing the emperor with false advice, although he sees the consequences of this from a much more personal perspective:

> He also gave false advice
> to the pious King,
> according to which I have done evil,
> and which allowed him to assail me,
> and to take me away by force.[66]

The friars, and especially the Franciscan Observants, clearly remained in the front rank of the enemies of the Gospel and of the German people.

That Eberlin looked to a synthesis of Luther's reforming vision with Hutten's in this group of pamphlets is significant to understanding the nature of his anticlericalism in these works and its place in the development of Eberlin's reforming thought. His denunciation of the friars as the agents of the papacy in its ongoing conflict with episcopal and parochial authority reflects Luther's reform programme in the 'Address to the Christian Nobility.' At the same time, his discussion of papal–imperial relations ties the preceding exposé into the parallel conflict for German liberties. In this way Hutten's political antipapalism is tied to Luther's antipapalism and anticurialism. Political autonomy under the emperor coincides with the national episcopalian church advocated by Luther. Although Eberlin's anticlerical polemics are radicalized in these pamphlets in terms of antipapalism and antifraternalism, his anticlericalism remains essentially medieval. The attack on the clergy is not anchored in Luther's soteriology and re-evaluation of the sacramental teachings of the medieval church. Rather, it remains a catalogue of clerical abuse. As did Luther in the 'Address to the Christian Nobility,' Eberlin merely revives and sharpens traditional anticlerical grievances and appends them to a radically antipapalist stance. Furthermore, central to the integration of the reforming visions

---

[65] 'Clag und vormanung gegen dem gewalt des Bapsts,' Böcking, vol. 3, pp. 509–10.
[66] Ibid., p. 510.

of Hutten and Luther is a reliance on this catalogue of clerical abuse to vilify the papal church.

The extent to which Eberlin's anticlericalism in this group of confederates remains medieval becomes clear as one investigates the specific crimes with which he charges the friars. Like Luther, Eberlin identified the nature and sources of conflict between the mendicants and the secular clergy in the later Middle Ages. Beyond this, Eberlin also revived crucial elements of the polemical tradition developed by the opponents of the friars in the course of these conflicts.

Investigations into antifraternalism in Middle English literature have indicated the importance of the polemics developed against the friars at the University of Paris in the middle of the thirteenth century for this genre and medieval estates satire in general.[67] Penn Szittya in particular has concentrated on the adaptability of William of St Amour's biblical exegesis and its importance in changed political circumstances in England a century later.[68] According to Szittya's interpretation, St Amour's criticism of the friars is determined not by realistic charges against them, but by their identification with three Biblical types: the Pharisees, the *psuedoapostoli* and the *antichristi*.[69] Eberlin's writings indicate that the versatility of St Amour's polemics was not exhausted in the fourteenth century, and that the friars continued to be identified with these biblical types into the sixteenth century.

Eberlin nowhere openly identifies the friars as Pharisees, although his allusions certainly imply that they are Pharisees. His comparison of contemporary events with the initial appearance of the Gospel in Judea and the characterization of the cloisters as 'synagogues of Satan' leave little doubt as to what role he assigns to his opponents.[70] Elsewhere he is even more explicit:

> In the Gospel, the Lord Jesus says to the evil scholars and clergy: You have taken away the key to the heavenly Kingdom, that is the understanding of the Holy Scriptures, and not only are you yourselves not entering the Kingdom, but you do not allow others to enter into it, that is, not only have you become evil, but also you

---

[67] See especially, Arnold Williams, 'Chaucer and the Friars,' *Speculum*, 28 (1953), pp. 499–513; Jill Mann, *Chaucer and Medieval Estates Satire: The Literature of Social Classes and the General Prologue to the Canterbury Tales* (Cambridge, 1973), pp. 37–54; Penn Szittya, 'The Antifraternal Tradition in Middle English Literature,' *Speculum*, 52 (1977), pp. 287–313; id., *The Antifraternal Tradition in Medieval Literature* (Princeton, 1986).

[68] Szittya, 'Antifraternal Tradition,' pp. 288, 313; *Antifraternal Tradition in Medieval Literature*, pp. 184, 200–1.

[69] Szittya, 'Antifraternal Tradition,' p. 290; *Antifraternal Tradition in Medieval Literature*, pp. 32–4.

[70] 'Der erste Bundesgenosse,' Enders, vol. 1, p. 3 (= Laube 2:709); 'Der VIIII. Bundesgenosse,' vol. 1, p. 105.

have denied the simple people the proper understanding of God's commands.[71]

This citation is from the introduction to the 'Eighth Confederate' in which Eberlin begins the historical investigation of the evils perpetrated on Christendom by the friars. Although Eberlin provides no biblical citations, this is obviously a paraphrase of Matthew 23:13 or Luke 11:52. William of St Amour's identification of the friars with the Pharisees took the form of an exegesis of Matthew 23, and this text retained its association specifically with the friars in the later Middle Ages.[72]

The proximity of Eberlin's polemics to the medieval antifraternal tradition becomes clearer with an investigation of the characteristics applied to the friars on the basis of St Amour's exegesis of Matthew 23. At Paris the immediate point of contention was the control of the theological faculty by the mendicants, and the key to St Amour's exegesis is the identification of the academic titles of the mendicant masters with the claim that the Pharisees desired to be called master and Christ's denunciation of this in Matthew 23:7–10.[73] By the early sixteenth century this charge played only a subsidiary role in the attack on the friars. Nonetheless, in his loose translation of *Praise of Folly* in the 'Sixth Confederate,' Eberlin alludes to it. In the spirit of the medieval antifraternal tradition, he plays on the title *magister* and charges that the aim of mendicant preaching is to 'master all men.'[74] Elsewhere Eberlin more directly denounces the friars' desire for academic titles. On this occasion he judges their activities not by the words of Christ, but by the criticism of St Francis, who often spoke of the lack of knowledge of his brothers.[75]

---

[71] 'Der VIII. Bundesgenosse,' Enders, vol. 1, p. 80. Luther had made use of this same text in the 'Address to the Christian Nobility,' but there applied it to canon law instead of the mendicants. See WA, 6:445.

[72] Szittya, 'Antifraternal Tradition,' p. 294; *Antifraternal Tradition in Medieval Literature*, pp. 34–6, 40–1, 201–7. See above, p. 31.

[73] Szittya, 'Antifraternal Tradition,' pp. 294–5; 'Sermo Magistri Wilhelmi de S. Amore, I,' in Ortwin Gratius, *Fasciculum rerum expetendarum*, ed. Edward Brown (London, 1690; reprint edn, Tucson, 1967), pp. 45–6.

[74] 'Der VI. Bundesgenosse,' Enders, vol. 1, p. 60: 'Auch mit solcher apostützlery und thorechten predigen wöllen sie alle menschen meisteren.' See also Alfred Götze, *Frühneuhochdeutsches Glossar* (Berlin, 1967), p. 157. This charge appears to have retained currency in Middle High German satire, see *Des Teufels Netz*, p. 172:

Wenn aber ainr von schuol kompt ...
Und macht denn ain grosz stimm,
Die ist so zornig und so grim
Und stelt sich gar maisterlich,
Niemann ist denn sin gelich.

[75] 'Der VIIII. Bundesgenosse,' Enders, vol. 1, p. 98.

In the verses of Matthew 23 adjacent to those cited above, William of St Amour found further characteristics of the Pharisees which he applied to the friars. The charge that the Pharisees loved the first place at dinners he identified with the friars' courting of the influential and wealthy that they might be delicately fed and honoured.[76] In the 'Sixth Confederate,' Eberlin repeats Erasmus's accusations that the mendicants pander to the merchants in order to receive a share of their plunder.[77] But he does not concentrate on this theme and emphasizes instead the friars' links to the papal curia. Unlike his medieval predecessors, Eberlin was willing to challenge openly the authority of Rome. It appears that, in the condemnation of both the mendicants and the papal curia, Eberlin combined this accusation with another, that of desiring greetings in the marketplace. The latter characteristic William of St Amour loosely identified with the friars' love of litigation, an activity expressly condemned by St Francis.[78] In Eberlin's view, the Franciscans, contrary to the specific commands of their founder, seek papal bulls with which they maintain their positions and overwhelm their opponents.[79] The same critique he applies elsewhere to all mendicants.[80] Should a layman challenge them, he soon finds himself entwined in the complexities of the ecclesiastical hierarchy and canon law.[81] The apex of their strength and depth of their degeneration lies, however, in the control of the Inquisition.[82]

On two other prominent charges linking the friars to the Pharisees, Eberlin is more traditional. On the basis of Matthew 23:15: 'Woe unto you, Scribes and Pharisees, hypocrites! for ye compass sea and land to make one proselyte, and when he is made, ye make him twofold more the child of hell than yourselves.' St Amour claimed that the friars stole children – that is, encouraged underaged novices.[83] On one occasion Eberlin makes specific reference to the stealing of children: 'The monks

---

[76] Szittya, 'Antifraternal Tradition,' p. 296; *Antifraternal Tradition in Medieval Literature*, pp. 37–8; 'Sermo Wilhelmi de S. Amore, I,' p. 44.

[77] 'Der VI. Bundesgenosse,' Enders, vol. 1, p. 60.

[78] Szittya, 'Antifraternal Tradition,' p. 296; *Antifraternal Tradition in Medieval Literature*, p. 38; 'Sermo Wilhelmi de S. Amore, I,' p. 45.

[79] 'Der VIIII. Bundesgenosse,' Enders, vol. 1, p. 98: 'Franciscus hat inen verbotten, sie solten kein bull umb etwas sach erwerben vom bapst, . . . das ist sein letst testament gsin, auch sein regel. Aber die graw kut wolt lob und eer haben, wolt vol und faul sein und nicht darumb thůn oder lyden, dann mit bǎpstlichem endchristlichem donder der bullen, do mit sie zwungen und bochten jedermann sy wolten wider ire regel und gebot.'

[80] 'Der V. Bundesgenosse,' Enders, vol. 1, p. 49.

[81] 'Der erste Bundesgenosse,' Enders, vol. 1, p. 10 (= Laube 2:714).

[82] 'Der VIII. Bundesgenosse,' Enders, vol. 1, pp. 82–3.

[83] Szittya, 'Antifraternal Tradition,' pp. 299–300; 'De periculis Ecclesiae,' in *Fasciculum rerum expetendarum*, p. 35.

seek everywhere to rouse children into a cloister.'[84] On the issue of the feigned piety of the friars, a charge which William of St Amour derived from Matthew 23:5: 'But all their works they do for to be seen of men,' Eberlin is not so reserved.[85] In his initial diatribe against the Franciscans in the 'First Confederate,' Eberlin accuses them of appearing better than they actually are.[86] The mendicants in general, he suggests, have had their success simply because of this appearance of holiness. When they first attempted to enter Germany, they were expelled by the people, who were subsequently won over by the friars' appearance of simplicity and piety.[87] However, the members of the mendicant orders themselves know how superficial this appearance is: 'There is a saying among us, and especially among the Franciscan Observants, that it doesn't matter what one does so long as the lay people don't know about it.'[88]

In the exegesis of William of St Amour and in the subsequent medieval antifraternal tradition the identification of the friars with the Pharisees was grounded only on their assumption of the title *magister*; the other characteristics which he applied to them were determined by the biblical type rather than any real life situation. The identity of the friars as the Biblical *psuedoapostoli* and *antichristi* – William treated both categories together and they were confused in the minds of most subsequent antifraternal authors – was much more broadly based in the competing claims of both the secular clergy and the mendicants to justify their office and priestly functions in terms of apostolic succession. Therefore, the claim that the friars did not truly imitate the lives of the apostles nor were they their true successors lies at the root of almost all thirteenth-century antifraternal tracts and is a unifying thread in most of the controversies involving friars in the fourteenth century.[89]

Eberlin again avoids the specific labels of the medieval tradition, but employs many of the prominent characteristics derived from them and alludes to the proof texts associated with these characteristics. He claims that the friars are the false prophets of Matthew 7 who appear in sheep's clothing, but are, in reality, ravenous wolves.[90] And, as the sworn servants of the antichristian pope, they are, by extension, to be

---

[84] 'Der VIIII. Bundesgenosse,' Enders, vol. 1, p. 101.

[85] Szittya, 'Antifraternal Tradition,' p. 298; *Antifraternal Tradition in Medieval Literature*, pp. 39–40; 'Sermo Wilhelmi de S. Amore, I,' p. 44.

[86] 'Der erste Bundesgenosse,' Enders, vol. 1, p. 5 (= Laube 2:711).

[87] 'Der VIII. Bundesgenosse,' Enders, vol. 1, p. 83.

[88] 'Der VIIII. Bundesgenosse,' Enders, vol. 1, p. 94.

[89] Szittya, 'Antifraternal Tradition,' pp. 301–3.

[90] 'Der VI. Bundesgenosse,' Enders, vol. 1, p. 63: 'Du einfältiget ley biss gewarnt vor den báttel München, dann offt kummen sy in schaffkleider und sind heimlich zuckent wölff und offt ist es, ye geistlicher schein ye flaischlicher sin'; 'Der VIII. Bundesgenosse,' Enders, vol. 1, p. 86: '. . . und yederman warnen vor den falschen propheten in schaffs

identified with the *antichristi*. Concentrating on the extremely contentious issue of the competing claims of the secular and mendicant clergy to the cure of souls, this line of argumentation provided fertile ground for reformers of the sixteenth century and furnished them with a particularly useful polemical weapon. The contrast between the themes developed here and the recommendation in the 'Fourth Confederate' that study, teaching, preaching and hearing confessions were the proper activity of the regular clergy indicates clearly the extent of Eberlin's radicalization over this brief span of time.

William of St Amour had identified 40 signs by which one could recognize the *psuedoapostoli*. The most famous of these was derived from the reference in 2 Timothy 3:6 to the false apostles who will enter houses and lead their occupants astray. This was interpreted in the medieval tradition as referring to those who, through preaching and the confessional, entered the house of the conscience illegally, that is without the legitimate cure of souls, and led the laity away from the duly constituted spiritual authority.[91] Eberlin's repetition of Erasmus's charge that the mendicants appealed particularly to women to extend their power over their husbands as well was a commonplace in this tradition.[92] However, Eberlin was able to continue making such accusations on his own: '. . . the begging monks seek secretly and openly in the confessional and the pulpit, in houses and on the streets to turn the people away from the emerging Christian teaching with lies and deception, . . .'[93] Nor does he shrink from drawing the consequences of this for the duly constituted spiritual authorities, the parochial clergy and the bishops: '. . . but the friars were supposed to preach and hear confessions where the priests required them, but afterwards they wished to be over the priests and, to this day, have been at odds with them to the great detriment of the people.'[94] This conflict between the secular and mendicant clergy he drew from the medieval antifraternal tradition. But again here he radicalized the position of his predecessors, largely on the basis of his willingness to denounce the papal curia along with the mendicants: 'Through them, all of Germany has become a vassal to the

---

kleideren, . . .' William of St Amour frequently makes the same identification. See 'De periculis,' pp. 23 and 26.

[91] Szittya, 'Antifraternal Tradition,' p. 305; *Antifraternal Tradition in Medieval Literature*, pp. 57–61; 'De periculis,' pp. 19–26.

[92] 'Der VI. Bundesgenosse,' Enders, vol. 1, p. 60: '. . . und die bättel münch richten ir sach dar uff das sy frawen und kouffleüten gefallen. . . . und die wiber sind darumb so günstig den bättel münchen, dann allen iren unwillen, so sy zů iren eemannen tragen, schütten sie den münchen in busen. Auch mit solcher apostützlery und thorechten predigen wöllen sie alle menschen meistern.'

[93] 'Der VIII. Bundesgenosse,' Enders, vol. 1, p. 87.

[94] 'Der VIIII. Bundesgenosse,' Enders, vol. 1, p. 96.

pope, all dioceses and all parishes. But the diocese of Salzburg is healthy which has to this day no mendicant cloisters within its boundaries.'[95]

Outside the universities the late medieval conflicts involving the mendicants revolved around three central issues: preaching, confession and burial of the laity. As we have seen, these remained points of contention from the thirteenth to the sixteenth century, and it appears that the biblical types associated with the performance of these services by the mendicants continued to have currency. Given the polemical exchanges in which Eberlin was involved, and the importance of preaching in Luther's theology and for the dissemination of his message, Eberlin's concentration on this theme comes as no surprise. That this topic also occupied a prominent place in the medieval conflicts involving the friars is indicated by its role not only in identifying them as *psuedoapostoli* and *antichristi*, but also in their identification as Pharisees. William of St Amour had linked the Pharisees' love of the first places in the Synagogue, contained in Matthew 23:6, to the friars' attempts to force their way into pulpits in which they have no authority.[96] Eberlin takes up fully the fundamentals of this position, including the principal medieval criticisms of mendicant preaching. The 'Fifth Confederate' recommends that this activity remain in the domain of the parish priest. If, however, for some reason he is unable to fulfil his duties, they can be entrusted to a monk, but only with the permission of the bishop.[97] This, however, does not apply to preachers remaining within the mendicant orders, whose obedience to their superiors, inexperience in the affairs of the parish and transient life disqualify them as suitable candidates.[98] When he turns to positive reform suggestions, Eberlin recommends that all foreign priests and monks be tested by the bishop before being allowed to preach.[99]

The accusation that the friars were shoving their way into pulpits was reinforced by the characterizations of mendicant preachers derived from their identification with the *psuedoapostoli* and *antichristi*. On this issue, the kernel of the antifraternal tradition lay in William of St Amour's exegesis of 2 Corinthians 11:7–15 and Paul's claim that the false prophets preach for personal gain.[100] Throughout 'The Fifteen Confederates,' Eberlin accuses the friars of preaching for the benefit of

---

[95] 'Der VIII. Bundesgenosse,' Enders, vol. 1, p. 83.

[96] Szittya, 'Antifraternal Tradition,' p. 296; *Antifraternal Tradition in Medieval Literature*, p. 38; 'Sermo Wilhelmi de S. Amore,' I, pp. 44–5.

[97] 'Der V. Bundesgenosse,' Enders, vol. 1, p. 47.

[98] Ibid., p. 48.

[99] 'Der VI. Bundesgenosse,' Enders, vol. 1, p. 63.

[100] Szittya, 'Antifraternal Tradition,' pp. 306–7; *Antifraternal Tradition in Medieval Literature*, p. 52; 'De periculis,' p. 35.

themselves and their order to the detriment of Christendom. To choose a representative passage, he claims in the 'Ninth Confederate' that 'they direct their activities to the winning of honours and their own good rather than the welfare of souls.'[101] In the gloss on Erasmus's critique of the mendicants' preaching practices in the 'Sixth Confederate,' Eberlin provides signs by which false preachers might be identified. Prominent among these is the claim that they encourage their hearers to give them alms. However, like Paul, they should preach for the sake of the Gospel, not personal gain.[102]

According to the medieval antifraternal tradition, the preaching of the friars is not only illegitimate but doctrinally false.[103] Here again we see the ease with which the medieval criticism of the friars could be adapted to the circumstances of the early sixteenth century. Throughout this group of the confederates, Eberlin portrays the mendicants as the chief opponents of the truth and purveyors of the heathen, scholastic doctrines. The medieval critics of the friars claimed that they employed all sorts of fables, lying and vain stories to make such falsity palatable to their audiences.[104] According to Eberlin, a sure sign of a false preacher is that he employs all manner of gestures, fables and examples which do not come from the Bible.[105] Naturally, this style is the antithesis of the true apostles' – and by extension the Reformers' – which is plain and direct.[106]

Closely related to the charge that the friars preach for gain is Paul's warning against false apostles who wish to live illegitimately from the Gospel. Paul's claim in 2 Thessalonians 3:6–12 that he lived from manual labour while at Thessalonica served as the basis for the medieval attack on the mendicancy of the friars.[107] In the 'Address to the Christian Nobility,' Luther, too, took up this criticism of the mendic-

---

[101] 'Der VIIII. Bundesgenosse,' Enders, vol. 1, p. 96: '. . . so ist all ir ding meer gericht uff gewin der eren und des eigen nutz dann uff selen heil.'

[102] 'Der VI. Bundesgenosse,' Enders, vol. 1, p. 61: 'Wann sie mit vil worten verkünden, das man geben soll almůsen, so sie samlen,'; p. 63: 'Wann die münch kummen allein und predigen, so sie samlen wőllen, oder so man wol soll leben, so geben yn nicht, dann sye sind schuldig offt eüch zů predigen und das umb gots willen.'

[103] Szittya, 'Antifraternal Tradition,' p. 306.

[104] Szittya, 'Antifraternal Tradition,' p. 307; *Antifraternal Tradition in Medieval Literature*, pp. 53–4; 'De periculis,' pp. 35, 41; 'Sermo Wilhelmi de S. Amore, I,' p. 45.

[105] 'Der VI. Bundesgenosse,' Enders, vol. 1, p. 61: 'Du hast jetz uss Erasmo gehőrt, wo by du erkennen solt ein bloderer, ein mårlin prediger, wann sie ungestůme gebård brauchen uff der kantzel, vyl fabel oder exempel sagen, die nit in der Bibel geschriben stond, . . . Wann sy vyl jauffthåding oder spőtwort brauchen, dar ab man lachen soll.'

[106] See 'Der VIII. Bundesgenosse,' Enders, vol. 1, pp. 84–5.

[107] Szittya, 'Antifraternal Tradition,' pp. 304–5; 'De periculis,' pp. 36, 39–40.

ancy of the friars.[108] The contrast between God's command to work and the mendicant life is a prominent and consistent theme throughout 'The Fifteen Confederates.' In the 'Eighth Confederate' it reaches a crescendo when Eberlin suggests that the Franciscan order be exterminated because it is the source of mendicancy among the monks and nuns.[109] Eberlin, however, safeguards Francis from this accusation. The saint had originally commanded his followers to live by the fruit of their labours, but they and the other friars subsequently perverted his teachings to live by the ill-gotten gains of begging.[110] Therefore, the friars live contrary not only to the commands of God, but also their own Rule.[111]

Living as they do from false teaching, the false prophets will not endure the testing of their doctrines and will persecute anyone who challenges them.[112] This, the 'First Confederate' implies, is the reason why the mendicants are Luther's chief opponents.[113] In a passage that sounds strongly autobiographical, Eberlin indicates that this is a common procedure: 'Or, if someone preaches the apostolic teaching, from which the baseless teachings and disgraceful lives of the monks will be noted, from that very hour they seek, both within and outside the cloister, an occasion to get rid of such a useful preacher to the detriment of God's Word.'[114]

Interestingly, Eberlin gives only scant attention to the other two chief points of contention between the mendicants and secular clergy: the hearing of confessions and burial in the cemeteries of mendicant churches. Other than identifying the confessional along with the pulpit as the pillars of mendicant power over the laity, Eberlin is strangely silent on this theme. His references to secular–mendicant disputes over burial of the laity are hardly more elaborate or detailed. The popularity of burial in the cemeteries of the mendicants and bequests to them instead of the parochial clergy seriously threatened not only the authority, but also the income of the parish priest.[115] On this subject, Eberlin makes only disapproving reference to the common myths that

---

[108] WA, 6:450–1.

[109] 'Der VIII. Bundesgenosse,' Enders, vol. 1, p. 87.

[110] 'Der VIIII. Bundesgenosse,' Enders, vol. 1, p. 96–9.

[111] Ibid., pp. 101–2.

[112] Szittya, 'Antifraternal Tradition,' p. 304; 'De periculis,' p. 40.

[113] 'Der erste Bundesgenosse,' Enders, vol. 1, pp. 6–7 (= Laube 2:712).

[114] 'Der V. Bundesgenosse,' Enders, vol. 1, p. 48.

[115] The bull *Super cathedram*, which attempted to regulate the juridical issues in the conflict between seculars and mendicants, dealt with burial dues in addition to the rights of preaching and hearing confessions.

association with the Franciscan order eased the way into heaven.[116] However, given the circumstances within which Eberlin found himself, his decision to concentrate on the denunciation of mendicant preaching practices is hardly surprising.

A further, very common charge in the English antifraternal tradition was that the friars' numbers were increasing without limit. Research into the demography of late medieval England suggests that such a charge has no basis in historical fact. Szittya argues, therefore, that it has more to do with a metaphysical than a physical conception of number. Wisdom 11:21, 'the keyword of the medieval world view,' suggests that all things exist within prescribed limits and proportions. From the perspective of the secular clergy, the friars, who were not true successors to the apostles and whose orders stood outside the normal ecclesiastical hierarchy, had no set place in the church and were, consequently, 'not numbered.'[117] Among his earliest criticisms of the friars in the 'First Confederate,' Eberlin claims that 'their great numbers are completely unknown.'[118] Nonetheless, in the 'Ninth Confederate,' he hazards a guess at the size of the mendicant orders and suggests the inflated figures of 24 000 friars in Germany alone and over 400 000 in Europe.[119] Shortly thereafter Eberlin comes directly to the issue at hand: the mendicants were not instituted to sing or read in the church or to say special prayers (the endowed orders are suitable for that) but to supplement the activities of the secular clergy whom they have attempted to supplant to the detriment of the church.[120] Eberlin shies away from completely adopting the charge that the mendicants are without metaphysical place, but in assigning them roles as helpers to the

---

[116] 'Der XIV. Bundesgenosse,' Enders, vol. 1, p. 158.

[117] Szittya, 'Antifraternal Tradition,' pp. 308–10; id., *Antifraternal Tradition in Medieval Literature*, pp. 221–30; 'De periculis,' p. 19.

[118] 'Der erste Bundesgenosse,' Enders, vol. 1, p. 5 (= Laube 2:711).

[119] 'Der VIIII. Bundesgenosse,' Enders, vol. 1, p. 95: 'Sunderlich haben es ermessen die bättel münch, deren in teütschland sind wol .xxiiij. tausent, und man hat es uber schlagen, das in Europa sind meer dann vier mol hundert tausent.' Steven Ozment, *The Reformation in the Cities. The Appeal of Protestantism to Sixteenth-Century Germany and Switzerland* (New Haven and London, 1975), p. 94 mistakenly identifies this as the number of people in orders in general.

[120] 'Der VIIII. Bundesgenosse,' Enders, vol. 1, p. 96: 'So sind sy nit angenummen vom römischen byschoff fürderlich zu singen und läsen in der kirchen, dann sölich örden waren vor hin gnüg, welche gestifft waren uff singen und läsen on den bättel, auch gnüg pfaffen, aber die bättel münch solten predigen und bychthören, wo die pfarrer ir bedörfften, aber dar nach wolten sy uber die pfarrer sein, und sind mit in zwiträchtig gesin biss uff die stund mit grossem schaden des volcks. So ist auch nit not gsin, das man bättel münch orden stiffte uff sunder gebät für das volck, dann ob in nit zu gehört auss der geschrifft, aber meer den pfarrern und seel sorgern.'

parochial clergy and then claiming that they have failed miserably in this task, he is denying them a place in the church.

Surprisingly, despite this virulent attack on the mendicant orders and the Franciscans in particular, Eberlin continues to honour St Francis throughout this group of the confederates. His first discussion of the origins of the Franciscan and Dominican orders refers to their founders in glowing terms.[121] Rather, it was the followers of these two who perverted the original vision.[122] Although the polemic against the friars escalates, the assessment of Francis and Dominic remains relatively constant. In the 'Ninth Confederate,' Eberlin continues to praise St Francis, although he voices some reservations about some of his undertakings.[123] Similarly, in the 'Fourteenth Confederate,' Eberlin defends the canonization of St Dominic, although he does this to take a back-handed swipe at the Preachers. To Dominic's credit, he cursed all who brought or accepted landed property into his order and, given the wealth of the Dominicans, has therefore cursed his own followers.[124]

Steven Ozment has commented on Eberlin's critique of the monastic orders:

> All are found wanting when measured by the *Testament* and other writings of St Francis, whom Eberlin finds to have bound his followers (and apparently all other true mendicants) to working with their hands, receiving only subsistence nourishment (never money or gold) for their labors, and remaining few in number in a nonconventual, simple lifestyle.[125]

Eberlin's perception of the ideals of the mendicant orders appears to be

---

[121] 'Der VIII. Bundesgenosse,' Enders, vol. 1, pp. 81–2: 'Es waren in Italia zwen frumm mann, Franciscus und Dominicus genant, die understünden sich das wort gottes zů predigen mit ettlichen iren gesellen, und begårten dess ein urlob von dem bapst und schafften vil nutz im volck, dann sie gar ein gaistlichen und unargwenigen lābens waren, sie namen nicht dann tåglich brot umb all ir arbeit, und waren gar innerlich andechtig lüt, und got was mit innen, . . .'

[122] Ibid., p. 82: '. . . aber dar nach vyl understünden sich im båttel neren, under deren zweien frummen mannen und under irer frummen gesellen tittel. Aber die vyle verderbt das spyl.'

[123] 'Der VIIII. Bundesgenosse,' Enders, vol. 1, p. 96: 'Franciscus ist ein ungelert einfeltig mensch gesin, und wie wol er für sich selbs ein frumm mensch ist gesin, hat er doch vyl dings understanden, das von verstendigen leüten nie gelopt ist worden.'

[124] 'Der XIIII. Bundesgenosse,' Enders, vol. 1, p. 160: 'Sie machen ein helgen auss irem Dominico und ich halt in darumb für hailig, dann er verflůcht alle prediger münch . . . dann sy biss uff dyse zyt von im verflůcht sind gewesen, dann an seim letzsten end verflůcht er alle, die ligend gůt in sein orden bråchten oder annemen, das stodt in siner legend.'

[125] Ozment, *Reformation in the Cities*, p. 94. As we have seen, this critique was applied by Eberlin specifically to the mendicant orders, not all monastic orders, a distinction that Ozment consistently overlooks.

often inconsistent and at times even contradictory. Despite his stinging criticism of them, he concludes the 'Ninth Confederate':

> But if the cloisters were organized according to a Christian form, they would gladly return to them; in the meantime they would not want to be in these synagogues of Satan, these schools of sin, these hypocritical assemblies, in which no one may lead a Christian life without great torment, . . .[126]

Much of this can be explained in terms of Eberlin's personal experiences. Hans-Herbert Ahrens suggested that St Francis remained for Eberlin, to the end of his life, the ideal of simple lay piety.[127] As we shall see, with the exception of one brief period of heated conflict, Eberlin did continue to speak fondly of the founder of the order to which he had belonged for much of his adult life.

However, Eberlin's continued respect for St Francis and his suggestion that the monasteries might still be reformed indicates as well the place of these pamphlets in the evolution of his reforming thought. On several important issues his polemics reflect not only the charges of the friars' opponents, but also the concerns of the Observant reform. At the beginning of the sixteenth century discussion continued, often in very heated terms, between reform-minded groups within the Franciscan order over the extent to which the Rule and Testament of Francis could be modified by papal Bulls.[128] This very likely sets the backdrop not only for Eberlin's apparent strict adherence to the ideals of Francis, but also for his denunciation of the friars' litigation. On other specific matters the Observant reform also often came close to reaffirming the charges of the friars' opponents. In the *Speculum imperfectionis*, Johannes Brugmann criticized the activities of the more lax members of the Observance in all too familiar terms: he denounced the vanity of the learned brethren; employed Matthew 23:15 against the treatment of novices; discussed the activities of unscrupulous mendicant confessors in terms of one of William of St Amour's favourite proof texts, 2 Timothy 3:6; and repeated many of the commonplace charges against mendicant preachers.[129] In the *Quaerimoniae* presented by a group of French Observant Franciscans to the Council of Constance in 1415, the friars

---

[126] 'Der VIIII. Bundesgenosse,' Enders, vol. 1, p. 105: 'Wo aber die klöster werden geordnet nach Christlicher form, wöllen sie gern wider dar in, hie zwischen wellen nit sein in dysen synagogen sathane, in disen sünden schulen, in diser glyssner samlung, do by niemandt mag christlich läben on grossen qual, . . .'

[127] Ahrens, p. 22.

[128] Niklaus Paulus, *Kaspar Schatzgeyer, ein Vorkämpfer der katholischen Kirche gegen Luther in Süddeutschland* (Strasbourg, 1898), pp. 35–42.

[129] G. G. Coulton, *Five Centuries of Religion*, vol. 6: *The Last Days of Medieval Monasticism* (Cambridge, 1950), pp. 440–3.

promised not to accept novices under the age of 20, or to hear the confessions of the laity or allow them to be buried in the churchyards of the friaries.[130]

It appears, then, that for very different reasons the Observant reformers had been applying some of the same rhetoric against their more lax brethren as that employed by the secular clergy against the friars as a whole. This shared rhetoric probably reinforced the stereotypes associated with the friars in the popular mind. Furthermore, it probably eased the transition of Reformers like Eberlin from being champions of reform within the order to becoming its opponents from without. As Hans-Herbert Ahrens has suggested, Eberlin did seem to return to an original Franciscan vision in his evolution as a Reformer. But this vision was indebted to the reform programs of the fifteenth-century Observance and was a short-lived phenomenon. Despite the continued respect for Francis, a respect shared by Luther in his statements in the 'Address to the Christian Nobility,' this group of pamphlets belongs to the literature generated by the opponents of the mendicant orders as they existed at the beginning of the sixteenth century. In the short time from his break with the order to the writing of the 'Ninth Confederate,' Eberlin developed a detailed, comprehensive attack on the mendicant orders. It is likely, then, that he was able to tap into an ongoing tradition of medieval origin which also manifested itself in the writings of both humanists and Reformers.

Wolfaria and beyond

Most likely the restful atmosphere of an extended stay with his cousin in Lauingen allowed Eberlin to write the next three confederates, the most reflective and abstract in the collection. The tenth claims to contain the ecclesiastical statutes of the imaginary land of Wolfaria as reported by Psittacus, one of its citizens. It envisions a national church, based on a system of semi-autonomous parishes, which is governed by a synod of equal bishops. Throughout, the system is democratic with all ecclesiastical officials, from the parish priests to the national bishops, freely elected by their constituents. Within the synod of bishops none has pre-eminence and synodal meetings rotate regularly to ensure that no primacy should develop. Monasticism appears to play no role in Wolfarian society. Psittacus suggests that the endowed orders should be allowed to die out slowly, but those relying on begging should be

---

[130] John Moorman, *A History of the Franciscan Order From Its Origins to the Year 1517* (Oxford, 1968), pp. 382–3.

disbanded immediately.[131] Much the same democratic spirit pervades
the statutes for the reform of secular life in Wolfaria which make up the
'Eleventh Confederate.' This work envisions a rational restructuring of
political life, in which all office holders, from the village mayor to the
elected king, are responsible to their subjects and must make room for
their voices in their councils. All upper-echelon office-holders are still of
noble birth, but emphasis lies on their functional role in society and not
the inherited rights of title. The agrarian basis of Wolfaria is clearly
indicated in the opening sentence: 'There shall be no more noble work
or livelihood than fieldwork.' Within this framework social life is firmly
regulated, sometimes to the point of absurdity. Unlike the ecclesiastical
statutes, which are presented as a *fait accompli*, those in the secular
realm must be ratified by all communities within the land, as must all
subsequent laws.[132]

Closely related to the Wolfarian statutes and probably written
immediately following them is 'A Friendly Answer by all Godfearing,
Respectable, Informed People in Germany to the Wretched Complaint
which Those in Orders have made to Them,' which occupies the twelfth
position.[133] The narrator claims to be answering the plea of monks and
nuns, dissatisfied with their life in the cloister. In the name of his
fourteen confederates, he offers a general dispensation to all wishing to
leave their orders. Monasteries should be reformed and supervised by
secular authority so that their independence is broken and the position
of the parish priest in the cure of souls is assured. However, departure
from the cloister must be voluntary and cannot be forced on the monks
and nuns by secular authorities or the laity in general.[134]

It is unclear whether Eberlin was still in Lauingen when he wrote the
final tract of 'The Fifteen Confederates,' 'A Wholesome Warning to each
and every Person who believes in Christ that They defend Themselves
against the New Harmful Teachings.' Here Eberlin sets out to prove that
scholastic theology and not the teaching of the Reformers is the novelty.
He defends the self-sufficiency of Bible reading, even by the simple
laymen, against the sophistic doctrines of the learned, which serve only
to bolster the elevated social position of the clergy and bilk the laity of
their hard-earned wages.[135] In the middle of this work Eberlin includes
a discussion of certain theological issues centring on works righteous-

---

[131] 'Der X. Bundesgenosse,' Enders, vol. 1, pp. 107–19 (= Laube 1:175–84).
[132] 'Der XI. Bundesgenosse,' Enders, vol. 1, pp. 121–31 (= Laube 2:721–9).
[133] Lucke, *Die Entstehung der 15 Bundesgenossen*, p. 90 and Geiger, 'Die reformatorischen Initia Eberlins,' pp. 183–4.
[134] 'Der XII. Bundesgenosse,' Enders, vol. 1, pp. 133–41.
[135] 'Der XV. Bundesgenosse,' Enders, vol. 1, pp. 163–70.

ness and the freedom of the human will, which, as Gottfried Geiger indicates, appear as 'foreign bodies' in the cycle.[136] Lucke argued that the 'Fifteenth Confederate' was written in the second half of August, on the basis of a reference in it to 'a little book on confession' which he identifies as Luther's 'On Confession,' then at the press. This would also indicate that Eberlin was in contact with Wittenberg, a possible reason for his deeper concern with theological issues.[137]

The Wolfarian statutes are likely the best known of Eberlin's writings and have encouraged most of the interest in his work in recent years. By their very nature, they suggest comparison with Thomas More's *Utopia*, the third edition of which was published by Froben in Basel in 1518. The cover illustration of the 'Eleventh Confederate' depicts a fool with cap and bells and both carry humorous, fictional dates: the tenth 'in our city of Baldeck on the 35th day of ubelis, in the year that Easter falls on a Monday' and the eleventh 'in our capital of Wolleck, in the month of Gutwyle, in the year that the mendicants' cowls are banished.'[138] Susan Groag Bell set the tone for most of the subsequent discussions of the Wolfarian Statutes by identifying them as 'the first Protestant Utopia.'[139] Although she found no evidence that Eberlin had read More's more famous work, Bell saw the parallels between the two works as significant. Furthermore, she claimed that on many of the points where Eberlin departs from More, one sees the influence of confessional allegiance on the authors. Eberlin drew many of the essentials for his reform programme from Luther, but drew on many other sources as well, especially the Swabian and South German apocalyptic tradition in which he was nurtured.[140] Most importantly, however, Eberlin differed from the general humanist approach in his pragmatism and practicality. The Wolfarian Statutes reflect many of the real concerns of the peasantry, from whom Eberlin likely stemmed, according to Bell. As such he provided a direct link between Luther and the German people.[141]

Subsequent work in English has further developed Bell's themes, although greater emphasis has been placed on the influence of Luther on Eberlin. Although he acknowledged Bell's identification of other influences on Eberlin, Richard Cole referred to Wolfaria as a 'Lutheran

---

[136] Geiger, 'Die reformatorischen Initia Eberlins,' p. 198.

[137] Lucke, *Die Entstehung der 15 Bundesgenossen*, p. 91.

[138] Enders, vol. 1, pp. 119, 121, 131.

[139] Susan Groag Bell, 'Johann Eberlin von Günzburg's Wolfaria: The First Protestant Utopia,' *Church History*, 36 (1967), pp. 122–39.

[140] Ibid., pp. 129–30, 134, 137.

[141] Ibid., pp. 131–2, 138–9.

Utopia,' derived from the dualism in 'Luther's political afterthoughts.'[142] Steven Ozment has argued that 'The Fifteen Confederates' were directly inspired by Luther's 'Address to the Christian Nobility' and, like it, contain much late medieval reform sentiment. However, they, too, are located in the process of transition from late medieval reform to the revolutionary changes of the Reformation. The Wolfarian Statutes, then, constitute 'an original Protestant version of what society should be.' Many of the secular ordinances hardly require a basis in Protestantism, but the religious statutes make clear the social benefits of the religious revolution.[143]

Bell's article has also inspired fruitful discussions among German-speaking historians about the utopian nature of Wolfaria. Ferdinand Seibt located the Wolfarian statutes within a tradition of early sixteenth-century German, intellectual utopias. Here it occupied a middle position between Michael Gaismair's prepared political programme and Hans Hergot's return to medieval Joachimist prophecy.[144] Seibt admits that Eberlin may have derived his fictional framework from More, but argues that the contents of the Wolfarian statutes indicate that he was dealing realistically with contemporary issues.[145] Of particular note is the distinction Seibt sees between the secular and ecclesiastical organiza-tions in Wolfaria. The former are presented by Eberlin as reform suggestions to be ratified by the individual communities of Wolfaria, while the latter are already statutes. This, says Seibt, indicates a greater earnestness in and demand for stricter adherence to the pattern of ecclesiastical reform.[146] The fundamentals of Seibt's interpretation have since held their ground: the Wolfarian Statutes continue to be characterized as a mixture of utopian and realist reform proposals, in which the ecclesiastical statutes betray greater urgency and clarity.[147]

The reaction of German-speaking historians to Bell's characterization of Wolfaria as Protestant has been somewhat less enthusiastic. Günther

---

[142] Richard Cole, 'Law and Order in the Sixteenth Century: Johann Eberlin von Günzburg and the Problem of Political Authority,' *Lutheran Quarterly*, 23 (1971), pp. 253–6.

[143] Ozment, *Reformation in the Cities*, pp. 90–108.

[144] Ferdinand Seibt, *Utopica: Modelle sozialer Planung* (Düsseldorf, 1972), p. 71.

[145] Ibid., pp. 73, 81.

[146] Enders, vol. 1, pp. 108, 122; Seibt, p. 76.

[147] Geiger, 'Die reformatorischen Initia Eberlins,' pp. 184, 193–4; Günther Heger, *Johann Eberlin von Günzburg und seine Vorstellungen über eine Reform in Reich und Kirche* (Berlin, 1985), pp. 47–64, 111–16; Günter Vogler, Max Steinmetz and Adolf Laube, *Illustrierte Geschichte der deutschen frühbürgerlichen Revolution* (Berlin, 1974), pp. 159–62; Günter Vogler, 'Reformprogramm oder utopischer Entwurf? Gedanken zu Eberlin von Günzburgs "Wolfaria" ' *Jahrbuch für Geschichte des Feudalismus*, 3 (1979), pp. 219–32.

Heger suggested that the novelty and radicalism of the 'Tenth Confederate' derived from Eberlin's reliance on the doctrine of the priesthood of all believers.[148] However, more recently, Christian Peters has summed up the general trend of interpretation among German scholars by describing Wolfaria as a utopia embodying medieval and humanist reform proposals, but certainly not a Protestant utopia.[149]

Indications are that in these last confederates Eberlin was beginning to come to terms with the dominant theological concerns of Wittenberg. But the extent to which this allows one to characterize the Wolfarian statutes as Protestant remains open. In his earlier writings Eberlin had conceived of reform in primarily ethical terms. The 'First Confederate' describes the essence of Christianity as the maintenance of a devout heart to God and an upright life toward one's neighbours.[150] The 'Fifth Confederate' claims that the Gospel is the 'pure Christian law' and the thirteenth indicates that this law is given by Christ in the Scripture.[151] This interpretation is still prominent in the 'Tenth Confederate' in which Psittacus explains that those Wolfarian villages too small to support a priest have a chapel where the villagers assemble on feast days and hear chapters five to seven of Matthew, for these chapters contain the sum of the evangelical law.[152] However, in the 'Eleventh Confederate,' Eberlin begins to include the Pauline epistles as part of his definition of the evangelical law.[153] This definition persists in the 'Fifteenth Confederate' in which Eberlin also begins to concern himself specifically with the central doctrines of Reformation theology.[154] Here Eberlin also complements his theological interests with frequent citations from the Bible, a form of argumentation which is all but absent in the earlier confederates.[155]

As Eberlin came closer to the central theological concerns of the Reformation, so, too, did his criticism of the first estate become more comprehensive and more radical. R. Po-Chia Hsia claims that in the 'Tenth Confederate' Eberlin presents a vision of an evangelical clergy

---

[148] Heger, pp. 81–7.

[149] Peters, pp. 38–9, 50.

[150] 'Der erste Bundesgenosse,' Enders, vol. 1, p. 2: 'Ain christlich wăsen stot darinn, das man ein andăchtig hărtz trag zu got, und ain erlichen uffrechten wandel zŭ dem năchsten menschen, . . .' (= Laube 2:709).

[151] 'Der V. Bundesgenosse,' Enders, vol. 1, p. 52; 'Der XIII Bundesgenosse,' Enders, vol. 1, p. 145.

[152] 'Der X. Bundesgenosse,' Enders, vol. 1, p. 116–17 (= Laube 1:82).

[153] 'Der XI. Bundesgenosse,' Enders, vol. 1, p. 127 (= Laube 2:725).

[154] 'Der XV. Bundesgenosse,' Enders, vol. 1, pp. 164–5.

[155] For example, see ibid., pp. 166–7.

which resembles closely the later reformed clergy of the territorial and urban churches. In this he reflects the moderate anticlerical tradition of clerical self-criticism stemming from Luther's writings.[156] Hsia's analysis assumes a continuity in Luther's anticlericalism which sees a direct development from his statements in the 'Address to the Christian Nobility' to the establishment of the territorial evangelical church. I have argued elsewhere that such an assumption disregards a phase of radical anticlerical invective in Luther's writings of 1521.[157] Nonetheless, in the Wolfarian statutes and the other pamphlets written in Lauingen, Eberlin begins to develop the more moderate anticlerical implications of the doctrine of the priesthood of all believers as formulated in the 'Address to the Christian Nobility.'

It appears that already in the 'Fifth Confederate,' Eberlin began wrestling with Luther's doctrine of the priesthood of all believers:

> . . . oh, you representatives of God in the secular estate, do not push the matter from you onto the bishops and others called spiritual, all Christians are spiritual people, they have received the Holy Spirit in baptism, they are part of the suffering of Christ and have the holy sacraments, one God, one belief, one promise, from which things one is truly called spiritual.[158]

But Eberlin did not begin drawing the further anticlerical implications of these expressions until he was in Lauingen. The 'Tenth Confederate' first defines the distinction between clergy and laity as one of function. It does away with the consecration of the clergy and describes the office of priest as purely an elective one.[159] Furthermore, Eberlin rejected the indelible character of the assumption of orders, arguing that one could

---

[156] R. Po-Chia Hsia, 'Anticlericalism in German Reformation Pamphlets: A Response,' in Dykema and Oberman, p. 495.

[157] 'Luther, Emser, and the Development of Reformation Anticlericalism,' *ARG* (forthcoming, 1996). See below, pp. 171–2.

[158] 'Der V. Bundesgenosse,' Enders, vol. 1, p. 51: '. . . o ir stathalter gotss in weltlichen stand, nit schieben die sach ab eüch uff byschoff und ander geystlich genant, alle christen sind geistlich leüt, sie haben den heiligen geist empfangen im touff, sy sind teilhafftig des lyden christi und haben die helgen sacrament, ein got, ein glouben, ein verheissung, von deren ding wegen wirt einer worlich geistlich genant.' Bernd Moeller ('Klerus und Antiklerikalismus in Luthers Schrift *An den Christlichen Adel deutscher Nation* von 1520,' in Dykema and Oberman, pp. 353–65) argues that in the 'Address to the Christian Nobility' Luther employs the doctrine of the priesthood of all believers to justify the reform of the first estate by the second. Clearly, this is how Eberlin first interpreted it.

[159] 'Der X. Bundesgenosse,' Enders, vol. 1, p. 111: 'Man soll nümmer kein pfaffen wyhen haben, aber so ein pfaff oder diacon stirbt oder ab godt, sollen die pfarr lüt am selben ort mit iren pfaffen einen anderen welen, den soll der vogt und gericht am selben ort mit dem byschoff intronisieren.' (= Laube 1:77).

return to the status of a layman if one saw fit.[160] This approach continues in the 'Fifteenth Confederate,' which repeats that the consecration of the clergy is not a sacrament and denies the distinction between evangelical commands and counsels.[161]

Despite Eberlin's developing awareness of the intricacies and the implications of the priesthood of all believers, he nowhere denies the necessity for the existence of a priesthood, nor does he root his attack on the clergy in Luther's sacramental theology. Furthermore, Eberlin did not drastically alter his reform proposals, which remained in the moderate tradition of the 'Address to the Christian Nobility.' His view of the ecclesiastical hierarchy remains true to the suggestions of the 'Eighth Confederate' and Luther's work, with the highest authority on religious matters given to a synod of German bishops.[162] Reform at the parish level looks to an end to many of the traditional abuses.[163] Eberlin also seeks to fully integrate the priest into the secular life of the parish, much in the manner of article 14 of Luther's 'Address to the Christian Nobility.' Henceforth the priest should be from the community he serves. He should not wear distinctive clothing or a tonsure and is to be subject to the same laws as his fellow citizens. He may own landed property and may pursue other occupations, but may not be a merchant, innkeeper or secular official. He is to be paid by the community, but will no longer receive the tithe.[164]

As Eberlin turns to the reform of monasticism, his position remains much as earlier, although he provides many more details. He continues to regard contemporary monastic practice as contrary to Christian teaching and counsels all so inclined to depart the monasteries without applying for dispensation.[165] The 'Fifteenth Confederate' takes the critique one step further and brands the claim that the monastic life is a surer way of following Christ as an error.[166]

---

[160] Ibid.: 'Wann einer kein pfaff me will sein, mag er das ampt uff geben und wider ein ley sein, wann man in wider erwelt mag er wider ein pfaff sein' (=Laube 1:78). See Heger, p. 81.

[161] 'Der XV. Bundesgenosse,' Enders, vol. 1, p. 166: 'Wer sagt, das etwas in der lere Christi sey ein radt und kein gebott, der irt. Allein küscheit halten ist ein radt.'; p. 167; 'Welcher sagt, das ölung, firmung, wyhe der pfaffen, eelicher stand sien göttliche sacrament, der irt und ist ein aigengesüchig lere.'

[162] 'Der X. Bundesgenosse,' Enders, vol. 1, pp. 110–12 and 118 (= Laube 1:77–8, 83–4).

[163] Ibid., pp. 108, 111–12 and 115–16 (=Laube 1:75, 77–8, 80–2).

[164] Ibid., pp. 110–12 (=Laube 1:77–8); see WA, 6:440–3.

[165] 'Der X. Bundesgenosse,' Enders, vol. 1, p. 112 (= Laube 1:78); 'Der XII. Bundesgenosse,' Enders, vol. 1, p. 134.

[166] 'Der XV. Bundesgenosse,' Enders, vol. 1, p. 167: 'Welcher sagt, das der orden stand mit dry gelübten gebunden sey sicherer zů dem hail dann eelicher stand, der irret.'

The 'Twelfth Confederate' demands that there be no more monastic reform on earlier models.[167] Eberlin, however, does provide concrete suggestions for reform which develop Luther's suggestion in the 'Address to the Christian Nobility' of returning the monasteries to schools of Christian doctrine as in the time of the apostles.[168] With this vision before it, the 'Tenth Confederate' provides a series of reform suggestions, many of which echo Luther's statements in the 'Address to the Christian Nobility': That the cloistered do away with distinctive clothing, that cloisters be consolidated and reduced in number, and that the age limit for the novitiate be raised.[169] All who wish to live a cloistered life other than by these stipulations must do so at home alone.[170] Eberlin's vision of primitive monasticism reaches its fullest development in the 'Twelfth Confederate.' The independence of the monasteries is to be broken, with most of the responsibility for their administration passing into the hands of the local secular authorities.[171] More importantly, the very nature of the monastic life is to be altered: the three vows are to be done away with and men are to live by the rule of St Augustine alone and women in free associations.[172]

However, these reforms do not apply to the mendicant orders, which must be immediately abolished.[173] This is to apply specifically to the Franciscan Observants and the Dominicans.[174] To ensure that the mendicants are quickly disbanded, Eberlin suggests further statutes aimed at rooting out support for them among the general populace: the mendicants are to lose all rights of citizenship; anyone giving alms to a friar will be punished; begging is no longer to be regarded as a form of religious profession and the mendicant orders are to receive no more novices.[175] Elsewhere his statutes look back to the sources of mendicant authority from the complaints of the medieval antifraternal tradition. He specifically attacks the practice of burial in the cemeteries of mendicant churches.[176] The friars may preach only on the express invitation of a community and should not be chosen as confessors.[177]

---

[167] 'Der XII. Bundesgenosse,' Enders, vol. 1, p. 140.

[168] 'Der X. Bundesgenosse,' Enders, vol. 1, p. 112 (= Laube 1:78).

[169] Ibid. (= Laube 1:78); WA, 6:438–40.

[170] 'Der X. Bundesgenosse,' Enders, vol. 1, p. 113 (= Laube 1:79).

[171] 'Der XII. Bundesgenosse,' Enders, vol. 1, p. 135.

[172] Ibid., pp. 135, 138.

[173] 'Der X. Bundesgenosse,' Enders, vol. 1, p. 117 (= Laube 1:82).

[174] 'Der XII. Bundesgenosse,' Enders, vol. 1, p. 140.

[175] 'Der XII. Bundesgenosse,' Enders, vol. 1, pp. 134–5, 137, 139; 'Der XV. Bundesgenosse,' Enders, vol. 1, p. 168.

[176] 'Der X. Bundesgenosse,' Enders, vol. 1, p. 114 (= Laube 1:80); 'Der XII. Bundesgenosse,' Enders, vol. 1, p. 136.

[177] 'Der XII. Bundesgenosse,' Enders, vol. pp. 135, 137.

To ensure that the mendicants are unable again to spread their poison, the 'Twelfth Confederate' declares as null and void all of their freedoms, bulls and papal letters.[178]

The increasing influence of Luther on this last group of confederates is clear. The view of clerical reform, with its emphasis on the German church, self-sufficiency of the local priest and perception of monasticism, is likely derived from the 'Address to the Christian Nobility.' However, it would be anachronistic to label Eberlin a 'Lutheran' at this stage in his reforming career. He continues to regard Luther's reform suggestions in a more general context of reform sentiment and there is no indication that he had rejected his earlier perception of the Wittenberg movement as an heir to the Reuchlin affair. Throughout the confederates, references to the Wittenbergers increase, but do not completely supplant those to others advocating reform. Most importantly, Eberlin's increasing identification with Luther is evident in his adoption of specific reform proposals from the 'Address to the Christian Nobility.' These are supplemented in the 'Tenth Confederate' by Eberlin's increasing awareness of the anticlerical implications of Luther's doctrine of the priesthood of all believers. But Eberlin first came to the central theological concerns of the Reformation in the 'Fifteenth Confederate.' Again, it appears that anticlericalism served as the bridge between the reforming movements of the early sixteenth century, as Goertz suggests.

In all of this, Eberlin takes Luther's reform proposals as the starting point for a much more comprehensive vision of a reformed church and society. This is most clearly evident in his treatment of the mendicant orders which grows out of the vision of them presented in the middle confederates. With regard to the prominence he attributes to them in the falsification of the Gospel, the stress which is usually placed on Eberlin's criticism of the friars is accurate. However, his is only the most extreme and best-developed example of a general tradition of antifraternalism. Both Luther and Hutten had called attention to the mendicants' close ties to the papacy. Luther had emphasized the implications of this for episcopal authority and the parochial cure of souls, while Hutten concentrated on its implications for imperial authority. Erasmus had revived much of the medieval catalogue of abuses associated with the friars. Eberlin adopted all of these currents of criticism and, on occasion, went beyond them directly to the medieval antifraternal tradition. The pervasiveness of the antifraternal criticism in the writings of humanists and Reformers suggests that it was a popular tradition inherited from the later Middle Ages and made commonplace in the society of

---

[178] Ibid., p. 139.

Renaissance Europe. If, as we suspect, conflict between the mendicants and secular clergy had again erupted in the first two decades of the sixteenth century, it is likely that the polemical weapons of earlier conflict would have been reinvigorated. Eberlin, rejected and expelled by his brethren, would have been able to turn to a living tradition of criticism to denounce his new enemies. As will later be evident, in so doing, he pointed the direction for a general assault on the Franciscan order.

Eberlin apparently left Lauingen in late August or early September 1521. Eberlin's intimate knowledge of the reforming movement in Augsburg and familiarity with those involved in it as revealed in later writings argue for a stop there while underway. He may also have stopped for a while in Nuremberg, although the evidence for this is much less firm.[179] While Eberlin was travelling toward Wittenberg, 'The Fifteen Confederates' appeared on the market with no indication of the author, publisher or date and place of publication. Eberlin himself admitted his authorship three years later in a signed pamphlet and, in another anonymous pamphlet, identified Basel as the place of publication and 1521 as the date.[180] Max Radlkofer was able to find a reference to the published version of 'The Fifteen Confederates' in a letter from Salandron to Vadian dated 26 October 1521. He further argued on the basis of the typeface that the printer was Pamphilius Gengenbach.[181] On the basis of a reference to it in a letter from Cochlaeus to Aleander dated 27 September, Lucke has argued 'The Fifteen Confederates' was published in time for the Frankfort book fair in September.[182] More recently, Christian Peters has argued convincingly that all of the confederates were published individually by Gengenbach prior to their publication in the collected work.[183]

---

[179] Riggenbach, *Eberlin und sein Reformprogramm*, pp. 80–1; 'Eine freundliche Vermahnung an die Christen zu Augsburg,' Enders, vol. 2, pp. 137–52; 'Klage der sieben frommen Pfaffen,' Enders, vol. 2, p. 59; 'Trost der sieben frommen Pfaffen,' Enders, vol. 2, p. 92.

[180] 'Wider die falschen Geistlichen, genannt die Barfüsser und Franziskaner,' Enders, vol. 3, pp. 85 and 88; 'Trost der frommen Pfaffen,' Enders, vol. 2, p. 93.

[181] Radlkofer, pp. 11–12.

[182] Lucke, *Die Entstehung der 15 Bundesgenossen*, p. 30; Walter Friedensburg, 'Beiträge zum Briefwechsel der katholischen Gelehrten Deutschlands im Reformationszeitalter,' *ZKG*, 18 (1897): 125.

[183] Peters, pp. 43–4.

CHAPTER FOUR

'A priest must be blameless, the husband of one wife'

The later confederates indicate that Eberlin was beginning to come to terms with the central theological issues of the Reformation in the latter half of 1521. This process was greatly accelerated with his arrival in Wittenberg in early 1522 and personal encounters with Luther, Melanchthon and Karlstadt. Eberlin's greater immersion in Reformation theology was paralleled by a toning down of his calls for social activism. Some of his earlier biographers, especially those on the fringes of the confessional camps, saw in this increasing mildness the influence of Melanchthon on Eberlin.[1] However, much more popular among the interpreters of Eberlin's writings is the opinion that his new social quietism reflects a social conservatism learned at the feet of Luther.[2]

More enduring, and ultimately more fruitful, than discussions of the respective influences of Luther and Melanchthon on Eberlin after his arrival in Wittenberg has been an ongoing debate over whether he passed through a radical Karlstadtian phase *en route* to the centre of the Reformation. In 1525 the Augsburg printer Heinrich Steiner published a radically anticlerical pamphlet by Eberlin entitled 'Against the Profaners of God's Creatures.' Bernhard Riggenbach, one of Eberlin's early biographers, claimed that this work is far too radical to have been written after Eberlin's personal acquaintance with Luther and Melanchthon. It must, therefore, have been composed in Leipzig in early 1522, as Eberlin was *en route* to Wittenberg, in support of Karlstadt, but first printed by a member of the Karlstadtian party in 1525.[3] Subsequent analysis of Eberlin's early Wittenberg writings has concentrated to a

---

[1] G. Strobel, 'Nachricht von Johann Eberlins von Günzburg Leben und Schriften' *Literarisches Museum* I (Altdorf, 1778), pp. 363–85; Kurt Stöckl, *Untersuchung zu Johann Eberlin von Günzburg*, Phil. Diss. (Munich, 1952), pp. 130–2.

[2] This line of interpretation was initiated by Max Radlkofer, *Johann Eberlin von Günzburg und sein Vetter Hans Jakob Wehe von Leipheim* (Nördlingen, 1887), pp. 572–4. It has been developed most fully in the recent biography of Eberlin by Christian Peters, *Johann Eberlin von Günzburg, ca. 1465–1533. Franziskanische Reformer, Humanist und konservativer Reformator* (Gütersloh, 1994), pp. 62–80.

[3] Bernhard Riggenbach, *Johann Eberlin von Günzburg und sein Reformprogramm: Ein Beitrag zur Geschichte des sechszehnten Jahrhunderts* (Tübingen, 1874), pp. 81–3.

large degree on assessing the extent and duration of Eberlin's 'radical Karlstadtian phase.'[4] More recently, however, Martin Brecht and Christian Peters have successfully challenged the very basis for this debate. Peters in particular has undercut the basis for Riggenbach's claim that 'Against the Profaners' was written in early 1522, arguing convincingly that it was much more likely written in the middle of 1523.[5] Interestingly, however, Eberlin's writings from 1522 and 1523 portray the Reformation in Wittenberg as a unified movement and in no way reflect an open split between Luther and Karlstadt which historians have assumed accompanied the former's return from the Wartburg. Furthermore, not only does Eberlin continue to mention Luther and Karlstadt in the same breath as the leaders of the Reformation, but he also draws freely from the writings of both men without any indication of tension between them, as earlier he had combined the reforming suggestions of Luther, Erasmus and Hutten. Only gradually do the arguments derived from Karlstadt's pamphlets disappear from Eberlin's writings and, even after they have been all but supplanted, Eberlin continues to mention Karlstadt along with Luther and Melanchthon as the leaders of the movement.

Peters's dismissal of the debate over Eberlin's 'radical Karlstadtian phase,' then, does not invalidate analysis of the respective importance of Luther and Karlstadt for the development of his reforming thought. Numerous arguments have been marshalled to indicate Eberlin's debts in his early Wittenberg writings to the works of Luther or Karlstadt. Many of these rely on passing comments made in Eberlin's writings,[6] or, more often, on an attempt to derive a distinctive Reformation theology with closer affinities to that of Luther or Karlstadt, from Eberlin's

---

[4] See Riggenbach, *Eberlin und seine Reformprogramm*, pp. 97–110; Radlkofer, pp. 52–62; Hans-Herbert Ahrens, *Die religiösen, nationalen und sozialen Gedanken Johann Eberlins von Günzburgs mit besonderer Berücksichtigung seiner anonymen Flugschriften*, Phil. Diss. (Hamburg, 1939), p. 31, n. 70; Gottfried Geiger, 'Die reformatorischen Initia Johann Eberlins von Günzburg nach seinem Flugschriften,' in *Festgabe für Ernst Walter Zeeden zum 60. Geburtstag am 14. Mai 1976*, ed. Horst Rabe *et al.* (Münster, 1976), pp. 197–200; Günther Heger, *Johann Eberlin von Günzburg und seine Vorstellungen über eine Reform in Reich und Kirche* (Berlin, 1985), pp. 23–4.

[5] Martin Brecht, 'Johann Eberlin von Günzburg in Wittenberg,' *Wertheimer Jahrbuch*, 1983 (1985), pp. 47–9; Peters, pp. 173–84.

[6] In the 'First Confederate,' Eberlin recommended to the emperor that he take as his confessor Luther, Erasmus or Karlstadt, see 'Der erste Bundegenosse,' Enders, vol. 1, p. 12. Gottfried Geiger ('Die reformatorischen Initia Eberlins,' p. 196) argued that this indicated Eberlin initially held Karlstadt in higher esteem than Melanchthon. Martin Brecht ('Eberlin in Wittenberg,' p. 47, n. 4) has countered that this reference is inconclusive; not being in orders, Melanchthon was ineligible for the confessor's post.

writings.[7] This attention to doctrine, however, is likely misdirected, and Geiger's claim that the theological discussions in 'The Fifteen Confederates' appear as foreign bodies in the context of the whole cycle may be enlightening on this point.[8] Newly arrived at the central theological issues of the Reformation, Eberlin failed to perceive the subtle differences in the theologies of justification upon which historians have since lavished so much attention. If, as I have suggested, Eberlin came only gradually to the theological concerns of the Reformation by way of a reforming vision which concentrated attention primarily on the shortcomings of the first estate, an analysis of the ongoing evolution of his anticlerical polemics should provide valuable insights into the evolution not only of Eberlin's thought, but also of the Wittenberg movement, in 1522 and 1523.

Eberlin's more complete immersion in the Wittenberg reform movement had a profound influence on the development of his anticlericalism. Two prominent themes are developed in his polemics from this period. On the one hand, Eberlin's overriding concern with the Franciscans and other friars retreats from centre stage, although this theme never completely disappears. In its place, he concentrates on distinguishing between the true and false clergy. The outlines of this distinction return to the perception, presented in the earliest confederates, and derived ultimately from Luther's 'Address to the Christian Nobility,' of the opposition between the bishops and parochial clergy on one side, and the temple servants, as Eberlin labelled the rest of the first estate, on the other. In Wittenberg, however, Eberlin develops much more fully than he had earlier the theological and biblical basis for this distinction. The other theme, which becomes increasingly visible in the writings from this period, is noticeable in the softened tone of Eberlin's anticlerical diatribes. He begins to defend the 'true priests and bishops' against some of the charges levelled at them, and implies a retraction of some of his earlier criticisms. This is complemented by a more gentle treatment of the clergy at all levels.

---

[7] Kurt Stöckl (*Untersuchung zu Eberlin*, pp. 85–6) and Riggenbach (*Eberlin und seine Reformprogramm*, pp. 87–8) mined Eberlin's scattered theological statements in the 'Fifteenth Confederate' to find a doctrine of justification parallel to Karlstadt's more orthodox Augustinian theology. On Karlstadt's Wittenberg theology see Herman Barge, *Andreas Bodenstein von Karlstadt*, vol. 1: *Karlstadt und die Anfänge der Reformation* (Leipzig, 1905; 2nd edn Nieuwkoop, 1968), pp. 182–3, 199, 208. Johann Heinrich Schmidt, '*Die 15 Bundesgenossen' des Johann Eberlin von Günzburg*, Phil. Diss. (Leipzig, 1900), p. 32, and Martin Brecht, 'Eberlin in Wittenberg,' p. 48, see instead in Eberlin's statements a reflection of Luther's doctrine of justification.

[8] See above, p. 88.

As has been noted, this new mildness in Eberlin's polemics is usually seen as a reflection of his conversion to a more conservative, Lutheran vision of reform. While there is some value in approaching the development of Eberlin's reforming thought in this manner, it treats as static Luther's own anticlerical polemics and it obscures the evolution of anticlericalism in Wittenberg and its place in the development of Reformation theology. I have argued elsewhere that Luther's most radically anticlerical polemics are contained in his writings of 1521. However, by early 1522, Luther was beginning to see the more destructive consequences of too rashly exploiting popular anticlericalism. Not only did Luther retreat from direct anticlerical agitation, but he also changed significantly the emphasis of his anticlerical polemics. Where earlier he had juxtaposed the priesthood of all believers directly with the first estate, he now set up opposite the false, papal clergy a new scripturally defined clerical order. But this change in tactics did not involve a retreat from an anticlerical standpoint *per se*.[9] Eberlin's new mildness itself is a reflection of this development of Wittenberg anticlericalism but, like Luther, Eberlin was not above the continued use of sharp language against the clergy when this seemed necessary.

In his last published work, written in 1526, Eberlin reflected back on his initial arrival in Wittenberg:

> Three and one-half years ago I came to Wittenberg and thought then that I knew much in the Gospel, but, when I consulted with the Wittenbergers, I knew nothing.[10]

The time of his arrival is confirmed by the appearance of his name in the matriculation records of the University of Wittenberg for the summer semester of 1522.[11] Beyond this Eberlin provides only two vague references to his activities during this time. In a pamphlet published in early 1522, he addresses the German bishops: 'I have advised you in an innocent and friendly manner in a small book addressed to you which I wrote while bedridden in Leipzig four weeks ago.'[12] Shortly thereafter,

[9] See my 'Luther, Emser and the Development of Reformation Anticlericalism,' *ARG* (forthcoming, 1996).

[10] 'Warnung an die Christen der Burgauischen Mark,' Enders, vol. 3, p. 275.

[11] Karl Edward Förstmann (ed.), *Album Academia Vitebergensis*, old series, vol. 1: *1502–1560* (Leipzig, 1841; reprint. Aalen, 1976), p. 113.

[12] 'Wie gar gefährlich, so ein Priester kein Eheweib hat,' Enders, vol. 2, p. 31.

he provided slightly more information about his stay in Leipzig and relationship with episcopal authority at that time:

> The bishop of Meersburg received an admonition to the German bishops, written by Johann Eberlin von Günzburg, and he sent a special messenger to Eberlin in Leipzig and requested that Eberlin come to him, because he wished to hear personally Eberlin's advice on such matters.[13]

At least part of Eberlin's admonition to the German bishops may survive in his first pamphlet to be written in Wittenberg, 'How Very Dangerous, that a Priest does not Have a Wife.'[14] The first half of this work deals with the issue of clerical celibacy on a theoretical level and opens by denouncing it as a teaching of the devil. Eberlin's basic premise is that God commanded marriage for humanity and has not exempted the clergy from this command. The Old Testament priests from Abraham to the prophets and Levites had wives. So, too, did some of the Apostles, and Paul's statements on church organization indicate that he envisioned the ministers of the Word as married men. On the other hand, the practice of celibacy by pagans is most evident from heathen sources. Celibacy is a special gift of God, and to attempt it without this special grace is to fight against heaven and nature. This theoretical discussion provides the background for Eberlin's subsequent treatment of the social issues involved in clerical celibacy. Identifying this practice as a great threat to the common good, Eberlin denounces the moral example provided by womanizing priests; even heathens know enough to guard the sanctity of marriage. Not only the priest's conduct, but also his sermons will improve with the experience of family life. Against those who maintain that, as a result of marriage, the priest's prebend will be over-taxed and his wife will offend the parishioners, Eberlin argues that the priest will administer his finances more carefully and grant his former concubine an honourable position in the life of the parish. Eberlin warns the bishops that, in maintaining clerical celibacy, they participate in the sinful lives of priests under their jurisdiction, and the pamphlet closes with a supplication to the bishops to do away with this practice.[15]

A reference by Eberlin to the discussion 'in a little book on monastic vows' has served as the focal point of an ongoing debate over the

---

[13] 'Trost der sieben frommen Pfaffen,' Enders, vol. 2, p. 92.

[14] Radlkofer, pp. 47–51; Enders, vol. 3, pp. vi–vii; Wilhelm Lucke, *Die Entstehung der '15 Bundesgenossen' des Johann Eberlins von Günzburg*, Phil. Diss. (Halle, 1902), pp. 21–2; Peters, p. 58.

[15] 'Wie gar gefährlich, so ein Priester kein Eheweib hat,' Enders, vol. 2, pp. 21–37.

Lutheran and Karlstadtian influences on this pamphlet.[16] Within its context Eberlin's reference is quite clear. Eberlin cautions against Jerome's excessive praise of virginity, which finds its parallel only in Luther's discussion of the conflict between Jerome and Jovinian on virginity.[17] However, the identification of this reference does not, in itself, resolve the debate on the influence of Luther and Karlstadt on 'How Very Dangerous.'

In the 'Address to the Christian Nobility,' Luther had laid the groundwork for subsequent discussions of clerical celibacy. On the basis of 1 Corinthians 7:7: 'For I would that all men were even as I myself. But every man hath his proper gift from God,' and Matthew 19:11–12:

> All men cannot receive this saying, save they to whom it is given. For there are some eunuchs, which were so born from their mother's womb: and there are some eunuchs, which were made eunuchs of men: and there be eunuchs, which have made themselves eunuchs for the kingdom of heaven's sake. He that is able to receive it, let him receive it,

he claimed that the grace to live a chaste life is given to only a few and, therefore, chastity is not commanded by Christ. Rather, 1 Timothy 3:2: 'A bishop must be blameless, the husband of one wife,' and 4: 'One that ruleth well his own house, having his children in subjection with all gravity,' and Titus 1:6–7: 'If any be blameless, the husband of one wife, having faithful children not accused of riot or unruly. For a bishop must be blameless, as the steward of God,' indicate that in apostolic times the priesthood was married. Clerical celibacy is, then, a human invention and 1 Timothy 4:1 and 3: 'Now the Spirit speaketh expressly, that in the latter times some shall depart from the faith, giving heed to seducing spirits, and doctrines of devils; . . . Forbidding to marry, and command-

---

[16] Ibid., p. 24. Riggenbach, *Eberlin und sein Reformprogramm*, p. 98 and Ahrens, p. 31 suggested that this refers to Karlstadt's 'Von gelubden unterrichtung.' Geiger, 'Die reformatorischen Initia Eberlins,' p. 197 suggests instead Karlstadt's 'De coelibatu, monachatu et viduitata axiomata.' On the other hand Lucke, *Die Entstehung der 15 Bundesgenossen*, p. 22; Heger, p. 24, Brecht, 'Eberlin in Wittenberg,' p. 48 and Peters, p. 58 opt for Luther's 'Judgement on Monastic Vows.' Radlkofer, p. 55 suggest the works of both authors.

[17] 'Wie gar gefährlich,' Enders, vol. 2, pp. 23–4: 'Ich gelaub auch, das Hieronimus an keym ort so fast erzaygt hab, wie er etwan menschliche kleyn verstendigkeit nit hab mügen gar abwerffen vonn ym, als da er will keuscheyt erhöchen, . . . were Hieronimus belyben bey sollichem zyl, da er lobt reynigkeyt, als ein leerer unserer zeyt in eym büchlein vonn klöster gelübtenn, were villeycht Christenheit nit so gar uberschwembt mit unseglicher unkeuscheit, . . .'; 'De votis monasticis iudicium,' WA, 8:611.

ing to abstain from meats,' indicate that it is of demonic inspiration.[18] These biblical citations and the arguments derived from them reappear in subsequent writings on this theme by both Luther and Karlstadt.[19] It is not surprising, then, that they form the basis of a significant part of 'How Very Dangerous' as well. Eberlin, too, frequently cites 1 Corinthians 7 and Matthew 19 to argue that the grace required to live a celibate life is a rare thing indeed.[20] Against the canonical strictures on clerical celibacy he also marshals 1 Timothy 3 and 4 and Titus 1:

> In 1 Timothy 3, Paul teaches how a priest should be recognized as qualified for his office, and he provides several characteristics: he should be the husband of one wife, should have well raised children and an upright, Christian wife. He also says the same of deacons in the first chapter of Titus and, shortly thereafter, warns in 1 Timothy 4 of doctrines which forbid marriage as the devil's teaching. I beg you, read the third and fourth chapters of the Epistle to Timothy and the first chapter of that to Titus and ponder well the text. You will certainly wonder at the seductive blindness of various texts in canon law.[21]

However, beyond this basic justification for his position, Eberlin avoided the theological complexity of Luther's rejection of a celibate clergy.[22] In its place, he mined the Old and New Testaments for examples of married clergy. In God's command to Adam and Eve, and later Noah and his family, to be fruitful and multiply Eberlin saw the command of marriage.[23] The first of these examples had been cited for

---

[18] 'An den christlichen Adel deutscher Nations von des christlichen Standes Besserung,' WA, 6:440–1.

[19] They play important roles in Luther's 'Judgement on Monastic Vows,' Karlstadt's 'Von gelubden unterrichtung' and 'Super coelibatu monachatu et viduitate axiomata.'

[20] 'Wie gar gefährlich,' Enders, vol. 2, p. 23: 'Ich wil auch die keuscheit dardurch nit nachgiltig machen, aber ich vermeyn keuscheit in sollichem grad lassen bleyben, darein sie Christus setzt. Math. xix. und Paulus. i. Corinthio. vij.'; pp. 24–5: 'Christus sagt Math. xix. Capi. der weyber sich enthalten vermag nit yederman, allein die es von oben herab haben, wer sollich gabe befindt bey im selbs, der erlass den Eelichen standt anzufahen. Inn diesen wortten will Christus meer abschrecken von frevenlichem furnemen an weyber zu leben, dan dartzu raytzen, Christus zeygdt wie schwer sey an Ee weyb zu leben, . . .'; p. 26: 'und das erkent Paulus, darumb sagt er, Es wer wol gut an weyb seyn. Aber unser boden leydet es nit, darumb soll yetlicher mann seyn eygen Ehe weyb haben, unnd yetliche fraw ein Ee man, . . .'; p. 29: 'Er hat auch sonderlich auss genummen die wunderbarlich keuscheit, das sie nicht yederman wirdt geben. Math. xix. als oben gnug gezeygt ist.'

[21] Ibid., p. 28.

[22] Geiger, 'Die reformatorischen Initia Eberlins,' p. 197.

[23] 'Wie gar gefährlich,' Enders, vol. 2, p. 23: 'Wir lesen im buch der schöpffung am ersten. ca. got hat den ersten man und fraw beschaffen, und sie gesegnet und gesprochen, wachssen und werden gemeret, und erfullen die erden. Solichs gebot hat got ernewret unnd meer bestettigt, redet zu dem Noe am .viij. un .ix. ca. dieses buchs, . . .'

the same purpose by Luther and Karlstadt.[24] Thereafter, however, Eberlin's argument follows more Karlstadtian lines. He traces a continuous line of married priests from Abraham to the Levites.[25] Similarly, there were married men among the apostles.[26] Karlstadt had developed the same argument in both his Latin and German pamphlets on vows.[27] Particularly convincing for Eberlin's dependence on Karlstadt is his use of the requirement' in Leviticus 21 that the high priest marry only a virgin as an indication that the Levitical priesthood was married.[28] Also common to both arguments is the assertion that clerical celibacy derives from heathen traditions. Karlstadt had made this claim with particular reference to the celibacy of monks and nuns. Eberlin widens its application to clerical celibacy in general.[29]

It appears again that the speculation on whether Eberlin was under the influence of Luther or Karlstadt is misplaced. Eberlin knew the writings of both on monastic vows and borrowed from them without

---

[24] 'De votis monasticis,' WA, 8:631; Calvin Pater, *Karlstadt as Father of the Baptist Movements: The Emergence of Lay Protestantism* (Toronto, 1984), p. 71.

[25] 'Wie gar gefährlich,' Enders, vol. 2, p. 23: 'Abraham was eyn priester, opffert got angenem opffer, und nam in seyn alten tagen die dryt haussfrau. Jacob was ein priester, het .iiij. Eefrawen, also fur und fur alle priester biss auff Aaron, habenn got gefallen wöllen inn fleyssiger gehorsam dieses gebots. Got hat auch im gsatz Moysi klerer wöllen anzeygenn, das seyn maynung sey, Die priester sollen weyber haben, darumb so eygentlich beschrieben wirt .Levit. xxi. und andes wo, welche frawen dem prister erlaubt seindt, welche vebotten zu freyen, . . .'

[26] Ibid., p. 27: '. . . wa das nit ist, wer auch besser ein weyb mit furen auch in mittel der arbeyt und geferlicheyt, als Cephas und ander Aposteln.'

[27] 'De coelibatu, monachatu et viduitate,' Köhler *et al.*, F 133, #361, Ciii(d): 'Novimus levitarum principes uxores primum habuisse, deinde etiam coniunctos ad officia tabernaculi coaptatos: quod cernere licet Exo 6. Accepit uxorem Aaron Elisabet. Eleazar accepit uxorē de filiabus Phutiel . . . Exo. 28. sic scribitur: Applica ad te Aaron, & filios suos, ut sacerdotio fungantur. Praeterea apostoli suas uxores secum duxerūt, ergo clarum est uxoratos fuisse. [1 Cor. 9]'; 'Von gelubden unterrichtung,' Köhler *et al.*, F 134, #362, Hiii(d): 'Aaron, Leviten, Propheten und Aposteln Christi sein eelich gewest; allein des Endchrist regiment is in unelichem und teufflischem stand.'

[28] 'Wie gar gefährlich,' Enders, vol. 2, p. 23: 'Die priester sollen weyber haben, darumb so eygentlich beschrieben wirt. Levit. xxi. und andes wo, welche frawen dem priester erlaubt seindt, . . .'; 'De coelibatu,' Köhler *et al.*, F 133, #361, Biii(d): 'Sequidem lex ait: Virginem ducat uxorem: viduam autem & repudiatem & fordidam, atque meretricam non accipiat, sed puellam dc populo, ne commisceat stirpem generis sui, volgo gentis: quia ego dominus qui sanctifico eum. [Levit. 21].'

[29] 'Super coelibatu, monachatu et viduitate axiomata,' Köhler *et al.*, F 125, #336, B(b): 'Quoniā Moniales suo cultu non imitantur Christianos, sed Ethnicos et divas suas illas Claras, Benedictinas et Dominicas in locū. Vestae posuerunt. . . .'; 'Von gelubden unterrichtung,' Köhler *et al.*, F 134, #362, D(b): 'Ich geschweig das unsere nonnen und monichen sso keuscheit geloben, den heyden mehr volgen dan gottlicher schrifft. Ich wolt auch gern einen sehen, der durch grundveste schrifften kund unterscheit geben tzwischen gelobdter keuscheit, so die junckfrawen der abtgotterin Veste gethan, und itzt unsere nonnen sanct. Clara oder Benedictus thuen.' E (b): 'Paulus hatt nicht von Nonnen wollen

any perception of contradiction between them. Granted, Luther had initially attacked both the methodology and some of the conclusions of Karlstadt's discussion of vows and monasticism. Luther's opinions, however, are apparent only from his exchange of letters with Melanchthon from the Wartburg and cannot be assumed to have been available to Eberlin at that time, especially if, as we suspect, Eberlin wrote the first draft of 'How Very Dangerous' while still in Leipzig.[30] Furthermore, one of Karlstadt's important conclusions initially rejected by Luther, that unrealizable vows are invalid, was later accepted in 'The Judgement on Monastic Vows.'[31]

Christian Peters has recently noted the topical nature of books on clerical celibacy in the spring of 1522. He suggests further that Eberlin may have intended this pamphlet as a form of self-recommendation to the Wittenberg Reformers.[32] If this were his strategy, it would help to explain Eberlin's apparently indiscriminate borrowing from both Luther and Karlstadt and his choice of subject matter in light of Karlstadt's own recent marriage.[33]

Eberlin's final 'humble supplication' to the bishops contained in this work, however, would seem to contradict his appeal to Karlstadt in light of the latter's more radical reform measures undertaken during the winter of 1521 to 1522. On the other hand, it does accord with the strong emphasis on the sufficiency of episcopalian authority contained in 'The Fifteen Confederates' and in Luther's 'Address to the Christian Nobility.' Furthermore, it is likely that events in Wittenberg around the time of Eberlin's arrival would have reinforced an appeal to the bishops. Throughout late 1521 and into 1522, Luther and other Wittenberg Reformers, including Karlstadt, wrestled with the practical problems of defining the extent and limits of episcopal authority. Luther's response was to advocate a reformed episcopacy as the basis for establishing a new reformed clerical order. This strategy appears most clearly first in 'Against the Spiritual Estate of the Pope and Bishops, Falsely So Called'

---

wissen / dan Nonschafft ist ein Heydnisscher / nit ein Christlicher stand.' 'Wie gar gefährlich,' Enders, vol. 2, p. 23: '. . . wan datzumal was nahe das teuflisch furnemen Der gotlosen under den Heyden, welche woltenn das yre Priester keuscheyt hielten, auch yre Münch und Nunne, . . .'

[30] Wilhelm Maurer, *Der junge Melanchthon zwischen Humanismus und Reformation*, vol. 2: *Der Theologe* (Göttingen, 1969), p. 173; Bernhard Lohse, 'Die Kritik am Mönchtum bei Luther und Melanchthon,' in *Luther und Melanchthon*, ed. Vilmos Vajta (Göttingen, 1961), pp. 142–4 and *Mönchthum und Reformation. Luthers Auseinandersetzung mit dem Monchsideal des Mittelalters* (Göttingen, 1963), pp. 356ff.; Pater, p. 126.

[31] 'De votis monasticis,' WA, 8:630–1, 654–5. See Maurer, p. 175; Lohse, *Mönchthum und Reformation*, p. 369.

[32] Peters, pp. 56–9.

[33] See Geiger, p. 197.

of July 1522. However, Luther was reaching for this solution already during the conflict with Archbishop Albrecht von Mainz which culminated in the writing of 'Against the Spiritual Estate.'[34] Eberlin's suggestion, then, that the positions of Luther and Karlstadt were similar was not as mistaken as it appears in hindsight. In early 1522, Luther, Karlstadt and the other Wittenberg Reformers were just beginning to come to terms with the structure of the new clerical order which would accompany wide-ranging reform of the church. The basic outlines of this order had been laid down in the 'Address to the Christian Nobility,' but the details of its structure remained open. The development of Eberlin's thought on the reformed clergy reflects not so much a decision between radical and moderate alternatives identified with Karlstadt and Luther as it does a decision for a Wittenberg reform movement which itself was not yet clearly defined on these issues.

Martin Brecht has called attention to a previously unnoticed break in Eberlin's publishing activity after 'How Very Dangerous.' All subsequent writings cite Luther's translation of the New Testament which came off the presses around 21 September 1522.[35] Christian Peters argues that during this period Eberlin was involved in an intensive study of Reformation theology which was a novelty to him at the time of his arrival in Wittenberg.[36] It is not surprising, then, that when Eberlin again began publishing, one of his first works summarized the fruits of a central component of those studies. 'On the Abuse of Christian Liberty' was likely completed in early autumn 1522 and published by W. Stöckel in Grimma. Peters suggests further that Eberlin's inability to find a publisher in Wittenberg indicates his continued residence on the periphery of the reforming circle, and he speculates that this pamphlet may have been part of Eberlin's theological rehabilitation.[37]

Certainly, this work indicates that Eberlin was indeed wrestling with

---

[34] Gottfried G. Krodel: ' "Wider den Abgott zu Halle." Luthers Auseinandersetzung mit Albrecht von Mainz im Herbst 1521, das Luthermanuskript Add. C. 100, S. C. 28 660 der Bodleian Library, Oxford und Luthers Schrift "Wider den falsch genannten geistlichen Stand des Papstes und der Bischöfe" von Juli 1522. Ein Beitrag zur Lutherbiographie aus der Werkstatt der Amerikanischen Lutherausgabe,' *Lutherjahrbuch*, 33 (1966), pp. 77–81; Ulrich Bubenheimer: 'Streit um das Bischofsamt in der Wittenberger Reformation 1521/22. Von der Auseinandersetzung mit den Bischöfen um Priesterehen und den Ablaß in Halle zum Modell des evangelischen Gemeindebischofs. Teil 1,' *Zeitschrift der Savigny-Stiftung für Rechtsgeschichte*. Kanonistische Abteilung, 73 (1987), pp. 160–2; Gottfried Krodel, 'Luther und das Bishofsamt nach seinem Buch "Wider den falsch genannten geistlichen Stand des Papstes und der Bischöfe," ' in Martin Brecht (ed.), *Martin Luther und das Bischofsamt* (Stuttgart, 1990), pp. 27–65; Dipple, 'Luther and Emser.'

[35] Brecht, 'Eberlin in Wittenberg,' p. 48.

[36] Peters, p. 59.

[37] Ibid., p. 68; see also Brecht, 'Eberlin in Wittenberg,' p. 49.

the fundamentals of Luther's theology. He discusses Christian freedom in terms of 1 Corinthians 13 and appeals to his readers to tarry for their weaker brethren and to preserve the unity of the evangelical cause. All should follow the example of Paul with regard to matters of adiaphora, living as a Jew among Jews and a heathen among the heathens. Having been loosed from the bonds of the law by Christ, the Christian should willingly return to its servitude through love for his/her neighbour. Eberlin warns against the dangers of freedom without faith and appeals to the authorities to take action against the free spirits. True reform lies in preaching, praying and waiting on the effects of the Word. Against those who claim that the Reformers have called for the breaking of papal laws, Eberlin argues that, while actions against impious laws have scriptural support, Luther, Melanchthon and Karlstadt live circumspect lives, ever mindful of their weaker brethren with regard to externals.[38]

There has been some dispute over whether 'On the Abuse of Christian Liberty' reflects more the arguments of Luther's 'The Freedom of a Christian' or the eight sermons he preached on his return from Wartburg.[39] Max Radlkofer has suggested, I believe correctly, that Eberlin worked from both sources.[40] Nonetheless, despite Eberlin's close adherence to Luther's theological statements and reforming vision, he continues to portray the Reformation movement as a unity. He frequently mentions Luther, Melanchthon and Karlstadt in the same breath and offers their lives as models of behaviour and their statements as authoritative.[41]

---

[38] 'Vom Missbrauch christlicher Freiheit,' Enders, vol. 2, pp. 39–55.

[39] Enders, p. x and Geiger, 'Die reformatorischen Initia Eberlins,' p. 199 argue for Luther's sermons as Eberlin's standard. Heger, p. 24, argues for 'The Freedom of a Christian.'

[40] Radlkofer, p. 61 noted in particular the close relationship of Eberlin's arguments to those in the second half of 'The Freedom of a Christian.' Equally strong parallels can be found to the first, second and fourth of Luther's sermons. See 'Von der Freiheit eines Christen menschen,' WA, 7:34–8; 'Acht sermon D.M. Luthers,' WA 10.III:1–20, 36–40; and 'Vom Missbrauch christlicher Freiheit,' Enders, vol. 2, pp. 42–52.

[41] 'Vom Missbrauch christlicher Freiheit,' Enders, vol. 2, p. 42: 'Kein sect umb bessers leben willen sol under uns auff kommen, noch von gewissers glauben, noch von genadenreichere sacrament wegen. . . . '; p. 45: 'Auch ist des Luthers leben anderst, . . . Des gleichen Melanchthon vil und ernstlich leret . . . Doctor Carlstat ist so ein erberer guthertziger man, . . . '; p. 51: '. . . und berauben auch das volck mit sollichen tzanckleren, das thundt Luther, Carlstat und Melanchthon nit. . . . '; p. 54: 'D. Lutherus, und M. Melanchthon, auch D. Carlstat haben offt do von geredt, wie ich schreyb, darumb mogeth ir euch mit innen nicht entschuldigen. . . . '; p. 55: 'Ob D. Luther, Carlstat, Melanchthon u. Etlich Papisten mutwilicher, auch nemlich antastent, sol darumb nit ein itzlicher freveler auch also thun, ...' Peters, p. 70, suggests that Eberlin's frequent defences of Karlstadt may indicate that he had heard rumours about disagreements between Karlstadt and Luther. This seems unlikely, given that Eberlin continued to hold Karlstadt up as a model Reformer into 1523.

Max Radlkofer has read Eberlin's statement in this pamphlet that, on his arrival in Wittenberg, he knew nothing of the Gospel as an admission that he had gone too far in some of his earlier writings.[42] 'On the Abuse of Christian Liberty' does appear to contain at least a partial retreat from some of Eberlin's earlier, more forceful statements, especially from the perspective of his anticlerical polemic. Against his earlier calls for monks and nuns to depart their cloisters and appeals that the mendicant orders be abolished, Eberlin now includes cowls and tonsures among the externals over which the enthusiasts fight to no avail.[43] Elsewhere, he remarks on Luther's concern for the weak in faith: 'Also, Luther's life is different than you claim. He lives in a cloister and wears a cowl. On Fridays, Saturdays and other fast days he does not eat meat.'[44] However, the extent to which this constitutes a retraction from Eberlin's earlier statements can only be ascertained in light of his subsequent writings.

In the heady early days of the Reformation two of the most prominent practical concerns dealt with clerical celibacy and the status of the cloistered life and of monastic vows. Eberlin's next work, 'Against the Imprudent, Unreasonable Departure of many Cloistered,' reassesses his position on the monastic life on the basis of his new understanding of the Gospel. Although the only extant version of this pamphlet bears the publication date of 1524, references by Eberlin to a work of this nature in pamphlets from 1522 and 1523 indicate that it was completed on 28 October 1522.[45] The content and style of 'Against the Imprudent Departure' indicates its proximity to 'On the Abuse of Christian Liberty.' Eberlin refers back to his earlier discussion of Christian liberty, and claims that the large numbers of runaway monks and nuns among those abusing this liberty have occasioned the present work.[46] He also reiterates the theme of the earlier discussion that spiritual freedom also demands discipline of the flesh.[47]

---

[42] Radlkofer, pp. 57–8.

[43] 'Vom Missbrauch christlicher Freiheit,' Enders, vol. 2, p. 51: '. . . vom fegfewer, von heyligen furbit, von bilden, von fastagen, von feyertagen, von farbentragen, von harr oder kolben u. fichtet man, fur und wyder, als von heuptsachen und schyrmet es mit Christlicher lere schein, . . . '

[44] Ibid., p. 45.

[45] 'Wider den unvorsichteigen, unbescheidenen Ausgang vieler Klosterleute,' Enders, vol. 2, p. 121; 'Eine freundliche, tröstliche Vermahnung an die Christen zu Augsburg,' Enders, vol. 2, p. 151; 'Wider die falschen Geistlichen, genannt die Barfüsser und Franziskaner,' Enders, vol. 3, p. 87. See Riggenbach, *Eberlin und sein Reformprogramm*, p. 200; Radlkofer, pp. 82–3; Enders, vol. 3, p. xv; Brecht, 'Eberlin in Wittenberg,' p. 50.

[46] 'Wider den unvorsichtigen Ausgang,' Enders, vol. 2, pp. 122–3.

[47] Ibid., p. 122: 'Darauss anzaygt wurdt, das ain glawbiger mensch ain gaystliche freyhayt habe, nit ain leypliche odder flayschliche, . . . Bey freyhayt des gaysts stat allerlay zwang und bandt des leybs, . . . '

Within this context, 'Against the Imprudent Departure' marks a new development in Eberlin's anti-monastic polemic. The emphasis in 'The Fifteen Confederates' on the harmful social effects of monasticism, the ungodly alliance between the mendicants and the papacy, and free dispensation for all those wishing to leave the monastery, now gives way to an almost exclusive concern for the spiritual well-being of the monks:

> When you read in certain writings of God-fearing teachers that the cloisters are antichristian and devourers of souls, don't understand this in terms of condition and buildings, of clothing and other external organization concerning the temporal life, such as fasting, vigils and labours, and those things relating to the mortification of the flesh. . . . Rather, understand the danger of cloisters in terms of the management of the soul, that one alleges the soul will be helped or hindered before God with the observance or non-observance of such monastic statutes. This is false, for belief in Christ alone helps and unbelief hinders.[48]

Throughout, 'Against the Imprudent Departure' relies heavily on Luther's 'Judgement on Monastic Vows' in its criticism of the institution of monasticism. At the outset Eberlin adopts Luther's contrast between the freedom of conscience conferred in baptism and the restriction of this liberty by monastic vows. Paul advised Christians to avoid servitude of this kind, but what greater bondage of the conscience is there than that imposed by monasticism.[49] Like Luther, Eberlin cites Matthew 24 as evidence that Christ denounced monasticism and labels it as devotion to Baal.[50]

Luther's 'Judgement on Monastic Vows' advised the departure from the monastery of those whose spiritual health was endangered therein. He was particularly concerned with those unable to fulfil the vow of chastity or troubled by the institution's denial of the Gospel and abuse of the mass.[51] Eberlin, too, encourages departure from the monastery to those whose spiritual welfare is endangered. These include monks and

---

[48] Ibid., p. 120. See above, pp. 90–1.

[49] 'Wider den unvorsichtigen Ausgang,' Enders, vol. 2, pp. 123–4: 'Ich bekenne auch, der hailig Paulus sagt, ain gekauffter knecht soll sich mit fůg fleissen, frey zůwerden und so eyner frey ist, soll er sich hůtten, das er nit ain knecht werde. . . . vil mer sol man diesem radt volgen in sollicher gefǎncknuss durch menschlich gsatz, das man fürderlich nach der gwyssen greyffet sy zů binden, und durch sie den gantzen menschen, als yetz im kloster stand geschicht, also das kayn mensch so hart under den hayden verkaufft ist, als die klosterleüt under den Christen, ...' See also Lohse, *Mönchtum und Reformation*, p. 369.

[50] 'Wider den unvorsichtigen Ausgang,' Enders, vol. 2, p. 125: 'Da wider auch Christus gelert hat Mat. 24. Wann sie zů euch sagen, sihe, nym war, Christus ist in der wůsten, gond nit hinauss, nymm war, er ist in der zell oder kǎmer, so glaubent es nit u. . . . Ist gleich dem dienst von priestern Baal gethon. iii Reg. 18.' 'De votis monasticis,' WA, 8:657, 616.

[51] 'De votis monasticis,' WA, 8:580–1, 632, 651 and 654.

nuns unable to fulfil their vow of chastity, those who are tempted by the works righteousness of their brothers and sisters, and those whose consciences are troubled because they must deny the Gospel or handle the sacrament in an idolatrous manner.[52] Like Luther, Eberlin frequently warns his readers against departure for the wrong reasons, but appears to contradict his mentor in his claim that the social problems posed by runaway monks and nuns outweigh the benefits of emptying the monasteries.[53] To those who would flee the monastery to escape persecution, he warns that suffering follows one in all stations of life.[54] As an example for anyone pondering this decision, Eberlin states that Luther and Johannes Lang still wear their cowls and that he has retained the tonsure and garb of a priest.[55]

Eberlin's advice betrays a generally more cautious tone about the departure from the cloisters than is found in Luther's discussion of monastic vows. Eberlin insists that, as the epistles of Paul indicate, with true faith, salvation is still possible in a state of bondage. All depends on faith and, in and of itself, the cloistered life is harmless.[56] Through

---

[52] 'Wider den Unvorsichtigen Ausgang,' Enders, vol. 2, ; p. 120: '. . . oder so du anfächtung halb deines fleisch nit magst on Eelichen standt sein, oder würdest gezwungen gottes Evangeliion verlaugnen, oder die Sacrament ungeschicklich gebrauchen, so hettest ursach auss dem kloster zůgon auss gebot gottes. . . . '; p. 128: 'Ettlich werden so vast gebrent durch leiplich anfächtung, das sy weder durch gebet zů gott, durch lesen unnd bemelten hailiger geschrifft, durch züchtigung jres leibs den brandt miltern mügen, disen ist geratten, das sy sollen herauss lauffen, ain eegemahl nemen, damit vil schendtliche grosse sünd vermeyden, davon ich jetzt nit sagen wil. Etlich wollen auss dem kloster darumb, das sye anders jre gewissen nit mügen erretten von verfůrung der gotlosshait, das sie durch exempel der andern, auff wolliche sy auch vil halten, gefůrt werden auff unglaubigen und eyteln won gůter werck und verdienst zů der säligkaytt.'

[53] Ibid., p. 129: 'Aber bewere vorhin deinen glauben, ob du frey seyest in deiner gwissen, das du on scrupel herauss gangest, dann gest on glauben herauss, so sündest und fallest dem teuffel mer in die hand, was nit auss glauben ist, ist sünd Ro. 14. . . . '; 'Ich wolt ain ungezogen mensch inn ain kloster helffen schliessen, lieber dann herauss lassen, in der welt seind vorhin gnůg mörder, rauber, hůrer, eebrecher, dieb, gassentretter, junckfrawschender, ist nit nott, das man die kloster auffthů unnd das Münich geschwürm gar auss lassen, eben sollichen losen kloster leütten seind die gsatz und kloster kercker gemacht 1. Thimo. 1. . . . '; 'Acht sermon D.M. Luthers,' WA, 10.III:23–4: 'Und wolte got alle Münch und Nonnen hörten diese predig und hetten den verstand und liessen alle auss den klöstern und hören alle klöster auff, die in der gantzen welt seind, das wolte ich. Aber nů sie den verstandt nit haben (dann es predigt jn niemants) und hören, das sie an andern enden hinauss geen, die nů wol gerůst sein, wollen sie denen volgen und haben jre gewissen noch nit gesterckt, wissen es auch nit, das es frey sey, das ist böse. Noch ist es besser, heraussen böse dann darjnnen.'

[54] 'Wider den unvorsichtigen Ausgang,' Enders, vol. 2, p. 128.

[55] Ibid., p. 131.

[56] Ibid., p. 124: 'Ain münich in aim kloster lasse sich geduncken, er sey ain gekauffter knecht, es mögen aber gekaufft knecht auch Christen sein, Als Paulus in vilen Episteln anzaigt, darinnen er sollichen glaubigen knechten underweyssung gibt in jrer berüffung.

dedication to Christian service and love of one's neighbour, one can justify leading a cloistered life.[57] According to Christian Peters, Eberlin's greater caution derives from his observation of the harmful social consequences resulting from the large numbers of monks and nuns fleeing their cloisters in the wake of the appearance of Luther's 'Judgement on Monastic Vows.'[58] Eberlin's own warnings about the social dislocation caused by the need to integrate large numbers of runaway monks and nuns into society indicate the validity of Peters's interpretation.

However, Eberlin's greater caution nowhere leads him to deny the fundamentals of Luther's assessment of monasticism at this time. In fact, it is likely that Eberlin's advice reflected the development of Luther's own perceptions of the religious life during the first half of 1522. Robert Bast has argued that into 1522 Luther's attitude toward monasticism remained 'reformist' rather than 'abolitionist.'[59] Certainly, in 'The Judgement on Monastic Vows,' Luther still allowed for the practice of such a life, and likely laid the groundwork for Eberlin's position:

> And so, if you vow to take up the religious life, and if you live with men of like mind, with a clear conscience that in monasticism you seek nothing to your advantage in your relationship with God, but because either your situation has brought you to embrace this kind of life, or it appeared the best way of life for you, without your thinking thereby that you are better than he who takes a wife or takes up farming, then in that case you are neither wrong to take vows nor wrong to live in this way, insofar as the propriety of the vow is concerned.[60]

A similar allowance for the validity of the religious life for those granted the grace to pursue it is contained in Luther's third sermon after his return from the Wartburg.[61] And in 'Against the Spiritual Estate' he again returned to the same point:

. . . '; p. 125: 'Unnd hatt ain kloster mensch waren glauben, mag es auch wol on schaden darinn sein. . . . '; p. 126: 'Also ist auch kloster standt an im selbs frey aim glaubigen und schadloss.'

[57] Ibid., p. 130: 'Die unverdienst pfründe im kloster sol dich auch nit ausstreyben, wann ob die stiffter wider vom tod auff stenden, sprechen sie dir dein pfründt nit ab, die weyl du doch so ser kommen bist in disem standt, auch wildt du Christlich leben im kloster, so gewinnest du so vil züschaffen mit brüderlichem dienst, das du wol damit dein brot verdienst.'

[58] Peters, pp. 73–80.

[59] Robert J. Bast, '*Je geistlicher . . . je blinder*: Anticlericalism, the Law, and Social Ethics in Luther's Sermons on Matthew 22: 34–41,' in Dykema and Oberman, pp. 367–72.

[60] 'De votis monasticis,' WA, 8:610.

[61] 'Acht Sermon D.M. Luthers,' WA, 10.III:24: 'Wer es on schaden thůn kan und zů liebe dem nechsten ein kappe tragen oder platten, die weyl dirs an deinem glaüben nit schadet: die kappe erwürget dich nit, wan du sie schon trügest.'

> Therefore, I have often said, and still say: Do not get involved with priestliness, monkery and nunnery where the Holy Scripture and pure faith are not studied and practised among them day and night. Religious foundations and monasteries must be the gates of hell if faith is not valiantly and vigorously exercised in them; then there is neither advice nor help for them. I warn you, beware of the clerical life *which is lived without Scripture.* [my emphasis][62]

Furthermore, Eberlin seems to apply to the monasteries Luther's programme for the reform of the clergy. In the middle of 'Against the Imprudent Departure,' he appeals to the 'Cloister-Prelates' as Luther appealed to the bishops in 'Against the Spiritual Estate.' He outlines a plan for the reform of monasteries by monastic superiors, and then concludes that it would be better for the religious to reform themselves than for Karsthans to undertake the task.[63]

None of this, however, changes Eberlin's evaluation of monasticism as it exists around him. 'Against the Imprudent Departure' includes a warning to parents not to place their children in monasteries and cautions that the preceding advice applies only to those already in the cloisters.[64] When Eberlin pauses to reflect on the social consequences of monasticism, his invective against the monks regains the virulence of his earlier writings. Interestingly, this time he makes little distinction between the mendicant and endowed orders. By begging, the friars are not only a great burden on society, but they also contravene the divine command to work and their own rules. The endowed orders, on the other hand, support themselves with usury and such thorough exploitation of their subjects that they are more oppressive than the worst tyrant.[65]

Furthermore, although he rarely deals explicitly with the topic in this group of pamphlets, Eberlin continues to regard all clergy who belonged to religious orders, including the mendicants, as the chief opponents of the Gospel and antithesis of the new evangelical clergy. On 14

---

[62] 'Wider den falsch genannten geistlichen Stand des Papsts und der Bischöfe,' WA, 10.II:129.

[63] 'Wider den unvorsichtigen Ausgang,' Enders, vol. 2, pp. 132–3.

[64] Ibid., p. 133. Luther made the same distinction. See above, p. 106, n. 51.

[65] Ibid., p. 135: 'Etlich örden leben allain vom bettel, in so grosser zale und reylichayt, da durch sie der welt ain bschwerd seind und gottes gebot wyderig, ja auch jren aygnen ordens Regel, Lyse Franciscus regel und andere. Etlich die leben on betel, aber sy schinden jre arme leüt hertter dann kain landtsherr, das ist warlich unträglich, auch habenn sy wůcher gilten von hundert fünff und der gleychen, das ist nit allein unträglich, sonder ergerlich unchristlich. Auch nemen sy wissenlich ab den leütten habe und gůt under scheyn des gebets für andere, und leben darin in aller überflüssigkait, mit beraubung der andern armen.'

November, Eberlin completed 'A Friendly, Encouraging Exhortation to the Christians at Augsburg' in which he sought to convey the fruits of his theological study at Wittenberg to his fellow Swabians.[66] The proximity of this work to its predecessors is obvious. Eberlin warns the Augsburgers against the over-hasty exercise of the new freedom conferred on them by the Gospel, and he cautions against the rejection of all external forms.[67] His primary purpose is to convey to the Augsburgers an overview of the essentials of Wittenberg theology and a report on the progress of reform in Wittenberg.[68] But within this framework, Eberlin is still able to cast the odd barb at his old foes. He warns against the teachings of the 'temples, schools and cloisters,' and contrasts living, true faith with that of the 'hearers' in the monasteries and schools.[69] The reference to the monasteries and schools is obvious. That to temples likely refers back to the designation in 'The Fifteen Confederates' of those who read private masses and say canonical hours as servants of the temple. All of these stand under God's curse.[70]

The objects of Eberlin's ire are more specific in another work penned during this period. Sometime after August 1522, Eberlin translated from Latin the history of the retraction of the evangelical Augustinian prior of Antwerp, Jacob Probst.[71] Eberlin's decision to translate this work likely stemmed from his perception that, like Probst, he too was a victim of mendicant intrigues, and his translation exploits every opportunity to utilize Probst's story as a polemic against the friars.[72] Chief among Probst's prosecutors was Eberlin's old nemesis, Johannes Glapion.[73] After his initial arrest, Probst was interrogated in the Franciscan cloister

---

[66] 'Eine freundliche, tröstliche Vermahnung an die Christen zu Augsburg,' Enders, vol. 2, p. 138.

[67] Ibid., p. 149: 'Lieben brieder, frewen euch, das jr frey seind von allen gesätzen, ewer gewissen halb, und das durch Christum. Aber hietten euch, das jr ewer freyhait nit gebrauchen zů ergernuss ewers nechsten noch zů rom ewers flaischs, als euch Paulus warnet zů den Römern und Galathern. . . . Aber in eüsserlichem schein sollen jr nit gar alle gesatz abwerffen, das nit unrů und ergernuss darauss erwachsse.'

[68] Enders, vol. 2, pp. 137–52. Peters, pp. 81–5, examines in detail the possibility that Eberlin had spent some time in Augsburg en route to Wittenberg.

[69] 'Eine freundliche Vermahnung zu Augsburg,' Enders, vol. 2, pp. 145–6.

[70] Ibid., p. 151: '. . . wann so grosse gotlosikait regiert in klöstern, und got, fürcht ich, Sein flůch über das Closter volck, schůl volck, und tempel volck gegeben hat.'

[71] 'Eine schöne und klägliche Historie,' Enders, vol. 2, pp. 95–117. Probst, who had studied in Wittenberg in 1519 and 1521, first returned there after the events of this story on 11 August 1522. Enders, vol. 3, p. 313. Furthermore, a letter from Karl Rose in Nuremberg to Nikolaus von Kniebis dated September 1522 refers to news of Probst provided by Eberlin. The relevant part of this letter is reproduced in Radlkofer, p. 81.

[72] Peters, p. 66.

[73] 'Eine schöne und klägliche Historie,' Enders, vol. 2, p. 99.

in Antwerp which is identified as Caiaphas's house, and the description of the proceedings makes clear the parallel to the interrogation of Christ. Throughout, the Franciscan hosts lived up to their reputation as hardened opponents of the Gospel.[74] Frightened for his life, Probst recanted his evangelical beliefs, much to the pleasure of the chief opponents of the Gospel, the friars. Sent to Ypres to avoid further trouble in Antwerp, Probst again began to preach the Gospel and soon ran foul of the friars; first the Franciscans and shortly thereafter the Dominicans. At Probst's second interrogation Glapion is cast in the role of Pilate.[75] With the story, Probst included a supplication to those who heard him preach in Antwerp in which he warns specifically against the false teachings of the mendicants.[76]

Eberlin's comments in 'A Friendly Exhortation' and his decision to translate Probst's story indicate that, despite the softened tone and partial retraction of his earlier criticisms of the clergy, and despite his concern with the establishment of a reformed clerical order, he still held the 'temple servants' responsible for the perversion of the Gospel. However, now his denunciations of them were linked to specific events and circumstances: the treatment of Probst by the mendicants and the strength of the anti-reform forces in Augsburg. Eberlin's subsequent writings from his first stay in Wittenberg continue to develop the same themes raised in the preceding pamphlets. It has long been acknowledged that Eberlin's writings fall easily into two distinct categories. On the one hand, one encounters his anonymous works, often in fictional form, which concentrate on pressing social concerns. On the other hand, Eberlin's signed works from this period are more explicitly theological in nature and reflect the political and social conservatism usually associated with the Wittenberg Reformation. The former group of pamphlets are usually thought to be more radical, and to reflect more closely the reforming tradition begun in 'The Fifteen Confederates.' Interestingly, from the perspective of Eberlin's anticlerical polemics, this distinction does not hold true. In his signed pamphlets, especially those addressed to a specific audience, Eberlin's ire against the 'temple servants' comes again to the fore as he dwells on their continued roles in the suppression of the Gospel within specific contexts. By way of contrast, Eberlin's anonymous works develop most fully his vision of a reformed clerical order.

In December 1522 and January 1523, Eberlin returned to the format

---

[74] Ibid., pp. 101–2.
[75] Ibid., pp. 108–10.
[76] Ibid., pp. 114–16.

of the anonymous pamphlet voicing social concerns.[77] In 'Seven Devout, but Disconsolate Priests Complain to One Another about Their Plight,' he introduces seven new characters to highlight the predicament of the godly clergy. Their complaints are answered by the fifteen confederates in the 'Consolation of the Seven Devout Priests.'[78] Read together, these pamphlets mark the culmination of Eberlin's first attempt to defuse some of the anticlerical tension he perceived around him and to define an evangelical priesthood. Several issues which escaped treatment in these two pamphlets come under consideration in the closely related 'Last Confederate.' Eberlin was in the habit of including short popular sayings and bits of advice on the title pages of his pamphlets and those from these three works clearly indicate their tone. The first claims that there are still devout priests and warns the laity not to take action against the clergy to avoid making the innocent suffer with the guilty.[79] The next two advise: 'Indeed, trust God' and 'Be patient, the hour approaches.'[80]

Eberlin himself regarded the contents of these pamphlets as something of a revision of 'The Fifteen Confederates.' Already in 'A Friendly Exhortation to Augsburg' he had criticized the writing of books dealing with religious themes and expressed some doubts about his earlier reform suggestions:

> I have written to you briefly, for I am completely against many writings beyond the Bible, and I wish that I had accomplished my preaching with my mouth alone and not my pen. Regarding matters of Scripture, there is little or no use in the writing of books. God wrote in the Bible and one should learn and teach from it.[81]

The conclusion to the 'Consolation of the Seven Devout Priests' makes this point more clearly: 'We ask that you would read judiciously our first fifteen little books, which appeared among many in Basel in 1521,

---

[77] In the first of these, Eberlin makes reference to a doctor-fool in Freiburg who is writing against 'The Fifteen Confederates.' 'Sieben fromme, aber trostlose Pfaffen klagen einer dem andern ihre Not,' Enders, vol. 2, p. 74. From this Martin Brecht concludes that Eberlin knew of Murner's intention to write against his work, but had not yet seen 'The Great Lutheran Fool' which appeared in December of that year. Therefore, he must have been working on this pamphlet and its sequel in December as well, Brecht, 'Eberlin in Wittenberg,' p. 51. Enders, vol. 3, p. 305 and pp. xii–xiii also noted the reference to Murner.

[78] Riggenbach, *Eberlin und sein Reformprogramm*, p. 117 and Radlkofer, p. 63 suggested that both pamphlets originally appeared as one. Enders, vol. 3, p. xii rejects this claim, but admits that they must have been written in close proximity to one another.

[79] 'Sieben fromme Pfaffen klagen ihre Not,' Enders, vol. 2, p. 57.

[80] 'Trost der sieben frommen Pfaffen,' Enders, vol. 2, p. 79; 'Letzter Bundesgenosse,' Enders, vol. 1, p. 171.

[81] 'Eine freundliche Vermahnung zu Augsburg,' Enders, vol. 2, p. 151.

for not all things found there are articles of belief.'[82] The 'Last Confederate' introduces a lengthy discussion of the dangerous consequences of writing books on religious issues with the claim that Luther and Melanchthon have wished that all books except the Bible be burnt.[83] While the main interest of this discussion is to denounce the glosses and scholastic theology, Eberlin does indicate reservations about his own publications.[84] The work then concludes by announcing the retirement of the fifteen confederates and encouraging their readers to turn their attention to the Bible.[85] Eberlin's statements indicate that his primary concern was to smooth over any contradictions on matters of belief between these two groups of pamphlets. Nonetheless, a new tone of conciliation pervades the later pamphlets.

This new tone reflects not so much Eberlin's conversion from a radical to a Lutheran vision of reform as it does the development of Wittenberg anticlericalism. As Goertz has suggested, with 'A Faithful Admonition to all Christians to Guard against Riot and Rebellion' Luther attempted in early 1522 to temper the anticlerical agitation he had earlier called forth. In it Luther cautioned against forceful action against the clergy, claiming that such tactics actually paled in comparison with what God had in store for the priests. He also warned against throwing out the good clergy with the bad:

> Alas, no such mild chastisement awaits them; an inexpressible severity and limitless wrath has already begun to break upon them. . . . God's purposes demand far more than mere insurrection. Since they are as a whole beyond the reach of help, would to God that we might extricate at least a few of them and save them from that horrible yawning abyss![86]

As an alternative strategy, he placed greater emphasis on exposing the evils of the papist clergy:

> From these texts we learn how the pope and his antichristian regime shall be destroyed. Through the word of Christ, which is the breath, the rod and the sword of his mouth, the pope's villainy, deceit,

---

[82] 'Trost der sieben frommen Pfaffen,' Enders, vol. 2, p. 93.

[83] 'Letzter Bundesgenosse,' Enders, vol. 1, p. 202.

[84] Ibid., pp. 204–5: 'Ain ietlicher gotzforchtiger mensch sol sich wol umbsehen, und vast forchten, bücher zeschriben in christlichen sachen, . . . Sihe fur dich, das du nit ufrichtest grossers ubel mit dynen geschriften.'

[85] Ibid., p. 205: 'Wyr .xv. bundtsgnossen haben vil geschryben, als unsere ersten .xv. biechlein zaigen mogen, auch die .vij. christlossen pfaffen, der pfaffen trost, und zcu letst diss biechlein, wir wollen auch uffhoren schryben, und alle menschen vermanen wir, das sie hailige schrift selbs lesen, betrachten, und mit mundt leren, do by blyben und bitten got fur uns.'

[86] 'Eyn treu vormanung Martini Luther tzu allen Christen. Sich tzu vorhuten fur auffruhr unnd Emporung,' WA, 8:677.

rascality, tyranny, and beguilements shall be revealed and laid open
to the world's derision. Lying and guile need only to be revealed and
recognized to be undone.[87]

Later, he commented on his own role in this process: 'Look what I have
done. Have I not, with the mouth alone, without a single stroke of the
sword, done more harm to the pope, bishops, priests, and monks than
all the emperors, kings, and princes with all their power ever did
before?'[88]

Already in the letter to the people of Augsburg, Eberlin echoed
Luther's assessment of his own activity:

> I believe that Luther has been sent by God to cleanse the Bible of the
> forced interpretations of the teachers, . . . and to strip from the
> clergy the title of Christ and his church, so that henceforth such
> great villainy will no longer be cultivated, protected and remain
> unpunished under God's holy name. I do not speak in order that, on
> account of this, the clergy will stop being evil, but so that one
> should know that they cannot defend their evil with God's name. If
> they wish to be evil, they must do this openly and be what they are
> without a holy title.[89]

And in the 'Consolation of the Seven Devout Priests' he recommends
Luther's 'Faithful Admonition' to his readers.[90]

Beyond this attempt to tone down the anticlerical agitation which he
earlier helped to call forth, Eberlin sought in these pamphlets to identify
the criteria for an evangelical clerical order. Scott Hendrix argues that in
these pamphlets Eberlin is 'taking the clergy's side' and presenting a
realistic picture of the plight of Catholic priests in the early years of the
Reformation.[91] The first four priests in 'Seven Devout Priests Complain
about Their Plight' do indeed discuss the most commonly mentioned
ecclesiastical abuses from the perspective of the clergy. The first
complains about the difficulties of remaining chaste and in the process
revives the principal arguments from 'How Very Dangerous.' He
accuses the pope and bishops of having brought great evil on
Christendom through their rejection of clerical marriage. The second
priest acknowledges the common charge that the clergy lead lazy lives
against the divine command to work for one's daily bread. In contrast to

---

[87] Ibid., p. 678.

[88] Ibid., p. 683.

[89] 'Eine freundliche Vermahnung zu Augsburg,' Enders, vol. 2, pp. 150–1.

[90] 'Der frommen Pfaffen Trost,' Enders, vol. 2, p. 92: 'Lieber freundt, behab dich wol,
und hastu nit geachtet des Luthers bücher, so nym doch zwen Quatern, welche er
geschriben hat wider solich uffrur wider pfaffen, darinn hastu trostliche antwurt.'

[91] Scott Henrix, 'Considering the Clergy's Side: A Multilateral View of Anticlericalism,'
in Dykema and Oberman, pp. 455–9.

the examples of Christ and the apostles, they live from usury and the sale of spiritual services. This theme is then revived by the third priest who charges that the whole Catholic cult is a perversion of true Christian worship aimed only at the accumulation of wealth. The fourth priest then complains of the difficulties of preaching in an age of rising literacy and increased production of books in the vernacular. The laity demand to hear the Gospel alone preached, but to do so indicates the hypocrisy of the clerical estate and tempts punishment from one's superiors. In each of these cases, the culpability of the clergy is admitted, but the difficulty of reform under current circumstances is highlighted. The tone of the pamphlet then shifts to indicate more clearly the impossible position in which devout priests find themselves. The fifth priest complains that, caught between Karsthans and the ecclesiastical authorities, the rank and file clergy have nowhere to turn. The books of the Reformers are banned – reference here is still made to the works of Luther, Karlstadt and Melanchthon – and no positive reform suggestions are being advanced from the orthodox side. The threat of Karsthans is discussed by the sixth priest, who challenges the common perception that priests lead easy lives. From the moment of his ordination, the priest suffers under a plague sent by God. Always a social pariah, he is increasingly the object of verbal and physical abuse. If the bishops do not act soon, the laity will. The final priest bemoans the conditions of the underpaid, overworked parish chaplain serving for an absentee priest. The present controversies have only aggravated the problems of the chaplain, who no longer knows which opinions are correct and yet must take responsibility for all that occurs in the parish.[92]

The answers of the fifteen confederates to these complaints in the 'Consolation of the Seven Devout Priests' indicate, however, that Eberlin's purposes went beyond merely identifying the 'clergy's side.' Rather, he was appealing to the Catholic priests to become true Christian priests, and outlining a model for them to follow in taking this step. The first priest had claimed that, on reading Paul's prescriptions for the servants of the church in 1 Timothy and Titus, he was frightened by the disparity with his own life.[93] This, however, is the model for behaviour that the fifteen confederates recommend to the priests. Whatever their reasons for entering the priesthood, God has called them

---

[92] 'Sieben frommen Pfaffen klagen ihre Not,' Enders, vol. 2, pp. 57–77.

[93] Ibid., p. 59: '. . . ich solt die .iij. epistel zů Timotheo und Tito lesen, darinn ich allen rath würd finden, eim priester nötig, ich hab jm gefolgt, und die epistel offt durch und uss gelesen, und ich sag warlich, mŭss ein pfarrer sein, wie darinn gelert würt, so helff mir got.'

to this office and will help them to persevere in it. Therefore, they should place their trust in him and rejoice in the role assigned to them.[94] In response to the sixth priest, the fifteen confederates maintain that an upright priest will be loved and honoured by his parishioners.[95] Taken together, these two answers contradict the position of the sixth priest that the priesthood as a whole stands under the curse of God.

The 'Consolation of the Seven Devout Priests' supplements this re-evaluation of the priesthood with practical advice to clergy inclined to the Reformation. The first priest is encouraged to read the books of the Reformers on clerical marriage and follow Luther's advice to marry in secret. Interestingly, some of Eberlin's suggestions are still drawn from Karlstadt's pamphlets on monastic vows.[96] The second priest is advised to employ his education for the benefit of the parish. If possible, he should buy and work his own field. However, Eberlin also echoes his advice to the monks in 'Against the Imprudent Departure' by allowing priests with the cure of souls to continue living from their benefice if they conscientiously perform their duties. Above all, the priest is warned against greed, which is as great a sin as adultery.[97] The third and fourth priests are encouraged to approach reform cautiously. While preaching the Gospel, one may continue to perform the old ceremonies in correct belief for weaker brethren. Furthermore, not all needs to be revealed immediately in one's sermons as numerous examples of preaching in the New Testament indicate.[98]

---

[94] 'Trost der sieben frommen Pfaffen,' Enders, vol. 2, p. 90: 'Bistu ein pfarrer, du seyest dazu kommen, wie du bist, ligt nit daran, hastu oder andere geirret darinn, so hat doch gott nit geirret, byss gern ein pfarrer, und halt dich noch den Epistelen Pauli zů Timo. und Tito. und predige die warheit, und die warheit wirt dich erlösen. . . . Der got welcher dich berůfft hat zů dem predigampt, wirt dich auch jm selbs also ussbereyten, das du wol wirst beston, damit far für, got geb dir glück.'

[95] Ibid., p. 93.

[96] Eberlin adopts the arguments first developed by Karlstadt that one does not know whether one has the gift of chastity until age 60 and that the priest is not bound by Mosaic law to marry a virgin. 'Der frommen Pfaffen Trost,' Enders, vol. 2, p. 81: 'Darumb Paulus .j. Timoth. v. das sechzigst jar gesetzt hatt zů der prob diser gnad der zeyt halb. . . .'; p. 82: 'Ist nit zeachten, ob sye iunckfraw sye oder witwen, so sag dann der frawen das gottes wort vom eelichen standt der pfaffen, uss der epistel .j. Tim. iij. und .iiij. ca. und Tit. j. ca.' See 'De coelibatu, monachatu et viduitate,' Köhler et al., F 133, #361, Cii (b)-Ciii. Luther dealt with the first of these issues in 'The Judgement on Monastic Vows,' WA, 8:666–9. Among the complaints of the seven priests, Eberlin continues to recommend the writings of Karlstadt along with those of Luther and Melanchthon: 'Sieben fromme Pfaffen klagen ihre Not,' Enders, vol. 2, p. 73: 'So wir aber wol erkennen, wie ubel es umb uns stot, wo wóllen wir rath darumb sůchen, die Lutherischen, Melanchtischen, Carlstadischen u. geschrifften dorffen wir by grosser peen nit haben oder lesen.'

[97] 'Trost der sieben frommen Pfaffen,' Enders, vol. 2, pp. 84–5.

[98] Ibid., pp. 87, 89.

In the complaints of the seven priests, responsibility for the problems of the clergy is frequently laid at the feet of the ecclesiastical authorities, and among these most often the bishops. The first priest charges the pope and bishops with seeking to make money from the vow of chastity rather than reform it.[99] The fifth and sixth priests accuse the bishops with opposing the cause of the Gospel and attempts for reform.[100] The second priest claims that the financial exactions of his superiors compel him to fleece his parishioners to survive, and the fourth complains that evangelical preaching is opposed by all levels of ecclesiastical authority who are backed up by the secular authorities and the Inquisition.[101] However, in 'Consolation of the Seven Devout Priests,' the fifteen confederates come out in defence of the bishops. They insist that the bishops are in the same predicament as the priests. They are surrounded by advisors who suppress the Gospel in their names.[102] Rather than condemn them, one should pity the bishops.[103] Their actions against the Gospel are much less forceful than they appear and many bishops are, in fact, inclined toward reform. As examples of these the bishops of Augsburg, Constance, Basel, Meersburg and Bamberg are mentioned.[104]

Martin Brecht describes this as the highpoint in Eberlin's relations with ecclesiastical authority.[105] And Christian Peters notes the contrast to the usual treatment of the bishops in reforming literature, and takes it as an indication of Eberlin's continuing trust in the ability of the church to reform itself.[106] However, as we have seen, the possibility of a reform of the church centred on the creation of an evangelical episcopacy was a serious option for the Wittenbergers in 1522. Furthermore, Eberlin's good will extends only as far as the bishops. Throughout these three pamphlets, he contrasts the diligent parish priest with the parasitic clergy involved in other pursuits. The cursed trinity of temples, cloisters and schools from the letter to Augsburg reappears in the 'Consolation of the Seven Devout Priests' as priests, monks and universities and in the 'Last Confederate' as schools, cloisters and papal law.[107] In this last

---

[99] 'Sieben fromme Pfaffen Klagen ihre Not,' Enders, vol. 2, p. 64.

[100] Ibid., pp. 73, 75.

[101] Ibid., pp. 66, 71–2.

[102] 'Der frommen Pfaffen Trost,' Enders, vol. 2, p. 91.

[103] Ibid.

[104] Ibid., pp. 91–2.

[105] Brecht, 'Eberlin in Wittenberg,' p. 51.

[106] Peters, pp. 103–4.

[107] 'Sieben fromme Pfaffen klagen ihre Not,' Enders, vol. 2, p. 74: 'Auch ist weder münchen, pfaffen, hohenschůlern zů trawen. sye seind eben die, weliche uns würden erstlich verfolgen, so sye uns erkanten.' 'Letzter Bundesgenosse,' Enders, vol. 1, p. 191: 'Die blům christlichs volcks ist in hohen schulen verderbt worden an sytten und

work, Eberlin traces the perversion of the tithe and with it the degeneration of the clergy. As they accumulated more wealth, the priests ceased to be servants of the church and became instead its lords.[108] In the 'Seven Devout Priests Complain about Their Plight,' Eberlin suggests that the monks initially criticized clerical greed, but soon came on side.[109] The 'Last Confederate' provides more details of how the endowed orders assembled wealth for themselves until they, too, were lords of powerful ecclesiastical institutions.[110] In the end, the priests and monks together established the kingdom of the Antichrist with which they rule the world.[111] These lords of the church Eberlin labels 'church thieves' because they rob the true preachers and the poor of their livelihood.[112]

Eberlin singles out specific groups of the 'church thieves' for further attention. He revives Luther's description of the 'mass-reading' priests. These, he says, provide no service to the community and celebrate the mass contrary to the instructions of Christ.[113] Similar scorn is directed against the monks. In 'A Friendly Exhortation to Augsburg,' he assigns them the role held by the mendicants alone in his earlier writings:

> It is also important to note that originally it was not the pure Gospel that was preached to the German nation but one mixed and authorized by the papists. For Saint Boniface and Saint Kilianus and others were sent by the popes, and thereafter the matter was handled by monks, as is indicated still by the old Irish cloisters in many large cities of the German nation and by many saints in German lands who were Irish monks.[114]

In the 'Last Confederate,' Eberlin turns his attention for the first time to the military orders. He attacks their very *raison d'être* by denying that

---

mainungen. Die ernstlichsten gwissen send durch Munchstand in Baals dienst gefurt worden. Alle welt ist durch bapsts gsatz verknupfft.'

[108] 'Letzter Bundesgenosse,' Enders, vol. 1, p. 176: 'Durch solliche wyse ist bald so vil gepracticiert worden, das uss den dienern herren send worden, uss den pflegern pfaffen, uss den pfaffen pfarrer, uss den pfarrern Junckerbischoff, welcher mer guts gehabt hat von dem zehenden, ist ains grössern gwalts gsyn.'

[109] 'Sieben fromme Pfaffen klagen ihre Not,' Enders, vol. 2, pp. 69–70.

[110] 'Letzter Bundesgenosse,' Enders, vol. 1, pp. 177–8 (= Laube 2: 1041–3).

[111] Ibid., p. 178: 'Also uss fraintlicher hilff und handtraychung der gmainen christen ist dem Antichrist und synem huffen uffgericht worden ain königklich rych, darin in gottes namen wider got taglich gehandelt wurt, als diser tag zaigt, und sendt münch und pfaffen worden herren aller welt.' (= Laube 2: 1042).

[112] Ibid. (= Laube 2: 1043).

[113] Ibid., p. 187: 'Ich hab offt gedacht, war zu doch die messerey pfaffin geordnet seyen. . . . Auch laisten sie kain hilff den pfarrern, wollen die pfarrer hilff haben, so miessen sie sonder helffer bestellen. Auch ist es widder die ordnung Christi, das man mess halte yn mainung wie man etlich hundert iar gehalten hatt.'

[114] 'Eine freundliche Vermahnung zu Augsburg,' Enders, vol. 2, p. 150.

the Gospel can be spread with the sword. Rather, the crusading ideal is the work of the devil. Satan established the military orders to enlist the nobility to defend his other villainous pursuits.[115]

With the retirement of the fifteen confederates and seven devout priests, Eberlin returned to the format of the signed pamphlet in his own voice. The question of what authority a council has to decide on matters of faith is the third of those considered in 'A Little Book Which Answers Three Questions' and indicates that Eberlin likely wrote this work in early spring 1523 when plans for a general council in Germany were being proposed.[116] Shortly thereafter, Eberlin wrote the first of two epistles to the council and citizens of Ulm, likely in preparation for his planned visit to the city in the summer of that year. 'A Short Written Report on Faith to the Citizens of Ulm' is dated 24 February 1523.[117]

Although these two works concentrate on matters of belief, they do provide further insight into the development of Eberlin's anticlerical polemic. The first letter to Ulm derives extensive biblical support for the claim that the pope, or for that matter anyone claiming to be the head of the church or Christ's vicar, is the Antichrist. Christ alone is the head of the church who calls and justifies its members. He has promised to be with his followers throughout time and consequently needs no vicar. All others are, therefore, servants of the church and should not claim the titles of head or vicar.[118] In addition, two of Eberlin's favourite scapegoats reappear: the professors and the monks. These he identifies with the Scribes and Pharisees who reject the Gospel.[119] To the monks Eberlin devotes a specific discussion. In relating the importance of faith to membership in the true church, Eberlin allows, in passing, that

---

[115] 'Letzter Bundesgenosse,' Enders, vol. 1, pp. 192–5.

[116] Riggenbach, *Eberlin und sein Reformprogramm*, p. 205 argued that the concerns of this work reflected Eberlin's experiences during his trip to southern Germany in the summer of 1523 and, therefore, it must have been written after his return to Wittenberg in November of that year. Radlkofer, pp. 90–2; Heger, p. 26 and Brecht, 'Eberlin in Wittenberg,' p. 52, all argue for the early spring. During the Nuremberg *Reichstag*, which was convened on 17 November 1522, a proposal was put forward for a council which would include secular representation. On 8 February 1523 this proposal was presented to the papal nuncio and on 6 March was proclaimed by imperial edict. In the meantime it was widely known through informal channels.

[117] 'Ein kurzer schriftlicher Bericht des Glaubens, an die Ulmer,' Enders, vol. 2, p. 174.

[118] Ibid., pp. 176–7.

[119] 'Ein Büchlein, worin auf drei Frage geantwortet wird,' Enders, vol. 2, p. 159: 'Und was die welt hin würfft, nimpt Gott an, was die welt uff hebt, würfft gott nider. Du meinst, Scribe und Pharisei der Juden, auch die Philosophi under den Heiden solten fürderlich Christus leer angenommen haben, auch die hohen schůler und Klosterleüth zů unsern zeyten, . . .'

salvation is possible within the monastery.[120] Nonetheless, he identifies the monasteries as places of the greatest godlessness and claims again that the cloistered are under the curse of God.[121] In contrast to the advice of 'Against the Imprudent Departure,' Eberlin here not only discourages the people of Ulm from committing their children to the monasteries, but also encourages monks and nuns to flee the cloisters if possible.[122]

In the introduction to 'A Short Report on Faith,' Eberlin had commented to the citizens of Ulm on the importance of his exodus to Wittenberg:

> God be praised, Who led me to the flowing, curative waters of the Gospel, to Wittenberg, there to hear God's Word and to have timely answers to pressing questions; praise God and rejoice with me, for He has done great things for me and His name is holy.[123]

Ultimately, the standard for Eberlin's new understanding of the Gospel and the reform it demanded was to be drawn from the teachings of Luther. However, throughout much of this period he regarded Luther as one of the trinity of Luther, Melanchthon and Karlstadt. Gradually Luther's specific vision of reform came to dominate Eberlin's. In this sense, Christian Peters's characterization of Eberlin as a conservative student of Luther is accurate. There is a corresponding waning of the influence of Karlstadt, but this is a gradual process and Eberlin continues throughout these writings to accord Karlstadt a place of prominence in the reform movement. Eberlin's continued respect for Karlstadt perhaps reflects a deep personal concern for the unity of the movement, but certainly it suggests that the perceived split between Luther and Karlstadt in 1522 was not as apparent to contemporaries, even in Wittenberg, as has been assumed.[124]

The growing influence of Luther on Eberlin throughout these works is reflected clearly by the softening of the anticlerical polemic in them. This does not suggest so much that Eberlin abandoned a radical reform

[120] 'Ein kurzer Bericht an die Ulmer,' Enders, vol. 2, p. 175: '... der gehört zu dem Christlichen hauffen, ... er sy arm oder reich, knecht oder frey, fraw oder man, Münnych oder lay, ...'; p. 180: '... welcher nit fliehen mag, leide sich als ainem thurn und begere hilf von got, deren gleichen fragen vil magstu auflösen, so du in deim glauben wol underricht byst.'

[121] Ibid., p. 180: 'Zu unsern zeiten ist der kloster stnd ain pfitz aller ungottssamkait, ...'; p. 189: '... wann ain grosser fluch gots ist über das kloster volck, ...'

[122] Ibid., p. 180: '... darumb sol sich kainer darein geben, und welcher darauss mag kommen, thü es, ...'; p. 189: '... thü kain künd auch inn reformiert klöster, ... und wa du mit radt und hylff magst ain person auss dem kloster stand erlösen, thü es zü lob dem theüren blut Jesu Christi, ...'

[123] 'Ein kurzer Bericht des Glaubens,' Enders, vol. 2, p. 174.

[124] Karl Müller, Luther und Karlstadt; Stücke aus ihrem gegenseitigen Verhältnis (Tübingen, 1907), p. 35.

programme for a more moderate Lutheran one as it indicates that he followed a general move among the Wittenbergers in toning down the unreserved use of anticlerical broadsides. This involved, on the one hand, following Luther's lead in 'A Faithful Admonition' by withdrawing from direct anticlerical agitation. On the other hand, Eberlin developed more fully the distinction outlined in 'The Fifteen Confederates' between the true and false priests. In this, the fruit of Eberlin's study in Wittenberg is also evident in the new practice of defining the true priesthood in terms of 1 Timothy 3 and 4, and Titus 1, and in his appeal to the episcopacy as the basis of a reformed clerical order. However, this involved for Eberlin, as it did for his mentor, not so much a retreat from anticlerical polemics as their redeployment. As Eberlin's treatment of the 'temple servants' indicates, anticlerical barbs remained an important weapon in the arsenal of the Wittenberg Reformers, although one which had to be used with greater caution than previously.

Interestingly, the prominent role of the friars among the temple servants fades into the background in the writings of 1522. In fact, aside from the translation of Probst's history, Eberlin's references to his former brethren and the mendicant orders generally are surprisingly infrequent. He touches on the common charge of the laxity of mendicant confessors when the first of the seven devout priests claims that rather than rebuke him for having a concubine, the Franciscan Observants admire him and grant the woman easy absolution.[125] Similarly, 'A Little Book Which Answers Three Questions' makes passing reference to the role of the friars in building an unnecessary number of churches.[126]

However, Eberlin's concern with the friars reappears when he speaks personally to the people of Ulm. 'A Short Report on Faith' opens with a description of Eberlin's former service to the Babylonian whore and expulsion from his order.[127] He warns his readers against the mendicant agents of the Antichrist and recommends that their preachers be replaced by evangelical pastors.[128] Eberlin concluded the short discussion of monasticism in this work: 'I will say no more at this time until my spirit prompts me to write further.'[129] He was, in fact, soon prompted to write on this issue. A series of conflicts between the Reformers and representatives of the Franciscan order soon called for responses not only from Eberlin, but from a number of his fellow apostates as well.

---

[125] 'Sieben fromme Pfaffen klagen ihre Not,' Enders, vol. 2, p. 62.
[126] 'Ein Büchlein worin drei Frage geantwortet wird,' Enders, vol. 2, p. 154.
[127] 'Ein kurzer Bericht des Glaubens,' Enders, vol. 2, p. 173.
[128] Ibid., pp. 190–1.
[129] Ibid., p. 189.

CHAPTER FIVE

'Against the profaners of God's creatures'

Christian Peters's redating of Eberlin's 'Against the Profaners of God's Creatures' raises a host of new questions about the nature of this work and its place in Eberlin's *corpus*. Riggenbach's identification of this pamphlet as a radical Karlstadtian polemic, written before Eberlin came under the moderating influences of Luther and Melanchthon, obscured the more problematic questions raised by it.[1] As Martin Brecht has claimed, despite the radicalism of its rhetoric, 'Against the Profaners' never really oversteps the boundaries of the Wittenberg theology of the time.[2] Yet, the radicalism of Eberlin's language and the general denunciation of the clergy contained in it contrast sharply with the tone and purposes of Eberlin's previous writings in Wittenberg. This discrepancy was noted by Christian Peters who suggested, as a result, that this work belonged with the pamphlets directed against the Franciscan order in the summer of 1523.[3] Despite certain specific criticisms of the Franciscans contained in this work, I prefer to regard it as a distinct salvo preceding the more general broadside against the order. Nonetheless, it does belong with the more radically anticlerical charges of the spring and summer of 1523 and, as such, provides interesting insights into the development not only of Eberlin's anticlerical polemics, but of those of the Wittenberg Reformers more generally.

'Against the Profaners' claims to revive a controversy from mid-1521 in which Karlstadt quarrelled with Johann Fritzhans and Franz Seyler, both of whom were Franciscans from the city of Annaberg, on the practice of consecrating water and salt.[4] In the midst of debate over the

---

[1] See above, pp. 94–5.

[2] Martin Brecht, 'Johann Eberlin von Günzburg in Wittenberg,' *Wertheimer Jahrbuch*, 1983 (1985), p. 49.

[3] Christian Peters, *Johann Eberlin von Günzburg ca. 1465–1533: Franziskanischer Reformer, Humanist und konservativer Reformator* (Gütersloh, 1994), p. 173.

[4] Eberlin refused to identify Karlstadt's opponents, but they and the controversy were identified by Max Radlkofer, *Johann Eberlin von Günzburg und sein Vetter Hans Jakob Wehe von Leipheim* (Nördlingen, 1887), p. 51. On the conflict between them and Karlstadt, see Hermann Barge, *Andreas Bodenstein von Karlstadt*, vol. 1: *Karlstadt und die Anfänge der Reformation* (2nd edn, Nieuwkoop, 1968), pp. 206–18. There appears no evidence to support the claim of Roberta Adamcyk that Eberlin was a participant in the original controversy while still in Ulm. Roberta Adamcyk, *Die Flugschriften des Johann Eberlin von Günzburg (1465–1533)* Phil. Diss. (Vienna, 1981), p. 6.

extent of Eberlin's radical Karlstadtian phase in early 1522, and the attempts to identify Lutheran and Karlstadtian elements in Eberlin's theological statements, Gottfried Geiger suggested that in assessing the relationship between 'Against the Profaners' and Karlstadt's earlier conflict with the Annaberg Franciscans, attention be shifted from the person of Karlstadt to his opponents. According to Geiger, 'Against the Profaners' was a form of self-recommendation, intended by Eberlin to introduce himself to Karlstadt, and the important element of the earlier controversy on which Eberlin wished to play was the identity of Seyler and Fritzhans as Franciscans. In so doing, he was able to indicate that he had left his Franciscan past behind him and was willing and able to enter the lists against the mendicants.[5] Recently Christian Peters has taken Geiger's approach one step further. Peters noted that in the introduction to 'Against the Profaners' Eberlin not only refers to the earlier conflict involving Karlstadt and the Annaberg Franciscans, but also that he charges Seyler with subsequently spreading false teachings.[6] Eberlin's pamphlet is, therefore, not a postscript to the original controversy, but a response to Seyler's activities in opposing the progress of the Reformation in Annaberg in late 1522 and early 1523. Tensions between Evangelicals and Catholics there reached a straining point in June 1523 when the local Evangelical preacher was expelled from his post. The Evangelical party responded with a flood of *Flugschriften*. According to Peters, 'Against the Profaners' was one of these.[7]

In the original conflict Karlstadt had indicated that the practice of consecrating water and salt had no basis in Scripture. In 'Against the Profaners' Eberlin declares his intention to prove that it is contrary to Scripture.[8] Nonetheless, 'Against the Profaners' has little to do with Karlstadt's two pamphlets from the quarrel with Fritzhans and Seyler. Karlstadt did not actually attack consecration, but sought to expose the abuses associated with it: 'I do not say that the holy water and salt hurt a person . . . but I only ridicule the foolish and blind usage which people attach to water and salt, placing their hope on the words and promises of men, when their hope should remain alone in God's Word.'[9]

---

[5] Gottfried Geiger, 'Die reformatorischen Initia Johann Eberlins von Günzburg nach seinen Flugschriften,' in *Festgabe für Ernst Walter Zeeden zum 60. Geburtstag am 14. Mai 1976*, ed. Horst Rabe *et al.* (Münster, 1976), p. 197.

[6] Peters, pp. 174–5.

[7] Ibid., pp. 179–84. Peters's interpretation has the added benefit of providing a more likely explanation for the delay until 1525 for the publication of this pamphlet. See Peters, p. 73.

[8] 'Wider die Schänder der Creaturen Gottes,' Enders, vol. 2, p. 2.

[9] 'Von geweychtem Wasser und salzc,' Köhler *et al.* F. 46, #127, Aiii(b).

Consequently, his task lay primarily in reinterpreting the biblical texts on which the church had based this practice. Eberlin, on the other hand, openly denounces the practice and thereby lays the basis for an open attack on the sacrament of ordination.

Eberlin adopts as his first premise the claim that all of God's creatures are good. This he derives from the obvious passages in Genesis 1, as well as statements in Psalm 145 [146:6] and 1 Peter 2. Even the heathens realize that apparently harmful creatures can be put to good uses.[10] However, the heart of the polemic lies in Eberlin's exegesis of 1 Timothy 4:1–6, and especially verses four and five: 'For every creature of God is good, and nothing to be refused, if it be received with thanksgiving: For it is sanctified by the word of God and prayer.' This allows him to claim that all are consecrated through the Word and prayer, not ecclesiastical rite, and that any distinctions (for example, between clean and unclean) derived from the Old Testament have been superseded.[11] Furthermore, he is able to identify his opponents as those who 'listen to deceitful spirits and doctrines that come from the devils.'[12]

Eberlin then shifts his tack and, citing Matthew 15 and 23 and Titus 1, argues that the moral worth of objects is not inherent, but dependent on the disposition of the one using them.[13] These citations have the added benefit of implicitly identifying Eberlin's opponents as Pharisees and false apostles. This becomes more explicit in the subsequent exegesis of Titus 1:14–15: 'Not giving heed to Jewish fables, and commandments of men, that turn from the truth. Unto the pure all things are pure: but unto them that are defiled and unbelieving is nothing pure; but even their mind and conscience is defiled.' The Jewish fables which Paul denounces Eberlin identifies as the consecration of churches and objects used in the mass. Given the opportunity for a sweeping denunciation of the ceremonialism of the church, Eberlin

---

[10] 'Wider die Schänder der Creaturen Gottes,' Enders, vol. 2, p. 4.

[11] Ibid., p. 5: 'Und Paulus 1. Thim. 4. Alle creaturen gotes seind gůt, Der schöpffer ist gůt und das beste gůt, unnd alle seine creaturen seind gut und fast gut.'; p. 13: 'Das aber gott etliche thier rain oder unrain urtaylt im gsetz, ist auffgehabt durch Paulum 1. Thim. iiij. unnd Thito am 1.'; p. 14: 'Also sagt Paulus, alle creatur gottes ist gůt, und nichts verwürflich, das mit dancksagung entpfangen wirdt, denn es wird gehayliget durch das wortt gottes und das gebet, . . .'; p. 19: '. . . wann Paulus sagt on allen zůsatz, alle creatur würt geweihet durch das wort gottes und gebet zů got, . . . nit allain von den pfaffen.'

[12] Ibid., pp. 11–12.

[13] Ibid., p. 6: 'Bist du gůt, so geschicht dir, wie Romanos am achten geschriben stat, wir wissen aber, das denen, die Got lieben, alle dinng zů dem besten dienen, die nach dem fürsatz berůfft seind, unnd bald darnach, ich bins gewyss, das weder tod noch leben, noch engel, noch Fürstenthum, noch gewalt, noch gegen wertigs noch zůkünfftiges, noch hohes, noch tiefes, noch kain ander creatur mag uns scheyden von der liebe gottes, die in Christo Jhesu ist unnserm herren.'

remains unusually subdued and restricts his argument to the alleged claim of his opponents that prayers offered in a church are somehow more efficacious than those offered elsewhere. In response, Eberlin argues that God must be worshipped in the spirit (John 4) and cites Christ's command to pray in one's own closet (Matthew 6:6).[14]

From the consecration of objects, Eberlin turns his attention to the consecration of individuals and ordination of the clergy. He begins by applying the curse contained in Malachi 2:2: 'I will even send a curse upon you, I will curse your blessings: yea, I have cursed them already ... [Malachi 2:2]' to the contemporary priesthood. From this he argues that consecration and ordination are, in fact, signs of all those under God's curse and in the domain of the devil, namely monks, nuns and priests.[15] Eberlin exhibits his ability as a popular writer in clarifying how ordination sets the clergy apart from the laity:

> ... as soon as one enters the clerical estate, his entire character and conduct indicate that he is more crooked than another person. They become pitiless, unbearable, unfriendly, untrue, false, knavish, reckless, greedy, etc. [It seems] as if God's curse works visibly in them, so that they are cursed in the consecration and God openly shows that the blessing and consecration of the invented soft-bishops is nothing other than a curse and malediction from God.[16]

In sharp contrast to his earlier Wittenberg writings, Eberlin here denounces the first estate as a whole. The religious generally are denounced as the enemies of God:

> In no place does one find more cursed, consecrated people in clothing, herbs, water, salt, candles, places, etc. than in the cloisters, and nowhere are there more of God's curses than there, according to Jeremiah, because one openly teaches and acts against God, and blasphemes all of God's truth and that of his confessors.[17]

While discussing the religious, Eberlin pauses to throw scorn on the mendicants in particular. He takes an oblique swipe at the burial privileges of the friars, arguing that neither the Patriarchs nor the first Christians were buried in consecrated ground, and that the consecration of graveyards and the whole burial ritual cause the greatest damage of

---

[14] Ibid., pp. 7–9. Eberlin here may be reflecting the argument developed by Karlstadt against the monastic profession and its justification on the basis of saying canonical hours. See 'Von gelubden unterrichtung,' Köhler *et al.*, F. 134, #362, F–Fiii.

[15] 'Wider die Schänder,' Enders, vol. 2, p. 15: 'Gott sagt durch den propheten, Ich will verflüchenn was jr segnen oder weyhen, ... Sihe aber ob nit sollich weyhung sey ain haymlich aber mal des teuffels, da mit er alle die zaychnet, so inn gottes flůch seind, Nämlich Munchen, Nunnen, pfaffen, kůrtz alles das zů gehört dem valschen reich, ...'

[16] Ibid., p. 16.

[17] Ibid., pp. 15–16.

all abuses associated with consecration.[18] In this context, he attacks specifically the Portiuncula indulgence of the Franciscans.[19] However, in the end Eberlin's concern is not specifically with the monks, but with all who disguise themselves under the appearance of holiness.[20]

The abusiveness of Eberlin's language against the clergy and the breadth of his denunciations of the first estate in this pamphlet stand in marked contrast to the language and goals of the works immediately preceding it. Eberlin's ongoing praise of Karlstadt and continued appeal to his writings raises yet again the question of whether this work reflects a more radical, Karlstadtian programme. Certainly there is some basis for such a claim. In the introduction to 'Against the Profaners,' Eberlin commented on the tactics of the Wittenberg leaders:

> . . . if, as one says, the gentle Christian teachers, Luther, Melanch-thon and others, were no longer on earth, if these dear men were strangled, the sophistic papists would have peace. No, no, these men hinder the misfortune of the Antichristians more with gentleness than they help it, . . . Oh, how earnest, zealous and sharp would be the attack with pen, mouth and sword if these mild teachers did not so greatly oppose it, . . .[21]

This Bernhard Riggenbach read, in connection with Eberlin's claim to be taking a stronger stand than had Karlstadt against Fritzhans and Seyler, as an indication that Eberlin was criticizing the mildness of Luther and Melanchthon.[22] Riggenbach's assessment has survived through much of the literature on Eberlin.[23]

Furthermore, elements of Eberlin's polemic accord better with the reforming vision traditionally associated with Karlstadt than that identified with Luther. Calvin Pater has indicated that Karlstadt avoids

---

[18] Ibid., pp. 18–19: 'Inn kaynem ding haben die lewtbescheysser betrüglicher scheinlicher hilff biss her für den teüffel gesůcht, dann in der weyhung der kirchoff, . . .'

[19] Ibid., p. 19: 'Als auch ain bůch der grawen münch leret, man soll am ersten tag Augusti in jr kirchen den vollkommnen ablass lassen beten für die todten, das beten vermŏge aber niemant dann die grawen gugler, unnd man erlangt auch gnadbrieff für die todten.' See Enders, vol. 3, p. 290.

[20] Ibid., p. 16: 'Ich rede jetzt nit allain von den seelosen Klosterleüten, in angesicht aller menschen, aber von denen, wŏlche auch erbarn haylgen scheyn haimlich unnd offentlich tragen.'

[21] Ibid., p. 4.

[22] Bernhard Riggenbach, *Johann Eberlin von Günzburg und sein Reformprogramm: Ein Beitrag zur Geschichte des sechszehnten Jahrhunderts* (Tübingen, 1874), p. 83.

[23] Radlkofer, p. 49; Wilhelm Lucke, *Die Enstehung der '15 Bundesgenossen' des Johann Eberlins von Günzburg*, Phil. Diss. (Halle, 1902), p. 21; Hans-Herbert Ahrens, *Die religiösen, nationalen und sozialen Gedenken Johann Eberlin von Günzburgs mit besonderer Berücksichtigung seiner anonymen Flugschriften*, Phil. Diss. (Hamburg, 1939), p. 31.

the distinction between the laity and clergy more firmly than Luther.[24] One might see in Eberlin's denunciation of the whole clergy as a cursed estate a reflection of this more radically laicized reforming impulse. In February 1522 Karlstadt preached a sermon on Malachi which was then printed in Wittenberg. In it Karlstadt does not denounce the clergy specifically with reference to Malachi 2:2, but he does provide a general indictment of the clerical estate.[25] Furthermore, there is some plausibility in regarding Eberlin's description of the primitive church as a reflection of Karlstadt's liturgical reforms in Wittenberg: 'Christ held his Testament in common sittings, clothes and places, and, without a doubt, so did the apostles and the first Christians.'[26]

However, none of this makes Eberlin a radical Karlstadtian or a critic of Luther's pace of reform. Eberlin's discussion of the mildness of the Wittenbergers continued: 'The time may come when one will wish said teachers and lords a long life and, nonetheless, all will be in vain.'[27] Throughout 'The Fifteen Confederates,' Eberlin frequently raised the spectre of popular unrest if the cause of the Gospel was endangered. It would seem that here again he is offering Wittenberg as an orderly alternative to unruly popular reform.

Martin Brecht's suggestion that 'Against the Profaners' remains within the boundaries of contemporary Wittenberg theology further undermines the characterization of this work as radical or Karlstadtian. Brecht himself did not undertake a re-evaluation of it. However, noting the differences between the enterprises of Eberlin in 'Against the Profaners' and Karlstadt in his two pamphlets on the consecration of water and salt, Christian Peters claimed that Eberlin develops an independent theological position from Karlstadt's. This is clear already in Eberlin's opening premise that all things as the creation of God are good, which rests on a creation theology derived from Luther's Genesis sermons of early 1523.[28] In fact, even the basis of Eberlin's attack on ordination develops out of a fundamentally Lutheran theological position. In his discussion of the importance of the disposition of a

---

[24] Calvin Augustine Pater, *Karlstadt as the Father of the Baptist Movements: The Emergence of Lay Protestantism* (Toronto, 1984), p. 66.

[25] 'Predig oder homilien uber den prophetē. Malachiam gnant,' Köhler *et al.*, F 64, #166, Aiii (b): 'Wir haben keine hefftiger und giffter feinde des heiligē Ewangelii / dan Bepst. Cardinalinen Bischoffen Pfaffen und Monichen. . . . Sie seind erger dan Heyden. und fechten offenlich wider gotis wort / und wellens doch kein wort haben.' See Pater, p. 186.

[26] 'Wider die Schänder,' Enders, vol. 2, p. 8.

[27] Ibid., p. 4. See also Günther Heger, *Johann Eberlin von Günzburg und seine Vorstellungen über eine Reform in Reich und Kirche* (Berlin, 1985), p. 24.

[28] Peters, p. 175.

person using morally neutral objects, Eberlin draws on Luther's arguments about the priesthood of all believers.[29] Elsewhere he juxtaposes faith with consecration and, on the basis of the absolute importance of the former, erases the distinction between the clergy and the laity.[30]

As Eberlin's argument develops, his proximity to Luther becomes even more apparent. The very basis for his rejection of the sacramental nature of ordination likely derives from Luther's discussion of extreme unction in 'The Babylonian Captivity of the Church.' Interestingly, Luther, too, bases his argument on 1 Timothy 4, and then illustrates his point with specific reference to the consecration of water and salt: 'Nevertheless, we shall number it among those "sacraments" which we have instituted, such as the blessing and sprinkling of salt and water. For we cannot deny that any creature whatsoever may be consecrated by the Word and by prayer, as the apostle Paul teaches us [1 Tim. 4:4–5].'[31]

It is possible, then, that Luther's words suggested to Eberlin the idea of opening his attack on ordination by concentrating on the consecration of water and salt, and thereby linking the current dispute to Seyler's earlier conflict with Karlstadt. This suspicion is reinforced when one turns to Luther's discussion of ordination in 'The Babylonian Captivity of the Church.' Luther assigned ordination, like other forms of consecration, to the realm of invented 'sacraments': 'I therefore admit that ordination is a certain churchly rite, on par with many others introduced by the church fathers, such as the consecration of vessels, houses, vestments, *water, salt*, candles, herbs, wine, and the like'[32] [my emphasis]. Shortly thereafter, he denied the validity of a priesthood instituted to read masses and recite the canonical hours:

> Therefore, those who are ordained only to read the canonical hours and offer masses are indeed papal priests, but not Christian priests, because they not only do not preach, but they are not even called to preach ... Thus they are hour-reading and mass-saying priests – sort of living idols called priests – really such priests as Jeroboam

---

[29] Cf. above n. 13 and 'Von der Freiheit eines Christenmenschen' WA, 7:27–8: '. . . wie S. Paulus leret Ro. 8. "Alle ding müssen helffenn den ausserwelten zu yhrem besten," es sey leben, sterben, sund, frumkeit, gut und bösses, wie man es nennen kan. . . . ich kann mich on allen dingen bessern nach der seelen, das auch der todt und leyden müssen mir dienen und nützlich seyn zur seligkeit, . . . da keyn ding ist sso gut, sso bösse, es muss mir dienen zu gut, sso ich glaube, und darff seyn doch nit, sondern meyn glaub ist mir gnugsam.' See also Peters, pp. 175–6.

[30] 'Wider die Schänder,' Enders, vol. 2, p. 17.

[31] 'De captivitate Babylonica ecclesiae praeludium,' WA, 6:570. Luther employs the same argument with regard to confirmation, p. 550.

[32] Ibid., p. 561.

ordained, in Beth-aven, taken from the lowest dregs of the people,
and not of Levi's tribe [1 Kings 12:31].[33]

Surprisingly, given his development of the concept of 'true prayer' in the
denunciation of consecration, Eberlin does not take this opportunity to
denounce again the reading of canonical hours and the clergy associated
with it. Nonetheless, other references indicate that he does adopt
Luther's criteria for judging the true and false priesthoods. His
definition of the true purpose of a church lays emphasis on preaching,
prayer and the reception of the sacraments to the exclusion of other
forms of worship.[34] Elsewhere, in denouncing the consecration of
church bells and the role of bishops in this practice, he makes the point
more clearly: 'I say, dear wine-bishop, that refers to other bells than
those you consecrate, . . . These bells are earnest, true preachers of
God's Word [Psalm 10]. Through hearing such bells, one believes and is
fit to pray and avert all of God's anger.'[35]

The point of Eberlin's attack on ordination is, however, much
broader than Luther's in 'The Babylonian Captivity of the Church.' He
is not content with merely a rejection of the 'hour-reading,' 'mass-
saying' priests or a recognition of ordination as a churchly rite. Rather,
he goes further in attacking all priests and religious and in defining
consecration and ordination as a sign of the devil. But even in this
Eberlin's charges were not novel. In 'On the Misuse of the Mass,' at the
height of his campaign to destroy the false papal priesthood, Luther,
too, denounced the papal clergy in such radical terms:

> He [the Pope] calls the clerics his priests, among whom he wants to
> be highest priest and prince. He alone has made them priestly by
> blessing them, anointing them with oil, and commanding them to
> wear long clothes; and he maintains that he has impressed an
> indelible mark on their souls, which, however, is nothing other than
> the mark of the beast in Revelation [13].[36]

Despite the sharpness of his polemic, when Eberlin looks to reform of
ordination, his suggestions are in line with his own earlier statements
and those of Luther. He advocates the continuance of the practice so
long as it is regarded as a tradition with no more significance than the

---

[33] Ibid., p. 113.

[34] 'Wider die Schänder,' Enders, vol. 2, p. 8: 'Bey den Christen soll ain Tempel nit
annderst geacht werden, dann als ain gemain haus, verordnet zů der versamlung
Christlichs volcks, zů hören predig, empfahenn die Sacrament, und andere Christliche
gemayne sachenn ausszůrichten.'

[35] Ibid., p. 9. Luther too made reference to the blessing of bells. 'De captivitate
Babylonica ecclesiae praeludium,' WA, 6:566.

[36] 'Vom Mißbrauch der Messe,' WA, 8:540.

conferral of office on local secular officials.[37] In this, Eberlin is only drawing the practical conclusion of Luther's distinction between clergy and laity as one of calling.[38] Eberlin himself had made similar suggestions in the tenth and fifteenth confederates.[39] And in Eberlin's discussion of the calling and installation of an evangelical pastor in this work one sees strong parallels to Luther's advice to the congregation in Leisnig.[40]

'Against the Profaners' is, then, not the radical departure from Lutheran orthodoxy which earlier interpreters of Eberlin's writings saw in it. Nonetheless, it does stand out as an anomaly within the context of Eberlin's Wittenberg writings, if for no other reason than by virtue of the radicalism of its language. That Eberlin's polemics became so embittered in early 1523 can hardly be explained in terms of the evolution of his reforming thought – as we have seen, the long-term trend there was towards increasing mildness. Rather, we must look to the immediate context for the writing of this work. Peters is correct, I believe, in his attempt to link it to the antifraternal campaign of 1523. As we shall see, in the spring of 1523 the Franciscans were coming out against the Reformation more forcefully than ever before. Seyler, as a member of the order and primary opponent of the Gospel in Annaberg, became for Eberlin a symbol of this new apostasy by the Franciscans, and the virulence of Eberlin's denunciation of him should come as no surprise.

---

[37] 'Wider die Schänder,' Enders, vol., 2, p. 16: 'Wann man die pfaffen weyhung der personen halb achtete als ain herrlichait, so man pflegt zů gebrauchenn in ainer erwölung gmainer diener, oder amptleüt, möcht man es erleyden und lassen fürgeen. Als ain yetliche stat ain sondere weyss hat zů erklärenn, das diser oder jhener Amptman sey erwölt. Also, so man ainen oder vile erwölet zů diener der Christlichenn gemain, zů pfarrern oder pfaffen, erzaigte man ain eusserlichen scheyn und geberd oder herlichait, dafür solte man halten die weyhung, und sonst für nichts u.'

[38] 'An den Christlichen Adel,' WA, 6:404–69; 'De captivitate Babylonica ecclesiae praeludium,' WA, 6:564. See Peters, p. 178.

[39] See above, pp. 89–90.

[40] Cf. 'Wider die Schänder,' Enders, vol. 2, p. 16; 'Daß ein christliche Versammlung oder Gemeine Recht und Macht habe, alle Lehre zu Urtheilen und Lehrer zu berufen, ein und abzusetzen, Grund und Ursach aus der Schrift,' WA, 6:408–16.

CHAPTER SIX

'A fool or an arch-rogue'

Eberlin's anticlerical asides in the works written in Wittenberg in 1522 and early 1523 suggest that, like his mentor, he withdrew from direct anticlerical agitation, but not from an anticlerical stance. This suspicion is confirmed by the appearance of 'Against the Profaners' with its scathing denunciations of the clergy and identification of ordination as a mark of the apocalyptic beast. That Eberlin would adopt such a radically anticlerical stance after his campaign to define and enlist support for an evangelical clergy, especially in the wake of the culmination of that campaign as embodied in the persons of the seven pious priests, indicates that anticlerical diatribes remained an important polemical weapon for the Reformers. The value of this weapon, and the importance which the Reformers attached to it, is indicated more clearly by the 1523 campaign against the Franciscans.

The opening salvoes of this campaign appear at first glance to be almost haphazard. Eberlin's 'A Second Admonition to the Council of Ulm' develops into a comprehensive attack on the friars, but only under the guise of exposing their opposition to the Reformation there. Heinrich von Kettenbach's work begins as an exegetical sermon on the text of Matthew 7. Johannes Schwan's 'An Epistle in Which He Shows From the Bible and Scripture Why He Left the Franciscan Order' and Francis Lambert's 'The Reasons Why He Rejects the Status of and Association With the Minors' appear to be merely personal justifications for departure from the Order. Only thereafter do the titles of the pamphlets betray more fully the intentions of their authors. Johannes Briesmann's 'Response to Caspar Schatzgeyer, OFM' indicates clearly the greater context in which these works were written. The other pamphlets, Schwan's 'A Brief Conception of the Frightful State of the Monks,' Lambert's 'An Evangelical Description of the Franciscan Rule,' Heinrich Spelt's 'A True Declaration or Explanation of the Profession, Vows and Life Which the Coloured False Religious Pursue Against Evangelical Freedom and Christian Love' and Eberlin's 'Against the False Religious Known as the Barefoot Friars or Franciscans,' are easily identifiable as more thorough denunciations of the Franciscans, other mendicants and, in some cases the religious more generally.

I have argued above that these pamphlets actually amount to a concerted campaign against the Franciscans, and to a lesser extent the mendicants more generally. Although there has been passing acknowledgement of a relationship between these works, no detailed analysis of this campaign has been forthcoming.[1] The failure to treat these works as a group has obscured not only their place in the development of Reformation anticlericalism, but also a crucial aspect of the evolution of this anticlerical tradition itself. The latter point becomes clear when one examines Luther's relationship to the campaign of 1523. Traditionally Luther's name is mentioned with reference to any of these pamphlets only insofar as they are seen to reflect some of his ideas or statements. Biographers of Eberlin have debated whether or not 'Against the False Religious' reflects Luther's arguments in 'Against the Spiritual Estate,' apparently on the basis of the similarities of the titles of these two works.[2] A more fruitful line of inquiry has been opened by those who have pointed to Eberlin's debt to Luther's 'Judgement on Monastic Vows.'[3]

However, Luther's role in this campaign was likely much more active than has traditionally been assumed. He can be tied directly to only two of the nine *Flugschriften* written against the Franciscans. But if Luther did not orchestrate this campaign, he certainly instigated it. In the autumn of 1522 Caspar Schatzgeyer responded to Luther's 'Judgement on Monastic Vows' and 'On Abolishing the Private Mass' in 'Revelation Against the False Writing.' In January 1523 Luther commissioned Briesmann's response to Schatzgeyer, and he provided Briesmann with specific instructions on how to answer the Franciscan Provincial Minister.[4] In early July Luther also wrote a prefatory letter for Lambert's 'Evangelical Description of the Franciscan Rule.'[5] In both cases he emphasized the status of the authors as former Franciscans to reinforce the veracity of their claims about their former order. If not

---

[1] See above, pp. 1–30.

[2] Bernhard Riggenbach, *Johann Eberlin von Günzburg und sein Reformprogramm: Ein Beitrag zur Geschichte des sechszehnten Jahrhunderts* (Tübingen, 1874), p. 144; Max Radlkofer, *Johann Eberlin von Günzburg und sein Vetter Hans Jakob Wehe von Leipheim* (Nördlingen, 1887), pp. 114–15; Günther Heger, *Johann Eberlin von Günzburg und seine Vorstellungen über eine Reform in Reich und Kirche* (Berlin, 1985), p. 27 have all argued for this dependence. Enders, vol., 3, p. xx has rejected it.

[3] Edmund Kurten, *Franz Lambert von Avignon und Nikolaus Herborn in ihrer Stellung zum Ordensgedanken und zum Franziskanertum im Besonderen* (Münster, 1950), p. 40, suggests that Eberlin's work is indebted to Luther's, but his analysis of that debt amounts to little more than a superficial comparison of chapter titles. Christian Peters, *Johann Eberlin von Günzburg ca. 1465–1533. Franziskanischer Reformer, Humanist und konservativer Reformator* (Gütersloh, 1994), p. 167, characterizes Eberlin's pamphlet as a 'concretization' of the arguments developed by Luther in 'The Judgement on Monastic Vows.'

[4] WA, 11:282–91.

[5] WA, 11:457–61.

personally called on to contribute, the other former Franciscans would certainly have seen this as an appeal to justify their own conversions and to strike a blow for the Reformation at the same time.

The timing of the campaign against the Franciscans was hardly fortuitous. The initial response of the Franciscans to Luther's writings was one of reserve. This reserve continued, at least among the German Friars Minor, after 1520. Although an attempt was made at the general chapter of the Franciscans in 1522 to stem the influence of Luther's writings within the order, Schatzgeyer had initially moved cautiously in the South German province.[6] In March of that year, he wrote a mildly worded response to Luther, in which he avoided specifically naming the Reformer. Conrad Pellican, the reform-minded guardian of the Basel Convent, saw this work through the press and took credit for an introductory epistle, likely written by Erasmus, published with it.[7] At the provincial chapter that year Schatzgeyer defended Pellican against charges of Lutheranism and agreed with him that educated members of the order should be allowed to read Luther's writings.[8] However, in Schatzgeyer's 'Revelation Against a False Writing' the conciliatory tone begins to disappear. Much of this work was written during Schatzgeyer's frequent visits to Ulm during that summer, and news of his activity was transmitted to Wittenberg by Wolfgang Rychard.[9] However, the conflict appears to have first come to a head in early 1523. A showdown between Martin Bucer and the Franciscans of Weissenberg in Alsace just before Lent may be indicative of a stronger stance taken by the superiors in the order.[10] Then, during Lent, Schatzgeyer attempted to transfer Pellican, his vice-guardian Johann Kreis and the preacher Johannes Lüthard from the Basel cloister, but was thwarted in his plans by the intervention of the city council.[11] At the chapter general of the order, convened in Burgos, Spain during Pentecost 1523, Schatzgeyer and Gilbert Nicolai were named inquisitors for the South German

---

[6] Heribert Holzapfel, *Handbuch der Geschichte des Franziskanerordens* (Freiburg, 1909), p. 463.

[7] Kurten, pp. 42 and 144. On the issue of Erasmus's authorship of the introduction to this work, see Peters, pp. 52–3.

[8] Theodor Vulpinus (ed.), *Die Hauschronik Konrad Pellikans von Rufach. Ein Lebensbild aus der Reformationszeit* (Strasbourg, 1892), pp. 79–80.

[9] Martin Brecht, 'Johann Eberlin von Günzburg in Wittenberg 1522–1524,' *Wertheimer Jahrbuch*, 1983 (1985), p. 52; Nikolaus Paulus, *Kaspar Schatzgeyer, ein Vorkämpfer der katholischen Kirche gegen Luther in Süddeutschland* (Strasbourg, 1898), p. 62; Peters, pp. 122–6.

[10] Paulus, *Schatzgeyer*, p. 57.

[11] Vulpinus, pp. 80–1.

province of the order.[12] These events were mirrored by an escalation in the war of words. Briesmann's pamphlet was intended as a response to 'Revelation Against a False Writing.' In late 1523, a response by Schatzgeyer to Briesmann appeared and was followed shortly by his reply to Spelt, Lambert and Eberlin.[13]

It appears, then, that the harsher stance against Luther within the Franciscan order and Schatzgeyer's consequent attack on Luther's teachings combined to call forth the response from Wittenberg. The nature of the polemics against the Franciscans indicates that while general, indiscriminate attacks on the clergy were now out of favour in Wittenberg, the full anticlerical venom of the earlier Reformation was still a viable tactic when dealing with specific clerics in specific circumstances. A logical starting point for the anti-Franciscan polemicists of 1523 was to revive the strategy of playing off secular-mendicant rivalries which had been developed in the 'Address to the Christian Nobility' and expanded in 'The Fifteen Confederates.' The debate had, however, moved significantly beyond the parameters of 1520 and 1521. In particular, the pamphleteers of 1523 had at their disposal Luther's fully developed criticism of monasticism and monastic vows. An analysis of these pamphlets, then, provides valuable insights into not only how Luther's teachings on monastic vows were applied to specific groups of religious, but also how these teachings were integrated with more traditional anticlerical themes. In 1523 pre-Reformation and Reformation anticlerical polemics were combined for a concerted assault on one of the main bulwarks of the old church.

Certainly the polemicists of 1523 saw in Luther's arguments against monastic vows a viable basis from which to attack the Franciscans. The extent to which Luther's arguments were reflected in these pamphlets naturally varies; Kettenbach's sermon and the short justifications for leaving the order make only passing reference to them, while the expositions on the Rule are much more detailed. Interestingly, Spelt's pamphlet indicates that proximity to Wittenberg did not necessarily determine the extent of dependence on Luther. Furthermore, the authors of these pamphlets make no secret of their debt to Luther. As a defence of Luther's work against the response of Schatzgeyer, Briesmann's pamphlet naturally remains firmly within the context of Luther's statements. The other authors are often more inventive, but indicate, nonetheless, their knowledge of Luther's position. Among Luther's writings recommended by Eberlin to his readers are 'The Judgement on

---

[12] Paulus, *Schatzgeyer*, p. 61.
[13] Ibid., pp. 66–7.

Monastic Vows' and 'The Church Postil,' which develops many of the same arguments against monasticism.[14] Schwan suggests 'The Judgement on Monastic Vows' as a standard with which to judge the arguments of his opponents in defence of monasticism and Lambert explicitly offers his 'Evangelical Description of the Franciscan Rule' as a supplement to it.[15]

Luther states at the outset of 'The Judgement on Monastic Vows' that his purpose is not to deny the validity of making vows, as this is clearly commanded in Psalm 76:11: 'Vow and pay unto the Lord your God,' but to determine which vows are godly, good and pleasing to God.[16] He then goes on to discuss monastic vows under five independent, but complementary headings: that such vows do not rest on God's Word, but are contrary to it; that they are contrary to faith; that they contradict evangelical freedom; that they oppose the commands of God; and that they are contrary even to human reason.

Luther begins the first section of his attack on monastic vows by stating that there is no basis for them in Scripture or the practices of the early church. Citing St Paul, he establishes as his basic principle: 'Whatever is commanded which is contrary to or beyond Christ is condemned, whether a man takes it upon himself or whether he is

---

[14] 'Die andere getreue Vermahnung an den Rath von Ulm,' Enders, vol. 3, pp. 31–2; 'Wider die falschen Geistlichen,' Enders, vol. 3, p. 86. On the similarities between Luther's 'Church Postil' and 'The Judgement on Monastic Vows,' see Hans-Christoph Rublack, 'Zur Rezeption von Luthers De Votis Monasticis Iudicium,' in Rainer Postel and Franklin Kopitzsch, eds. *Reformation und Revolution. Beiträge zum politischen Wandel und den sozialen Kräften am Beginn der Neuzeit. Festschrift für Rainer Wohlfeil zum 60. Geburtstag* (Stuttgart, 1989), pp. 224–37.

[15] 'Ein Sendbriff Johannis Schwan,' Köhler *et al.*, F ll86, #2980, Aiii; Schwann, 'Ein kurtzer begriff des Erschrocklichē stands der munch,' Köhler *et al.*, F 208, #593, Aiii (d); Lambert, 'Ein Evangelische beschreibung über der Barfüsser Regel,' Köhler *et al*, F378, #1050, Bii.

[16] 'De votis monasticis iudicium,' WA, 8:577. Studies of Luther's 'Judgement on Monastic Vows' stress that in this work Luther still allowed for the possibility of a reform of monasticism; see Bernhard Lohse, 'Die Kritik am Mönchtum bei Luther und Melanchthon,' in Vilmos Vatja (ed.), *Luther und Melanchthon. Referate und Berichte des zweiten internationalen Kongresses für Lutherforschung Münster 8.–13. Aug. 1960* (Göttingen, 1961), pp. 129–45; id., *Mönchtum und Reformation. Luthers Auseinandersetzung mit dem Monchsideal des Mittelalters* (Göttingen, 1963); Heinz-Meinolf Stamm, *Luthers Stellung zum Ordensleben* (Wiesbaden, 1980); Robert Bast, '*Je geistlicher . . . je blinder*: Anticlericalism, the Law, and Social Ethics in Luther's Sermons on Matthew 22:34–41,' in Dykema and Oberman, pp. 367–78. However, Luther's reform proposals in the 'Address to the Christian Nobility' indicate as well that his treatment of the mendicant orders remained distinct from his treatment of other religious. It should come as no surprise, then, that the opponents of the Franciscans would adopt arguments from 'The Judgement on Monastic Vows' to demand the abolition, not just the reform, of the mendicant orders.

following the example of the saints.'[17] The remainder of this section is devoted to proving that monastic vows oppose or exceed the commands of Christ. Luther strikes at the very root of the monastic ideal by denying the distinction between the precepts and counsels of Christ and by rejecting the division of the Christian life into perfect and imperfect states. The vows of obedience and poverty rest not on evangelical counsels but, properly understood, they are precepts binding on all Christians. Therefore, to vow to fulfil these is meaningless. Chastity alone is an evangelical counsel, and it is impossible to make a counsel into a precept as this goes beyond the Gospel.[18]

Luther then juxtaposes monastic vows with faith, taking as his first principle the words of Paul in Romans 14:23: 'Everything that is not of faith is sin.' Compulsory vows, as commands derived from the so-called evangelical counsels, are by their very nature law. But Paul has indicated in the epistles to the Galatians and Romans that salvation comes through faith not the law. In taking vows, the monks believe that they are performing a service to God and indicate that they are attempting to be justified by the law rather than faith. They even go so far as to equate their vows with a second baptism, thereby implying that the grace of baptism is insufficient.[19]

Having indicated that monastic vows oppose both faith and the Word of God, Luther turns next to proving that they contradict the fruit of these, namely, evangelical freedom. As a form of law, vows are unnecessary for salvation and, therefore, valid before God only if they are not compulsory. The conscience, however, must depend on Christ alone and cannot be bound. This is the evangelical liberty which, unlike vows, cannot be renounced. Luther allows that Christians may continue to observe the law, and therefore vows, if the conscience remains free.[20]

The arguments of these first three sections of Luther's work are clearly reflected in the pamphlets against the Franciscans. As a specific response to Schatzgeyer encouraged by Luther, Briesmann's work contains naturally the most accurate and detailed reflection of Luther's arguments. However, Spelt, Schwan and Lambert also indicate a clear understanding of the central themes of 'The Judgement on Monastic Vows.' Schwan concludes his justification for leaving the order on the same note on which Luther opened his attack on vows: 'Since God nowhere in Scripture orders or commands monasticism, it is clear that it

---

[17] 'De votis monasticis,' WA, 8:578–79.
[18] Ibid., pp. 580–7.
[19] Ibid., pp. 591–604.
[20] Ibid., pp. 605–17.

has been invented and fabricated by men.'[21] His 'A Brief Conception of the Frightful State of the Monks' states even more explicitly that vows go against Christ and God's grace.[22] Spelt takes as his point of departure the attempt to identify monastic vows with the Gospel, a practice he labels the highest form of idolatry.[23] Lambert makes the same point with specific reference to the Franciscan Rule. Luther argued, on the basis of Francis's claim that his Rule was the Gospel, that the saint had wanted his followers to live free from vows and that he had erred when he instituted the order with them.[24] Lambert prefers to lay the blame for this perversion on Clement V's gloss of the Rule, *Exivi de paradiso*.[25] Both Spelt and Lambert reject the traditional distinction between evangelical precepts and counsels, and identify obedience and poverty as precepts binding on all Christians and chastity as the only counsel.[26] Lambert also rejects the division between perfect and imperfect states in the Christian life.[27] Although he avoids the discussion of precepts and counsels, Schwan does return to Luther's argument in denouncing as a perversion of the Gospel the identification of the monastic way as more perfect.[28]

Luther's claims that monastic vows oppose faith and Christian liberty are also taken up. Lambert and Spelt both cite Romans 14:23 to claim that without faith all is sin. Lambert adds that the true imitation of Christ is a matter of faith not statutes or special clothing and Spelt accuses the religious of doubting the sufficiency of Christ's atonement and attempting to be justified by the law.[29] Schwan makes general reference to the epistles to the Romans and Galatians and contrasts the

---

[21] 'Ein Sendbriff Johannis Schwan,' Biii(b).

[22] 'Ein Kurtzer begriff des Erschrocklichē stands der munch,' A(b).

[23] Spelt, 'Ain ware Declaration oder Erklärung,' Köhler *et al.*, F 47, #131, Aiii(d).

[24] 'De votis monasticis,' WA, 8.579–80.

[25] 'Ein Evangelische beschreibung über der Barfüsser Regel,' Dii(b).

[26] Spelt, 'Ain ware Declaration oder Erklärung,' Bii; Lambert, 'Ein Evangelische beschreibung über der Barfüsser Regel,' Dii(b).

[27] 'Ein Evangelische beschreibung über der Barfüsser Regel,' E.

[28] 'Ein Sendbriff Johannis Schwan,' Aii.

[29] 'Lambert, Ein Evangelische beschreibung über der Barfüsser Regel,' Diii(c)–Diii(d): 'Uñ zuñ Romern. xiiij. was nit ist uss dē glauben / ist sünd . . . Hierüb Christū nachvolgen ist nit dz man die cloysterey annem / oder mit disem oder yenem kleyd angethon sey / sond glauben.' Spelt, 'Ain ware Declaration oder Erklärung,' Biii(d): 'O lieber mensch / die weyl du des sins bist / so gelaubest du nymmer meer in Christum / alle deine werck seindt sund unnd sund / wie der haylig Paulus spricht Roṁ. 14 Was da nit geschicht auss dem glawben ist sund / . . . Paulus Gal. 2 . . . Jr sollent wissen dz kain mensch würt gerechtfertigt durch das gesetz, sonder allain durch den glauben in Christū damit kayn mensch gloryret.' C: 'Das ist dein mainung / suma summarum / die gerechtigkait Christi / der unentlich schatz seines leydens / dunckt dich nit genug sein zū volkömner verzeyhung / oder bezalung deiner sunde / zū deiner erlösung und seligkait / . . .'

uselessness of monastic ceremonies with the efficacy of faith in baptism.[30] Both Lambert and Spelt also revive Luther's point that the conscience must remain free and cannot be bound by vows.[31] However, on this matter Schwan most clearly indicates his knowledge of Luther's treatise:

> ... it is perfectly clear that of a thousand monks, not one has entered the cloister who did not think that his life was better than the common Christian life, who did not seek through this to become pious, pleasing to God and holy. . . . In this way it is evident that their very essence is against Christ and is an imprisonment of the conscience without God's Word. For the Christian conscience can be bound by no laws, but alone by the Word of God.[32]

While they provide fewer details from Luther's arguments, Eberlin and Kettenbach indicate that they, too, were familiar with 'The Judgement on Monastic Vows.' Edmund Kurten noted that several of Eberlin's chapter titles in 'Against the False Religious' are similar to those in 'The Judgement on Monastic Vows,' and that his third chapter deals with the contradiction between the Rule and the Gospel.[33] However, his exposé on the Franciscans lacks the theological complexity of Luther's work, and Eberlin does not so much repeat Luther's statements as take them as a point of departure. Like Lambert, he begins by answering the claim that the Rule of St Francis is the Gospel, and he contrasts the Gospel with the glosses on the Rule not only by Clement V, but also Nicholas

---

[30] 'Ein Sendbriff Johannis Schwan,' B: 'Sondern das ich weyss / das seyn todt meyn ist / seyn leyden uñ aufferstehüg meyn ist / macht mich alsso reych / das ich weytter keynes eusserliches dinges bedarff zur frumkeytt / es sey fasten / blatten / kleyder u. was es wolle. Also redt der Apostel / ynn der Epistel zun Römern und Gal: die unsser münche / und bauch diener / nie recht verstanden habē.' Bii: 'Das bedeutt unssere tauff / die eyn sigel ist / der gottlichen zusagung / und versicherung / das Christus leben / und todt / unsser sey ... Wer nun den glawben ynn Christo hatt / der ist schon frum / und kan durch keyn kloster / gelübd / kappen / platten / stryck / odder gürrtel u. frümer werden / ssondern hat schon volkomlich alles / durch seyn glawben.'

[31] Spelt, 'Ain ware Declaration oder Erklärung,' Fiii(d): 'Wie oben gesagt ist / unnd das ist die ware Christenliche / oder Evangelisch freyhait / welche dir kain mensch oder creatur nymmer mere nemē / noch du dir selber mit kainem gelubdt ūwandeln kanst / . . .'; 'Ein Evangelische beschreibung über der Barfüsser Regel,' Fii–Fii(b): 'Wee wee denen so vilen verflüchten menschlichē satzungen / die nichts zů einer christlichē sachē thůn / sunder nur strick anwerffen / mit welchē mā unzeliche sünd thůt. O gott wólt / das der gātz umbkreyss der erdē wisst was für ein heylige freyheit sey der kinder gotts / in welche wir durch die gnad Christi gesetzt seind. . . . Hyerüb ist zů radten allen Christē / das sye nit werdē knecht der menschen .j. Cor. vij. das sye sich den menschē mit eynicher gelübd verstricken / sund allweg in Christo frey bleiben.'

[32] 'Ein Sendbriff Johannis Schwan,' Bii(b).

[33] Kurten, p. 40.

III and Julius II.[34] Although not specifically addressing the issues of counsels and precepts in those terms, both Eberlin and Kettenbach do claim that the vows as taken contradict scripture and that obedience and poverty are binding on all Christians and chastity is a matter of free choice.[35] Both authors also indicate that monastic vows oppose faith and Christian liberty. Eberlin's epistle to Ulm charges that vows contradict faith and denigrate the sole mediatory role of Christ, and 'Against the False Religious' contrasts the freedom of the Gospel with compulsory vows and accuses Francis of attempting to make the Gospel into law.[36] Kettenbach compares the 'chains of hell and ropes of Judas' with the freedom of the Gospel and warns the Franciscans of their fate on the day of judgement:

> Then I [Christ] will say to them: 'I have never known you as a friend, therefore depart from me, all you workers of evil.' As if he said: 'You suppose that your works are truly good and have made you pious and great before me, since you have held your orders, vows, statutes and rules. But I say, they are all vain sin and evil, also your miracles, for they have taken place without faith.'[37]

As a sermon, Kettenbach's work might be expected to simplify theological arguments. On the other hand, one would expect more detailed arguments from Eberlin, especially in the lengthy tract specifically against the Franciscan Rule. However, Eberlin had already written a work on monastic vows, 'Against the Imprudent Departure,' to which he directs his readers at the end of 'Against the False Religious.'[38] In the earlier pamphlet Eberlin denies the greater perfection of the monastic way and develops more fully the contrast between faith and the law and the need to safeguard the freedom of the conscience obtained in baptism.[39]

In his fourth section, Luther endeavours to prove that monastic vows contradict the commandments of God by comparing them to both tables of the Decalogue. The first commandment demands complete faith in God, which, as he has already indicated, is impossible when the conscience is bound by vows. In praising the founders of their orders and adopting their names instead of Christ's, the monks violate the

---

[34] 'Wider die falschen Geistlichen,' pp. 49–50.

[35] Ibid., pp. 56–7; Kettenbach, 'Eine Predigt auff den achten Sonntag nach dem Pfingsttag,' Clemen, pp. 219–20 and 222.

[36] 'Die andere getreue Vermahnung an den Rath von Ulm,' pp. 34–5; 'Wider die falschen Geistlichen,' p. 56.

[37] 'Eine Predigt auf den achten Sonntag nach dem Pfingsttag,' pp. 221–2.

[38] 'Wider die falschen Geistlichen,' p. 87.

[39] Eberlin, 'Wider den unvorsichtigen Ausgang vieler Klosterleute,' Enders, vol. 2, pp. 123–5.

second commandment. Similarly, they contravene the third commandment when, instead of observing the order of prayer and preaching of the primitive church, they commit themselves to all manner of idolatrous ceremonies which they regard as good works.[40] The second table of the Decalogue Luther sums up as the commands to obey one's parents and love one's neighbour. The monks, however, avoid these, citing Matthew 10:37: 'He that loveth father or mother more than me is not worthy of me,' and Matthew 19:29: 'And every one that hath forsaken houses, or brethren, or sisters, or fathers, or mother, or wife, or children, or lands for my name's sake, shall receive an hundredfold, and shall inherit everlasting life,' and claim that they are dead to the world and wish to obey only their superiors and practise love only among their *confreres*. This they claim as a higher form of obedience and love when, in fact, they are in this way limiting a command made general by God. One need only observe the bitter infighting between monastic orders to understand their definition of the love of one's neighbour.[41]

Luther here provided a model for an equally detailed comparison of the monastic life with the Decalogue by Heinrich Spelt:

> You have already heard how they promote idolatry, deny Christ, etc. Now, I will briefly show with the ten commandments how they take their vows, and in what matter they hold none of God's commandments, or wish to hold them, but rather are obedient to the devil in all things.[42]

His analysis of the relationship of monastic vows to the first three commandments follows Luther's closely. The cloistered break the first commandment by relying on their own works for salvation.[43] However, for the second and third commandments Spelt relies on Luther's definition of the third: in their canonical hours and other duties in the choir, which are performed mechanically without reflection, they frequently take God's name in vain, and they hold the sabbath only with such external observances.[44]

In his discussion of the second table of the Decalogue, Spelt departs somewhat from Luther's arguments and expands on them. Like Luther, he charges the monks with refusing obedience to their parents and

---

[40] 'De votis monasticis,' WA, 8:618–19. On the importance of the Law and especially the second table of the Decalogue in Luther's criticism of monasticism and in the development of his anticlericalism, see Bast, pp. 367–78.

[41] 'De votis monasticis,' WA, 8:623–4, 627–8.

[42] 'Ain ware Declaration oder Erklärung,' Cii(b).

[43] Ibid., Biii–Biii(b).

[44] Ibid., Cii(b)–Ciii(c).

breaking the fourth commandment under the guise of greater obedience to their superiors. Luther's further charge that vows contradict the divine command to love one's neighbour is implied in Spelt's claim that obedience to the order often precludes helping one's parents in times of need.[45] Thereafter, Spelt applies a spiritualized interpretation of the remaining six commandments to indicate how the monks break them. While not physically harming others, they are guilty of murder for the numerous souls they lead astray with their works righteousness. They break the sixth and tenth commandments by depriving the laity of the fruit of their labour with specious claims of providing spiritual services. Even more importantly, their evil example deprives others of the grace of God and God of his due honour. With reference to the seventh and ninth commandments, Spelt has recourse to Luther's denunciation of the monastic vow of chastity. Finally, against the eighth commandment, the monks give false witness to God with the example of their evil lives and thereby lead others astray.[46]

Besides Spelt's pamphlet, this criticism of vows finds its greatest resonance in Schwan's discussion of monasticism. Schwan concentrates his attention on the second table of the Decalogue and contrasts the monastic vows with the divine commands to obey one's parents and love one's neighbour.[47] Beyond this, however, references to Luther's argument are scarce. The fifth chapter of Lambert's description of the Rule discusses the vow of obedience and follows Luther in contrasting this with the commandment of obedience to parents.[48] In one of his numerous points of contrast between the Gospel and the Rule, Eberlin revives the argument that monastic obedience is a more limited, inferior

---

[45] Ibid., Ciii(d). See WA, 8:625.

[46] 'Ain ware Declaration oder Erklärung,' Ciii(d)–D(b).

[47] 'Ein kurtzer begriff des Erschrocklichē stands der munch,' A(b)–Aii: 'Ich hab dir gebotten / vatter uñ mutter tzu eren / uñ ynen gehorsam tzu seyn / sso hastu gebot lasszen gebott seyn / uñ bist hyn getretten / tzu eyner geselschafft / die keynen hat willen annemen / ehr ubergeben dan tzuvor / vatter und mutter / das ist / Ehr ubertret dan gleich / in seinez anfang / mein gebot / . . . Des gleichenn / sso mein regel gelautet hatt / uff gemeine bruderliche liebe / . . .'

[48] 'Ein Evangelische beschreibung über der Barfusser Regel,' Diii(b): 'Jr etlich auch der aller schentlichstē gleissner scheinen sich nit / ir sect der verderbung also hoch zumachen / das sye sagē / vatter und muter mog man under sich tretten und sich jrer unseligen geselschafftē oder convent zufugen / also unzeliche jungē verfure sye / und under dē erlognen schein der haltung des Evangeliō / verfuren sye sye zu offentlicher übertrettung des gottlichen befelchs. Von jnen selbs legen sye dises uss. Matt. x. Welcher sein vatter und muter meer lieb hat dañ mich / ist mein nit würdig. gleich als wer es Christo nachgefolgt / uñ sein crütz getragē / wañ einer zu jnē hyn ein gieng.' 'De votis monasticis iudicium,' WA, 8:623–4.

form of the obedience commanded by God for all Christians.[49] However, beyond these instances, this argument does not figure prominently in the rest of the anti-Franciscan *Flugschriften*.

Luther's final critique of monastic vows, that they are contrary to human reason, has even less impact. He suggests that, as vows are invalidated in circumstances in which their fulfilment is impossible, they are necessarily conditional. This he bases on the example of vows to make a pilgrimage, but, as all vows are equally valid before God, what applies to one must apply to all. However, a superior is unable to dispense a monk from the vow of chastity, even if he is unable to fulfil it.[50] Although he adopts the opposition between the Franciscan Rule and human reason as the theme for the third chapter of 'Against the False Religious,' Eberlin avoids Luther's arguments and concentrates instead on what he perceives to be the excessive harshness of the Rule.[51] Schwan touches on the issue, suggesting that his position can also be supported by an argument from reason, but pleads lack of space in the present work as grounds for not elaborating.[52]

None of the pamphlets against the Franciscans repeat the full argumentation of Luther's work on monastic vows. Nonetheless, it is also clear that the authors knew and adopted elements of Luther's work. It is also important to note that they develop arguments against the religious life which derive from the central motifs of Reformation theology: the use of scripture as the criteria against which to judge vows, the identification of vows as law and the consequent opposition between them and faith and Christian liberty. Moreover, these authors were involved in a different enterprise than Luther. Lambert's justification for writing may serve as an indication of the nature of this enterprise:

> On this, one has a book by the most Christian teacher of holy scripture, Martin Luther, in which is contained everything required to expose the senselessness of monastic vows, and nothing further could be desired. But because the Franciscan sect above all others leads the world astray, it is well deserving of its own book.[53]

To indicate the particular dangers posed by the Franciscans, the former

---

[49] 'Wider die falschen Geistlichen,' p. 57: 'Christus. Meyne junger sollen so underthenig sein, ainer dem anndern auch die füss wäschen, Johan. xiij. cap. Auch frembden und feinden, allen menschen. 1.Pet.2. frantz. Das Evangeliion stelt die gehorsam oder underthenigkait nur Francisko bewysen zewerden und meynen nachkommlingen, wie dann ich geschworen hab gehorsam dem bapst honorio. u. cap. ij. reg.'

[50] 'De votis monasticis iudicium,' WA, 8:629–41.

[51] 'Wider die falschen Geistlichen,' Enders, vol. 3, pp. 63–6.

[52] 'Ein Sendbriff Johannis Schwan,' Aiii(c)–(d).

[53] 'Ein Evangelische beschreibung über der Barfüsser Regel,' Bii.

members had to go beyond the general indictment of monasticism by Luther. The ongoing tradition of antifraternalism and the biblical types it identified with the friars provided a logical point of departure. Erasmus had revived in print the characteristics which this tradition associated with the friars, although he was less explicit in identifying the Franciscans with the biblical types of Pharisees, false prophets and *psuedoapostoli*. Closer to home, Eberlin had reinforced many of these characteristics in 'The Fifteen Confederates.' The anti-Franciscan polemics from 1523 do not develop these characteristics as fully as Eberlin had done two years previously. Rather, they adopt the characteristics from the literary types which were especially applicable to the context in which they were writing.

If, as we suspect, the identification of the friars with the biblical types of Pharisees, false prophets and *psuedoapostoli* was commonplace in late medieval society, it is not surprising that elements of this appear in Luther's writings. Particularly useful for Luther's purposes were the apocalyptically coloured warnings in the New Testament against the advent of false apostles and false prophets and servants of the Antichrist. However, the nature of Luther's criticism of monasticism generally dictated a different set of proof texts than that of the medieval antifraternal tradition. And, when he does share the same sources with this tradition, his exegesis emphasizes different characteristics of his opponents. Luther, then, injected new meaning into the traditional biblical types and laid the groundwork for a more scathing attack on the friars deriving from the central elements of his Reformation theology. In the first section of 'The Judgement on Monastic Vows,' he cites the words of Christ in Matthew 24 and applies them to monasticism:

> Christ speaks most clearly against monastic vows in Matthew 24 [:23–26], 'Then if any man shall say to you: Behold, here is Christ, or there, do not believe it. For false Christs and false prophets shall arise and they shall show great signs and wonders, so that if it were possible even the elect would be led into error. Behold, I have told you beforehand. If therefore they shall say to you: Behold, he is in the desert, do not go there; Behold, he is in the secret chambers, do not believe it.' . . . In other words, they are the ones who call people to the wilderness and secret chambers, that is, to the cloister or the monastery.[54]

Even more appropriate to Luther's purposes is Paul's warning in 1 Timothy 4:1–3 against those going astray in the last days. Already in 'The Babylonian Captivity of the Church,' Luther had identified these with the religious orders:

---

[54] 'De votis monasticis iudicium,' WA, 8:657.

> Moreover, I greatly fear that these votive modes of life of the religious orders belong to those things which the Apostle foretold: 'They will be teaching lies in hypocrisy, forbidding marriage and enjoining abstinence from foods which God created to be received in thanksgiving.' [1 Tim. 4:2–3][55]

In 'The Judgement on Monastic Vows,' Luther is willing to absolve all monks from their vows and declare the vows unacceptable in the sight of God on the authority of this text alone.[56]

Elsewhere, Luther draws on some of the biblical texts central to the medieval antifraternal tradition and the metaphors associated with them. In 'The Babylonian Captivity of the Church,' he identified false priests and bishops with the ravenous wolves in sheep's clothing of Matthew 7:15–20.[57] 'The Judgement on Monastic Vows' makes this identification specifically with the monks.[58] In the latter work he also relies heavily on Paul's warning against self-serving hypocrites contained in 2 Timothy 3:1–7 to claim that monks are servants of the belly who seek to introduce divisions into the body of Christ.[59] And in his 'Church Postil,' he provides a lengthy exegesis of 2 Timothy and applies Paul's statements specifically to the mendicants.[60] However, Luther uses these texts primarily to denounce the works righteousness of the monks rather than to revive the attributes associated with the friars in the medieval antifraternal tradition.

Penn Szittya argues for the overriding importance of the identification of the friars with these biblical types in the medieval antifraternal tradition.[61] Given this tradition and Luther's use of the same biblical types, it is not surprising to see them reappear in the anti-Franciscan polemics of 1523. In these, our authors rely primarily on Luther's proof texts but, as will later be evident, they continue to be influenced by the characterizations of the medieval tradition. Both Kettenbach and Eberlin take as their point of departure an exegesis of Matthew 7:15–20. Eberlin begins 'Against the False Religious' by indicating the importance of guarding against false prophets and devotes the rest of the pamphlet to identifying these with the Franciscans.[62] Kettenbach identifies the false prophets, who appear as sheep but in reality are ravenous wolves,

---

[55] 'De captivitate Babylonica ecclesiae praeludium,' WA, 6:540.

[56] 'De votis monasticis iudicium,' WA, 8:596–7.

[57] 'De captivitate Babylonica ecclesiae praeludium,' WA, 6:567.

[58] 'De votis monasticis iudicium,' WA, 8:600 and 607.

[59] Ibid., pp. 607, 647, 652 and 655.

[60] 'Kirchenpostille,' WA, 10.I:634–709. See especially p. 635.

[61] Penn Szittya, 'The Antifraternal Tradition in Middle English Literature,' *Speculum*, 52 (1977), pp. 302–3; id., *The Antifraternal Tradition in Medieval Literature* (Princeton, 1986), pp. 31–61.

[62] 'Wider die falschen Geistlichen,' Enders, vol. 3, p. 43.

with monks in general and especially with the Franciscans.[63] Lambert
and Schwan fail to cite this passage, but do make reference to wolves in
sheep's clothing.[64]

Given its prominence in Luther's critique and particular applicability
to monasticism, surprisingly little use is made of Matthew 24:23–6 by
the anti-Franciscan polemicists. Kettenbach cites this text in conjunction
with Matthew 7 to indicate that even some of the elect will be led into
error by these false prophets.[65] Spelt makes the same claim, without
specifically referring to the false prophets.[66] Only Lambert adopts *in
toto* the essence of Luther's exegesis and identifies the desert and secret
chambers with the monasteries and cloisters.[67] Not surprisingly,
Briesmann plays off this theme, and apparently combines it with the
criticism of the friars based on Matthew 23:7, 'And [they love] greetings
in the market,' when he claims that the mendicants are found in the
marketplace rather than the desert.[68]

Luther's other prominent proof text, 1 Timothy 4:1–3, serves as a
rallying point for these authors. In general, they are very Lutheran in
their use of this passage to denounce the statutory nature of the
monastic life. Eberlin employs it to denounce the dietary restrictions and
celibacy of the Franciscans as teachings of the Devil.[69] Kettenbach uses
it to the same effect against their clothing and diet.[70] Lambert, on the
other hand, is chiefly concerned with the implications of this text for the
vow of chastity.[71] Schwan applies this passage more generally in
connection with 2 Peter 2:1–3, which Luther also employs for the same

---

63 'Eine Predigt auf den achten Sonntag nach dem Pfingsttag,' Clemen, p. 215.

64 Lambert, 'Rationes propter quas,' Aii; Schwann, 'Ein kurtzer begriff des Erschrocklichē stands der munch,' A(b).

65 'Eine Predigt auf den achten Sonntag nach dem Pfingsttag,' Clemen, p. 216.

66 'Ain ware Declaration oder Erklārung,' Gii–Gii(b).

67 'Ein Evangelische beschreibung über der Barfůsser Regel,' E: 'Hör du verfürer der du
das wort gotts also verfelschest / uñ dise ding dychtest / weystu nit dz geschribē ist. Matt.
xxiiij. Welcher zů eüch sagt. Sych hye ist Christus / da / oder dört / jr solts nitt glauben.
Und kurtz darnach sagt er. Wañ sye eüch sagen werdē. sych in der wůsti / so geend nit
hynauss. sych in den beschlosznen gemachē / jr solts nit glaubē.'

68 'Ad Gasparis Schatzgeyri,' p. 26 (b): 'Quero igitur a plicatore, ad quod Monachorum
genus pertinebunt fratres mendicantes, qui non in heremo, sicut Iohannes, sed prope
macellum (ubi omnia quae ad lauticiam attinent, veneunt) monestaria sua constituerůt,
nimirum ventris negotium agentes.'

69 'Die andere getreue Vermahnung an den Rath von Ulm,' Enders, vol. 3, p. 6. The
prominence of this text in the attack on monasticism in general is indicated by the
attention paid to it by Briesmann in his response to Schatzgeyer. See 'Ad Gasparis
Schatzgeyri,' pp. 37–8.

70 'Eine Predigt auf den achten Sonntag nach dem Pfingsttag,' Clemen, pp. 216–19.

71 'Ein Evangelische beschreibung über der Barfůsser Regel,' F(b)–Fii.

purpose, to warn against the dangers of human teachings.[72] Heinrich Spelt, however, provides the clearest identification with the false prophets and reinforces his claim with 2 Timothy 3:1–7, another text cited frequently by Luther:

> ... they are those of whom St Paul prophesied and predicted to his beloved disciple Timothy in the fourth chapter of the first epistle to him. There he says the Spirit predicted openly that in the last times some would depart from faith and heed spirits of error and the teachings of devils, etc. Furthermore, in the third chapter of the second epistle to his disciple, he says the same and warns him to guard against them and to avoid those who have an appearance of godliness, but in reality are full of blasphemy.[73]

On the other biblical type of the antifraternal tradition, the Pharisee, Luther is strangely silent in 'The Judgement on Monastic Vows.' In fact, he never explicitly identifies the monks with the Pharisees. He does, however, cite Matthew 23, which served as the cornerstone of William of St Amour's exegesis, to denounce the legalism of monastic superiors:

> Could it not be fairly argued that monasticism is both iniquitous and cruel, and on this ground alone is highly suspect as Satan's charade, for it is so merciful in matters of no moment, but so severe in matters which are of moment? What can anybody say to such perversity, except the words of the Gospel, 'You strain at a gnat and swallow a camel' [Matt. 23:24]? or again, 'You tithe your cumin and mint, but neglect the weightier matters of the law' [Matt. 23:23]. Or again, 'You lay on men's backs heavy burdens they cannot even bear' [Matt. 23:4].[74]

Elsewhere, he makes reference to the pharisaic righteousness of the monks, but does not make explicit the identification of the two groups or concern himself with the metaphors of the medieval exegesis which do.[75]

In contrast, the anti-Franciscan polemicists frequently identify the Franciscans as Pharisees, either directly or by clear implication. Eberlin refers to the activities of these Pharisees against the Word of God and Kettenbach denounces the false teachings of the Pharisees, murderers of souls and apostles of the Antichrist.[76] Schwan, too, calls them Pharisees and argues that daily experience indicates the pharisaical cunning of his

---

[72] 'Ein Sendbriff Johannis Schwan,' Biii(b).

[73] 'Ain ware Declaration oder Erklärung,' Aiii(d)–B.

[74] 'De votis monasticis iudicium,' WA, 8:634.

[75] Ibid., pp. 608 and 609.

[76] Eberlin, 'Die andere getreue Vermahnung an den Rath von Ulm,' Enders, vol. 3, p. 37; Kettenbach, 'Eine Predigt auf den achten Sonntag nach Pfingsttag,' Clemen, p. 215.

former brethren.[77] Other identifications are made through allusions to biblical texts dealing with the Pharisees, especially Matthew 23. Eberlin cites this chapter in general in support of his claim that the Franciscans as a group are damned.[78] Spelt introduces an identification of all monks with the Pharisees, false apostles and *antichristi* with reference to Matthew 23:

> Christ when he reviled so angrily, grievously and sharply the hypocrites and learned ones (as we learn in the twenty-third chapter of Matthew) on account of their false, evil, tyrannical lives, charged, reproached and cursed them with so many woes, saying, 'Woe unto you learned ones and hypocrites' . . . and truly, this woe the Lord cries out still, and much more in these last times than ever before, to the tyrannical servants and bondsmen of the Antichrist, . . .[79]

Elsewhere he implies the same identification when he cites the reproaches of both John the Baptist and Jesus against the Pharisees and Sadducees.[80] Similarly, Schwan turns Christ's denunciation of the Scribes and Pharisees against his former brethren, again designating them as hypocrites.[81] Lambert, however, comes closer to Luther's use of this text when he cites Matthew 23:2: 'The Scribes and Pharisees sit in Moses' seat,' against the vow of obedience.[82]

The extent to which the Reformation polemicists were able to adapt the conventions of the medieval antifraternal tradition to their needs becomes clear as one investigates the characteristics derived from the biblical types identified with the friars. As we have seen, the Reformation propagandists were fortunate to inherit from the medieval intraclerical disputes three crucial points of conflict which were easily adapted to their purposes: the contests over preaching, confessing and burial dues. And the evidence suggests that tensions between the mendicants and the secular clergy over these matters were again heightened at the end of the fifteenth century and the beginning of the sixteenth.[83] Central to the mendicant–secular conflicts of the later Middle Ages was the competition that the better-trained friars posed to the preaching of the parochial clergy. William of St Amour was able to

---

[77] 'Ein Sendbriff Johannis Schwan,' Biii; 'Ein kurtzer begriff des Erschrocklichē stands der munch,' Aiii − Aiii(b).

[78] 'Die andere getreue Vermahnung an den Rath von Ulm,' Enders, vol. 3, p. 8.

[79] 'Ain ware Declaration oder Erklärung,' A(b).

[80] Ibid., Aiii(d)–B.

[81] 'Ein Sendbriff Johannis Schwan,' Biii(b).

[82] 'Ein Evangelische beschreibung über der Barfüsser Regel,' Diii(b): 'Wee eüch / die ir böser seind dan die gleisszner und schrifftgelertē / die ir nit allein im stůl Mosi wie die selben / sond in dē stůl d pestilenz sitzē / wan pestilenzisch und unreyn ist all ewer satzūg.'

[83] See above, pp. 27–8.

identify the friars with the Pharisees, *psuedoapostoli* and false prophets by claiming they had an inordinate love of the pulpit, abused Christ's instructions to the disciples prior to the preaching journey, and preached for their own gain.[84] Such criticism of mendicant preaching retained currency into the Renaissance. Erasmus pilloried the mendicants' style of preaching, and suggested that the motivation behind their antics was greed and egoism.[85] Luther, too, denounced mendicant preaching in the 'Address to the Christian Nobility,' and Eberlin took up this theme in 'The Fifteen Confederates.' Concerned with monasticism in general, 'The Judgement on Monastic Vows' generally avoids these issues, but does make reference to the preaching of monks and on this occasion encourages it as the proper expression of the spiritual office.[86] However, in his 'Church Postil' Luther returned to the theme of mendicant preaching and denounced it with specific reference to 2 Timothy 3, a central text in St Amour's attack on the spiritual services provided by the friars.[87]

The pamphlets of 1523 follow this lead in returning to the conventions of the antifraternal tradition and adapting them to the specific needs of the Reformation. Johannes Schwan reiterates the charge that the preaching of the Franciscans is self-serving:

> For what have they preached to us other than themselves – as the Apostle says – and their begging. . . . for the monks have preached nothing other than, 'whoever gives us something, whoever does good to our convent, whoever builds a cloister for us or helps us poor brothers, he will receive God's grace, he will inherit eternal salvation, etc.'[88]

Eberlin warns the council of Ulm that it is impossible for a friar to preach the Gospel while still a member of an order. As an example of this, he offers his own earlier activity as a preacher for the Franciscans.[89] Spelt comments on the willingness of the Franciscans to adopt the roles of preachers and confessors with reference to how lucrative these posts are. As preachers, they are more concerned with justifying

---

[84] Szittya, 'Antifraternal Tradition,' pp. 296, 304 and 306–7; id., *Antifraternal Tradition in Medieval Literature*, pp. 38, 43–7, 51–4; 'De periculis Ecclasiae,' in Ortwin Gratius, *Fasciculum rerum expetendarum*, ed. Edward Brown (London, 1690; reprint edn, Tucson, 1967), pp. 35, 37 and 39; 'Sermo Wilhelmi de S. Amore, I,' pp. 44–5.

[85] A.H.T. Levi (ed.), *Collected Works of Erasmus*, vol. 27, pp. 132–5.

[86] 'De votis monasticis iudicium,' WA, 8:648. The relative insignificance of the office of preaching in the initial conflict between Luther and Schatzgeyer is suggested by Briesmann's citation of Matthew 23:6 to denounce the false religion of the monks without mentioning preaching. See 'Ad Gasparis Schatzgeyri,' p. 22 (b).

[87] 'Kirchenpostille,' WA, 10.I:662–6.

[88] 'Ein Sendbriff Johannis Schwan,' Aij(b).

[89] 'Die andere getreue Vermahnung an den Rath von Ulm,' Enders, vol. 3, pp. 7, 18.

their own estate than spreading the Gospel.[90] The charge that the friars preach with an eye to financial gain reappears with Lambert, who charges that they tailor their sermons particularly to women in the audience, who can most easily be convinced to give more.[91] Perhaps the matter is best summed up in Kettenbach's sermon:

> We should also have paid attention to what they preached to us, whether they preached Christ or themselves. What have they preached other than their holy orders, which God has not instituted? Furthermore, the saints of their orders, their indulgences, the Roman see, the power of the pope, the freedom of their order, signs of their saints, and only such simple monkey business? They have led us from Christ to the pope, to themselves, to their orders.[92]

Kettenbach's indictment of indulgences, the papacy and the cult of saints indicates how easily traditional charges against the friars could be expanded to meet the needs of the sixteenth-century Reformers. Eberlin and Lambert take this tactic one step further. Traditionally opposition to the mendicants' preaching centred on its implications for parochial self-sufficiency and parochial and episcopal discipline. Eberlin's attack on the preaching of the friars in 'The Fifteen Confederates' remains within this tradition.[93] However, the issue in 1523 was not that the mendicants preach without proper episcopal authority, but rather that, contrary to the command to preach the Gospel to all nations, they remain bound by the medieval settlements which limited mendicant preaching in a diocese to those friars licensed by the bishop. Lambert takes this as the basis for an indictment of the bishops and Eberlin provides it as another example of how the Rule contradicts the Gospel.[94]

As we have seen, according to Spelt's assessment the other lucrative post to which the mendicants aspired was that of father confessor.[95] William of St Amour had denounced this activity by the friars in his exegesis of 2 Timothy 3:6: 'For of this sort are they which creep into houses, and lead captive silly women laden with sins, led away with divers lusts.' St Amour had explained this as the house of the conscience

---

[90] 'Ain ware Declaration oder Erklärung,' Eii–Eii(b).
[91] 'Ein Evangelische beschreibung über der Barfüsser Regel,' Kij.
[92] 'Eine Predigt auf den achten Sonntag nach Pfingsttag,' Clemen, p. 218.
[93] Szittya, 'Antifraternal Tradition,' pp. 296, 304; id., *Antifraternal Tradition in Medieval Literature*, pp. 52, 131–40, 210–12. For Eberlin's treatment of mendicant preaching in 'The Fifteen Confederates,' see above, pp. 77–9.
[94] Lambert, 'Ein Evangelische beschreibung über der Barfüsser Regel,' Kiii; Eberlin, 'Wider die falschen Geistlichen,' Enders, vol. 3, pp. 54–5, 59.
[95] See above, p. 148.

which the mendicants enter illegitimately through the office of confession and lead the women and their husbands away from the legitimate authority of the parochial clergy.[96] As an important source of the friars' power and livelihood, confession lay at the centre of attacks on them.[97] The nature of that attack is familiar to most readers of English literature in the person of Chaucer's friar granting easy penance for financial reward to 'frankeleyns over-al in his countree' and to 'worthy wommen of the toun.'[98] In 'The Devil's Net,' the friars' roles as preacher and confessor are intimately linked: 'Now the same preachers come / They bring the people to them with their teaching / And tell them much about God, / So that one brings them money and lays it on the altar / And must confess to and trust in them.'[99]

Erasmus, too, sees the source of mendicant power in the pulpit and confessional:

> And although they are segregated from civil life, no one can afford to belittle them, least of all the mendicants, who know all about everyone's secrets from the confessional as they call it. They know it's forbidden to publish these abroad, unless they happen to be drinking and want to be amused with enthralling stories, but then no names are mentioned and the facts are left open to conjecture. But if anyone stirs up his hornets' nest they'll take swift revenge in their public sermons, pointing out their enemy by insinuations and allusions so artfully veiled that no one who knows anything can fail to know who is meant.[100]

Shortly thereafter, he implies the connection between confession and leading women astray which figures so prominently in the medieval antifraternal tradition: '. . . and the friars find favour with women for many reasons, the main one being that a priest can provide a bosom where a woman can pour out her troubles whenever she quarrels with her husband.'[101] Arnold Williams has commented on the ease with which charges of spiritual seduction could become charges of bodily seduction.[102] Both charges seem to be implied by Briesmann's citation of

---

[96] Szittya, 'Antifraternal Tradition,' p. 305; id., *Antifraternal Tradition in Medieval Literature*, pp. 57–61; 'De periculis,' pp. 19–26.

[97] Williams, p. 505.

[98] Geoffrey Chaucer, *Canterbury Tales*, ed. John Manly (New York, 1928), pp. 154–5. Jill Mann, *Chaucer and Medieval Estates Satire: The Literature of Social Classes and the General Prologue to the Canterbury Tales* (Cambridge, 1973), pp. 38 and 47–50, provides numerous other examples of this charge in medieval satirical literature.

[99] *Des Teufels Netz*, pp. 173–4.

[100] *Collected Works of Erasmus*, vol. 27, p. 132.

[101] Ibid., p. 135.

[102] Williams, p. 512.

2 Timothy 3.[103] The latter, however, predominates in Eberlin's charges. In the 'Second True Admonition to the Council of Ulm,' he identifies the confessional as an occasion for illicit sexual affairs.[104] A little later, he warns the men of Ulm against allowing their wives and children to run to the friars for confession. Above all, the father confessor should be kept from the house: 'Do not summon your wife's father confessor to your house to eat or gossip unless it is a case of pressing urgency – it is not necessary to place fleas on a hide.'[105]

Closely related to the contests between the friars and the parochial clergy over preaching and confessing was the bread-and-butter issue of the revenue lost by the parish priest to mendicant competitors in the form of burial dues. This point of conflict the polemicists were able to take up and adapt to their own purposes by turning it against the anniversary masses held by the friars and by opening these to Luther's criticism of private masses and the Catholic theology of the mass more generally. William of St Amour, in an inventive exegesis on Jesus's denunciation of the Pharisees' decorating of the graves of the prophets in Matthew 23:29, had attacked the practice of burial in the church-yards of mendicant churches, and argued that the friars' concern with the dying was purely financial.[106] St Amour's charge was repeated in much of the late medieval satirical literature in both Latin and the vernacular.[107] The point is particularly well stated in the 'Viri fratres, servi Dei': 'They note with great assiduity where the rich fall sick, and run there, not stopping their visits until they have buried them. But none of them will go to the houses of the poor.'[108] Both of Eberlin's works under consideration take up his cursory treatment of this theme in 'The Fifteen Confederates.' In 'The Second True Admonition to the Council

---

[103] 'Ad Gasparis Schatzgeyri,' p. 11 (b): 'Atque (quod pene exciderat) dum auriculares matronarum confessiones religiosissime audiunt, hoc est, dum captivas ducunt mulier-culas, oneratas peccatis, quae ducuntur variis desideriis, semper discentes, et nunquam ad scientiam veritatis per venientes. 2. Timoth. 3.'

[104] 'Die andere getreue Vermahnung an den Rath von Ulm,' Enders, vol. 3, p. 24: ' . . . also wan man bulschafft nit anderst mag verglimpfen, so richt man an langen und vilen trost yn der beicht.'

[105] Ibid., p. 30.

[106] Szittya, 'Antifraternal Tradition,' p. 300.

[107] Szittya, 'Antifraternal Tradition,' p. 300; id., *Antifraternal Tradition in Medieval Literature*, p. 206; *Des Teufels Netz*, p. 174:

> Darzuo hand si vil grosz spehen,
> Wo ain richer krank lit.
> Da hept sich denn erst ain strit,
> Wie er den bring mit der grebt.

[108] As quoted in Mann, p. 51. The translation is Professor Mann's. For other examples of this charge, see Mann, pp. 41 and 231, n. 134.

of Ulm,' he reminds his readers of how jealously the mendicants guard their cemeteries.[109] Later in the same work he indicates that their concern with the souls of the departed is purely financial.[110] In 'Against the False Religious,' he goes even further, denouncing as superstition the desire to be buried in the Franciscan cowl and denying the validity of the prayers for the dead.[111]

Luther's attack on the cloistered added a whole new dimension to this charge. The anniversary masses so long popular with the patrons of the friars now were denounced as part of the general attacks on canonical hours and the mass. In 'The Babylonian Captivity of the Church' Luther had attacked the 'hour-reading' and 'mass-saying' priests.[112] 'The Judgement on Monastic Vows' applies this criticism specifically to the monks, whose liturgical activities he identifies as perversions of the divine forms of worship mentioned by Paul. As Erasmus and Eberlin had done earlier, he denounces the performance of masses in Latin without any reflection as mere 'braying and mumbling.'[113] Luther also denounces the monastic divine service as a chief pillar of monkish indolence:

> Because manual labour is prohibited, they do not work. They are supported by the rest of the world, devouring everyone else's substance although they are perfectly hale and hearty. This is to the great detriment of the genuinely poor. They repay their benefactors by spiritual works of mercy, that is, by the worship of God which we described earlier, a lot of mumbling and bellowing, of sighing and reading, and so on. Above all, the masses are among the most execrable abominations in God's sight.[114]

The denunciation of canonical hours and masses is a prominent theme throughout the anti-Franciscan polemics. Eberlin contrasts the canonical hours with true prayer from the heart and true worship anchored in faith.[115] Spelt denounces these prayers said without reflection or understanding and warns against saying prayers like the hypocrites who

---

[109] 'Die andere getreue Vermahnung an den Rath von Ulm,' Enders, vol. 3, p. 9.

[110] Ibid., p. 23: 'Sagen mir, yr münch, selen mörder zu Ulm, warumb lassen ir so vil alter yartag abgehen bey euch, warumb tilgen ir uss odder unterlassend so vil gedechtnus der selen yn ewerm seelbuch. . . . Das ist mein rede, yr seynt eygengesuchig lewt, suchen anderer heil noch nutz nit, wan man nit gebe bauchfulle, yr werden des fegfewrs wol vergessen.'

[111] 'Wider die falschen Geistlichen,' Enders, vol. 3, pp. 47, 60.

[112] See above, pp. 128–9.

[113] 'De votis monasticis iudicium,' WA, 8:621–2. See also 'Praise of Folly,' *Collected Works of Erasmus*, vol. 27, p. 131 and above p. 47.

[114] 'De votis monasticis iudicium,' WA, 8:628.

[115] 'Wider die falschen Geistlichen,' Enders, vol. 3, p. 59; 'Die andere getreue Vermahnung an den Rath von Ulm,' Enders, vol. 3, p. 22.

wish only to be seen. God is a spirit and must be prayed to in the spirit.[116] All of these charges are reproduced in detail in Lambert's eleventh chapter devoted specifically to the divine office of the Franciscans.[117] Even more common is the claim that the friars exploit their prayers as a means to extort goods from the laity. Kettenbach makes this charge with specific reference to masses and vigils.[118] Spelt charges that the monks are worse than the moneychangers in the temple or Judas when they 'sell' their spiritual services to the laity. Furthermore, they implicate the unsuspecting laity in their idolatrous activity.[119] Lambert applies Luther's charge that the monks perform divine services as an excuse to avoid real work specifically to the Franciscans and then takes the opportunity for a swipe at the Catholic theology of the mass.[120]

Several other charges levelled at the Franciscans were determined even less by historical factors and indebted more to the characteristics of the biblical types with which the friars were identified. Closely related to the accusation that the friars preach for personal gain was an attack on their mendicancy itself. William of St Amour had charged the friars with living illegitimately from the Gospel and contrasted their begging with Paul's claim that the apostles worked with their hands to feed themselves [2 Thessalonians 3:6–12].[121] This remained a crucial element in the medieval controversies involving the friars, and it was sharpened in the later fourteenth century when they were accused of depriving the more deserving poor of their livelihood.[122] These charges are clearly reflected in the characterization of friar Huberd in the general prologue to the *Canterbury Tales*:

---

[116] 'Ain ware Declaration oder Erklärung,' Ciii(b).

[117] 'Ein Evangelische beschreibung über der Barfüsser Regel,' Hiii(d)–Jiii(c). Kurten, p. 68 noted Luther's influence on this chapter.

[118] 'Eine Predigt auf den achten Sonntag nach Pfingsttag,' Clemen, p. 217.

[119] 'Ain ware Declaration oder Erklärung,' Eii – Eii(b).

[120] 'Ein Evangelische beschreibung über der Barfüsser Regel,' K(b): 'Nun volgt / damit wir sehe / warinne die Barfüsser arbeyten und alle andere münch. Dañ all vō des Endtchrists reich seind die im mit gehellen oder mit würcke / gelebet sye nit yrer hand arbeyt / damit sye selig seyent keins wegs / sunder in iren löchern und hüle ligen sye zü heülen / und opffern täglich Christum (wie sye rede) und widerüb creützige sye yn / . . .'

[121] Szittya, 'Antifraternal Tradition,' p. 304; id., *Antifraternal Tradition in Medieval Literature*, pp. 47–52; 'De periculis,' pp. 36 and 39–40.

[122] Williams, pp. 505–6; Katherine Walsh, *A Fourteenth-Century Scholar and Primate: Richard FitzRalph in Oxford, Avignon and Armagh* (Oxford, 1981), pp. 349–451. On the development of the charge that mendicancy of the friars endangered the livelihoods of the more deserving poor, see Wendy Scase, *'Piers Plowman' and the New Anticlericalism* (Cambridge, 1989); Geoffrey Dipple, 'Uthred and the Friars: Apostolic Poverty and Clerical Dominion Between FitzRalph and Wyclif,' *Traditio*, 49 (1994), pp. 235–58.

> He was he beste beggere in his hous.
> And yaf a certain ferme for the graunt:
> Noon of his brethreren cam there in his haunt.
> For though a widwe hadde nought a sho,
> So pleasant was his *In principio*
> Yit wolde have a ferthing er he wente;[123]

'The Devil's Net' makes the same point more forcefully:

> So the collectors of alms go out,
> Then they sell the truth
> To peasant women and maids
> For cheese, fat and eggs.
> Throughout the land
> Here cultivating the greatest dishonour
> Which everywhere is a blemish.
> There bringing such evil, false sorcery,
> As they fleece the people
> With their false prattle.[124]

This characterization must have retained its force into the sixteenth century. Sebastian Brant denounces clerical begging in general: 'And the priests want to support themselves by begging, / The monks' orders are very rich / And complain as if they were poor.'[125] Erasmus, on the other hand, restricts himself to the mendicancy of the friars and sharpens the implicit accusation that they deprive the more deserving poor of their sustenance: 'Many of them too make a good living of their squalor and beggary, bellowing for bread from door to door, and indeed making a nuisance of themselves in every inn, carriage or boat to the great loss of all other beggars.'[126] Luther made much the same point in his denunciation of mendicancy in the 'Address to the Christian Nobility.'[127]

These charges, stripped of their satirical veneer, reappear in the polemics against the Franciscans. Spelt contrasts the deserving poor with the devil's 'fattened pigs' who vow the highest poverty, but whose begging sack has no bottom.[128] Eberlin reprimands the citizens of Ulm for giving alms to the mendicants, who smear their mouths with sweet poison, instead of to the deserving poor. In the same pamphlet, he also contrasts the begging of the Franciscans with Paul's example.[129]

---

[123] Chaucer, pp. 155–6. See also the description of the friar's begging in the summoner's tale, pp. 320–1.

[124] *Des Teufels Netz*, pp. 170–1.

[125] Sebastian Brant, *Das Narrenschiff*, ed. Manfred Lemmer (Tübingen, 1962), p. 96.

[126] *Collected Works of Erasmus*, vol. 27, p. 131.

[127] 'An den Christlichen Adel,' WA, 6:450–1.

[128] 'Ain ware Declaration oder Erklärung,' Diii(c)–Diii(d).

[129] 'Die andere getreue Vermahnung an den Rath von Ulm,' Enders, vol. 3, pp. 6, 11.

Lambert cites the same example of Paul against the begging of the Franciscans and accuses them of employing every effort and trick to ensure that their begging sacks are filled.[130]

In 'The Judgement on Monastic Vows,' Luther did not concern himself specifically with the mendicancy of the friars, although he did touch on their poverty doctrines as part of his general attack on the monastic vows of poverty. True evangelical poverty he defines on the basis of Matthew 5:3: 'Blessed are the poor in spirit, for theirs is the kingdom of heaven.' This poverty which is enjoined on all Christians is a matter of disposition not material deprivation. In contrast, the monks vow a false material poverty in leaving behind a world of deprivation for a life of indolence and plenty in the cloister. This is not even the material poverty of the early church in Jerusalem, but rather that of children and the mentally defective who live in plenty, but do not administer to their own needs. It is merely a pretence to live idly from the work of others and a flagrant violation of spiritual poverty.[131] Within this context, Luther makes specific reference to the Franciscan prohibition against touching money: 'Obstinately applying this kind of obedience, then, the Minorite does not give his neighbour a helping hand or offer him a red cent even if he is dying and in dire need.'[132]

Luther's contrast between false material poverty and true spiritual poverty as a way to refute mendicant teachings on apostolic poverty was not novel.[133] However, the use made of this argument in the campaign against the Franciscans to reinforce more traditional attacks on the mendicancy of the friars reflects Luther's formulation of it. Kettenbach repeats the distinction between spiritual and material poverty and the charge that the cloistered life is one of plenty and indolence.[134] Lambert and Spelt begin chapters specifically on the vow of poverty with similar statements.[135] Eberlin adopts not only the distinction between spiritual

---

[130] 'Ein Evangelische beschreibung über der Barfüsser Regel,' K(b)–Kii.

[131] 'De votis monasticis iudicium,' WA, 8:641–3 and 645.

[132] Ibid., p. 625.

[133] For a fourteenth-century example of the use of this tactic, see Dipple, 'Uthred and the Friars,' pp. 250–8.

[134] 'Eine Predigt auf den achten Sonntag nach Pfingsttag,' Clemen, p. 220: 'Christus spricht Mat. am 5. [v. 3]: Beati pauperes spiritu, Selig seynd die armen yhmm geyst. und solich armut ist allen Christen gebotten. so machen sye eyn armut auf solichen sinn: Selig seind, die in der welt wenig güts übergeben odder verlassen Und kommen in eyn reych klöster, da sie kein armut oder mangel leyden.'

[135] Lambert, 'Ein Evangelische beschreibung über der Barfüsser Regel,' Eii(b): 'Darumb was es für ein armüt sey / wirt uss der rede Christi offenbar. . . . Sychstu wie die armüt sein mussz / die allen Christen zůmal hoch von nöten. Allen sag ich / nit allein den Barfüssern.' Eiij: 'dañ es vō geist můssz verstandē werdē. ye nit ein yeder armer ist selig / sonder der im geist arm ist / der ist warlich selig. Spelt, 'Ain ware Declaration oder Erklärung,' Diij(b): '. . . wann es ist der recht verstandt / war lebendig Gayst der hayligen geschrifft nit / noch

and material poverty, but also Luther's criticism of the Franciscan's refusal to touch money.[136]

However, to further drive home the attack on the friars' begging, the polemicists of 1523 turned to another characteristic traditionally associated with them. William of St Amour took Jesus's charge in Matthew 23:6 that the Pharisees loved the 'uppermost rooms at feasts' as an opportunity to accuse the friars of currying the favour of the wealthy in order to extract alms from them.[137] Chaucer makes this point, clearly contrasting the profession of the friar with his actual preferences:

> For unto swich a worthy man as he
> Acorded nat, as by his facultee,
> To have with sike lazars a queyntance.
> It is nat honeste – it may nat avance –
> For to deelen with no swich poraille,
> But al with riche and selleres of vitaille.[138]

Jill Mann has discovered evidence of similar charges in French and Latin works from the Continent.[139] This characterization, too, must have retained currency into the Renaissance. In *Praise of Folly*, Erasmus satirizes the friars and merchants in one blow: 'There are plenty of sycophantic friars, too, who will sing their praises and publicly address them as honourable, doubtless hoping that a morsel of these ill-gotten gains will come their way.'[140] Kettenbach's warning to the wealthy and noble listeners in his sermon in all likelihood reflects this charge:

> Oh, you nobles, you wealthy ones, if you had recognized them by Christ's teaching, you and your heirs would still have the good manors, fields, meadows, vineyards, lease rents, incomes, interests, villages and castles! Now, however, you have been deceived by the

---

will / oder mainung Christi in seinen worten / das die volkommenhait der armůt / stee in verlassung der zeytlichen ding (wie du mainst) und allein von ander leüt gůt sich zůerneren / das magest du mercken auss andern seinen worten. Als nemlich Matt. 5.'

[136] 'Wider die falschen Geistlichen,' Enders, vol. 3, p. 60: 'Christus Hat geriten. Math. xxj. und gelt genommen durch mittel person. Johann xiij. auch selbs angriffen. Mar. xij. frantz. Das verpeut ich bey todsünd. 3. ca. und 4. ca. re. Also das man auch für krancke personen und zu andern grossen notturfften des leibs nit soll gelt nemen. . . . christus. Sălig seind die armen am gaist. Math. v. franntz. Sălig seind die eüsserlich betlen, darumb sag ich trützlich, solche leipliche armůt und betlen macht erben und künig im himelreich. vj. cap. reg.'

[137] Szittya, 'Antifraternal Tradition,' p. 296; id., *Antifraternal Tradition in Medieval Literature*, p. 38; 'Sermo Magistri Wilhelmi de S. Amore, I,' p. 44.

[138] Chaucer, p. 155.

[139] Mann, pp. 51–3.

[140] *Collected Works of Erasmus*, vol. 27, p. 121. Erasmus repeats this charge when he satirizes the friars themselves. See p. 135.

false prophets of Baal who revel and carouse from one midnight to the next on your goods.[141]

Eberlin does not specifically address his comments to the wealthy, but reprimands his readers in 'The Second True Admonition to the Council of Ulm' for leaving inheritances to these servants of Satan instead of their rightful heirs.[142]

The Reformation attack on the begging of the friars indicates the extent of Luther's debt to medieval criticisms of the mendicant orders, and the difficulty at times of distinguishing pre-Reformation from Reformation anticlericalism. This difficulty is even more pronounced when dealing with two other charges levelled at the friars in 1523: complaints that they were sectarians and that they stole children by encouraging underaged novices. The charge that the friars constitute a new sect, distinct from the sect of Christ, appears to have been a catchword of the Wycliffite attack against them.[143] Wyclif charged on the basis of 1 Corinthians 3:3–5:

> For ye are yet carnal: for whereas there is among you envying, and strife, and divisions, are ye not carnal, and walk as men? For while one saith, I am of Paul; and another, I am of Apollos; are ye not carnal? Who then is Paul, and who is Apollos, but ministers by whom ye believed, even as the Lord gave to every man?

that the individual orders opposed the one order instituted by Christ, and he contrasted the simplicity and freedom of the Gospel with the myriad of statutes enjoined on the various orders.[144] This charge probably became a commonplace of antimendicant sentiment even among the orthodox. While it is not readily discernible in late medieval satiric literature, it reappears fully blown in Erasmus's *Praise of Folly*:

> But nothing could be more amusing than their practice of doing everything to rule, as if they were following mathematical calculations which it would be a sin to ignore. . . . In short, they all take remarkable pains to be different in their rules of life. They aren't interested in being like Christ but in being unlike each other.[145]

Although Luther mentions the charge of sectarianism, it is not particularly prominent in 'The Judgement on Monastic Vows.' As we have seen, it lies behind his claim that vows contradict the second

---

[141] 'Eine Predigt auf den achten Sonntag nach Pfingsttag,' Clemen, p. 216.

[142] 'Die andere getreue Vermahnung an den Rath von Ulm,' Enders, vol. 3, p. 11.

[143] Williams, p. 504.

[144] Lohse, *Mönchtum und Reformation*, pp. 179–83.

[145] A.H.T. Levi (ed.), *Collected Works of Erasmus*, vol. 27: *Literary and Educational Writings*, vol. 5 (Toronto, 1986), p. 131.

commandment.[146] In a later discussion of evangelical freedom, he cites Romans 16:17–18 and charges: 'This is exactly what the monastic institutions do. We never see divisions and sects except among the monks. Among them we find servitude to the belly.'[147] In support of this claim, Luther then cites 2 Peter 2:1: 'On this very point Peter, in 2 Peter 2[:1] calls them sects of perdition, and with a grim and terrible statement he warns us against sects and opinions which have nothing to do with Christ.'[148] Luther's criticisms are levelled at monasticism in general, although on one occasion he specifically charges St Francis with being a schismatic.[149]

Albeit with varied emphasis, the charge of sectarianism appears in all of the pamphlets aimed at the Franciscan order in 1523. In his justification for leaving the order, Schwan refers to having left the 'cloister sects.'[150] Kettenbach does not specifically call the Franciscans a sect, but reprimands them for living apart from the general brotherhood of Christ.[151] In his second letter to Ulm, Eberlin touches on a key element of the medieval secular–mendicant conflict when he refers to the implications of this division for episcopal and parochial discipline. Shortly thereafter, he appeals to the interests of the Ulm council by pointing out the social implications of mendicant sectarianism.[152] In a more general denunciation of monasticism, Spelt claims that the division of Christendom by the sects began shortly after the time of the apostles and that they have expanded to the point that they are without number.[153]

Spelt's point is repeated by Lambert, who includes a table listing 94 such sects and explains that this table is far from comprehensive, but includes only the sects of which he personally has heard.[154] Like Wyclif, he cites 1 Corinthians 3 against this introduction of divisions into the body of Christ.[155] Later, he charges the Franciscans specifically with observing their statutes instead of the Gospel and denounces the chapters of the order for vainly promulgating new statutes which have nothing to do with Christ, are rarely observed and frequently altered.[156]

---

146 See above, pp. 139–40.
147 'De votis monasticis iudicium,' WA, 8:655.
148 Ibid.
149 Ibid., pp. 579–80.
150 'Ein Sendbriff Johannis Schwan,' Bii(b).
151 'Eine Predigt auf den achten Sonntag nach Pfingsttag,' Clemen, p. 218.
152 'Die andere getreue Vermahnung an den Rath von Ulm,' Enders, vol. 3, pp. 6, 10.
153 'Ain ware Declaration oder Erklärung,' Aiii(b).
154 'Ein Evangelische beschreibung über der Barfüsser Regel,' Bii(b)–Biii(d).
155 Ibid., Bii(b).
156 Ibid., Kii(b).

In the final chapter of his description of the Rule, Lambert again ties the statutory life of monasticism to sectarianism:

> For at all times they set one statute over another, none of which they hold to . . . Woe to these godless people who vainly praise God and follow and teach alone their own fabrications. Truly, if there were no other reason, nonetheless this is sufficient to do away with monasticism, that they do not follow God's Word, but instead their own inventions and sins . . . But who will ensure that in the holy community of Christ no more sects will be invented? That all peoples will unanimously follow Christ? That no one will any longer say, 'I am a Dominican, I am a Benedictine, I am a Franciscan, I am this or that,' but each will say with one confession, 'I am a Christian.'[157]

This same theme also underlies Eberlin's 'Against the False Religious.' He begins the attack on his former order by claiming it has more statutes than the Jews have laws and more sects than days in the year.[158] In 36 points he summarizes details of the Rule and argues that these not only do not appear in the Gospel, but are also contrary to it.[159]

Similarly, the accusation that the friars encouraged underaged novices was little changed in the hands of the Reformers. On the basis of the description of the proselytizing activity of the Pharisees in Matthew 23:15, St Amour had charged the friars with stealing children.[160] In 'The Babylonian Captivity of the Church,' Luther cites the same text in his appeal to abolish priestly vows: 'But now we traverse sea and land to make many proselytes [Matt. 23:15]; we fill the world with priests, monks and nuns, and imprison them all in lifelong vows.'[161] In 'The Judgement on Monastic Vows,' his allusion to the medieval charge is somewhat clearer: 'And yet our present-day monks, although they teach neither faith nor sound doctrine, but rather everything blasphemous, dare to snatch sons away from their parents into a permanent bondage.'[162]

In this latter work, Luther devotes his attention at one point to a discussion of the novitiate year. This was likely to be the motivation for similar concern with this topic by Lambert. However, Kurten observes that, while Luther concentrates on the probationary period as an improper test of the grace required for the vow of chastity, Lambert emphasizes other vices: the lack of evangelical instruction during the

---

[157] Ibid., Kiii(b)–Kiii(c).
[158] 'Wider die falschen Geistlichen,' Enders, vol. 3, p. 48.
[159] Ibid., pp. 55, 61.
[160] Szittya, 'Antifraternal Tradition, pp. 299–300; id., *Antifraternal Tradition in Medieval Literature*, p. 40; 'De periculis,' p. 35.
[161] 'De captivitate ecclesiae Babylonica praeludium,' WA, 6:539.
[162] 'De votis monasticis iudicium,' WA, 8:627.

novitiate and the tricks employed by the monks to ensnare the novices.[163] Both Lambert and Eberlin attack this practice by admonishing parents not to place their children in cloisters. In an excess of rhetorical zeal, Lambert suggests that placing children in a monastery is worse than murdering them or burying them alive.[164] Eberlin uses Saint Bonaventure as an example of a child novice to the Franciscans.[165] Elsewhere, he frequently warns parents against dedicating their offspring to the Antichrist by placing them in cloisters.[166]

Penn Szittya has attributed the versatility and longevity of the medieval antifraternal tradition to its reliance on eternal, unchanging biblical types for its characterizations of the friars. A further characteristic attributed to them indicates clearly how the literary type continued to dominate the perception of the friars and how easily this perception could be adapted to the needs of the Reformers. In the exegesis of St Amour the Pharisees' broad phylacteries and the enlarged borders of their garments mentioned in Matthew 23:5 were an occasion for an attack on the alleged feigned piety of the friars. St Amour had identified these distinctive costumes with the friars' practice of going barefoot. However, in the English antifraternal literature, this charge took an unusual twist and became identified with excessive clothing worn by the friars.[167] This is evident in the depiction of Chaucer's friar: 'For there he was not lyk a cloysterer, / With a thredbare cope, as is a poure scoler, / But he was lyk a maister, or a pope. / Of double worstede was his semycope, / That rounded as a belle, out of the presse.'[168]

On the Continent, however, it appears that the tradition remained true to the characterization of St Amour. It is not clear whether the term 'Barfusser,' applied specifically to the Franciscans by these authors, traditionally carried derogatory connotations. However, in the pamphlets of 1523 it soon took on such connotations. As we have seen, both Eberlin and Ulrich von Hutten referred to Glapion as 'wooden shoe.'[169] Lambert devotes a chapter of his description of the Franciscan Rule to the shoes of the friars and the hypocrisy associated with them:

---

[163] Kurten, pp. 65–6. See 'De votis monasticis iudicium,' WA, 8:659–61 and 'Ein Evangelische Beschreibung über der Barfüsser Regel,' Fiii(c)–Gii(b).

[164] 'Ein Evangelische beschreibung über der Barfüsser Regel,' Giii(c).

[165] 'Wider die falschen Geistlichen,' Enders, vol. 1, pp. 46–7.

[166] Ibid., p. 69; 'Die andere getreue Vermahnung an den Rath von Ulm,' Enders, vol. 3, pp. 31, 33.

[167] Szittya, 'Antifraternal Tradition,' pp. 298–9; id., *Antifraternal Tradition in Medieval Literature*, p. 39; 'Sermo Wilhelmi de S. Amore, I,' p. 43.

[168] Chaucer, p. 156.

[169] See above, p. 72.

The bare-footed friars cut their shoes with the top open. The reason for this, as I understand it, is that they want their shoes to be regarded as sandals, that is, as the shoes of bishops or apostles, as the shoes of the apostles are so described in Mark 6. . . . With this they reveal wonderfully their hypocrisy, that by their shoes alone they wish to be regarded as evangelical.[170]

This charge was also linked to other distinctive features of the Franciscan order. Later in this work, Lambert denounces the statutes specifying the robe of the Minors and prohibiting them from riding as fabrications contrary to both the Rule and the Gospel.[171] Eberlin cites these same characteristics together with the practice of not wearing shoes as the feigned simplicity by which the Minors lead the world astray, and later refers to the statutes regulating these matters as a clear indication that the Rule contradicts the Gospel.[172]

The anti-Franciscan polemics of 1523 took as their basic premises Luther's attack on the institution of monasticism in 'The Judgement of Monastic Vows.' These they supplemented with charges that were applicable to the Franciscans, and often the other mendicants, in particular. Parallels between these charges and the characterizations of the friars in medieval and Renaissance antifraternal satirical literature tend to indicate that they were commonplaces generally associated with the friars. However, these characterizations were chosen and adapted on the basis of their applicability to the task at hand. This is most apparent in the complete neglect of William of St Amour's charge that the friars unjustly desired the status of *magister*, the charge that occupied a central place in both the conflicts at the University of Paris and his exegesis of Matthew 23.[173] In 1523, the universities and learned ones come under fire as a group, but the concrete issues of contention are those of the cure of souls and the relationship of the Franciscans with the laity.

In their reliance on Luther's work, these authors provided an important vernacular channel for the transmission of his criticisms of monasticism to the Reformation public. In so doing, they took Luther's arguments from an abstract to a concrete plane, directing them at a specific, easily identifiable group within the clerical estate. However, the real strength of the campaign against the Franciscans lay in the ability of these authors to tap into a popular tradition identifying particular vices with the friars on the basis of their association with certain biblical types. Robert Scribner has argued that a basic technique of Reformation propaganda was the gradual shift from one 'symbolic universe' to

---

[170] 'Ein Evangelische beschreibung über der Barfüsser Regel,' Hiii(d).

[171] Ibid., Jiii(c), Kiii(c)–Kiii(d).

[172] 'Wider die falschen Geistlichen,' Enders, vol. 3, pp. 45, 63.

[173] Szittya, 'Antifraternal Tradition,' pp. 294–5; id., *Antifraternal Tradition in Medieval Literature*, pp. 35–7.

another through the transformation of images and symbols familiar to the audience.[174] This the polemicists of 1523 achieved through the incorporation of themes from Luther's 'Judgement on Monastic Vows' into the tradition of antifraternalism.

The continued currency of this tradition is attested to by the appearance of elements from it in the writings of Renaissance satirists, particularly Erasmus, and in the writings of Luther. That they appear in Luther's earlier writings suggests a modification, although not a refutation, of Lohse's claim for the originality of Luther's attack on monasticism. The novelty of Luther's theological arguments denying the validity of monasticism is not to be challenged, but these arguments should be understood within the context of the late medieval and Renaissance criticism of the monks and friars, and the social and spiritual evils associated with them. This suggests as well that caution be exercised in dealing with the anticlerical polemics of the early Reformation. Rublack indicates that, in the reception of Reformation pamphlets, associations are made where the text is able to touch on experience, in the form of traditional criticism of the clergy or the lived experience of the reader.[175] The results of research into the medieval antifraternal tradition cautions against attributing to the friars all of the vices of which they are accused by their foes. This polemic may have stemmed not so much from living experience as from the incendiary application of a new theology to traditional criticisms that had been around ever since there were friars.

---

[174] R.W. Scribner, *For the Sake of Simple Folk: Popular Propaganda for the German Reformation* (Cambridge, 1981), p. 9.

[175] Rublack, p. 237.

CHAPTER SEVEN

Variations on a theme

In certain crucial ways the anti-Franciscan campaign of 1523 was a controlled outburst. Luther had called it forth against a specific group within the first estate, and all of the pamphleteers involved had close personal connections with Wittenberg, with the possible exceptions of Heinrich Spelt and Heinrich von Kettenbach. The mendicants were an obvious threat to the spread of the Reformation and their traditional ties to the papacy and autonomy from episcopal jurisdiction immediately excluded them from the ranks of the reformed clerical order. Schatzgeyer's response to Luther, then, set the stage for the employment of anticlerical sentiment for a limited tactical objective.

The writings of Kettenbach and Johann Rot-Locher, another apostate from the Ulm Franciscan Observants, provide an interesting perspective on the development of Wittenberg anticlericalism. Neither man became personally connected to Wittenberg, although both of them regarded their activity as a part of Luther's Reformation. However, both also have subsequently been characterized as exponents of what are traditionally considered non-Lutheran elements of the Reformation age: Kettenbach of the Knights' Revolt and Rot-Locher of the Reformation, or revolution, of the common man. Finally, both men took part in the denunciation of their former brethren: Kettenbach, as we have already seen, in 1523, and Rot-Locher in a belated attack in early 1524. But their approaches to the anti-Franciscan campaign are significantly different to those of the other authors studied here. Instead of singling the friars out as a specific group distinct from the evangelical clergy, these two men come to the attack on the friars from comprehensive anticlerical visions which identify all clergy as the enemies of God and the truth.

The different perspectives from which Kettenbach and Rot-Locher approach the antifraternal campaign relate directly to the distance they remained from the centre of the Reformation. However, this is not to suggest that somehow their visions were intentionally less 'Lutheran.' Rather, their reading of Luther's message was filtered through the prism of personal experiences which did not include the moderating effect of direct contact with the Wittenbergers.

The prophets of Baal

Heinrich von Kettenbach's reforming career appears as a classic example of the development of a Reformation radical. He began agitation for the Reformation in late 1521 or early 1522 as a preacher in the Franciscan priory in Ulm. While still in Ulm, he produced three *Flugschriften* aimed at elucidating elements of Wittenberg theology. Forced from the city around the middle of July 1522, he migrated probably to Bamberg, where he penned an additional seven *Flugschriften*. In these later pamphlets, Kettenbach begins to supplement his espousal of Luther's reform with explicit references to and enthusiasm for the activities of Franz von Sickingen.

But Kettenbach's writings do not provide evidence that his career breaks down into distinct moderate and radical phases. In the middle of his polemics in support of the activities of the imperial knights, he produced two *Flugschriften* with explicitly theological concerns: 'A Sermon to the Commendable City of Ulm in Farewell' and 'A New Apology and Justification for Martin Luther against the Murderous Braying of the Papists.' Rather, the notion that Kettenbach's allegiance had changed appears to have more to do with our perceptions of the relationship between the Reformation and Knights' Revolt than his own affiliations. In one of his later writings, Kettenbach himself established the relationship between the politics of the German estates and the Reformation:

> There [at Worms] you were faced with the affair of Martin Luther, the truly Christian, devout, innocent, learned doctor, who defended not only the honour, dignity, rank, goods, fiefs, and lives of the superstitious, foolish, servile German land, but also the salvation of all Christians on earth, for he defended the true Christian belief, through which we all must be saved and not through our own works.[1]

Research into Sickingen's activities before and during the Knights' Revolt has begun to close the gap between it and the Reformation.[2] Hans-Jürgen Goertz, in particular, has emphasized the importance of anticlericalism as the primary bridge by which the lower nobility came

---

[1] 'Ein Practica,' Clemen, p. 185 (= Laube 2:821).

[2] William R. Hitchcock, *The Background of the Knights' Revolt* (Berkeley and Los Angeles, 1958), pp. 42–56. Heinrich Steitz, 'Franz von Sickingen und die reformatorische Bewegung,' *Ebenburg-Hefte*, 2 (1968), pp. 19–28. Martin Brecht, 'Die deutsche Ritterschaft und die Reformation,' *Ebenburg-Hefte*, 3 (1969), pp. 27–37. Ulrich Oelschläger, 'Der Sendbrief Franz von Sickingens an seinen Verwandten Dieter von Handschuchsheim,' *Ebernburg-Hefte*, 4 (1970), pp. 71–85. Wolfgang Jung, 'Oekolampad an Hedio,' *Ebenburg-Hefte*, 5 (1971), pp. 87–94. 'Kaspar Aquilas "Predigt" auf der Ebernburg,' *Ebernburg-Hefte*, 9 (1975), pp. 124–32. Karlheinz Schauder, 'Martin Bucer und Franz von Sickingen,' *Ebernburg-Hefte*, 16 (1982), pp. 226–33. Volker Press, 'Ein Ritter zwischen Rebellion und Reformation: Franz von Sickingen (1481–1523),' *Ebernburg Hefte*, 17 (1983), pp. 151–77.

over to the Reformation.[3] Goertz's primary concern is with the response of the lower nobility general to the Reformation, and the subjects of his research go well beyond those who actively supported Sickingen. But, given the nature of Sickingen's campaign against Trier, the suggestion that anticlerical sentiment and agitation served as the cross-over from Reformation to the Knights' Revolt seems particularly relevant.

When Eberlin began his agitation for reform in the Ulm Franciscan cloister, Kettenbach was master of the novices there.[4] But the exact relationship between these two men remains a mystery, and the problem is compounded by Kettenbach's failure to mention his more famous *confrere* in any of his writings. The fact that Kettenbach was able to remain in the cloister more than a year after the departure of Eberlin suggests that in 1521 he had not yet openly identified himself as a proponent of reform. Kettenbach himself indicates that he preached three times on the consolation of a troubled conscience in Advent 1521, and the context in which he makes these claims would indicate that the sermons were delivered in an evangelical manner.[5] However, the first clear statement of his reforming activity in Ulm is 'A Profitable Sermon to all Christians of Ulm on Fasting and Feasting,' which he delivered on the first Sunday of Lent (9 March) 1522.[6]

In a later discussion of the nature of the Christian church, Kettenbach concludes: 'Had Peter Nestler known this, he would not have prattled so many lies and errors about the church.'[7] From the beginning, Kettenbach's chief opponent in Ulm was Nestler and in winter and spring 1522 Kettenbach and Martin Idelhauser, a reforming canon in the Ulm cathedral, squared up against Nestler and the Ulm Dominicans.[8]

---

[3] Hans-Jürgen Goertz, *Pfaffenhaß und groß Geschrei: Die reformatorischen Bewegungen in Deutschland 1517–1529* (Munich, 1987), 107–8, 117–18; id., *Antiklerikalismus und Reformation* (Göttingen, 1995), pp. 45–62.

[4] For the details of Kettenbach's career in the order see Hans Volz, 'Heinrich von Kettenbach,' *NDB*, vol. 8 (Berlin, 1969), p. 412.

[5] 'Ein Gespräch mit einem frommen Altmütterlein von Ulm,' Clemen, p. 73 (= Laube 1:210); 'Sermon zu Ulm,' Clemen, p. 110.

[6] 'Eine nützliche Predigt zu allen Christen von dem Fasten und Feiern,' Clemen, p. 5.

[7] 'Ein Sermon von der christlichen Kirche,' Clemen, p. 100.

[8] For the details of Kettenbach's conflict with Nestler, compare Bernhard Riggenbach, *Johann Eberlin von Günzburg und sein Reformprogramm: Ein Beitrag zur Geschichte des Sechszehnten Jahrhunderts* (Tübingen, 1874), p. 171 with Stadtarchiv Ulm, *Ratsdekreten*, X. 19. 1, fasz. 11 #1 and M. Georg Veesenmeyer, 'Verantwortung der Evangelischen Bürger zu Ulm gegen Peter Hutz, genannt Nestler,' in Veesenmeyer, *Beitrage zur Geschichte der Litteratur und Reformation* (Ulm, 1792), pp. 117–26. On Martin Idelhauser see Veesenmeyer, 'Revocationsacte Martin Idelhausers von 1522, nebst einer Einleitung dazu, worinn die Nachrichten von diesem Kaplan am Münster zu Ulm gesammelt sind,' in Veesenmeyer, pp. 127–51; Bernd Breitenbruch, *Predigt, Traktat und Flugschrift im Dienst der Ulmer Reformation* (Ulm, 1981), p. 38; Max Radlkofer, *Johann*

Kettenbach himself indicates that an important point of contention had been the efficacy of lighting memorial candles in the church and establishing endowed masses.[9] The controversy must have generated significant attention and disturbance. Finally, on 21 March the city council intervened, fearing 'trouble among the common people,' cited the parties involved before it and enjoined them to more peaceful activity.[10]

This controversy gave rise to Kettenbach's second *Flugschrift*, 'A Sermon against the Pope's Kitchen Preacher in Ulm.' He claims to be responding to Nestler's assertion that the church has the power to alter Scripture, although the suggestion that this 'alteration' includes 'perversion through glosses' may indicate that Kettenbach exaggerated his opponent's position.[11] The text for the sermon is Luke 21:33, 'Heaven and earth will pass away, but my words will never pass away.' This provides the groundwork not only for an attack on papal power and the rejection of the teachings of scholastic theology, but also an indictment of the activities of all levels of the clerical estate.[12]

Kettenbach's suggestion that someone should scrape, or even tear out the tongues of his opponents may be taken as an indication of the tone of the dispute, and it may soon have become too hot for Kettenbach in Ulm.[13] Wilhelm Rem's *Augsburger Chronik* states that a Franciscan monk preaching support for Luther was forced to flee Ulm in 1522 after Jacob Fugger placed a price on his head.[14] Like the 'Sermon on Fasting and Feasting,' that against Nestler was first published by Melchior Ramminger in Augsburg. This led Otto Clemen to suggest that, with apparent recklessness, Kettenbach went directly to the camp of the enemy. He must, however, have soon returned to Ulm and re-entered the fray. A discussion by Kettenbach of Idelhauser's revocation on 2 July in Kettenbach's planned *Abschiedspredigt* and later references to sermons he preached in Ulm on the festivals of Sts Peter and Paul (29

Eberlin von Günzburg und sein Vetter Hans Jakob Wehe von Leipheim (Nördlingen, 1887), pp. 78–9.

[9] 'Gespräch mit einem Altmütterlein,' Clemen, pp. 55–6 (= Laube 1:201–2).

[10] Stadtarchiv Ulm, *Ratsdekreten, 2 – Reformation, 1522*; Keim, p. 46; Clemen, p. 229.

[11] Nikolaus Paulus, *Die deutschen Dominikaner im Kampfe gegen Luther (1518–1563)* (Freiburg, 1903), pp. 283–4.

[12] 'Ein Sermon wider des Papsts Küchenprediger zu Ulm,' Clemen, pp. 32–50.

[13] Ibid., p. 33.

[14] Historische Kommission bei der Bayerischen Akademie der Wissenschaft (ed.), *Die Chroniken der deutschen Städte vom 14. bis ins 16. Jahrhundert*, vol. 25: *Augsburg* (Leipzig, 1896; reprint edn, Göttingen, 1966), pp. 170–1; Clemen, pp. 230–3.

June) and St Bonaventure (15 July) indicate that he could not have quit the city for good before the middle of July.[15]

According to his own testimony, Kettenbach preached on the nature of the Christian church on three occasions in Ulm. It is likely that one of these was subsequently published as 'A Sermon on the Christian Church.'[16] Kettenbach's stated purpose in this work is to provide a comprehensive definition of the term 'church' to clarify matters under debate. He contrasts a strongly Augustinian ecclesiology with suggestions identifying the church with various elements of the ecclesiastical hierarchy. Although he adopts a more academic tone here than in his earlier pamphlets, Kettenbach's polemics are no less virulent. As a clear statement of his ecclesiology, this pamphlet provides valuable insights into Kettenbach's anticlericalism.[17]

Kettenbach must have been forced to leave the city for good shortly after this. He apparently did not even have time to address a farewell sermon to his flock. A pamphlet written after his departure from the city was intended to fulfil this function: 'In conclusion, I hope that, with this sermon, I have fulfilled in part what I neglected at my departure.'[18] Shortly thereafter he suggests the reason for his haste: 'But then I knew that I could not remain or I would have been guilty of a mortal sin; I did not want to cause them to murder me, . . .'[19]

Already in these early pamphlets Kettenbach develops the outlines of the general anticlericalism that pervades all of his later writings. The central theme, that the clergy as a whole opposes the Gospel, is evident already in 'A Sermon on Fasting and Feasting,' which charges 'priests, monks, pope, bishops and all who wear a tonsure or cowl' with opposing the Christian church.[20] Shortly thereafter, in 'A Sermon on the Christian Church,' he returns to this charge, claiming: 'The priests and clergy with their prelates have always been against God and Christ, against the prophets and apostles, just as they are at this time.'[21] The contrast between Kettenbach's comprehensive anticlericalism and Eberlin's

---

[15] Clemen, pp. 231–3. See 'Sermon zu Ulm,' p. 116; 'Von der Kirche,' p. 102; and 'Gespräch mit einem Altmütterlein,' p. 69 (= Laube 1:208).

[16] 'Gespräch mit einem Altmütterlein,' Clemen, p. 69 (= Laube 1:208). M. Georg Veesenmeyer, 'Nachricht von Heinrich von Kettenbach, einer der ersten Ulmischen Reformatoren, und seinem Schriften,' in Veesenmeyer, pp. 108–9, identified this as the sermon delivered on the feast of St Bonaventure, although Clemen (p. 232) insists that it was not written down in the published form until after 15 July. It certainly postdates the sermon on the feast of Sts Peter and Paul which is mentioned in its conclusion.

[17] 'Von der Kirche,' Clemen, pp. 80–102.

[18] 'Sermon zu Ulm,' Clemen, p. 120.

[19] Ibid., p. 121.

[20] 'Vom Fasten und Feiern,' Clemen, p. 15.

[21] 'Von der Kirche,' Clemen, p. 94.

more limited attacks on the friars a year earlier is striking. However, much had happened in the intervening year. The status of Luther and his reform had been decided at Worms, and the lines between the Reformers and those faithful to the old church had hardened considerably. Part of this process was the development of Reformation anticlerical polemics. As will become apparent, Kettenbach had at his disposal not only the more limited anticlerical diatribes of Luther's 'Address to the Christian Nobility,' but also his more radical statements in 'On the Misuse of the Mass.'

A clear indication of the extent to which circumstances had changed is Kettenbach's awareness from his earliest writings of the essential features of Wittenberg theology. Whereas Eberlin initially saw Luther's activity as an extension of that of the humanists in 1521, in 1522 Kettenbach has a pretty clear idea of the distinctive themes of the Wittenbergers. Not only does he adopt Luther's emphasis on the primacy of Scripture, but he is also aware of his distinction between Law and Gospel.[22] This lays the basis for detailed contrasts between Christian liberty and the legalism of the papists and between the doctrines of salvation *sola fide* on the basis of predestination and the works righteousness of Luther's opponents.[23]

Furthermore, Kettenbach was able to exploit elements of Luther's teachings to underscore his own anticlerical programme. This he integrated carefully with existing anticlerical sentiment. On occasion he denounces clerical wealth and refers to excessive gifts to the church as theft.[24] The hypocrisy of clerical and monastic fasts he contrasts with the unwilling fast of the impoverished laity, and he attacks the use of the ban to enforce unjust demands of the church.[25] The clergy generally are charged with being servants who wish to be lords.[26] At the same time, Kettenbach effectively used Luther's theology as an anticlerical weapon. This is particularly prominent in his treatment of the clerical abuse of sacred power, an abuse which Robert Scribner identifies as the source of all other resentment of clerical power.[27] He is able to claim that the clerical monopoly on sacred power derives from heathen teachings,

---

[22] 'Vom Fasten und Feiern,' Clemen, pp. 16, 21; 'Wider des Papsts Küchenprediger,' Clemen, p. 35.

[23] 'Vom Fasten und Feiern,' Clemen, pp. 20–4; 'Von der Kirche,' Clemen, pp. 87–90.

[24] 'Von der Kirche,' Clemen, p. 100.

[25] 'Vom Fasten und Feiern,' Clemen, pp. 12–13, 17–18.

[26] 'Vom Fasten und Feiern,' Clemen, p. 15; 'Wider des Papsts Küchenprediger,' Clemen, p. 36.

[27] Robert Scribner, 'Anticlericalism and the German Reformation,' in id., *Popular Culture and Popular Movements in Reformation Germany* (London, 1987), p. 249.

which serve not only to exploit the laity, but also lead their souls to damnation.

Kettenbach focuses squarely on the theme of the sacred power exercised by the clergy in the last of his pamphlets written in Ulm, 'A Sermon on the Christian Church.' This pamphlet opens with the claim that there is no salvation outside of the church. Kettenbach denies that the true church can be identified with the papal church by appealing to Luther's teaching on the invisible church and a detailed exposition of predestination.[28] In this way he undercuts the clerical monopoly on sacred power and lays the basis for a denunciation of orthodox theology as heretical. He then turns the Bible against scholastic theology and canon law to clarify their demonic origins.[29] When the opportunity arises, Kettenbach explains how specific teachings and practices contradict true theology and lead to damnation. This polemic is sharpened with reference to the money extorted from the laity, thereby revealing the full extent of clerical deception in both the sacred and profane realms.[30]

However, despite his use of Reformation theology against the clergy, Kettenbach fails to employ the assumedly most potent of Luther's weapons, the doctrine of the priesthood of all believers. Rather, he concentrates his attention on the use of biblical types of the opponents of the Gospel to drive home his denunciations of the clergy. Particularly prominent in his attack on the clergy is the biblical type of the *antichristi*. 'A Sermon on Fasting and Feasting' identifies the oppressors of the church as the vicar or viceroy of the Devil, that is the Antichrist, and his mercenaries, whose chief crime is the binding of consciences which Christ has set free.[31] On this point, Kettenbach is probably indebted to Luther, whose identification of the papacy with the Antichrist in the 'Address to the Christian Nobility' rested also on the charge that the popes had robbed the church of the freedom given by Christ:

> Now we see how they handle Christendom, taking away its freedom without any proof from Scripture, at their own whim. Those whom

---

[28] 'Von der Kirche,' Clemen, 80–102.

[29] 'Vom Fasten und Feiern,' Clemen, 19–22; 'Wider des Papsts Küchenprediger,' Clemen, pp. 46–9. In the sermon on fasting he appears to still trust a purified version of canon law, but the sermon against Nestler denounces the institution outright.

[30] For specific examples, see 'Vom Fasten und Feiern,' Clemen, p. 23; 'Von der Kirche,' Clemen, pp. 93, 101.

[31] 'Vom Fasten und Feiern,' Clemen, p. 23: 'es thut es auch niemant dann des teüfels vicari und stathalter, der entchrist und sein söldner . . . . wer des bapst vych wil sein, der hört den bapst. wer Thome oder schoti, Ambrosy oder Dominici schaff will sein oder bock, der hört sy und hölt nit frey, das got frey gemacht hat in speiß und trank, sunder legen bann und sünd darauf, das auch solich lerer doch nit geton haben.'

God and the apostles have subjected to the temporal sword. It is to be feared that this is a game of the Antichrist or his immediate precursor.[32]

Like Luther, Kettenbach distinguishes between an earlier mystical Antichrist and the subsequent true Antichrist, and links his outlook to papal presumptions of superiority, not only to the emperor but also to God.[33] He was probably also familiar with Luther's conflict with Alveld on the authority of the papacy. In 'A Sermon on the Christian Church,' Kettenbach, too, dismisses claims of Petrine primacy based on Matthew 16:18: 'On this rock I will build my Church.'[34] Shortly thereafter, he takes up the theme of the papalist distinction between the office and its occupant, which had also come to the fore in Luther's conflict with Alveld.[35]

As suggested earlier, the identification of the papacy with the Antichrist also forms the basis for an indictment of those associated with it. Kettenbach again follows Luther's lead in declaring the papal church a 'synagogue of Satan' on the basis of Revelation 2:9: 'I know the blasphemy of them which say they are Jews, and are not, but are the synagogue of Satan.'[36] For both authors, papal authority and the synagogue of Satan are closely linked to canon law and scholastic theology:

> So you see that, with your teaching, you have preached against the Gospel, that you have remained with human teaching, with the pope's spiritless law, with your Aristotle the 'Foolosopher' and his disciples such as Thomas and Scotus, etc.[37]

Luther's rejection of papal authority initially led him to the call for the establishment of a German national church led by a reforming

---

[32] 'An den christlichen Adel deutscher Nation,' WA, 6:411.

[33] 'Wider des Papsts Küchenprediger,' Clemen, pp. 36, 38. See also Clemen, p. 51, n. 4; 'An den christlichen Adel deutscher Nation,' WA, 6:433–5 and 'Vom Missbrauch der Messe,' WA, 8:496.

[34] 'Von der Kirche,' Clemen, pp. 80–1. See 'Resolutio Lutheriana super propositione sua tercia decima de potestate papae,' WA, 2:185–240 and 'Von dem Papstthum zu Rom wider den hochberühmten Romanisten zu Leipzig,' WA, 6:314.

[35] 'Von der Kirche,' Clemen, pp. 81–2. 'Von den Papstthum zu Rom,' WA, 6:312.

[36] This type appears in various forms in Kettenbach's works: 'Wider des Papsts Küchenprediger,' Clemen, p. 49: '. . . des Bapsts sinagoga oder hoff . . .'; 'Von der Kirche,' Clemen, p. 95: '. . . die synagogen satane [Apoc. II] . . .'; p. 101: '. . . bleib bey des teüfels synagog, deren seind hie vil und mit den besten geacht. Aber was hilfft es, das man vil sagt? die leüt wöllen bleiben in der Babilonischen gefencknus, ...' This last reference suggests strongly a debt to 'De captivitate Babylonica ecclesiae praeludium,' WA, 6:565.

[37] 'Wider des Papsts Küchenprediger,' Clemen, p. 33. See 'An den christlichen Adel deutscher Nation,' WA, 6:457–8; 'De captivitate Babylonica ecclesiae praeludium,' WA, 6:536–7 and 'Vom Missbrauch der Messe,' WA, 8:541–2.

episcopacy. However, in 'On the Misuse of the Mass,' he denounced papal bishops in terms no less virulent that those he used against the papacy itself. Kettenbach, too, implicates the bishops and other prelates in the crimes of the pope and labels them servants of the devil and mercenaries of the Antichrist.[38] He challenges them to prove their claims of apostolic succession by leading lives conformable to the examples provided by the Apostles.[39] And those who fail to comply he denounces as successors of Annas and Caiaphas, who unjustly assume the seat of Moses [Matth. 23:2] [sic].[40] Instead of concerning themselves with spreading the Gospel, they follow their own desires and, when judged according to the standards of the Gospel, appear to be more like heathen princes than Christian bishops.[41]

Kettenbach's treatment of the papal bishops suggests that he has taken up Luther's criticism of them in 'On the Misuse of the Mass.' This suspicion is reinforced by Kettenbach's treatment of the rank and file clergy. In his criticism of the Catholic theology of the mass, Luther identified the papal priesthood as the priesthood of the devil and his apostle, the pope.[42] Kettenbach, too, denounces the papal priesthood as a whole. He accuses the priests and monks of leading debased lives which provide evil examples for the laity. They show no inclination to reform, but instead appear committed to the destruction of the church. To justify their evil ways, they, like their superiors, pervert the Gospel and teach instead their own doctrines. Whoever follows their teachings will, like them, end up dancing to the devil's tune.[43]

However, the full impact of Kettenbach's denunciation of the papal priesthood becomes apparent in his identification of it with the biblical types of the opponents of the Gospel. Citing 1 Timothy 4, he is able to identify the clergy generally as those who adhere to teachings of the devil, that is, the pope.[44] This allows him to link the priests and monks

---

[38] 'Von der Kirche,' Clemen, p. 84. See 'Vom Misbrauch der Messe,' WA, 8:499–503.

[39] 'Wider des Papsts Küchenprediger,' Clemen, p. 41.

[40] Ibid.

[41] 'Von der Kirche,' Clemen, pp. 91–3. See 'Vom Missbrauch der Messe,' WA, 8:500–5. Albrecht Classen, 'Anticlericalism in Late Medieval German Verse,' in Dykema and Oberman, pp. 98–9 and 103–5 indicates the importance of this charge in criticisms of the bishops in late medieval German verse.

[42] WA, 8:486–92, 504–5, 541–2.

[43] 'Von der Kirche,' Clemen, pp. 94–5. On the importance of the bad example provided by an immoral priest in medieval criticisms of the clergy, see Gerald Owst, *Literature and Pulpit in Medieval England* (Oxford, 1961), pp. 246, 259, 267, 274 and Classen, pp. 106, 108.

[44] 'Vom Fasten und Feiern,' Clemen, p. 22; 'Wider des Papsts Küchenprediger,' Clemen, p. 37. Luther made extensive use of this text, see 'De captivitate Babylonica ecclesiae praeludium,' WA, 6:540; 'De Votis Monasticis Iudicium,' WA, 8:595–7, 627; 'Vom Missbrauch der Messe,' WA, 8:547.

to the antichristian papacy, whose false doctrines they expound and whose executioners and hangmen they are.[45] Elsewhere he calls the priests Pharisees who sit on Moses' stool or the lying elders of Daniel 13 who bear false witness against Susanna, that is, the church. On the basis of clerical greed and the willingness of the clergy to pervert the truth in the service of that greed, he also identifies them as devotees of Baal.[46] The application here of Old Testament types to the contemporary clergy again suggests the influence of Luther's extensive use of this tactic in 'On the Misuse of the Mass.'[47]

In his first pamphlet written after the departure from Ulm, 'A Conversation with a Pious Little Old Mother from Ulm,' Kettenbach opts for a dialogue instead of his usual sermon format. It is tempting to see as a model for this any of Hutten's numerous dialogues – *Vadiscus* is the most likely candidate. In 'A Conversation' and all of his subsequent works, Kettenbach adopts some of the anticlerical themes of Hutten's works, as well as his programme for the reform of the nobility. G. Kawerau has labelled as *Alarmschriften* Kettenbach's later writings, which concentrate on the social and political conditions within the empire and advocate support for the cause of Franz von Sickingen.[48] Kawerau does not include 'A Conversation' among these, but in it Kettenbach turns his attention for the first time to Sickingen's feud against the archbishop of Trier and the general political context of the Reformation. The mixture of local and national concerns in this work indicates that it forms a bridge between Kettenbach's activity as a Reformer in Ulm and his role as the propagandist of the *Alarmschriften*. However, the gulf between these two phases of his career is not as wide as is often assumed. This is indicated already in Kettenbach's first reference to the goings-on at the Ebernburg which includes a discussion not only of the opposition between Sickingen and the archbishop of Trier, but also a detailed explanation of the reforms initiated there by Oecolampadius.[49]

Kettenbach next wrote the pamphlet which was to serve as the *Abschiedspredigt* he had been unable to deliver when he left Ulm. 'A Sermon to the Commendable City of Ulm in Farewell' takes as its theme the words of Paul in Galatians 1:6: 'I marvel that ye are so soon

---

[45] 'Vom Fasten und Feiern,' Clemen, pp. 13, 18.

[46] Ibid., pp. 12–13.

[47] 'Von Missbrauch der Messe,' WA, 8:555ff. On the use of this type to pillory clerical vice in medieval sermons, Owst, pp. 257, 259, 269, 280.

[48] G. Kawerau, 'Heinrich von Kettenbach,' *Realencyklopädie für protestantische Theologie und Kirche*, vol. 10 (3rd edn; Leipzig, 1901), p. 267.

[49] 'Ein Gespräch mit einem Altmütterlein,' Clemen, pp. 66–7 (= Laube 1:206–7). For likely sources of Kettenbach's information about events at the Ebernburg, see Clemen, pp. 77, n. 1, 277, n. 1; Breitenbruch, p. 46.

removed from him that called you into the grace of Christ unto another gospel.' In 43 short articles, Kettenbach contrasts the Gospel with the teachings of the papists on such issues as fasting, confession, the cult of saints and indulgences. This provides an opportunity for the denunciation of the proponents of this other, papalist gospel, and his derision of the clergy at all levels surpasses that of any of his earlier *Flugschriften*.[50]

In Kettenbach's next pamphlet, 'A Comparison of the Holy Lord and Father the Pope with Jesus,' the influence of Hutten is even clearer. In 66 short articles, Kettenbach indicates how the pope fails to follow the example given by Christ, who is the true head of the Church. These articles are taken over verbatim from Hutten's 'Comparison of the Pope's Statutes with the Teachings of Christ.' Kettenbach's debt to Hutten is further indicated by his 'Complaint to the Nobility of the Empire,' which is appended to the list of articles. Kettenbach calls on the nobles to oppose the soldiers of the Antichrist, who, if left unchecked, will soon enslave all citizens of the empire. If necessary, force is permissible in the reform of the clergy.[51]

Thereafter concerns of the Wittenberg Reformation and of the Knights' Revolt continue to appear side by side in Kettenbach's writings. His next pamphlet, 'A New Apology for Martin Luther,' concentrates primarily on theological issues in its defence of Luther against ten of the most common accusations levelled against the Reformation by its detractors.[52] Much more political are his next two *Flugschriften*: 'A Practica for Many Future Years Drawn from the Holy Bible' and 'An Exhortation From Junker Franz von Sickingen to His Host.' In the first of these Kettenbach takes as his literary model the numerous Practica current at the time, but suggests that the Bible offers a surer guide to present and future events than do the stars and other portents. Nonetheless, his work loses none of the apocalyptic tone of its more vulgar counterparts. This apocalypticism is lent greater urgency by the deteriorating political situation in the empire. Kettenbach addresses primarily the imperial cities and directs them to the oracle on Ariel in Isaiah 29. Like Jerusalem, the cities will be saved by God if they hold to his Word. However, the situation in the empire is not conducive to favourable divine intervention; the emperor is blind and the cities have

---

[50] 'Sermon zu Ulm,' Clemen, pp. 107–23.

[51] 'Vergleichung des aller heiligsten Herrn und Vater des Papsts gegen Jesus,' Clemen, pp. 131–49. 'Vergleichung der Bäpst satzung gegen der leer Christj Jesu,' Böcking, vol. 5, pp. 386–95.

[52] This work was likely published by May 1523; see Theodor Hampe, 'Archivalische Miszellen zur Nürnberger Literaturgeschichte' (Volkslied und Kriegslied im alten Nürnberg, II. Teil) *Mitteilungen des Vereins für Geschichte der Stadt Nürnberg*, 27 (1928), p. 262, for a decree by the Nuremberg city council likely referring to it.

failed thus far to support the knights. If they are not careful, the princes and knights may soon make common cause against them.[53]

'A Practica' was likely written before Sickingen's death on 7 May 1523.[54] The 'Exhortation of Junker Franz,' despite its title, likely postdates Sickingen's death. In this work Kettenbach provides what purports to be the words of Sickingen to his troops on the eve of battle, as well as an appeal for class solidarity to the members of the lower nobility in the armies of his opponents. The knights of Christ are reminded that all victory comes from God alone, often in miraculous ways, as the examples of Gideon, Samson and Jonathan indicate. Towards the end of this work, Kettenbach appears as the narrator to caution the reader against assuming that Sickingen's defeat indicates the judgement of God against him. God's plans remain hidden until the last judgement. There is still time and God may yet raise up another Sampson who will fight with the sword of the Spirit.[55]

There has been some disagreement among historians over where Kettenbach wrote these pamphlets. Like his earlier writings, 'A Conversation' was first printed in Augsburg.[56] It is probable, then, that after his departure from Ulm, Kettenbach remained in Swabia, likely in the area around Ulm or Augsburg. Thereafter his trail becomes fainter. His obvious support for the Knights' Revolt suggests the Ebernburg as an obvious possibility, but more convincing is Otto Clemen's suggestion of Bamberg, in which city several of these writings were initially printed.[57] Interestingly, however, the only surviving edition of the 'Exhortation of Junker Franz' comes from an Augsburg printer. This merely adds to the mystery surrounding the end of Kettenbach's life. After the profusion of *Flugschriften* in 1522 and 1523 his pen suddenly

---

[53] 'Ein Practica practiciert aus der heiligen Bibel auf viel zukünftig Jahr,' Clemen, pp. 183–200 (= Laube 2:820–7).

[54] Kettenbach's frequent references on the proper preparation for death suggest it was written during the darkest days of the Knights' Revolt. It must have been published by late August when the Nuremberg city council again turned its attention to 'a little book' by Kettenbach. The continued popularity of this work is indicated by yet another Nuremberg decree from January 1524. See Hampe, pp. 262–3.

[55] 'Ein Vermahnung Junker Franzen von Sickingen zu seinem Heer,' Clemen, pp. 203–12. This work was likely published in early 1524. In January it, too, came to the attention of the Nuremberg authorities; see Hampe, p. 263.

[56] Clemen, pp. 52–3.

[57] Veesenmeyer, 'Nachricht von Kettenbach,' pp. 97–101 suggested both the Ebernburg and Wittenberg as possibilities. His discovery of a reference to a Heinrich von Kettenbach among the Nuremberg Augustinians further confused the issue, although he was sceptical about the identification of this man with the Franciscan from Ulm. Keim, pp. 46–7 took the Nuremberg reference more seriously and suggested that Kettenbach travelled not only to that city, but also to Augsburg and Strasbourg before settling in Wittenberg. For the argument in favour of Bamberg, see Clemen, pp. 233–4.

becomes quiet. This has led to a general agreement among historians that he died in 1524, but as to where and how there is no information.[58]

The anticlerical polemics presented in these pamphlets continue to develop the themes of Kettenbach's earlier writings, but provide significantly more details on the vices of the clergy and the ways in which they can be identified with various types of biblical and extra-biblical idolatrous priests. The themes that Kettenbach develops indicate not only a more complete immersion in the works of Luther, but also an acquaintance with the writings of Hutten and the Reformers assembled around Franz von Sickingen. Of the latter group, Kettenbach betrays especially the influence of Hutten's historical works – 'Remonstrance and Warning,' *Vadiscus* and 'Disclosure of How the Popes Have Acted Against the Emperors' – and Martin Bucer's 'New Karsthans.' These produce a close identification between the perception of the papacy as the Antichrist and the history of papal–imperial relations and show great concern for the plight and the cause of the nobility.

To further his case against the clergy in these works, Kettenbach exploits even more fully the traditional resentment of clerical power and privilege. He pillories clerical vows of poverty by contrasting them with the obvious wealth of many members of the first estate, and he denounces clerical exemptions from the legal and financial responsibilities of the laity.[59] The sacred power exercised by the clergy over the laity again is identified as devilish or heathen. Pilgrimages, the cult of saints and endowed masses are lampooned as *Totenfresserei*, the 'devouring' of the dead.[60] The confessional is exposed as a source of unwarranted influence of the clergy over the laity.[61] The complaints presented to this point were common stock of the reforming literature and Kettenbach likely derived them from a variety of sources. However, his most comprehensive list of *gravamina*, that developed in 'A Comparison of the Pope with Jesus,' is taken over directly from Hutten.[62]

Interestingly, Kettenbach fails to develop even in these works the anticlerical implications of Luther's priesthood of all believers. In 'A

---

[58] Karl Schottenloher, who maintained that Kettenbach and Rott-Locher were the same person, of course disagreed with this conclusion. The abiding concern with death and the preparation for it in Kettenbach's last writings suggest that he may have been ill or aged in 1523.

[59] 'Vergleichung des Papsts gegen Jesus,' Clemen, pp. 147–8 (= Laube 2:815–16); 'Gespräch mit einem Altmütterlein,' Clemen, pp. 72–5 (= Laube 1:209–11).

[60] 'Ein Gespräch mit einem Altmütterlein,' Clemen, pp. 56–74 (= Laube 1:201–11).

[61] 'Sermon zu Ulm,' Clemen, pp. 113–14.

[62] Compare articles 12–16, 21, 26, 28–31, 44–5, 49, 51–2 and 60 in 'Vergleichung des Papsts gegen Jesus,' Clemen, pp. 131–44 with the same articles in Hutten's 'Vergleichung der Bäpst satzung gegen der leer Christi Jesu,' Böcking, vol. 5, pp. 388–95.

Sermon to Ulm,' he makes reference to this doctrine, but fails to develop it further.[63] Instead, he expands considerably the discussion of biblical types of the opponents of the Gospel. This tactic served him most effectively as the bridge between the Reformation and the Knights' Revolt. And its versatility is immediately apparent. Already in 'A Conversation,' Kettenbach begins to describe the identification of the papacy with the Antichrist much like Hutten in terms of the conflict between *imperium* and *sacerdotum*: 'The pope has taken such power onto himself and freed his mercenaries; he has stolen from the worldly power its legitimacy and subjected the emperor and kings to him, so that he should be servant of all (2 Thess. 2:4).'[64] Kettenbach's citation of Paul's discussion of the Antichrist reflects a wide use of this text which likely had its impetus from Luther.[65] However, the close identification of the kingdom of the Antichrist with the rise of the papal monarchy suggests the influence of Hutten, whose historical writings trace the same perversion of the church. Hutten develops this theme most fully in 'How the Popes Have Always Been Against the German Emperors,' in which work is also contained 'A Comparison of the Pope's Statutes with the Teaching of Christ Jesus.'[66] It is not surprising, then, that Kettenbach's discussion of the papacy in 'A Comparison of the Pope with Jesus' most clearly reflects Hutten's stance:

> Many await and look for the Antichrist, but his kingdom has already stood for many hundreds of years and began with force with the first pope who wanted to be above a Roman emperor, . . . Therefore, when the Antichrist's Kingdom comes to an end, only then will we recognize who the Antichrist was. That will be when the papacy at Rome perishes and when the pope, bishops, priests and monks again are servants of the church and when their servants – the emperor, kings, lords, princes, and nobles – again become lords in the church. When they and not the clergy are given power to rule lands and people.[67]

This theme he again picks up in 'A Practica,' when he identifies the claim that the pope transferred the empire from the Romans to the Germans as a pillar of papal power and sure sign of the pope's antichristian qualities.[68]

Kettenbach's treatment of the bishops, however, is much less

---

[63] 'Sermon zu Ulm,' Clemen, p. 113.

[64] 'Ein Gespräch mit einem Altmütterlein,' Clemen, p. 74 (= Laube 1:211).

[65] This text, which appears frequently in Luther's writing, is employed for the same purpose in 'New Karsthans.' See 'Gesprech Büechlin Neuw Karsthans,' Berger, p. 201.

[66] 'Wie die Pắpst allwegen wider die Teutschen Keyser gewest,' Böcking, vol. 5, pp. 366–7.

[67] 'Vergleichung des Papsts gegen Jesus,' Clemen, pp. 131–2.

[68] 'Ein Practica,' Clemen, p. 187 (= Laube 2:822).

consistent in these pamphlets. 'A Conversation' specifically denounces the archbishop of Trier, who tricks money out of the laity to pay for his war against the defenders of the Gospel.[69] At the end of the 'Complaint to the Nobility of the Empire,' Kettenbach includes the bishops among the enemies of the Gospel, but implies that they are compelled by the papacy to take this stance.[70] However, in 'An Exhortation of Junker Franz' he returns to his earlier denunciation of papal bishops who live not according to evangelical example, but like heathen princes and kings.[71]

He also continues to implicate the priests and monks as the assistant hangmen of their superiors.[72] To reinforce his claims, Kettenbach returns to the characterizations of his opponents as false prophets and minions of the Antichrist. The priests and monks appear as apostates and apostles of the Antichrist, and Kettenbach continues to rely on 1 Timothy 4:1ff. for this identification.[73] The theme of 'A Sermon to Ulm' makes apostolic warnings against false prophets and apostles particularly relevant, and here Kettenbach expands the biblical basis for this identification.[74] Later, this apocalyptic imagery is again expanded, and the church of Rome is identified as the whore of the apocalypse arrayed in purple and scarlet and its servants as Gog and Magog.[75] However, given the apocalyptic contexts of several of these references, especially those in 'A Practica,' Kettenbach makes surprisingly little use of this imagery.

Instead, the types of false priests from the Old and New Testaments come to the fore in Kettenbach's *Alarmschriften*. In 'A Practica,' he claims that at Augsburg Luther's opponents included 'the hypocrites and learned ones, the false prophets and the raving, drunken priests of Baal.'[76] The hypocrites and learned ones are the Scribes and Pharisees, and Kettenbach relies heavily on this characterization of the clergy. He portrays the contemporary struggle between the Gospel and the clergy as parallel to Jesus' constant sparring with the Pharisees.[77] This allows him to employ denunciations of the Pharisees by both Jesus and John

---

[69] 'Ein Gespräch mit einem Altmütterlein,' Clemen, p. 60 (= Laube 1:204).

[70] 'Vergleichung des Papsts gegen Jesus,' Clemen, p. 149 (= Laube 2:817).

[71] 'Ein Vermahnung Junker Franzen,' Clemen, pp. 204–5.

[72] 'Ein neu Apologia Martini Luthers,' Clemen, p. 158 (= Laube 1:575).

[73] 'Ein Gespräch mit einem Altmütterlein,' Clemen, pp. 64, 68 (= Laube 1:205); 'Vergleichung des Papsts gegen Jesus,' Clemen, p. 148 (= Laube 2:816).

[74] 'Sermon zu Ulm,' Clemen, pp. 108–9.

[75] 'Ein neu Apologia Martini Luthers,' Clemen, p. 173 (= Laube 1:584); 'Ein Practica,' Clemen, p. 187–8, 192 (= Laube 2:823, 826).

[76] 'Ein Practica,' Clemen, p. 187 (= Laube 2:822–3).

[77] 'Ein neu Apologia Martini Luthers,' Clemen, p. 119.

the Baptist against his opponents.[78] Interestingly, Kettenbach avoids limiting his identification of the Pharisees specifically to the friars. Rather he remains true to the general anticlerical denunciations of his earlier works. In 'A Sermon to Ulm,' he notes how the Jewish religious leaders, with whom he identifies the contemporary clergy, have always opposed true prophets, Christ and the apostles.[79] This theme reappears in his subsequent writings.[80] In his identification of the first estate with the Jewish religious establishment, Kettenbach is able to isolate specific groups for closer scrutiny. For example, he frequently identifies the bishops and prelates with Annas and Caiaphas.[81]

As Kettenbach became increasingly concerned with the activities of the imperial knights, the identification of the clergy with the biblical types of false priests provided the context for interpreting the political events associated with the Reformation. In his first discussion of political affairs of the empire, he identifies the clergy as Jews.[82] Thereafter, the comparison becomes much more explicit. In the 'Sermon to Ulm,' he casts the ecclesiastical authorities as the high priests plotting the crucifixion of Luther.[83] In 'A Comparison of the Pope with Christ,' a similar comparison is extended to include some secular figures and in 'A New Apology for Martin Luther' Luther's opponents become the descendants of Annas, Caiaphas, Herod and Pilate.[84] The obvious implication of this assessment was that political support for Luther was comparable to political support for Christ.

Even more important for Kettenbach's attack on the clergy, however, is his identification of them with a range of false priests and prophets from the Old Testament. The discussion of the excessive ceremonial in the church, with which 'A Conversation' opens, provides Kettenbach with the opportunity to cite Jeremiah's warning to the exiled Jews against the idolatry of the Babylonians in Baruch 6.[85] Elsewhere this tactic takes different forms. On several occasions he uses the account of

---

[78] 'Ein Gespräch mit einem Altmütterlein,' Clemen, pp. 56–7 (= Laube 1:201–2); 'Ein neu Apologia Martini Luthers,' Clemen, p. 158 (= Laube 1:575).

[79] 'Sermon zu Ulm,' Clemen, pp. 119–20.

[80] 'Ein neu Apologia Martini Luthers,' Clemen, pp. 172, 174 (= Laube 1:583–4); 'Ein Practica,' Clemen, p. 190 (= Laube 2:824–5).

[81] 'Ein Sermon zu Ulm,' Clemen, p. 120; 'Ein neu Apologia Martini Luthers,' Clemen, p. 174 (= Laube 1:584); 'Ein Practica,' Clemen, p. 190 (= Laube 2:824).

[82] 'Ein Gespräch mit einem Altmütterlein,' Clemen, p. 67 (= Laube 1:207).

[83] 'Sermon zu Ulm,' Clemen, p. 123.

[84] 'Vergleichung des Papsts gegen Jesus,' Clemen, p. 149 (= Laube 2:817); 'Ein neu Apologia Martini Luthers,' Clemen, p. 159 (= Laube 1:575).

[85] 'Ein Gespräch mit einem Altmütterlein,' Clemen, p. 58: 'Jn dem buch des propheten Bar. ca. ulti. lesen wir, das Hiere. schrib den in der gefenknis zů babilone also: Zů babylone werdt jr sehen guldin, silbrin, hültzin und stainin göter, . . .' (= Laube 1:202).

Susanna and the elders from Daniel 13 as a metaphor for the contemporary church.[86] More common is his identification of his opponents with the priests of Baal, an identification he has established already in 'A Sermon on Fasting and Feasting.'[87] Thereafter, he treats this as an established analogue, referring to his opponents as the priests of Baal and Baalites.[88] In some of the later works he supplements this identification with reference to other types of false priests: those of Bel, Moloch and Astoroth.[89]

These identifications, although much less prevalent and obvious in Reformation polemics than those drawn from the Gospels, were not without precedent. They were, in fact, stock types used to pillory clerical vice in medieval homiletic literature.[90] Luther himself had tapped into this tradition. His identification of the true and false priesthoods in 'On The Misuse of the Mass' made extensive use of these images, and especially that of the priests of Baal.[91]

Like Luther, Kettenbach exploits these types to further highlight the connections between heathen teachings and clerical vice. In 'A Sermon on Fasting and Feasting' he uses the identification of the monks and priests with the prophets of Baal, the stomach god, to highlight the hypocrisy of clerical fasts.[92] The identification of his opponents with the Babylonian priests described in Baruch chapter 6 allows Kettenbach not only to apply Jeremiah's warnings against idolatry, but also to emphasize clerical avarice and lechery.[93] The summary description of false priests in 'A Sermon to Ulm' opens a whole range of clerical vice to ridicule. The example of Egyptian priests holding land independently of pharaoh ties clerical deception to ecclesiastical wealth. The priests of Bel, described in Daniel 14, highlight clerical greed, hypocrisy and sexual misconduct; and the priests of Baal point to clerical deception of the laity.[94]

In addition to opening up charges of clerical vice, the use of these

---

[86] 'Vom Fasten und Feiern,' Clemen, p. 23; 'Von der Kirche,' Clemen, pp. 91, 99; 'Ein neu Apologia Martini Luthers,' Clemen, p. 169 (= Laube 1:582).

[87] 'Vom Fasten und Feiern,' Clemen, p. 23.

[88] 'Sermon zu Ulm,' Clemen, p. 109; 'Ein neu Apologia Martini Luthers,' Clemen, pp. 159–60, 169 (= Laube 1:582).

[89] 'Sermon zu Ulm,' Clemen, pp. 118–19; 'Ein neu Apologia Martini Luthers,' Clemen, p. 167 (= Laube 1:580).

[90] Owst, pp. 257, 259, 269, 280.

[91] 'Vom Missbrauch der Messe,' WA, 8:482, 488, 493, 498–9, 554–60.

[92] 'Vom Fasten und Feiern,' Clemen, pp. 12–13.

[93] 'Ein Gespräch mit einem Altmütterlein, Clemen, p. 58 (= Laube 1:202).

[94] 'Sermon zu Ulm,' Clemen, pp. 118–19. The example of the Egyptian priests Kettenbach may have lifted from 'New Karsthans.' See 'Gesprech Büechlin Neuw Karsthans,' Berger, p. 174.

types further anchors the Reformation in its historical and apocalyptic context. The clearest example of this occurs in 'A Sermon to Ulm,' where Kettenbach draws all of the historical types together in one lengthy catalogue of clerical vice.[95] Later, he draws together the apocalyptic and the historical types. In 'A Sermon on the Christian Church,' he identifies the priests of Babylon with the Babylonian whore of the apocalypse.[96] Elsewhere, he links this identification to Luther's discussion of the Babylonian captivity of the church, thereby firmly integrating the present into this context.[97] This in turn further strengthens the identification of the Reformation with the godly of all ages. Luther is frequently cast in the role of Daniel defending Susanna or opposing the priests of Bel, or Elijah overcoming the 400 priests of Baal.[98]

The full import of Kettenbach's development of this historical context only becomes clear when one turns to his demand for action to remedy the situation. Kettenbach's appeals to positive action are scattered in his earliest writings. In 'A Sermon on the Christian Church,' he claims that since the priests and monks refuse to reform the church, secular authorities must undertake this task.[99] This appeal remains consistent, but the identification of secular authority is clarified in the later pamphlets. Under the increasing influence of Hutten's writings in 'A Comparison of the Pope with Jesus' he calls on the nobility to reform the church, by force if necessary.[100] Here the importance of historical example and the analogues of Old Testament types of the false priest become clearer. References to the destruction of the Baalites in 1 Kings 18 and 2 Kings 10, both of which Kettenbach alludes to, suggested a possible extreme response to obstinate clergy. This response Kettenbach made explicit in his final pamphlet, 'An Exhortation of Junker Franz,' by casting Sickingen in the role of the Old Testament warrior heroes Gideon, Samson and Saul.[101]

But even on this point Kettenbach's statements are not so far from

---

[95] 'Sermon zu Ulm,' Clemen, pp. 118–19.

[96] 'Von der Kirche,' Clemen, pp. 99–100.

[97] 'Ein Gespräch mit einem Altmütterlein,' Clemen, pp. 59–60 (= Laube 1:203–4).

[98] 'Ein neu Apologia Martini Luthers,' Clemen, p. 169 (= Laube 1:582), 'Vergleichung des Papsts gegen Jesus,' Clemen, p. 148 (= Laube 2:816). On occasion Kettenbach also extended the list of godly witnesses to include prominent medieval heretics who opposed the papacy and the Roman church. The most fully developed reference appears in 'A Conversation' and likely reflects an even longer list in Bucer's 'New Karsthans.' Compare 'Ein Gespräch mit einem Altmütterlein,' Clemen, p. 74 and 'Gesprech Büechlin Neuw Karsthans,' Berger, p. 193.

[99] 'Von der Kirche,' Clemen, p. 94.

[100] 'Vergleichung des Papsts gegen Jesus,' Clemen, p. 146 (= Laube 2:815).

[101] 'Vermahnung Junker Franzen,' Clemen, pp. 203–4.

Luther's as they might initially appear. In the preface to 'On Confession,' which Luther addressed to Franz von Sickingen, Luther compared the papal clergy with the 31 Canaanite kings who would not yield to Joshua, as described in Joshua 11: 19–20. He suggested that God had hardened the hearts of the clergy, as He did earlier those of the Canaanites and concluded:

> They still have time to change that which one cannot, should not and will not endure from them; but if they do not change, then another will change them, without their thanks, who will teach them, not like Luther with letters and words, but with deeds.[102]

Luther himself, then, provided a clue to the identity of the new Joshua. In so doing he implicitly conferred on Sickingen and his activities the mantel of legitimacy associated in his writings with the exercise of secular authority on behalf of the Gospel. Sickingen had already gone a long way toward realizing the claim to such legitimacy through his sponsorship of the reforms of Oecolampadius, Bucer and others in his territories. It was a small step from this position to Kettenbach's that the feud against Trier was a divinely sanctioned crusade against those whose hearts God had already hardened.

The comprehensive denunciation of the clergy contained in Kettenbach's writings is the backdrop for his development of specifically antifraternal themes in the 'Sermon on the Eighth Sunday After Pentecost.' While Kettenbach's anticlerical vision easily provided room for specifically antifraternal themes from the outset, these were not developed in his earliest writings. Rather, in those works he deals with the Franciscans and other friars only insofar as he mentions the religious generally. And when Kettenbach turns his pen on the religious in these writings, he integrates traditional criticisms of them with attacks on them developed by Luther in 'The Judgement on Monastic Vows.'[103] However, the Franciscans and other friars come more to the fore in Kettenbach's writings from mid 1523, and it is likely that he wrote his anti-Franciscan polemic at this time. There is even some indirect evidence that he was in contact with the other former Franciscans in

---

[102] WA, 8:138–9.

[103] For example, see Kettenbach's criticism of the *Totenfresserei* of the monks in 'Von der Kirche,' Clemen, p. 89; his denunciation of the hypocrisy of monastic self-denial in 'Ein Gespräch mit einem Altmütterlein,' Clemen, pp. 71–2 (= Laube 1:209–10); and his denunciation of the preaching activities of his opponents in 'Sermon zu Ulm,' Clemen, p. 110. His debts to Luther's criticisms of the monastic life are clear in his attacks on the works righteousness of the monks, his criticisms of the pretensions of the monastic life and his treatment of childhood novitiates as a contravention of the fourth commandment; see 'Von der Kirche,' Clemen, p. 89; 'Sermon zu Ulm,' Clemen, pp. 114, 117, 118.

Wittenberg.[104] This concern with the Franciscans reaches a highpoint in 'A New Apology for Martin Luther' when Kettenbach turns his attention specifically to Glapion.[105] In the same text he applies several of the biblical texts and characteristics from the antifraternal tradition specifically to the religious.[106] And these themes are easily integrated into Kettenbach's greater vision. Specific denunciations of the friars are merely added to the scorn heaped on the clergy as a whole. But the fact that Kettenbach observed such apparently unrestrained polemics against an important element of the first estate emanating from Wittenberg itself must have confirmed his suspicions about the diabolical nature of the clergy.

The Big Jacks and the heretical followers of the Whore of Babylon

Just as Heinrich von Kettenbach sought to reconcile Wittenberg with the Ebernburg, so did Johann Rot-Locher attempt to carry through a Reformation of the common man from a Lutheran context. Rot-Locher has long been identified as one of the firebrands of the early Reformation. The earliest interpreters of his writings saw in him a *Schwärmer* in the spirit of the Zwickau prophets.[107] This judgement was softened somewhat at the turn of the last century. More than their predecessors, Ernst Fabian and Ludwig Keller emphasized the Lutheran elements in Rot-Locher's theology, although Fabian continued to regard him as a *Feuergeist* and Keller initially attributed his first pamphlet to Nichlaus Storch.[108] In 1925, Karl Schottenloher portrayed Rot-Locher

---

[104] During the same period in which he printed 'A Sermon to Ulm' and 'A Comparison of the Pope with Christ,' Erlinger also produced editions of Eberlin's 'Seven Devout Priests Complain about Their Plight' and 'Consolation of the Seven Devout Priests.' See Karl Schottenloher, *Die Buchdruckertätigkeit Georg Erlingers in Bamberg von 1522 bis 1541 (1543). Ein Beitrag zur Geschichte der Reformationszeit* (Leipzig, 1907; reprint edn, Wiesbaden, 1969), pp. 59–60. Still in 1523, editions of 'A Comparison of the Pope with Jesus' and of 'A New Apology for Martin Luther' appeared from the press of Nickel Schirlentz in Wittenberg, the printer of several of Eberlin's *Flugschriften*. 'A Comparison of the Pope with Jesus' also appeared in Strasbourg in 1523, possibly from the press of Johannes Schwan; see Clemen, pp. 127–9, 156.

[105] 'Ein neu Apologia Martini Luthers,' Clemen, p. 159; see also p. 173.

[106] Ibid., pp. 161–3, 168, 172.

[107] M. Georg Veesenmeyer, 'Nachricht vom Heinrich von Kettenbach,' in Veesenmeyer, p. 103 and C. Th. Keim, *Die Reformation der Reichstadt Ulm. Ein Beitrag zur schwäbischen und deutschen Reformationsgeschichte* (Stuttgart, 1851), p. 47.

[108] Ernst Fabian, 'Die Einführung des Buchdrucks in Zwickau 1523,' *Mitteilungen des Altertumsvereins für Zwickau und Umgegend*, 6 (1899), pp. 55–6; Ludwig Keller, 'Aus den Anfangsjahren der Reformation. Nachrichten über Hans Greifenbach, Hans Sachs, Hans Locher und Heinrich von Kettenbach,' *Monatshefte der Comenius-Gesellschaft*, 8 (1899), pp. 181–4.

as a Reformation radical without, however, using the term *Schwärmer* or any of its negative connotations. According to Schottenloher, in his earliest writings Rot-Locher recognized a difference between secular and ecclesiastical authority and sought to undermine only the latter, but his later writings chronicle his disenchantment with all authority. In particular, two later works addressed as letters to the mythical evangelical peasant Karsthans call for open resistance to the tyrants and, as the voice of the oppressed, are among the most prominent harbingers of the Peasants' War.[109] To this interpretation Paul Kalkoff responded that, although the rhetoric in the later pamphlets becomes more impassioned than in the earlier, there is no significant departure from the Lutheran teaching on obedience to secular authority in them.[110]

Subsequent historical writing has sought out a middle ground between these two interpretations. Walter Zöllner has argued that, despite the Lutheran context in which he worked, Rot-Locher's concern with social reform places him in what historians of the former German Democratic Republic called 'the bourgeois-radical camp.' His reform programme reflects primarily the concerns of the urban bourgeoisie, but he was perceptive enough to realize the need to appeal to the people's movement, as indicated by the *Flugschriften* addressed to Karsthans.[111] Werner Packull concurs with the general outlines of this interpretation. Noting that the later *Flugschriften* encourage Karsthans to lay down his flail, Packull, nonetheless, sees Rot-Locher as an unconscious ally of Thomas Müntzer. In these two pamphlets, one sees 'a shift in the Karsthans image from its religious, polemical function to a symbol of social agitation.'[112] More recently, Susan Karant-Nunn has reflected more closely Kalkoff's position and claims that Rot-Locher was hardly unrestrained, although the authorities would have found irksome his expressions of sympathy for the peasants in 1524.[113]

Johann Rot was an apostate Franciscan Observant from Ulm. He departed the cloister in 1521 or 1522 and afterward wandered widely, apparently with the authorities dogging his every step, eventually

---

[109] Karl Schottenloher, 'Wer ist Johann Locher von München?' in *Der Münchner Buchdrucker Hans Schobser 1500–1530* (Munich, 1925), pp. 109–42.

[110] Paul Kalkoff, 'Die Prädikanten Rot-Locher, Eberlin und Kettenbach,' *ARG*, 25 (1928), pp. 128–50.

[111] Walter Zöllner, 'Johann Locher – Ein Kämpfer der Bauernkriegszeit,' in *Der deutsche Bauernkrieg und Thomas Müntzer*, ed. Max Steinmetz, Siegfried Hoyer and Hans Wermes (Leipzig, 1976), pp. 194–7.

[112] Werner Packull, 'The Image of the "Common Man" in the early Pamphlets of the Reformation,' *Historical Reflections*, 12 (1985), pp. 272–3.

[113] Susan Karant-Nunn, *Zwickau in Transition, 1500–1547: The Reformation as an Agent of Change* (Columbus, Ohio, 1987), pp. 196–7.

arriving in Zwickau in the second half of 1523 under the name Locher. Here his luck changed for the better. He was befriended by the reform-minded *Bürgermeister* Hermann Mühlpfort, who offered him his sister's hand in marriage and a position as the municipal secretary. It was apparently here that he received communion in both kinds as a mark of his commitment to Lutheranism and began to preach and write pamphlets.[114] There is no clear evidence of when exactly Rot-Locher arrived in Zwickau. However, his first pamphlet, 'A Long-Time Silent Christian Brother,' was printed there by Jörg Gastel in 1523.

This first pamphlet Rot-Locher addresses to the members of Christ's 'band' and to friends in Munich, especially those persecuted for Jesus's sake. He immediately informs the reader that he will deal with three issues: a review of the contemporary Christian life and comparison of it to God's commandments; a discussion of the fraternity of Christ as an example to his followers; and an admonition to them to persevere in the face of adversity, including a discussion of the activities of the Franciscan Observants and their idol. The remainder of the pamphlet, however, deals only with the first issue, and Rot-Locher delivers a stinging indictment of contemporary society in his comparison of it with the Ten Commandments.[115]

Karl Schottenloher suggests that Rot-Locher took up the previously announced discussion of Christian fraternity shortly thereafter in 'A Delightful Sermon Produced on Christmas.'[116] At the beginning of this work, he refers back to his discussion of the Ten Commandments which has recently appeared.[117] The sermon was first printed in 1524, but, as the subject matter indicates, likely written in December 1523. It contrasts the spiritual joy and peace of the Gospel message with the bacchanal of contemporary celebrations. Responsibility for this perver-sion of the Christmas message Rot-Locher lays at the feet of the wealthy and influential. The announcement of the birth to the shepherds

---

[114] The pamphlets of Rot-Locher, published under the name of Johann Locher, provide only meager details of his biography. However, in 1925 Karl Schottenloher published the confession, discovered in a Munich archive, of a runaway Franciscan, Johann Rot. Schottenloher convincingly identified Rot with Locher, although his further attempt to identify this man with Kettenbach as well has been rejected; see Kalkoff, pp. 131–2; Zöllner, p. 191; Packull, pp. 267–8. The 16 articles of Rot's confession have been reproduced in Schottenloher, 'Wer ist Johann Locher?' pp. 127–8. Unfortunately, they follow no apparent chronological or thematic order. The accepted outline of Rot-Locher's activity is that established by Schottenloher (pp. 129–35), although with corrections on some details by Kalkoff, pp. 132–4.

[115] 'Ein tzeitlang geschwigner Christlicher Bruder,' Köhler *et al.*, F 574, #1477.

[116] Schottenloher, 'Wer ist Johann Locher?' p. 115.

[117] 'Ein lieplicher Sermon Colligiert an dem heyligē Christag,' Köhler *et al.*, F. 1198, #3018, Aii(b).

becomes a metaphor for the preaching of the Gospel. It is the simple and humble who receive its message in the correct spirit.

Early in 1524 Rot-Locher produced three more pamphlets in rapid succession. 'On Singing the Ave Maria' is an attack on the immoderate veneration of the Virgin, which can lead to idolatry and detract from the honour due to God alone. Although Rot-Locher sticks closely to his subject matter, his advice on the correct veneration of the Virgin is generally applicable to veneration of the saints and reflects the suggestions of other Reformers. It is not her own merit, but rather her humble obedience to the will of God that has earned Mary a place of honour among the saints. Instead of trusting in her merit, the true Christian must emulate her humble obedience.[118]

The next two *Flugschriften* indicate, if not Rot-Locher's connection to the authorities of Zwickau, certainly his desire to curry favour with them. 'A Practicable Report to Those at Zwickau' draws on the tradition of the *Prognostica* to predict the end of the Antichrist's reign in 1524, an indication that it was written very early in the year. It certainly preceded Rot-Locher's Lenten tractate which makes reference to it.[119] Dedicated to the *Bürgermeister* and council of the city, this work denounces the activities of the *Schwärmer* and praises the actions of the city fathers in the cause of the Reformation.

During his interrogation, Rot-Locher admitted to eating meat with others in Zwickau during Lent, although this was not the practice there.[120] 'A Grace-Filled Privilege of Christian Freedom,' likely written in early Lent and dedicated to Hermann Mühlpfort, is a discussion of the practice of fasting and a defence of those breaking the fast. Rot-Locher touches on a prominent theme of the preceding work when he exhorts his readers to be always mindful of their weaker brethren, and when he describes true fasting as a means of castigating the flesh.[121]

Rot-Locher's next pamphlet, 'A Serious Understanding of Good and False Preachers,' is addressed to the nobility of Voigtland. It suggests that he had undertaken a preaching tour of that region, although it is unclear when this occurred. Rot-Locher's citation of Christ's command to the apostles to shake from their feet the dust of villages which rejected them suggests a sense of failure with his enterprise. In contrast to his praise of the Zwickau Reformation, he here bemoans its lack of

---

[118] 'Vom Ave Maria Leuthen,' Köhler *et al.*, F 248, #689.

[119] 'Müglichen bericht an die zů Zwickau,' Köhler *et al.*, F 857, #2160, Dii; 'Ein gnadenreichs Privilegium Christlicher freyheyt,' Köhler *et al.*, F 982, #2483, Bii(b).

[120] Schottenloher, p. 128. On the response of the Zwickau *Rat* to breaking of the fast in 1524 see Karant-Nunn, p. 134.

[121] The final part of 'A Practicable Report' discussed good works, when performed in the proper spirit, as a means of subjecting the flesh to the spirit.

progress in Voigtland and elsewhere.[122] This provides a basis for an open attack on the oppression of the laity by the church.

Karl Schottenloher argued that the moderate tone of Rot-Locher's works of early 1524 gives way in this pamphlet to a 'boundless hatred' of the clergy.[123] This is a rather extreme assessment of the tone of this work, but its subject matter does allow Rot-Locher's anticlericalism to come more clearly into view. It may be as well that the resistance Rot-Locher encountered on his preaching journey, and an apparent lack of success of the Reformation more generally, led to a sense of embitterment and sharpened the tone of his writings. This is especially apparent in the next two works, the letters addressed to Karsthans. 'A Woeful Missive of the Peasant Enemy to Karsthans, his Confederate' bewails in strongly apocalyptic terms the lack of social reform that has accompanied the reawakening of the Gospel. The same themes are taken up in an even sharper tone in 'An Unusual, Second Missive of the Peasant Enemy to Karsthans.'[124] Even before completing the second letter to Karsthans, Rot-Locher probably left Zwickau.[125] The only evidence we have for the time of his departure is a letter from his publisher, Jörg Gastel, to Stephen Roth in Wittenberg dated 18 May 1524:

> Also, with regard to the King of Denmark, I ask my lord that you go to the Chancellor and say that Locher is not in Zwickau, he has ridden away, but we hope for him constantly; when he comes, I will send him to you . . .[126]

Fabian suggests that the Danish King sought Locher's help in reforming the church in his realm and that Locher must have been well known and favourably regarded in Wittenberg.[127] The letter does reveal that Locher had left Zwickau, apparently promising to return, and that this had

---

[122] 'Ernstlicher verstand guter und falscher Prediger,' Köhler *et al.*, F 583, #1517, Aiii (= Laube, p. 977).

[123] Schottenloher, 'Wer ist Johann Locher?' p. 118. Kalkoff, pp. 135 and 139, rejects this characterization and sees this pamphlet more as advice to the evangelical preacher than as a denunciation of the clerical estate.

[124] 'Ein Cläglicher Sendtbrief des bauernveyndts zu Karstenhansen seynem Pundtgnossen,' Köhler *et al.*, F 1044, #2637 (= Laube 2:964–73); 'Ein ungewöhnlicher zweiter Sendbrief des Bauernfeinds an Karsthans,' in *Flugschriften der Bauernkriegszeit*, ed. Adolf Laube and Hans-Werner Seiffert (Berlin, 1975), pp. 99–108.

[125] Ernst Fabian, p. 60, discovered a possible reference to these two pamphlets in a letter written in early 1524 by the Zwickau Chancellor Valentin Hertel to Stephen Roth: 'Quidam nomine Kasthans subinde nouos edit libellos.' On the dating of the two letters to Karsthans and the circumstances surrounding their composition, see Schottenloher, 'Wer ist Johann Locher?' p. 135; Kalkoff, p. 149; Laube and Seiffert, p. 580; Zöllner, p. 193.

[126] 'Brief Jörg Gastels an Roth, 18. Mai 1524' in Fabian, pp. 101–2.

[127] Fabian, p. 60.

occurred under favourable circumstances. However, his likely first destination was Erfurt.

In his confession, Locher stated: 'When he came to Erfurt, he met a member of his order who helped him to write and undertake the articles.' Elsewhere he admitted that he had disparaged the order and charged its members with sodomy.[128] Article eight of Locher's *Flugschrift* 'Article 15' accuses the Franciscans of not only breaking their vows of celibacy, but of also being 'sodomous fools.'[129] Karl Schottenloher suggested that 'Article 15' was Locher's third *Flugschrift*, fulfilling the promise in 'A Long-Time Silent Christian Brother' to deal with the issue of the Franciscan idol. The articles written in Erfurt he identifies as the anonymous *Flugschrift* 'The Reformation of Kaiser Friedrich III.' Kalkoff rightly challenges Schottenloher's evidence for this identification and maintains that the work in Erfurt was 'Artikel 15.' Both men agree that Locher's helper with the articles was Eberlin, who Locher confesses wrote a book in Erfurt against the Bavarian princes and Schatzgeyer, obviously 'I Wonder that there is no Money in the Land.'[130] But the earliest evidence we have for Eberlin's activity in Erfurt stems from May 1524. 'Artikel 15' then was probably Locher's last work prior to his trip to Munich.

There is no indication of how long Locher remained in Erfurt, whether he returned to Zwickau to deliver the manuscript of 'Artikel 15' personally to Gastel or, in fact, why he decided to return to Munich despite the obvious danger. He had probably not long been active in Munich before his arrest and interrogation on 24 November. There is some indication in the record of the interrogation that he attempted to soften his sentence by distancing himself from the reforming radicals and repenting his past actions. He explicitly distanced himself from Müntzer and expressed his willingness to be corrected on any issues in which he was proven wrong.[131] Given his situation, one is not inclined to doubt the sincerity of the final article of the confession, the wish that he had never left the order.[132] It is generally agreed that Rot-Locher was executed shortly after his interrogation, either in late 1524 or early 1525.

The reputation of Rot-Locher as a radical derives especially from the sharp language and explicit details of social inequality in the two missives to Karsthans. However, already in his first pamphlet, Rot-Locher did not shrink from upbraiding the wealthy and influential for

[128] Schottenloher, 'Wer ist Johann Locher?' p. 127.

[129] 'Artikel 15,' Köhler *et al.*, F 1078, #2726, Ai(b).

[130] Schottenloher, 'Wer ist Johann Locher?' p. 128. See also p. 130 and Kalkoff, p. 133.

[131] Schottenloher, 'Wer ist Johann Locher?' p. 128.

[132] Ibid.

their failure to conform to the ideals and mandates of Scripture. This scolding is a consistent theme throughout his *Flugschriften*, although it becomes milder in the earliest pamphlets of 1524, when Rot-Locher apparently enjoyed his greatest success as a reforming preacher and closest ties to the powerful in Zwickau; and later it reaches unprecedented virulence in the pamphlets addressed to Karsthans. This scolding forms the backdrop for his discussions of specific forms of oppression in contemporary society. Within this context, it may be more fruitful to consider Rot-Locher in the tradition of late medieval penance preachers than as a spokesman for the 'revolution of the common man.'

As an explicit comparison of social realities with divine mandates, 'A Long-Time Silent Christian Brother' exemplifies especially well Rot-Locher's primary concern with moral reform. Like the great medieval preachers, his main targets are the degenerate lives of the influential and wealthy.[133] It is they who, concerned more with their own advantage than the common good, set the standard for the evils so prevalent in society.[134] Even when they do establish useful, godly laws, they themselves are the first to break them.[135] As Rot-Locher works his way through the catalogue of sins which have beset Christendom, the powerful remain the most visible culprits. They are the greatest blasphemers and regularly deceive, defame, cheat and bear false witness against friend and foe alike.[136] They are no less given to sexual indiscretions than the poor, but quick to use their influence to cover these up.[137] Indeed, the proverb is true which states: 'one hangs only the small thieves, [but] tips the hat to the great.'[138]

Against this picture of the debauchery of the upper social orders, Rot-Locher juxtaposes a vision of the virtuous, although misled, poor which Packull characterizes as the 'religious, polemical function' of the Karsthans image.[139] This becomes particularly clear in his Christmas sermon in which the lowly status not only of the shepherds, but also of Mary and Joseph, becomes a metaphor for God's use of and concern for the poor and downtrodden.[140] This same point is emphasized again in 'A Practicable Report to Those at Zwickau': 'But He reveals his secrets

---

[133] Owst, pp. 287–8.

[134] 'Ein tzeitlang geschwigner Christlicher Brůder,' Köhler *et al.*, F. 574, #1477, Diii.

[135] Ibid., F(b).

[136] Ibid., Biii(b). See Owst, pp. 319–31 for a discussion of the vices traditionally attributed to the nobility.

[137] 'Ein tzeitlang geschwigner Christliche Brůder,' Köhler *et al.*, E(b).

[138] Ibid., Diii(c). This proverb also appears in the fourteenth-century *Summa Predicantium* of the English Dominican John Bromyard. See Owst, pp. 302–3.

[139] Packull, p. 272.

[140] 'Eyn lieplicher Sermon,' Köhler *et al.*, F 1198, #3018, Aiii; B(b).

only to the little [people], that is the simple, as He has demonstrated among you.'[141]

Rot-Locher's scolding of the powerful could, at times, lead him dangerously close to open defiance of the authorities and rejection of the established social order. In 'A Long-Time Silent Christian Brother,' he asks why one should continue to pay rents and taxes to such princes and lords.[142] Despite this rhetorical flourish, however, he advises Karsthans, who appears already in this pamphlet, to hold his peace, for Christians are forbidden to oppose evil with force.[143]

Throughout his confession, Rot-Locher connected his activity as a Reformer with Wittenberg, and in one article he specifically distanced himself from Müntzer's teaching on baptism and maintained that he held to the Lutheran understanding of this sacrament.[144] Rot-Locher has left no systematic statement of his theology, and it is not my purpose here to attempt to systematize it and compare it with Luther's. However, on the crucial issue of the legitimacy of secular authority he claimed: 'His and the other Lutherans' opinion was to maintain themselves free and unbound to the spiritual authority, for there is no spiritual authority; [but] he knew well that there must be a secular authority.'[145] At the beginning of 'A Long-Time Silent Christian Brother,' he makes the same point, again in terms which indicate his adherence to Luther's teaching on obedience to secular authority:

> I am not [attacking] the power which is ordained for the frightening and punishment of evil people, for this also is sufficiently grounded in Scripture. Rather, [I am speaking] of the power, whether self-styled spiritual or secular, with which they wish to intrude into the administration of our Lord and Captain [Jesus Christ], to do violence to our consciences and freedom according to their pleasures.[146]

Throughout his early pamphlets, Rot-Locher maintained a consistent position on this matter. In 'A Practicable Report to Those at Zwickau,' he denounces the *Schwärmer* for their fleshly misunderstanding of Christian liberty and, in the process, appears to make a rueful assessment of the outcome of his own scolding of the secular authorities:

> So if one preaches to [the *Schwärmer*] how the spiritual authority and its adherents are not at all founded upon the holy, godly

---

141 'Müglichen bericht an die zů Zwickaw,' Köhler *et al.*, F 857, #2160, cii(b).
142 'Ein tzeitlang geschwigner Christlicher Brůder,' Köhler *et al.*, F 574, #1477, Diii(d).
143 Ibid., Cii, Diii. In the medieval homiletic tradition, the oppressed were encouraged to stand steadfast and await the day of judgement, Owst, pp. 296–302.
144 Schottenloher, 'Wer ist Johann Locher?' p. 128.
145 Ibid.
146 'Ein tzeitlang geschwigner Christlicher Brůder,' Köhler *et al.*, F 574, #1477, Aiii.

> Scriptures, and how secular authority is applied more for the
> tyranny of heathens than Christian protection of the poor, then
> these wild Christians, becoming unreasonable, want to give nothing
> more to the clergy and wish no longer to be obedient to secular
> authority.[147]

If, he continues, the *Schwärmer* knew that this abuse of authority was
caused by God himself in his anger, they would be moved to compassion
rather than raving against it.[148] This work, too, contains a strong
warning against bloodshed.[149]

As has generally been noted, Rot-Locher's denunciation of the
influential becomes sharper in the later pamphlets. 'A Serious Understanding of Good and False Preachers' suggests that the prevailing
problems in society can be traced to the lack of unity among rulers on
issues of the Spirit and truth. Toward the end of this work, Rot-Locher
remarks with surprise that the princes and lords wish to aid the
unrighteous.[150] In 'A Woeful Missive of the Peasant Enemy to
Karsthans, his Confederate,' he returns to the characterization of secular
authority as heathen, and spiritual authority as antichristian, although
now they are mentioned together:

> They see the handwriting on the wall, that the pomp, pride and
> presumption of the *grossen Hansen* has little foundation and no
> better legitimacy than that of the heretical followers of the Whore
> of Babylon and her regiment of all Papists and persecutors of
> Christ.[151]

The tone becomes even sharper and the proximity of the two kingdoms
even closer in 'An Unusual Second Missive of the Peasant Enemy to
Karsthans':

> Therefore, most beloved brother, you have in haste the two
> kingdoms which the Devil has noted in his register, unless they are
> soon to be redeemed. The first you have noted through its heathen
> life and tyranny. The second, with which God wishes to have even
> less to do, is the pope's greedy, truly antichristian kingdom, and this
> is not fabricated, for all the signs appear among his followers.[152]

A chief source of frustration for Rot-Locher was obviously the alliance

---

[147] 'Müglichen bericht an die z$\overset{o}{u}$ Zwickaw,' Köhler *et al.*, F 857, #2160: Aiii(b).

[148] Ibid., Aiii(c).

[149] Ibid.

[150] 'Ernstlicher verstand guter und falscher Prediger,' Köhler *et al.*, F 583, #1517, Aiii(c), E (= Laube 2:978).

[151] Cited in Packull, p. 270. 'Ein Cläglicher Sendtbrieff des Bauernveyndts zu Karstenhansen seynem Pundtgnossen,' Köhler *et al.*, F 1044, #2637, Aiii (= Laube 2:965).

[152] 'Ein ungewöhnlicher zweiter Sendbrief des Bauernfeinds an Karsthans,' Laube and Seiffert, pp. 107–8.

between the emperor and pope and the attempts to enforce the Edict of Worms. In the second letter to Karsthans, his invective against Charles V is unprecedented.

> Oh, you poor Christian name, but what are you called? I am called: I Thirst After The Blood Of Men, to crucify again the God of heaven through his members; for this reason He has given me power and for this reason I am always described as an increaser of empire and have so many lands that I don't know how to rule them all and keep them in peace.[153]

However, Rot-Locher does not reserve his venom for the emperor or the rulers in Voigtland alone. Authorities throughout the secular hierarchy are accused of ruling according to their own whims rather than the precepts of Scripture.[154] Suggestions for peaceful reform offered to them 'go in one ear and out the other.'[155] In fact, the problem extends even to the councillors and assemblies which advise the lords.[156]

Despite this denunciation of the powerful, Rot-Locher continues to maintain the legitimacy of established secular authority and insists that the emperor must be given his due as outlined in Scripture.[157] On occasion he does raise the spectre of popular action against abuses of temporal power but, as we have seen, this tactic was not unusual among Reformation supporters then.[158] Elsewhere he stresses that the ban, not rebellion, is the Christian community's weapon against its enemies.[159] And much more prominent than threats of force are his appeals to Karsthans to lay aside his flail and await God's plan.[160]

Karl Schottenloher aside, the interpreters of Rot-Locher's pamphlets have noted his aversion to the use of force in the service of the Reformation. They emphasize rather the clear instances of social oppression outlined in detail by Rot-Locher in the second letter to Karsthans. Walter Zöllner sees in these the concerns of both the

---

[153] Ibid., p. 99.

[154] 'Ein Cläglicher Sendtbrieff des Bauernveyndts zu Karstenhansen seinem Pundtgnossen,' Köhler, *et al.*, F 1044, #2637, Aiii(*c*) (= Laube 2:966).

[155] Ibid., Aiii(d) (= Laube 2:967).

[156] 'Ein ungewöhnlicher zweiter Sendbrief des Bauernfeinds an Karsthans,' Laube and Seiffert, p. 100.

[157] Ibid., pp. 102–3: 'so lass ichs kaysers ambt und gab in seinen wirden, als vil die gschrift gibt und Got erlaubt hat.'

[158] Ibid., p. 107: 'Dann warlich brůder, es wirt sein nymmer also thun wie pissher, das spils ist zů vil, die stett nit weniger die baurn werden sein urtitz.' Packull, p. 272. See above, pp. 126–7.

[159] 'Ernstlicher verstand guter und falscher Prediger,' Köhler *et al.*, F 583, #1517, B–B(b) (= Laube 2:980).

[160] 'Ein Cläglicher Sendtbrieff des Bauernveyndts zu Karstenhansen seynem Pundtgnossen,' Köhler *et al.*, F 1044, #2637, B–Bii (= Laube 2:968–9); 'Ein ungewöhnlicher zweiter Sendbrief des Bauernfeinds an Karsthans,' Laube and Seiffert, p. 107.

peasants and city dwellers, although the bourgeois elements are predominant.[161] Werner Packull, on the other hand, stresses the proximity of these complaints to those contained in the peasant articles of 1525.[162] This similarity appears most clearly in Rot-Locher's charge that the peasants are prohibited from defending their crops against wild animals reserved for the sport and tables of the nobility.[163] Also denounced are the legal system, in which the poor are unable to obtain justice, the activities of the merchant monopolies, inflation, and tolls and duties, all of which endanger the livelihood of the poor.[164] Particular attention is paid to the activities of robber-barons and the general lack of peace and security in the land, which makes travel over even the shortest distance a dangerous undertaking.[165]

Packull has noted that Rot-Locher's overall vision of reformed society remains strikingly medieval.[166] While the vividness of Rot-Locher's description of the oppression of the poor suggests a very clear perception of, and concern with, existing social conditions, his catalogue of the elements of this oppression is neither as original nor specifically contemporary as assumed. In fact, most of his vignettes of social oppression had been commonplaces of medieval penance sermons for several centuries. Complaints against the effects of hunting on peasant crops appear in John Bromyard's fourteenth-century *Summa Predican-tium*. Denunciations of lawyers and the legal system and of the false practices of merchants and of those involved in regulating trade were even more commonplace.[167] Rot-Locher's debt to the medieval tradition is apparent throughout the letters to Karsthans, which, when viewed as a whole, are exhortations aimed primarily at the moral rather than the structural reform of Christendom. As prominent among the obstacles to reform, Rot-Locher identifies the loss of Christian unity.[168] The specific instances of the oppression of the poor are discussed at the end of the second letter to Karsthans, and it appears Rot-Locher intended them as

---

[161] Zöllner, p. 196.

[162] Packull, p. 271.

[163] Ibid., 'Ein ungewöhnlicher zweiter Sendbrief des Bauernfeinds an Karsthans,' Laube and Seiffert, p. 105.

[164] 'Ein ungewöhnlicher zweiter Sendbrief des Bauernfeinds an Karsthans,' Laube and Seiffert, pp. 104, 106, 107.

[165] Ibid., pp. 101, 106.

[166] Packull, pp. 271–2.

[167] Owst, pp. 317, 329, 338–49, 353–61.

[168] 'Ein ungewöhnlicher zweiter Sendbrief des Bauernfeinds an Karsthans,' Laube and Seiffert, pp. 105–6: 'Ainer spricht: Ich bin kayserisch, der ander ich bin endtchristisch, der dritt pfaltz-gräffisch, ainer ist fürstlich, der annder adelisch, ainer ist stettisch, der ander beurischs, wie dann all nation yren namen haben. Welliche sindt dann Christi? Da hört nyemant nicht von sagen. All unser thun unnd lassen ist yn die welt gebaut.'

a series of examples to highlight the preceding discussion. They are introduced by several quotations from classical and patristic sources, the most prominent of which is taken from Saint Bernard:

> Saint Bernard described the fellows masterfully in one place: You sit, he says, in secret councils in order to kill the innocent. You lay hidden snares to catch the poor. Then your right hand will be filled with gifts. Then the goods of the poor will be taken from them by force, as in war. Then the sinner is praised and the unrighteous blessed; you praise evil and do what should not be done.[169]

Behind the oppression of the poor, Rot-Locher sees the twin vices of pride and greed: 'What is the result and cause? The cursed money which one loves more than one's neighbour, . . . Oh, you cursed greed for honour and money, you destroy our limbs and lives, our love of our neighbour, and finally our eternal life.'[170] Gerald Owst has described these two vices as the 'burning problems of the hour' for late medieval moralists.[171] Rot-Locher's citation of Bernard reinforces the perception that he was working within the same tradition of pulpit jeremiad. When he turns his attention specifically to the nobility, the catalogue of vices grows. Their disunity and incessant quarrelling are traced to drunkenness and overweening pride.[172] Like the late medieval moralists, he contrasts the depravity of the contemporary knighthood with an ideal of a golden age of chivalry in the past.[173] In general, grasping pride prevents the true exercise of authority.[174] And the kingdom of Christ will replace this state of affairs with the re-establishment of brotherly love.[175]

---

[169] Ibid., p. 104.

[170] Ibid., p. 100.

[171] Owst, pp. 307–8.

[172] 'Ein ungewöhnlicher zweiter Sendbrief des Bauernfeinds an Karsthans,' Laube and Seiffert, p. 101: 'Wee ymer und ewigklich dem, der yn solichem hochmůt erstochen wirdt, das des merertheyls des verflůchten hellischen zů trinckens schuld ist, dann wo sie yetz zůsamen kummen, haben sie kain andre freüdt dann sauffen.'

[173] Ibid., p. 106: 'Dann lieber her Got man wayss wol wer adel ist; oder von wann der adel herkumbt, oder das sollich verordent wurden, die rauberey, morderey auffzůheben, die strassen frydlich zů halten, sich yn allen redlichen thatten dapffer erzaygten, das were adelisch, dann mit tugenden můss man den erheben.' See Owst, pp. 331–8 and Classen, pp. 106–7.

[174] 'Ein ungewöhnlicher zweiter Sendbrief des Bauernfeinds an Karsthans,' Laube and Seiffert, p. 103.

[175] 'Ein Cläglicher Sendtbrieff des Bauernveyndts zu Karstenhansen seynem Pundtgnossen,' Köhler et al., F 1044, #2637, Aiii(c)–Aiii(d): 'Christus wil alhie auch herr seyn / auch ein Reych haben darynñe die seynigen solen Regiern . . . was wirt dañ das hieig Reych Christi seyn? So er doch spricht sein Reych sey nit vō diser Welt? Also wirt es genant: zehalten die lieb gegen den negsten / das ist Christi / die letzte mainung und bevelch gewesen / und ein Newes gebot.' (= Laube 2:967).

The preceding is not an attempt to deny Packull's claim that Rot-Locher had 'become a spokesman for the Reformation of the common man' or that for him 'the Christian mandate carried social implications.'[176] His discussion of the evils so prominent in the society of his day indicates a very real awareness of the concerns of the peasantry. More importantly, there is lacking in the writings of Rot-Locher the criticism of the lower social orders which makes an appearance in the medieval homiletic literature.[177] But it is important to note that he turned to an established homiletic tradition to give voice to his social concerns. The context in which Rot-Locher made these points had changed from that of his medieval predecessors; complaints about the mighty in vernacular *Flugschriften* are a completely different enterprise than criticisms of them in sermons at court, whether in Latin or the vernacular. But the nature of this tradition suggests caution when interpreting Rot-Locher's more 'revolutionary' rhetoric. This rhetoric does not make him a spokesman, intentional or not, for the 'revolution of the common man.' His primary aim throughout his writings remained to effect a transformation in morals not in social structures. Furthermore, this transformation in morals he perceived to be fully in line with the aims of the Wittenberg Reformation. And Gastel's letter to Stephen Roth suggests that, at least prior to the appearance of the letters to Karsthans, Rot-Locher's activities were favourably regarded in Wittenberg.

While his identification of secular authority with the heathen empire appears to have fluctuated somewhat with his personal fortunes, throughout his writings Rot-Locher consistently identified the papacy and clergy as the Antichrist's empire. Behind the scolding of secular authority lies a more forceful damning of traditional spiritual authority and, as has been indicated, it is the perceived alliance of the two which encourages the sharpest language against the former. Rot-Locher is concerned, however, not with exposing the evils of the clergy so much as tracing their influence in society. Nonetheless, his scattered references to the antichristian empire reveal an anticlericalism as comprehensive as Kettenbach's, from which it was likely derived.[178] Furthermore, like Kettenbach, Rot-Locher integrated criticisms of the clergy derived from Reformation theology into more traditional critiques.

Interest in Rot-Locher's criticisms of secular authority and social

---

[176] Packull, p. 271.

[177] See Owst, pp. 361–70.

[178] Rot-Locher frequently made reference to Kettenbach and his *Flugschriften*. For example see 'Ein tzeitlang geschwigner Christlicher Bruder,' Köhler, *et al.*, F 574, #1477, Cii, Eiii; 'Ernstlicher verstand guter und falscher Prediger,' Köhler, *et al.*, F 982, #2483, Diii.

relations has generally obscured the extent of his anticlericalism. However, he himself indicates that the term *grossen Hansen* ('big Jacks') should be applied not only to the princes and nobles, but to the prelates as well (the lords of cloisters are mentioned specifically).[179] In fact, this term is especially fitting for the popes, false bishops and their followers.[180]

Central to Rot-Locher's attack on the clergy is the identification of the papacy with the Antichrist. Like Kettenbach, he repeats Luther's charge that the papists have stolen the freedom given by Christ and compel Christians to live as heathens.[181] He takes the doctrine of papal plenitude of power as an indication that the pope is the Antichrist and as an opportunity to identify him as a successor of Caiaphas.[182] The whole system of canon law is nothing more than a disguised attempt to steal German money and increase the power of the papal empire.[183] And Rot-Locher's debt to the medieval criticism of the exercise of secular authority by the episcopacy is clear in his treatment of the archbishop of Salzburg and the bishop of Trent:

> Therefore they refuse to come together. Why? Because one wants to sit, walk and stand before another, and if one is not raised up above another, they grumble and fume and endlessly bear jealousy and anger. Indeed, on one occasion, the better part of an Imperial Diet was wasted on such important matters as whether the armoured servant of Salzburg or the great councillor of Trent should sit before the other . . .[184]

It appears that this eclectic anticlerical vision was inherited from Kettenbach. Rot-Locher cites specifically Kettenbach's calculation of the numbers martyred under the papal empire.[185] More impressive is the

---

[179] 'Ein tzeitlang geschwigner Christlicher Brůder,' Köhler *et al.*, F 574, #1477, Biii(b).

[180] Ibid., Aiii(b)–Aiii(c): 'Das auch die grossen Hansen (Redt von dem schuldigen die Christum und die seynigen verfolgen) . . . Sunderlich die heylliglosen götzen zů Rom / und ander Niklas Bischoff mit sambt yren todtenpfeyffern / . . .'

[181] 'Ein tzeitlang geschwigner Christlicher Brůder,' Köhler *et al.*, F 574, #1477, Aiii(c): 'Urssach sy syndt eingefüert falsch Brůder / unnd neben eynkumen / züverkundtschafften unser freyheyt / die wir haben in Christo Jhesu / das sy uns gefangen haben / . . . Denn so sie Christen genendt wöllen werden unnd Heydnisch leben / warumb wöll wir uns dañ auch Heydnisch zů leben zwingen lassen /.'

[182] Ibid., Ciii(d)–D(b).

[183] 'Müglichen bericht an die zů Zwickaw,' Köhler *et al.*, F 857, #2160, Dii.

[184] 'Ein ungewöhnlicher zweiter Sendbrief des Bauernfeinds an Karsthans,' Laube and Seiffert, p. 102. Rot-Locher also used the example of Imperial Diets to indicate the heathen nature of secular authority in the first letter to Karsthans. See 'Ein Cläglicher Sendtbrieff des Bauernveyndts zu Karstenhansen seinem Pundtgnossen,' Köhler *et al.*, F 1044, #2637, Bii–Bii(b) (= Laube 2:970–1).

[185] 'Ein tzeitlang geschwigner Christlicher Brůder,' Köhler *et al.*, F 574, #1477, C(b)–Cii.

identification of the papacy with the Jewish priesthood in his Christmas sermon:

> But Isaiah says: 'He shall come from a royal stem.' But then how can he be poor? Yes, it is true, but hear that this royal race was so much in decline that it was no longer distinguished. The mother Mary was born of David's blood, but the papistical patriarchs, the priests, had usurped the dominion.[186]

Like Kettenbach, Rot-Locher does not limit his attack to the upper echelons of the ecclesiastical hierarchy. Here again reforming themes mix with more traditional criticisms of the rank and file clergy. Rot-Locher calls a curse upon all monks, nuns and priests who lead debauched lives yet claim to follow a path of greater perfection.[187] In this they, too, share a primary responsibility for the evils in society. On the one hand, their false piety encourages trust in works righteousness.[188] On the other hand, their laziness serves only to increase anger and sin among the people, and Rot-Locher lists monks and priests along with highwaymen, thieves and murderers as those whose lives provide examples most damaging to the whole community.[189] Christendom has the monks and priests above all to thank that God's anger has descended upon it.[190] Such unlearned, lazy, greedy dream preachers pose the greatest threat to Christendom because they lead it away from Christ.[191] In terminology reminiscent of the attacks on the Franciscans, he labels the clergy stomach preachers who exploit the cult of saints to fill their sacks.[192] Elsewhere, he denounces the sale of spiritual services as an outgrowth of clerical greed.[193]

While Kettenbach may have provided the model for a comprehensive denunciation of the clergy, Rot-Locher reveals his knowledge of Eberlin's works in his concern with the particular dangers posed by the cloistered. As a consequence, Rot-Locher's attacks on the mendicants are much more frequent and more completely integrated into his anticlerical vision than are Kettenbach's. He frequently notes that his charges levelled against the clergy as a whole are especially applicable to the monks. The widespread blasphemy in society is apparent above all

---

[186] 'Eyn lieplicher Sermon,' Köhler et al., F 1198, #3018, Bii.

[187] Ibid.

[188] 'Ein Gnadenreichs Privilegium,' Köhler et al., F 982, #2483, Diii.

[189] 'Ernstlicher verstand guter und falscher Prediger,' Köhler et al., F 583, #1517, Ciii(b); 'Ein tzeitlang geschwigner Christlicher Brůder,' Köhler et al., F 574, #1477, Diii(b).

[190] 'Ein tzeitlang geschwigner Christlicher Brůder,' Köhler et al., F 574, #1477, Biii.

[191] 'Ernstlicher verstand guter und falscher Prediger,' F 583, #1517, Ciii.

[192] Ibid., Biii.

[193] 'Müglichen bericht an die zů Zwickaw,' Köhler et al., F 857, #2160, C.

in the cloisters.[194] Christ's denunciation of the Pharisees and Sadducees is especially relevant for the 'damned sects of monks.'[195] Monks appear as the clerical counterparts of the lawyers; and the cloistered as a whole serve as the most glaring example of those trusting in works righteousness.[196]

Like Eberlin, Rot-Locher bemoans the plight of those in the cloisters and warns against entering monastic orders at the same time as he denounces the institution. In 'A Long-Time Silent, Christian Brother,' he laments the numbers locked away in cloisters and comments that much has already been written on this subject.[197] In terms strongly reminiscent of 'The Fifteen Confederates,' he scolds the parents of monks and nuns for their failure to trust in God and provides some insight into the hardships of the monastic life.[198]

Indeed, Rot-Locher adopted not only Eberlin's concern for the monks and nuns and critique of monasticism, but his antifraternalism as well. In 'A Long-Time Silent, Christian Brother' he indicated his intention to expose the Franciscans, much in the spirit of 'The Fifteen Confederates' and the campaign against the order:

> . . . and on a related issue, which Rot has shown to me, to disclose the evident [facts] concerning the beloved sons of the pope, namely the Franciscan Observants, what their idol through them and they, for their part, through him have brought to pass. In sum, of what their life consists.[199]

Karl Schottenloher identified the 'Franciscan idol' as Schatzgeyer.[200] A more likely candidate is St Francis himself. Unfortunately, Rot-Locher did not write his exposé on the Franciscans until 1524 and it is unclear whether or not he knew of the pamphlets being prepared against the order when he wrote 'A Long-Time Silent, Christian Brother.' He may

---

[194] 'Ein tzeitlang geschwigner Christlicher Brŭder,' Köhler et al., F 574, #1477, Biii(b).

[195] Ibid., Ciii.

[196] Ibid., Diii(c); 'Müglichen bericht an die zŭ Zwickaw,' Köhler et al., F 857, #2160, D.

[197] 'Ein tzeitlang geschwigner Christlicher Brŭder,' Köhler et al., F 574, #1477, Eiii. Fabian, p. 57 has pointed to the parallels between the discussions of monasticism in the works of Rot-Locher and Kettenbach. On this issue, at least, it is most likely that both men were indebted to Eberlin.

[198] 'Ein tzeitlang geschwigner Christliche Brŭder,' Köhler et al., F 574, #1477, Eii(b): 'Dunckt eüch nit / von wann es yetz kumbt / das man sovil frumer kinder / der welt gleych wider Gottes gebot / Ere uñ recht in die Clŏster hat gestossen / Wee eüch jr verzweyffelten vätter und muetter / jn den keyn Barmhertzigkeit nit ist noch erscheynt / . . . Auwe des yamers / So sy dañ zŭ jarn kummen und die anfechtungen nahnen / fragt man sye dañ / dürffen sy jr not nit klagen / Es stet die Ebtässin oder ander ein hauff an der winden / müessen zŭ horchen / damit sye sich nitt verredt.'

[199] Ibid., Aiii(b).

[200] Schottenloher, 'Wer ist Johann Locher?' p. 112 n. 6.

have known of the defences of Schwan, Lambert and Spelt for their
departures from the order and planned something of the same himself.

While no explicit denunciation of the Franciscans appears in Rot-
Locher's works until 'Article 15,' he revives some of Eberlin's charges
against the mendicants generally in his earlier writings. This is most
evident in 'A Grace-Filled Privilege' when he discusses the prayers and
fasts of the monks in terms of Matthew 6:

> The fourth and last are the dissembling and hypocritical people,
> regarded to some extent as great before the blind world, as the
> plump, fatted pigs in the cloisters and their followers, the feeders on
> saints, etc. Certainly, they do not wish to be like the others just
> discussed, and like the hypocrites in the temple [stand] openly
> before [all] eyes . . .[201]

In addition to their hypocrisy, Rot-Locher also denounces the monks'
substitution of formula prayers for useful work and their involvement of
the laity in this specious path to salvation.[202] These charges were
levelled against the mendicants by other polemicists, but are easily
applicable to the monks in general. However, as he continues, Rot-
Locher indicates that the mendicants are his primary targets:

> Still, the treacherous fools, the monks, do not trust Him, especially
> the fat-eaters, who nonetheless take upon themselves to raise not
> only themselves but also others with them up to heaven. Why? They
> run out into all the world, land and houses; they set themselves up
> with the appearance of a monkey in the marketplace with their
> masquerade, as when a conjuror will raise up a heavenly kingdom,
> [saying]: 'Give us meat, give us fish, in sum, everything on which we
> feast.' Indeed, a cudgel for the lazy fellows; drive them to the Devil,
> to work, and say freely that all who help them, who give cover to
> their heresy, are as pious as they.[203]

Elsewhere, in laying down the criteria for good preachers, Rot-Locher
refers to Eberlin's denunciations of mendicant preaching in the 'Fifth
Confederate.'[204]

The charges against the monks mentioned above reflect many of
Eberlin's prominent accusations against the Franciscans in 'The Fifteen
Confederates.' However, when one turns to 'Article 15,' the influence of
the anti-Franciscan pamphlets of 1523 is apparent. This is not surprising,
given the likelihood that Eberlin helped Rot-Locher to compose this
work. Like Eberlin, he identifies the Franciscans specifically with the

---

[201] 'Ein Gnadenreichs Privilegium,' Köhler et al., F 982, #2483, Aiii(d).

[202] Ibid.

[203] Ibid., Aiii(d)–B.

[204] 'Ernstlicher verstand guter und falscher Prediger,' Köhler et al., F 583, #1517, Ciii,
Ciii(c), Eii.

ravenous wolves of Matthew 7 and as the greatest enemies of the Gospel.[205] The basic thesis of this work, like that of Eberlin's 'Against the False Religious,' is that the Rule and life of the Friars Minor oppose the commands of God and Christian love.[206] Consequently, they can be neither evangelical nor apostolic as claimed.[207] Rot-Locher does not shrink from implicating St Francis himself and charges that the Rule was a fabrication dreamed up by the saint.[208]

The bulk of the remaining parts of 'Article 15' discuss specific aspects of the Franciscan Rule in terms, like the polemics of 1523, which combine Luther's critique of monasticism with more traditional criticisms of the mendicants. The opposition between the Rule and the Gospel provides the basis for a warning against entering the monastery and the rationale for leaving it.[209] The vows of chastity and poverty are attacked; the friars sport a false chastity to hide their unchaste lives, and exploit their false vow of poverty to fool not only the simple but the wise as well.[210] In connection with the latter vow, Rot-Locher attacks the mendicancy of the friars which, he claims, has no scriptural basis.[211] All of these characteristics of the life of the friars had been denounced by Luther. However, Rot-Locher also adopts the arguments of the anti-Franciscan polemicists on two important functions of the friars: preaching and hearing confessions. His discussion of preaching suggests strongly the influence of Eberlin on this work: 'That it is impossible that a barefoot monk can preach the clear Word of God from a pure and innocent heart to the common people.'[212]

Despite the comprehensiveness and virulence of his indictment of the first estate, Rot-Locher, too, remained true to distinct limits on anticlerical activity as laid down in Luther's 'A Faithful Admonition.' Nowhere in his writings did he call for direct action even against the antichristian kingdom. Indeed, his response to the activities of the *Schwärmer* in 'A Practicable Report to Those in Zwickau' indicates that he looked askance at any sort of anticlerical direct action.[213] Rather, throughout his writings, he continued to exhort secular authorities, albeit with increasingly abusive language, to dethrone the Antichrist.

---

[205] 'Artikel 15,' Köhler *et al.*, F 1078, #2726, A(b).
[206] Ibid.
[207] Ibid.
[208] Ibid.
[209] Ibid., Aiii.
[210] Ibid., A(b).
[211] Ibid.
[212] Ibid., Aii.
[213] See above, pp. 189–90.

And his upbraiding of the big Jacks stemmed from their failure to free themselves from the heretical followers of the Whore of Babylon.

As he claimed in his confession, Rot-Locher adhered to the Lutheran teaching on the two swords, at least as that teaching was understood in Zwickau. Secular authority was legitimate and divinely sanctioned; the spiritual authority of the papacy was antichristian and an abomination. However, this stance did not preclude the expectation of significant social renewal with the reawakening of the Gospel. Many of the reasons for Rot-Locher's commitment to the 'Reformation of the common man' must remain hidden in his personal psychology and experiences. However, he was certainly not alone in his expectations of the reform of society to be engendered by the reawakened Gospel. 'The Fifteen Confederates,' which Rot-Locher certainly knew, looked to a much more comprehensive reform than anything he suggested. Eberlin himself had only begun to see the Gospel divested of wide-reaching social implications after a period of study in Wittenberg in 1522. Rot-Locher, preaching reform in Zwickau in 1523 and 1524, still had not shorn the Gospel of its social implications, and it is tempting to regard his as the more common understanding of Luther's message prior to 1525.

CHAPTER EIGHT

'The agents of Satan'

The likelihood that Eberlin assisted Rot-Locher in the composition of 'Article 15' raises the issue of ongoing polemics against the Franciscans by former members of the order after 1523. With the exception of Eberlin, these men dropped the issue as quickly as they had picked it up. Eberlin himself continued to make disparaging remarks about members of the order and, on occasion, revived some of the earlier accusations against the group as a whole. These instances, however, become increasingly isolated in his writings after 1523. Less than a year after he had called St Francis 'a fool or an arch-rogue,' Eberlin appealed to the example of his piety:

> Saint Francis endeavoured to let no divine visitation pass over without fruit; he waited on it always, and, as he walked in rain or snow, if his heart was excited by God, he stood still and heard what his God spoke to him and did.[1]

As Eberlin's antifraternal and anticlerical polemics waned, his denunciation of those demanding a more rapid or complete Reformation waxed. Where he had earlier identified the mendicants as the greatest danger to the cause of the Gospel, he now turned this charge on the enthusiasts, the agents of Satan.

The anticlerical polemics of Eberlin's later works reflect not only the fruits of his continued study at Wittenberg, but also the experiences of an extremely active career as a wandering preacher. Already in the midst of the pamphlet war against the Franciscans, he departed Wittenberg for a preaching journey through south Germany. His first destination was probably Basel. Bernhard Riggenbach suggests that he may have taken part in the disputation held there by Oecolampadius on 30 August 1523. There is no direct evidence for this and more likely is Max Radlkofer's suggestion that, if he was present at the disputation, he was not a participant.[2] From Basel he went to Rheinfelden where he

---

[1] 'Wie sich ein Diener Gottes Worts in seinem Thun halten soll,' Enders, vol. 3, p. 196.

[2] Bernhard Riggenbach, *Johann Eberlin von Günzburg und sein Reformprogramm: Ein Beitrag zur Geschichte des sechszehnten Jahrhunderts* (Tübingen, 1874), pp. 151–2 and 156; Max Radlkofer, *Johann Eberlin von Günzburg und sein Vetter Hans Jakob Wehe von Leipheim* (Nördlingen, 1887), p. 124. Citing a letter from Rychard to Magenbuch dated 11 August 1523 which mentions Eberlin, Radlkofer suggests that he stopped in Ulm *en route* to Basel. However, there is no indication as to why he only passed through the city and later returned to preach. The best summary of Eberlin's itinerary during his travels in 1523 is Christian Peters' *Johann Eberlin von Günzburg ca. 1465–1533*.

remained four weeks, preaching in the church and leading Bible studies in private homes. Although well received by the local populace, his preaching led to investigations by officials from the imperial government in Ensisheim and deputations from the university and cathedral chapter of Basel.[3] The warmth with which Eberlin was received by the people of Rheinfelden is attested to by his dedication to them of a short catechetical work, 'A Splendid Mirror of the Christian Life.'[4]

Eberlin probably next returned to Basel, where he delivered the manuscript of 'A Splendid Mirror' to the printer Pamphilius Gengenbach. He then travelled in Alsace, eventually making his way to Strasbourg where he stayed with Johannes Schwan, who had taken over the press of Reinhard Beck.[5] Eberlin may also have visited Conrad Sam, the reforming preacher in Brackenheim and later Reformer of Ulm, who, he claims, was forced to take a 'vacation without pay' merely for entertaining him for three hours.[6] He then took to the road again, travelling extensively in the southwest before stopping in Rottenburg am Neckar, one of his old haunts from his Tübingen days. There is no indication of how long he remained in Rottenburg, although we do have the published version of a sermon he preached there in the house of Andreas Wendelstein.[7]

Eberlin must have arrived in Ulm by the middle of October and begun preaching immediately. The atmosphere heated up quickly and on 26 October he appealed to the city council for protection from his opponents and the opportunity to confront them in an organized disputation. On the same day, the Dominicans of Ulm, presumably led by Peter Nestler, requested that the council have Eberlin arrested. The

---

Franziskanische Reformer, Humanist und konservativer Reformator (Gütersloh, 1994) pp. 185–222.

[3] For Eberlin's description of his activities in Rheinfelden and Basel, see 'Mich wundert, dass kein Geld im Land ist,' Enders, vol. 3, pp. 156–8 (= Laube 2:1129–31) and 'Ein freundlich Zuschreiben an alle Stände deutscher Nation,' Enders, vol. 3, p. 128.

[4] 'Ein schöner Spiegel des christlichen Lebens,' Enders, vol. 3, pp. 97–109.

[5] Peters, pp. 192–205. Schwan printed a revised version of 'A Splendid Mirror' which Enders used as the basis for his critical edition of this work. Although earlier scholars had suspected that Gengenbach had published the original edition of this work, only recently has an exemplar of it been found; see Peters, pp. 192–3.

[6] 'Mich wundert,' Enders, vol. 3, pp. 167–8 (= Laube 2:1138). See Riggenbach, *Eberlin und sein Reformprogramm*, p. 190 and Radlkofer, p. 132.

[7] 'Predigt von zweierlei Reich, gehalten zu Rottenburg,' Enders, vol. 3, pp. 89–95. Riggenbach, *Eberlin und sein Reformprogramm*, p. 159, suggests that the publication was undertaken by an appreciative member of Eberlin's audience. Peters, p. 211, allows that the work was probably delivered to the press by a member of Eberlin's audience, but insists that the manuscript came from Eberlin's pen.

city council, however, refused to take sides, rejected both appeals and encouraged Eberlin to move on.[8]

Eberlin may then have visited his cousin Hans Jakob Wehe, the reforming priest in nearby Leipheim. Wehe's sermons had enjoyed considerable popularity locally, and among his listeners were citizens of Günzburg. The priest of Günzburg responded by having the town magistrates throw several of them into the tower.[9] An anonymous pamphlet entitled 'The Clocktower,' which champions the cause of Wehe and denounces the priest and magistrates of Günzburg, has been attributed to Eberlin, although the authenticity of Eberlin's authorship of this work has been a matter of ongoing debate for more than a century.[10] On the basis of the obscurity of the style of this work when compared to the clarity of Eberlin's writings, I am inclined to side with those who reject his authorship. This work also adds little to an understanding of Eberlin's anticlericalism and, consequently, will be left out of consideration.

Available evidence would indicate that Nuremberg was Eberlin's next destination. References in his next pamphlet, 'A Friendly Epistle to All Estates of the German Nation,' indicate that it was written there between 8 and 11 November.[11] Riggenbach argued that Eberlin was motivated to write the pamphlet on the occasion of the second Nuremberg *Reichstag*, planned to convene on 13 November.[12] Although accepting Riggenbach's suggestions, Radlkofer insisted that the intended readership was not the assembled representatives, but all Germans of every estate.[13] Eberlin's dedication of this work to Susanna Truchsassin of Rheinfelden and its primary concern with the activities and treatment of runaway monks and nuns and married clergy rather than with a comprehensive reform programme suggest that Radlkofer's identification of the intended audience is the correct one. Nonetheless, if Eberlin was awaiting the convening of the *Reichstag*, he probably

---

[8] *Stadtarchiv Ulm, Ratsprotokollbände der Jahre 1517–1555*, vol. 7, f. 380; Riggenbach, *Eberlin und sein Reformprogramm*, pp. 188–9; Radlkofer, pp. 136–7; Bernd Breitenbruch, *Predigt, Traktat und Flugschrift im Dienste der Ulmer Reformation* (Ulm, 1981), p. 22.

[9] Radlkofer, p. 137.

[10] 'Der Glockenthurm,' Enders, vol. 3, pp. 111–24 (= Laube 2:926–37). See also Riggenbach, *Eberlin und sein Reformprogramm*, pp. 194–6; Radlkofer, pp. 143–4; Enders, vol. 3, p. xxv; A. Leitzmann, 'Zu Eberlin von Günzburg,' *Beiträge zur Geschichte der deutschen Sprache und Literatur*, 43 (1918), p. 277; Martin Brecht, 'Johann Eberlin von Günzburg in Wittenberg 1522–1524,' *Wertheimer Jahrbuch*, 1983 (1985), p. 49 n. 8; Laube, p. 937; Peters, p. 242.

[11] 'Ein freundlich Zuschreiben an alle Stände deutscher Nation,' Enders, vol. 3, pp. 129–30 and 145.

[12] Riggenbach, *Eberlin und sein Reformprogramm*, p. 197.

[13] Radlkofer, p. 146 n. 37.

became impatient with its postponement until January 1524 and continued on to Wittenberg. En route he may have stopped in Coburg to visit Matias Vischer, whom he mentions in a later pamphlet.[14]

Eberlin, then, probably returned to Wittenberg in late autumn 1523 and wintered there. During this time he appears to have continued actively writing. 'How a Servant of God's Word Should Conduct Himself' is a comprehensive set of instructions for the aspiring evangelical preacher, dedicated to Eberlin's cousin Wehe. Mixed with advice on preaching, Bible study and upright conduct is the exhortation to Wehe to proceed cautiously in matters of reform, and, in a possible partial retraction of his own earlier writings, Eberlin indicates that he has adopted the mildness of Melanchthon. More so than in any of his earlier works, he indicates a concern for the activities of the *Schwärmer*, who, he claims, are more detrimental to the cause of the Gospel than the Papists.[15] Although probably not published until 1525, this work indicates the date of its completion as 24 March 1524.[16]

During this period Eberlin also appears to have devoted himself to a reflection on the experiences of his travels. 'I Wonder that there is no Money in the Land' revives the character of Psittacus and the social concerns of 'The Fifteen Confederates.' Modelled closely on Hutten's 'The Robbers,' this work purports to be the written transcript of the discussion between Psittacus and three south German commoners on the reason for the widespread poverty in a land so richly endowed by God.[17] Eberlin reiterates many of his earlier concerns, and the clergy comes in for no small part of the blame for this deplorable state of affairs. Nonetheless, Eberlin continues to show concern for the activities of the enthusiasts and this work contains his most detailed critique of the writing and publishing of books. Among those denounced as having foolish titles which mislead readers is 'The Fifteen Confederates.'[18]

Statements in this pamphlet suggest that it was written piecemeal throughout 1523 and early 1524, and a reference to Eberlin's marriage and preaching in Erfurt indicates that it must have been completed after he moved there in 1524.[19] Furthermore, the first edition of it appears to have been printed in Eilenberg and, as we have seen, Rot-Locher confessed that Eberlin wrote it in Erfurt.[20] When exactly he arrived

---

[14] 'Mich wundert,' Enders, vol. 3, p. 148 (= Laube 2:1123). Radlkofer, p. 178.

[15] 'Ein Diener Gottes Worts,' Enders, vol. 3, p. 211.

[16] Ibid., p. 184.

[17] Peters, pp. 222–36, indicates clearly the extent of Eberlin's debt to Hutten's dialogue.

[18] 'Mich wundert,' Enders, vol. 3, pp. 147–81 (= Laube 2:1123–48).

[19] 'Mich wundert,' Enders, p. 165 (= Laube 2:1136). See also Radlkofer, pp. 173–5, Enders, vol. 3, pp. xxvii–xxix, Laube 2:1148–9 and Peters, pp. 223–34.

[20] Enders, vol. 3, p. xxvi. See above, p. 187.

there, however, is unclear.[21] His next pamphlet, 'A Sermon in Erfurt on Prayer,' is the printed version of a sermon he said he preached in Erfurt on 1 May 1524.[22] Elsewhere he claimed that his preaching in Erfurt was the model of mildness and order, and this sermon continues to exhibit his concern with the activities of the enthusiasts and desire for slow, peaceful reform.[23] This mildness did not preclude upbraiding those who used the Gospel for licence:

> I came to Erfurt in Thuringia in 1524 and preached there an entire year. I said to each estate what Peter and Paul had prescribed for them. It was very odd what I taught: that being a Christian consisted of more than being abusive to priests, eating flesh, not offering, and not confessing. I also rebuked the gluttony, drunkenness, etc. of the assembled, so called Christian band.[24]

Eberlin's account of his activities in Erfurt suggests that he preached regularly there. There has been some suggestion that Luther recommended him for a clerical position, but Eberlin's own statements in 'I Wonder' indicate that he was still in search of fixed employment.[25] A contemporary of Eberlin states that he had been barred from the chancel at some point during his stay in Erfurt, but provides no reason for this.[26] Perhaps this explains Eberlin's statement that he had his sermon on prayer printed so that all could judge its contents.[27] To maintain himself and his wife during this period, Eberlin may also have contributed a translation of Psalm 114/115 and the introduction to Johannes Loersfelt's *Erfurt Enchiridion*.[28]

Prior to his departure from Erfurt in spring 1525, Eberlin claims to have played a prominent role in stilling unrest among the peasants assembled before the gates of the city and the townspeople within. He then performed the same service in the neighbouring town of Ilmenau and the territories of the counts of Arnstat.[29] He apparently next visited Ansbach, where, with the support of Georg Vogler, the over-secretary of

---

[21] Peters suggests April. For a summary of Eberlin's activities in Erfurt, see Peters, pp. 257–78.

[22] 'Predigt zu Erfurt, vom Gebet,' Enders, vol. 3, p. 238.

[23] 'Mich wundert,' Enders, vol. 3, p. 165 (= Laube 2:1136).

[24] 'Warnung an die Christen der Burgauischen Mark,' Enders, vol. 3, p. 282.

[25] 'Mich wundert,' Enders, vol. 3, p. 166 (= Laube 2:1136).

[26] Radlkofer, pp. 513–15.

[27] 'Predigt zu Erfurt,' Enders, vol. 3, p. 237.

[28] Konrad Ameln, 'Psalmus in excitu Israel verdeutscht,' *Jahrbuch für Liturgik und Hymnologie*, 28 (1984), pp. 65–7 and Wilhelm Lucke in WA, 35:18, n. 1; Peters, pp. 274–8.

[29] 'Warnung an die Christen der Burgauischen Mark,' Enders, vol. 3, pp. 282–7. Radlkofer, pp. 513–15 discovered confirmation of several of Eberlin's claims. For a summary of this period of Eberlin's life, see Peters, pp. 279–91.

the chancellery and later chancellor of the Margravate of Brandenburg-Ansbach-Kulmbach, he applied on 9 September for the position of vicar in Rothenburg ob der Tauber. His application was rejected by the conservative council.[30] Even before receiving the reply from Rothenburg, Eberlin went to visit Friedrich von Schwarzenberg in Hohenlandsburg.[31] It was likely that through this benefactor Eberlin received his first post as an evangelical pastor in the service of Duke Georg II of Wertheim.[32] In support of his appeal for a position he wrote the last of his works to be published, 'A Warning to the Christians of the Burgauischen Mark.' Ostensibly a warning to Eberlin's friends and relatives not to heed those attempting to foment renewed rebellion, this pamphlet attempts to disassociate the Gospel from the events of the preceding year and to justify Eberlin's own activities during the Peasants' War.[33]

Eberlin spent the next four years in the service of the Duke of Wertheim, first in the small parish of Remlingen and later in Wertheim itself. In the latter post he appears to have risen to prominence as a close advisor of the Duke on matters pertaining to the Reformation in the territory. Unpublished writings from this period indicate a strong interest in practical matters of reform and the establishment of a humanist pedagogical programme. Eberlin's influence and position came to an abrupt end on 17 April 1530 with the death of the Duke. Political pressures both within and outside the territory made his further activity there untenable and he accepted a new position in the parish of Leutershausen. However, conflicts and personalities from Wertheim followed him to the new post and the three years spent there were filled with bitter strife. Throughout these conflicts, Eberlin's health continually worsened and he died in early autumn 1533.[34]

---

[30] Th. Kolde, 'Zur Geschichte Eberlins von Günzburg,' BbKG, 1 (1895), p. 267; Aug. Schnizlein, 'Zu Johann Eberlins Berufung nach Rothenburg,' BbKG, 22 (1916), pp. 88–90.

[31] Ehmer, p. 56.

[32] Günther Heger, Johann Eberlin von Günzburg und seine Vorstellungen über eine Reform in Reich und Kirche (Berlin, 1985), p. 35.

[33] 'Warnung an die Christen der Burgauischen Mark,' Enders, vol. 3, pp. 253–87.

[34] On the last years of Eberlin's life see Karl Schornbaum, 'Leutershausen bei Beginn der Reformationszeit und das Ende Eberlins von Günzburg,' BbKG, 11 (1905), pp. 5–34 and 78–92; Kurt Stöckl, Untersuchungen zu Johann Eberlin von Günzburg, Phil. Diss. (Munich, 1952); Helmut Weidhase, Kunst und Sprache im Spiegel der reformatorischen und humanistischen Schriften Johann Eberlins von Günzburg, Phil. Diss. (Tübingen, 1967); Matthias Simon, 'Zur Geschichte der Kirchenbücher. Das Konfitentenregister Eberlins von Günzburg 1531 als Kommunikantenbuch,' ZbKG, 36 (1967), pp. 99–105; Ehmer, pp. 55–71; Eric Langguth, 'Einmutig in der neuen Lehre: Dr Johann Eberlin – Graf Michael II – Dr Andreas Hoffrichter. Der Wechsel im Wertheimer Pfarramt 1530,' Wertheimer Jahrbuch, 1983 (1985), pp. 73–102; Heger, pp. 34–42; A. Enzo Baldini, 'Uno Scritto di Johann Eberlin sull' Educazione di un Principe all' Indomani della Guerra dei Contadini,' in Studi Politici in Onore di Luigi Firpo, ed. Sylvia Rota Ghibaudi and Franco Barcia (Milan, 1990), vol. 1, pp. 431–79; Peters, pp. 292–314.

Throughout the pamphlets written after the campaign against the Franciscans, Eberlin's frequent references to the mildness of his own preaching are paralleled by a significant reduction in polemics against the clergy. In 'A Friendly Epistle to All Estates of the German Nation,' Eberlin cautions monks and nuns against hasty departure from their cloisters, much in the spirit of 'Against the Imprudent Departure.' Nonetheless, he continues to regard the essence of monasticism, the priesthood and the universities as inherently opposed to God.[35] 'A Splendid Mirror of the Christian Life' makes the same point on the basis of the laziness of the clergy and monks, who are identified as latter-day Pharisees much more dangerous than their predecessors.[36] Interestingly, in 'I Wonder' the anticlerical polemics again return to centre stage. The clergy share a major part of the blame for the impoverishment of the land according to this work. Eberlin cleverly unites the charges of clerical greed and sexual immorality by claiming that women succumb to the advances of the priests and monks in order to receive luxury items from them.[37] The clergy appear among the laziest and yet best-provisioned groups in society.[38] More fully developed here is the pun on *Pfaffen* and *Affen* to indicate that the priests are descended from apes.[39] In a passage obviously written before his travels, Eberlin suggests that the activities of Franz von Sickingen indicate that the nobility have begun to recognize this and no longer wish to tolerate such monkey

---

[35] 'Zuschreiben an alle Stände deutscher Nation,' Enders, vol. 3, p. 132: 'Der münchen, pfaffen, nunnen und hohen schulen wesen und stand ist so manigfaltig wider Got, das keyner so einfeltig ist, der die Biblia liset, er findet, wie ungötlich die stend seind, auch ynn menschlicher vernunfft so vil erkant wurt, das solich stend seind ein grewel der welt.'

[36] 'Ein schöner Spiegel,' Enders, vol. 3, p. 101: 'Im buch der geschöpfft im .iiij. capitel spricht Gott zů dem man. In dem schweyss deines angesichts solt du essen dein brot. . . . Folget aber, das pfaffheyt und kloster stånd wider Gott ist, darinn man zů ergerniss der anderen, und zů grosser unrůw und spitzfindigkeit müssig ist. . . . Von disem phariseischen Gottes dienst der tempel knecht weisst Gott nichts, als wenig er von dem tempel weisst. Sonderlich so die phariseer unserer zeit meer gebråchtlich und begirlich seind der menschen eer, dann die alten.'

[37] 'Mich wundert,' Enders, vol. 3, p. 159 (= Laube 2:1131–2).

[38] Ibid., p. 167: '. . . und sovil mussiggeher pfaffen, monch, nunnen, hochbuler, sprich ich, hochschuler und ander schutzen und bachanten. . . . Ist nit das ein gross wunderwerck, unnd das thon allein wir armen, wan man erst ansihet der reychen uberfluss, auch der pfaffen und der Clösterleuth, wilchs ytzlichs fur .vi. menschen genug hette und fur sich aussgibt, so find man gross reylichkeit gottis.' Eberlin goes into greater detail about how each of the groups within the clerical estate exploit money from the laity on pp. 176–8 (= Laube 2:1137–8, 1144–6).

[39] Ibid., p. 154: '. . . dan die affen haben vortzeitten erkeufft ein erhebung yres geschlechts und mehrung yres namens, und sein zwen buchstaben kommen zu yrem namen, P. und F., und werd ytzt genant Pfaffen, die affisch art hangt ynen noch an, . . . Die affen wolten sich gesellen zu den Fursten und adel, und durch sie erhöcht werden und ist ynen wol gelungen, als man sicht zu diser zeit' (= Laube 2:1127).

business.[40] Much of Eberlin's anticlericalism in this work can be explained by his use of Hutten's dialogue as a model. In addition, Max Radlkofer has suggested that in this work Eberlin retreats as narrator and simply voices the grievances of the commoners.[41] Certainly, the invective here is more coarse than in many of Eberlin's other pamphlets and it probably reflects opinions he heard voiced during his travels.

However, when Eberlin turns his attention to the Franciscans, his own voice reasserts itself. Both 'A Splendid Mirror of the Christian Life' and 'I Wonder' repeat the common charges against the mendicancy of the friars.[42] Beyond this, however, he develops a personal invective against members of the Franciscan Observants. The brothers in Kaisersberg are denounced for their opposition to the Gospel.[43] This introduces a lengthy discussion of Caspar Schatzgeyer, who appears as a good but misguided and intolerant man.[44] Eberlin provides a valuable insight into the origins of the pamphlet war of the preceding year in his discussion of Schatzgeyer's writings:

> This Schatzgeyer has written much about the free will, in praise of monkish begging, in praise of monastic vows, and about merits of the individual, so that our Lord God will need 600 acres of arable land to pay these holy people for their merits, . . .[45]

Eberlin also indicates how firmly the lines had been drawn when he denounces Conrad Pellican for writing the preface to Schatzgeyer's first pamphlet and having it printed, and Sebastian Münster for translating it into German.[46]

This outburst against his former brethren aside, the predominant theme in these pamphlets is concern with the activities of the *Schwärmer* rather than those of the clergy. The development of this concern suggests that it was occasioned both by Eberlin's continued contact with Wittenberg and by his experiences during his travels. In the first pamphlets written while he was *en route*, Eberlin does not concern himself with the activities of the enthusiasts. However, they soon appear in his discussion of the plight of runaway monks and nuns and married priests in 'A Friendly Epistle to All Estates of the German Nation.' At the beginning of this work, Eberlin marvels at the numbers of monks, nuns and priests who have accepted the Gospel and suffered for its

---

[40] Ibid.

[41] Radlkofer, p. 172.

[42] 'Ein schöner Spiegel,' Enders, vol. 3, p. 101. 'Mich wundert,' Enders, vol. 3, pp. 176–7 (= Laube 2:1145).

[43] 'Mich wundert,' Enders, vol. 3, pp. 169–70 (= Laube 2:1139).

[44] Ibid., p. 172 (= Laube 2:1141).

[45] Ibid., p. 173 (= Laube 2:1142).

[46] Ibid., pp. 172–3 (= Laube 2:1141).

sake.[47] In terms strongly reminiscent of 'Against the Imprudent Departure,' he cautions the monks, nuns and priests against acting too rashly but, on the other hand, reprimands those who persecute them for their change of status.[48] However, in contrast to the earlier work, the latter now include many 'so-called Evangelicals.'[49] At the end of the pamphlet he emphasizes the need for caution:

> ... many evil people are found in good callings; God may also keep many good people in evil callings, like the three youths in the furnace in Babylon, and there are still many good persons imprisoned in cloisters and the priesthood, waiting patiently until God will attend to them.[50]

After his return to Wittenberg, Eberlin developed this theme more fully. In his advice to evangelical preachers, he warns against those who see in the Gospel nothing more than railing against priests, monks and the conventions of the old church.[51] The pastor should be concerned with the inner transformation of his flock and not with such externals as leaving the cloister or priesthood.[52] In 'I Wonder,' Eberlin's warnings become more urgent and he claims that the enthusiasts pose a greater threat to the cause of the Gospel than the Papists who have been laid low.[53] In his criticism of writing books in this work, he identifies a new

---

[47] 'Zuschreiben an alle Stände deutscher Nation,' Enders, vol. 3, pp. 126–7.

[48] Ibid., pp. 135–6.

[49] Ibid., p. 129.

[50] Ibid., p. 137.

[51] 'Ein Diener Gottes Worts,' Enders, vol. 3, p. 205: 'So kome ich und mancher fischer daher, und nehmen uns an, wyr sind Lutherisch, odder Evangelisch, wie man sagt, und wollen nicht weniger gehalten seyn, denn sie gehallten werden, und on kunst, on zucht, on geystliche erfarung und on Christliche bescheydenheyt wollen wyr schellten die Pfaffheyt, Muncheyt, und alte gebräuche ...'; p. 209: 'Also fahen etliche an, und reytzen das volck widder Pfaffen und Münche, sagen yhr wessen sey böss und gottloss, yhre lere sey falsch, ...'

[52] Ibid., pp. 219–20: 'Wenn yhr mercken mugt, lieber Er vetter, das eyn mensch gefasset hat Gottes wort, solt yhr euch nicht fast bekümmern umb die veranderung seynes eusserlichen wessens und wandels halben, als etliche thun, die mit allem vleyss radten und treyben, die Pfaffen von yhren pfronden zu lassen, die Münch und Nonnen auss den Clöstern zugehen, und der gleychen eusserlichs dings mehr zu thun, als ob keyn heyl were, wo man nicht auch diss alles nicht alleyn ynnerlich, sondern auch eusserlich von sich abwürffe, ...'

[53] 'Mich wundert,' Enders, vol. 3, p. 164: 'Aber ytz fahet an herfur zu dringen was verborgen lag, so die untzucht so gross wurt, das wol geordnete gemut ein grawel darab haben, und so mann nit mehr gross ursach hat wider Papisten zu handeln, sie ligen schon darnider, aber der lossen Evangelischen (also genant) schwirmer gotlossigkeit und stolz erligt nit, so fahen sie an widereynander zu streben, die lossen verfolgen die guten prediger, und wan sie yres schwirmen halb gestrafft werden, auch auss des Luthers lere, dörffen sie sich auch furtragen uber den Luther und Melanchton, und uber andere Christliche lehrer, und sagenn, was geht mich Luther an et cetera. Ich hab so wol gottis geyst als ehr et cetera' (= Laube 2:1135).

idolatry which has supplanted the old and consists of nothing more than scolding and threatening priests, monks and universities.[54] With the approach and arrival of the Peasants' War these warnings intensify even more. In 'A Sermon in Erfurt on Prayer,' he maintains that the Devil is behind those who are concerned only with iconoclasm, abusing the clergy and violating fasts.[55] 'A Warning to the Christians of the Burgauischen Mark' clearly identifies these types as the agents of Satan.[56] In this work Eberlin avoids denouncing the clergy and, in fact, he casts himself as a defender of the cloistered and clergy during the disturbances in Erfurt.[57]

Aside from Eberlin, the only other propagandist among the former Franciscans later to deal specifically with monasticism was Francis Lambert. The last of the articles he defended at the 1526 Homberg Synod dealt with the nature of the monastic life and, according to Edmund Kurten, revived issues from his commentary on the Rule. The concern here is, however, with monasticism in general and Lambert concentrates more on the themes of Luther's 'Judgement on Monastic Vows' than the specifically antimendicant polemics.[58]

Given Eberlin's early concern with the mendicants and his prominence in the campaign against the Franciscans, it is hardly surprising that he would continue to cast the occasional barb in the direction of the friars. More noteworthy are his claims that the *Schwärmer* rather than the mendicants, or for that matter any other element of the first estate, pose the greatest danger to the Reformation. Undoubtedly, this emphasis on the activities of the enthusiasts stemmed in part from Eberlin's experiences during his travels and subsequently in Erfurt. However, it appears to reflect also the beginnings of proto-confessional

---

[54] Ibid., p. 163: 'Das ist ein newe abgötterey, dem gotis wort also frembd namen geben, und ist nit besser dan der vorig heilgen dienst, und Sophistische sprach in der lehre heilger geschrifft, unnd so man schier alle buchlin ausslieset, find man nicht dan schelten, fluchen, toben, schwirmen wider Mönch, Pfaffen, Hochschulen, als ob das Christenthumb daryn stunde' (= Laube 2:1134).

[55] 'Predigt zu Erfurt, vom Gebet,' Enders, vol. 3, p. 237: 'Der teuffel yst uns nit mynder uffsatzig dan yhnen, . . . were ain erlicher Christlicher bluts tropf yn uns, wir solten ernstlicher zu der sach thon. Sollichs thon aber stat nit yn bylden schenden, yn flaisch fressen, pfaffen schmähen u.'

[56] 'Warnung an die Christen der Burgauischen Mark,' Enders, vol. 3, p. 255: '. . . der sathan hat aussgesandt seyne postbotten under Gottis kinder (deren jhr auch send durch Christum) zů seen bösen samen under sie, anzünden ein verderblich feur, und alles under gůttem scheyn, . . .'; p. 266: 'Aber der teuffel hat (laider) fast gewunnen, auch auff diser seytten, so man yhe nit mehr will achten des Bapsthumbs, so richt er an ain bissigs, zankischs (und alss man sagt) gut knechtisch lesteren wider das Bapsthumb, . . .'

[57] Ibid., p. 286.

[58] See Kurten, pp. 72–3 and 116–38.

camps within the Reformation. Eberlin's warnings against the enthusiasts come to the fore most clearly in his writings of early 1524. At the
same time, Rot-Locher was explicitly distancing himself from the
activities of the *Schwärmer*. Although Eberlin speaks of the enthusiasts
only in general terms, in his last writings he no longer mentions
Karlstadt among the Reformers and begins to refer to Johannes
Bugenhagen in his place, again suggesting that the boundaries of
orthodoxy were being drawn more clearly in Wittenberg.[59] This
suggests a wider concern on the part of those associated with
Wittenberg that their movement was now imperilled more from the left
than the right.

---

[59] 'Ein Diener Gottes Worts,' Enders, vol. 3, p. 193; 'Warnung an die Christen der
Burgauischen Mark,' Enders, vol. 3, pp. 266–7.

Conclusion:
Antifraternalism and Reformation
anticlericalism

The 1523 broadside against the Franciscans was an affair of the moment, although Rot-Locher's 'Article 15' appears as a delayed volley. It was occasioned by Schatzgeyer's responses to Luther, particularly that defending monasticism, and his firmer action against those sympathetic to the new teaching within the order. But this fact should not diminish the importance of this event. Luther and his followers were not lashing out at an annoying but ineffectual opponent. In many important ways the friars remained in the early sixteenth century the spiritual and intellectual leaders of the Christian west which they had been since the fourteenth century. The anti-Franciscan campaign of 1523, then, was an integral part of the Reformation's repudiation of the central organs of the old church.

Despite the brief span of time in which the pamphlets against the Franciscans were written, their authors were able to develop a consistent and comprehensive denunciation of their former brethren. In prefatory letters to the works of Briesmann and Lambert, Luther claimed that the experiences of these authors as Franciscans qualified them especially to write against the order. But their attacks rested much less on their experiences as Franciscans than on characterizations of the friars as a whole developed during the medieval intra-clerical rivalries and adopted by the satirical literature of the later Middle Ages and Renaissance.[1] The consistency of themes developed in the pamphlets against the Francis-

---

[1] Robert Scribner, *For the Sake of the Simple Folk: Popular Propaganda for the German Reformation* (Cambridge, 1981), p. 243 has commented on evangelical propaganda as myth: 'There are two important transformations or shifts of coding in the signs used by evangelical propaganda. One is the transformation of connotation into denotation, that is, the secondary or implied significations of a term become its primary significations, and describe it exhaustively. For example, monks no longer denote a class of religious persons, who may have connotations of irreligious or immoral life, as in *The Abbot on the Ice*. They are now essentially an irreligious group, indeed, in *The Origins of the Monks* an anti-religious group.' Interestingly, from this perspective the 1523 polemicists stand closer to St Amour and Wyclif than to the medieval and Renaissance satirists, although there is no indication that they knew directly the works of the former group. Rather, the medieval and Reformation opponents of the friars were involved in much the same enterprise.

cans indicates that this was a concerted effort. The use made of these same themes in 'The Fifteen Confederates' suggests as well that Eberlin may have provided a model for a successful campaign against the friars. However, Eberlin's antifraternalism was only the most detailed manifestation of a much more general phenomenon. Hutten denounced the friars as agents of the papacy and Erasmus's satiric treatment of them is rooted firmly in the antimendicant literature of the Middle Ages. Luther himself had played off the traditional rivalries between the secular clergy and the friars in the 'Address to the Christian Nobility,' and he revived many of the central themes of the medieval antifraternal polemics in his 'Church Postil.'

The campaign of 1523 took the attack to a new level by applying specifically to the mendicants Luther's criticisms of monastic vows. Thus it integrated traditional antifraternal themes with Luther's novel criticism of an important element of the first estate. But this amounted to more than placing new wine in old skins. Rather, a symbiotic relationship was established between the two traditions of criticism. The biblical types traditionally associated with the friars, and the characterizations derived from them, clearly and effectively identified the Franciscans and other mendicants as anti-Christian, and set the stage for the detailed exposition of their opposition to the Gospel. The criticism of vows and the religious life derived from Luther's theology in turn reinforced and deepened the anti-Christian characterization of the friars.

Given the strength and vitality of the late medieval antifraternal tradition, it is hardly surprising that Eberlin, and later other former Franciscans, adopted elements from it. Rather, one is impressed by how quickly and completely Eberlin turned on the order to which he had earlier been so strongly committed. This suggests a strong sense of betrayal at the hands of those he expected to share his vision of reform. The earliest 'Confederates' indicate that Eberlin initially viewed the activities of both the humanists and the Reformers in terms of the medieval perception of reform as the removal of abuses. In this process he envisioned an important role for the 'reformed' clergy, and his anticlericalism in this period must be understood as a call to return the first estate to its ideals and proper functions. The recognition of the Observants as the true sons of Francis in 1517 probably raised hopes that they might lead the way in a wider reform of the Church. Certainly, statements by other members of the Franciscan Observance indicate that initially the writings of Luther, who was also a member of a recently reformed order, were favourably received. In 1521 the terms 'reform' and 'reformation' were hardly clear-cut.

By way of contrast, Eberlin first began to deal with the central themes of Reformation theology in the 'Fifteenth Confederate.' But, as he studied in Wittenberg, these themes quickly hedged out denunciations of clerical laxity and abuse as the central motifs in his pamphlets. Nonetheless, his works from the period of his first stay in Wittenberg continue to discuss the clergy, but turn to the more constructive task of defining the evangelical priesthood. Although he continues to denounce those who do not fit into this category, his tone softens considerably and he begins to relegate many of the distinguishing features of the clergy, which earlier had occasioned so much abuse from him, to matters of externals.

The shift in focus in Eberlin's pamphlets away from anticlericalism mirrors Luther's own attempts in 1522 and 1523 to disassociate the movement from growing anticlerical agitation, and his early attempts to begin to define a new evangelical clergy. The contrast between these activities and the renewed attacks on elements of the first estate in 1523 is striking. Equally impressive is Luther's role in calling forth the anti-Franciscan polemics. But the campaign against the Franciscans did not violate Luther's warnings against anticlerical agitation or undermine the new clergy. The pamphlets of 1523 remained within acceptable limits by relying on the power of the Word to lay low the friars – the most detailed were direct comparisons of the Franciscan Rule with the Gospel – rather than direct action against the foes of the Gospel. As traditional agents of the papacy and foes of episcopal and parochial authority, the friars had no place in an evangelical clerical order. And Schatzgeyer's activity indicated that the Franciscans remained hardened opponents of the Gospel. In 1523 anticlerical propaganda had a recognized tactical role in the spread of the Reformation.

However, the extent to which Luther's programme was successful beyond the walls of Wittenberg is less sure. The writings of Kettenbach and Rot-Locher indicate that warnings against direct anticlerical agitation were being heeded. Kettenbach's support for the Knights' Revolt assumed that Sickingen was a legitimate secular ruler who undertook reform of the church as Luther had requested. Rot-Locher's fulminations against the *Schwärmer* denounced over-hasty action against even the heretical followers of the Whore of Babylon. But both men continued to adhere to comprehensive anticlerical visions which saw the clergy as a whole opposed to the Gospel. Furthermore, these anticlerical visions were a key element in tying the Reformation to other 'less Lutheran' activities: for Kettenbach the Knights' Revolt and for Rot-Locher 'the Reformation of the common man.'

By 1524 matters had changed again as the social tumult leading up to the Peasants' War escalated. Things were clearly getting out of hand and lines had to be drawn more clearly between those advocating legitimate reform and the enthusiasts who were going too far. Certainly, the criteria for theological orthodoxy at Wittenberg had not yet been firmly established. But the replacement of Karlstadt's name with Bugenhagen's in Eberlin's writings, and Rot-Locher's attempts to distance himself from Müntzer in his confession, suggest that the boundaries separating those within the fold from those outside of it were beginning to be constructed. And the warnings against the activities of the *Schwärmer* in the writings of both Eberlin and Rot-Locher indicate that agitating against monks and priests clearly placed one outside the fold. The contrast between these warnings and earlier Reformation polemics is striking. In his last published work, Eberlin portrayed himself as a defender of monks, nuns and priests against the unbridled passions of the rabble during the Peasants' War. Five years earlier he had lamented the fact that there was not enough water in the Rhine to drown all the friars in Germany.

Bibliography

Primary sources

Barack, K.A. (ed.), *Des Teufels Netz. Satirisch-didaktisches Gedicht aus der ersten Hälfte des fünfzehnten Jahrhunderts* (Stuttgart, 1863; reprint edn, Amsterdam: Editions Rodopi, 1968)

Brant, Sebastian, *Das Narrenschiff*, ed. Manfred Lemmer. Neudrucke Deutscher Literaturwerke, n.s., vol. 5 (Tübingen: Max Niemeyer Verlag, 1962)

Brieger, Theodor (ed.), *Quellen und Forschungen zur Geschichte der Reformation*, Vol. 1 *Aleander und Luther 1521. Die vervollständigen Aleander Depeschen* (Gotha: Friedrich Andreas Perthes, 1884)

Briesmann, Johannes, 'Ad Gasparis Schatzgeyri plicas responsio pro Lutherano libello de Missis et Votis Monasticis' in Köhler *et al.*, F 374, #1042

Bucer, Martin, 'Gesprech Büechlin Neuw Karsthans' in *Sturmtruppen der Reformation. Ausgewählte Schriften der Jahre 1520–1525*, ed. Arnold E. Berger. Deutscher Literatur Sammlung Literarischer Kunst – und Kulturdenkmäler in Entwicklungsreihen. Reihe Reformation, vol. 2 (Leipzig: Philipp Reclam jun. Verlag, 1931)

Chaucer, Geoffrey, *Canterbury Tales*, ed. John Manly (New York: Henry Holt and Company, 1928)

Eberlin von Günzburg, Johann, 'Sendtbrieff an Pfarrer von Hohensynn. Doctor Martini Luthers Leer betreffennde. Oder eynem Jedē Prelatischen Pfarrer seynes vatterlandts,' in Alfred Götze, 'Ein Sendbrief Eberlins von Günzburg,' *Zeitschrift für deutsche Philologie*, 36 (1904), pp. 145–54

———— 'Der erste Bundesgenosse. Ein klägliche klag an dē christlichē Rŏmischen kayser Carolum, vō wegē Doctor Luthers und Ulrich von Hutten. Auch von wegen der Curtisanē und bǎttel münch. Das Kayserlich Maiestat sich nit lass sollich leüt verfüren' in Enders, vol. 1, pp. 1–14 (= Laube 2:709–20)

———— 'Der andere Bundesgenosse. Vom fasten der .xl. tag vor Osteren und andern, wie do mit so jǎmerlich wirt beschwǎrt das Christenlich volck' in Enders, vol. 1, pp. 15–22

———— 'Der III. Bundesgenosse. Ein vermanung aller christē das sie sich erbarmē uber die klosterfrawē' in Enders, vol. 1, pp. 23–33

———— 'Der IIII. Bundesgenosse. Von dem langē verdrüssigen geschrey, das die geistlichē Münch, Pfaffen und Nunnen die syben tag zeit heissen' in Enders, vol. 1, pp. 35–43

———— 'Der V. Bundesgenosse. Ein vermanung zu aller oberkeit Teütscher Nation, das sy den Predig stül oder Cantzel reformieren' in Enders, vol. 1, pp. 45–53

———— 'Der VI. Bundesgenosse. Erasmus von rotherodam ein fürst aller gelerten zů unseren zytē, schreibt jm̄ bůch genāt Encomion morias, vom predigen der bǎttel münch' in Enders, vol. 1, pp. 55–65

———— 'Der VII. Bundesgenosse. Dz lob der pfarrer' in Enders, vol. 1, pp. 67–78

———— 'Der VIII. Bundesgenosse. Warūb man herr Erasmus von Roterodam in Teütsche sprach transferiert. Warumb doctor Luther und herr Ulrich von Hutten teütsch schriben' in Enders, vol. 1, pp. 79–88

———— 'Der IX. Bundesgenosse. An alle christenliche oberkeit jn wǎltlichem und geystlichem stand Teütscher nation, ein klǎglich ernstlich klag aller gotsfǒrchtigē Münch Nunnen und pfaffen, dz man inen zů hilff kum̄ do mit sy vō irē endtchristenlichen by wonerē erlǒst werden' in Enders, vol. 1, pp. 89–105

———— 'Der X. Bundesgenosse. New statutē die Psitacus gebracht hat uss dem lād Wolfaria welche betrǎffendt reformierung geystlichen stand' in Enders, vol. 1, pp. 107–119 (= Laube 1:75–89)

———— 'Der XI. Bundesgenosse. Ein newe ordnǔg weltlich städts das Psitacus anzeigt hat in Wolfaria beschriben' in Enders, vol. 1, pp. 121–31 (= Laube 2:721–30)

———— 'Der XII. Bundesgenosse. Ein früntliche antwort aller gotzförchtigen, erberen, verstēdigē in Teütschem land auff die jǎmerliche klag der ordens leüt an sie gethon' in Enders, vol. 1, pp. 133–41

———— 'Der XIII. Bundesgenosse. Ein zuversichtig ermanung an die redlichen, erberen starcken und christlichen herren obern und underthon gemainer Eydgnoschafft (genant Schwitzer) das sy trewlich helffen handthaben Ewangelische leer und frumme christen' in Enders, vol. 1, pp. 143–51

———— 'Der XIIII. Bundesgenosse. Herr erasmus vō Rotherodam im bůch Encomion Morias, zeigt an dē spǒtlichen dienst so wir jetz bewysen den hailigen' in Enders, vol. 1, pp. 153–61

———— 'Der XV. Bundesgenosse. Alle und ietlichē christgelǒübigē menschen ein heylsame warnūg das sy sich hǔten vor nüwen schedlichen leren' in Enders, vol. 1, pp. 163–70

———— 'Letzter Bundesgenosse' in Enders, vol. 1, pp. 171–205 (= Laube 2:1038–50)

———— 'Wider die Schänder der Creaturen Gottes' in Enders, vol. 2, pp. 1–19

————— 'Wie gar gefährlich, so ein Priester kein Eheweib hat' in Enders, vol. 2, pp. 21–37

————— 'Vom Missbrauch christlicher Freiheit' in Enders, vol. 2, pp. 39–55

————— 'Klage der sieben frommen Pfaffen' in Enders, vol. 2, pp. 57–77

————— 'Trost der sieben frommen Pfaffen' in Enders, vol. 2, pp. 79–93

————— 'Schöne und klägliche Historie Bruder Jacobs Probst in Antwerpen' in Enders, vol. 2, pp. 95–117

————— 'Wider den unvorsichtigen Ausgang vieler Klosterleute' in Enders, vol. 2, pp. 119–36

————— 'Eine freundliche Vermahnung an die Christen zu Augsburg' in Enders, vol. 2, pp. 137–52

————— 'Ein Büchlein, worin auf drei Fragen geantwortet wird' in Enders, vol. 2, pp. 153–69

————— 'Ein kurzer schriftlicher Bericht an die Ulmer' in Enders, vol. 2, pp. 171–92

————— 'Die andere getreue Vermahnung an die Ulmer' in Enders, vol. 3, pp. 1–40

————— 'Wider die falschen Geistlichen, genannt die Barfüsser und Franziskaner' in Enders, vol. 3, pp. 41–88

————— 'Predigt von zweierlei Reich, gehalten zu Rottenburg' in Enders, vol. 3, pp. 89–95

————— 'Ein schöner Spiegel des christlichen Lebens' in Enders, vol. 3, pp. 97–109

————— 'Der Glockenthurm' in Enders, vol. 3, pp. 111–24 (= Laube 2:927–39)

————— 'Ein freundlich Zuschreiben an alle Stände deutscher Nation' in Enders, vol. 3, pp. 125–45

————— 'Mich wundert, dass kein Geld im Land ist' in Enders, vol. 3, pp. 147–81 (= Laube 2:1121–55)

————— 'Wie sich ein Diener Gottes Worts in seinem Thun halten soll' in Enders, vol. 3, pp. 183–232

————— 'Predigt zu Erfurt vom Gebet' in Enders, vol. 3, pp. 233–52

————— 'Warnung an die Christen der Burgauischen Mark' in Enders, vol. 3, pp. 253–87

Erasmus, Desiderius, *The Colloguies of Erasmus*, trans. Craig R. Thompson (Chicago and London: University of Chicago Press, 1965)

————— 'Praise of Folly' in *Collected Works of Erasmus*, ed. A.H.T Levi. Vol. 27: *Literary and Educational Writings*, vol. 5, trans. and annotated by Betty Radice (Toronto: University of Toronto Press, 1986) pp. 77–153

————— 'Antibarbarians' in *Collected Works of Erasmus*, ed. Craig R. Thompson. Vol. 23: *Literary and Educational Writings*, vol. 1:

Antibarbari / Parabolae, trans. and annotated by Margaret Mann Phillips (Toronto: University of Toronto Press, 1978) pp. 1–122

———— *Opera Omnia Desiderii Erasmi Roterdami*, ed. Clarence H. Miller. Ser. 4, vol. 3: *Moriae Encomium id est Stultitiae Laus* (Amsterdam and Oxford: North-Holland Publishing Company, 1979)

Förstemann, Karl Edward (ed.), *Album Academiae Vitebergensis* (old series) Vol. 1: *1502–1560* (Leipzig, 1841; reprint edn, Aalen: Scientia Verlag, 1976)

Güettel, Caspar, 'Vom Evangelischer / allerbestendigsten Warheyt dem Antichristischen klůgen hauffen erschröcklich / Und doch den einfeltigen schefflein Christi Jhesu fast freüdsam uñ tröstlich' in Köhler *et al.*, F 271, #772

Historische Kommission bei der Bayerischen Akademie der Wissenschaft (ed.), *Die Chroniken der deutschen Städte vom 14. bis ins 16. Jahrhundert*. Vol. 25: *Augsburg* (Leipzig: Salomon Hirzel, 1896; reprint edn, Göttingen: Vandenhoeck und Ruprecht, 1966)

Hochstratten, Jakob von, 'Defensorium fratrum mendicantium contra curatos illos qui privilegia fratrum iniuste impugnant' in Köhler *et al.*, F 1085, #2751

Hutten, Ulrich von, 'Huttenus ad Carolum' in Böcking, vol. 1, pp. 371–83

———— 'Ein Clagschrift des Hochberůmtem und Eernueste herrn Ulrichs vō Hutten gekrōnten Poeten uñ Orator an alle stend Deütscher nation' in Böcking, vol. 1, pp. 405–19

———— 'Clag und vormanung gegen dem gewalt des Bapsts' in Böcking, vol. 3, pp. 473–526

———— 'Vadiscus oder die Römische Dreyfaltigkeit' in Böcking, vol. 4, pp. 145–268

———— 'Vergleichung der Bǎpst satzung gegen der leer Christj Jesu' in Böcking, vol. 5, pp. 386–95

———— 'Ein trewe Warnung, Wie die bǎpst allwegen wider die Teutschen keyser gewest' in Böcking, vol. 5, pp. 364–86

Karlstadt, Andreas Bodenstein von, 'De coelibatu, monachatu et viduitate' in Köhler *et al.*, F 133, #361

———— 'Super coelibatu monachatu et viduitate axiomata' in Köhler *et al.*, F 125, #336

———— 'Antwort Andreas Bo. von Carolstad Doctor: geweicht wasser belangend' in Köhler *et al.*, F 92, #250

———— 'Predig oder homilien uber den prophetē. Malachiam gnant' in Köhler *et al.*, F 64, #166

———— 'Von gelubden unterrichtung' in Köhler *et al.*, F 134, #362

———— 'Von geweychtem Wasser und salzc' in Köhler *et al.*, F 46, #127

Kettenbach, Heinrich von, 'Eine nützliche Predigt zu allen Christen von dem Fasten und Feiern' in Clemen, pp. 5–26

———— 'Ein Sermon wider des Papst Küchenprediger zu Ulm' in Clemen, pp. 27–51

———— 'Ein Gespräch mit einem frommen Altmütterlein von Ulm' in Clemen, pp. 52–78 (= Laube 1:201–17)

———— 'Ein Sermon von der christlichen Kirche' in Clemen, pp. 79–103

———— 'Ein Sermon zu der löblichen Stadt Ulm zu einem Valete' in Clemen, pp. 104–25

———— 'Vergleichung der aller heiligsten Herrn und Vater des Papsts gegen Jesus' in Clemen, pp. 126–52 (= Laube 2:815–19)

———— 'Ein neu Apologia und Verantwortung Martini Luthers wider der Papisten Mordgeschrei' in Clemen, pp. 153–75 (= Laube 1:575–89)

———— 'Ein Practica practiciert aus der heiligen Bibel auf viel zukünftig Jahr' in Clemen, pp. 176–201 (= Laube 2:820–29)

———— 'Ein Vermahnung Junker Franzen von Sickingen zu seinem Heer' in Clemen, pp. 202–13

———— 'Eine Predigt auf den achten Sonntag nach dem Pfingsttag' in Clemen, pp. 214–25

Lambert, Francis, 'Ein Evangelische beschreibung über der Barfüsser Regel' in Köhler et al., F 378, #1050

———— 'Rationes propter quas Minoritarum conversationem habitumque reiecit' in Köhler et al., F 779, #1959

Luther, Martin, 'Resolutio Lutheriana super propositione sua tercia decima de potestate papae,' WA, 2:180–240

———— 'Von dem Papstthum zu Rom wider den hochberühmten Romanisten zu Leipzig,' WA, 6:277–324

———— 'An den christlichen Adel deutscher Nation von des christlichen Standes Besserung,' WA, 6:381–469

———— 'De captivitate Babylonica ecclesiae praeludium.' WA, 6:484–573

———— 'Von der Freiheit eines Christenmenschen,' WA, 7:12–38

———— 'Vom Missbrauch der Messe,' WA, 8:477–563

———— 'De votis monasticis Martini Lutheri iudicium,' WA, 8:564–669

———— 'Eyn treu vormanung Martini Luther tzu allen Christen. Sich tzu vorhuten fur auffruhr und Emporung,' WA, 8:670–87

———— 'Wider den falsch genannten geistlichen Stand des Papsts und der Bischöfe,' WA, 10.II:93–158

———— 'Acht Sermon D.M. Luthers,' WA, 10.III:1–64

———— 'Daß ein christliche Versammlung oder Gemeine Recht und Macht habe, alle Lehre zu urtheilen und Lehrer zu berufen, ein und abzusetzen, Grund und Ursach aus der Schrift,' WA, 11:401–16

————— *D. Martin Luthers Briefwechsel*, ed. Otto Clemen, vol. 2: *1520–1522* (Weimar: Hermann Böhlaus Nachfolger, 1931)

Mayer, Hermann (ed.), *Die Matrikel der Universität Freiburg i. Br.*, vol. 1 *1460–1656* (Freiburg i. Br.: Herdersche Verlagshandlung, 1907)

Mekum (Myconius), Friedericus, 'Eyn Freuntlich Ermanung und trŏstung aller freündt und liebhaber gottis wort yn der loblichen berŭmptē Pergkstadt S: Annapergk' in Köhler *et al.*, F 934, #2329

Melanchthon, Philip, 'Didymi Faventini adversus Thomam Placentinum pro Martino Luthero theologo oratio' in *Melanchthons Werke in Auswahl*, ed. Robert Stupperich, vol. 1: *Reformatorische Schriften*, pp. 56–140 (Gütersloh: C. Bertelsmann Verlag, 1951)

Pellican, Conrad, *Die Hauschronik Konrad Pellikans von Rufach. Ein Lebensbild aus der Reformationszeit*, ed. Theodor Vulpinus (Strasbourg: J.H. Ed. Heitz (Heitz u. Mündel), 1892)

Pölnitz, Götz Freiherr von (ed.), *Die Matrikel der Ludwig-Maximilians-Universität Ingolstadt-Landschut-München* (Munich: J. Lindauersche Universitätsbuchhandlung, 1937)

Rot-Locher, Johann, 'Confession' in Karl Schottenloher, 'Wer ist Johann Locher von München,' in *Der Münchner Buchdrucker Hans Schobser 1500–1530*, (Munich: Verlag der Münchner Drucke, 1925), pp. 127–8

————— 'Ein tzeitlang geschwigner Christlicher Bruder' in Köhler *et al.*, F 574, #1477

————— 'Ein lieplicher Sermon Colligiert an dem heyligē Christag' in Köhler *et al.*, F 1198, #3018

————— 'Vom Ave Maria Leuthen' in Köhler *et al.*, F 248, #689

————— 'Müglichen bericht an die zŭ Zwickau' in Köhler *et al.*, F 857, #2160

————— 'Ein Gnadenreichs Privilegium Christlicher freyheyt' in Köhler *et al.*, F 982, #2483

————— 'Ernstlicher verstand gutcr und falscher Prediger' in Köhler *et al.*, F 583, #1517 (= Laube 2:977–81)

————— 'Ein Cläglicher Sendtbrieff des Bauernveyndts zu Karstenhansen seynem Pundtgnossen' in Köhler *et al.*, F 1044, #2637 (= Laube 2:964–76)

————— 'Ein ungewöhnlicher zweiter Sendbrief des Bauernfeinds an Karsthans' in *Flugschriften der Bauernkriegszeit*, ed. Adolf Laube and Hans-Werner Seiffert (Berlin: Akademie-Verlag, 1975), pp. 99–108

————— 'Artikel 15' in Köhler *et al.*, F 1078, #2726

Schwan, Johannes, 'Ein kurtzer begriff des Erschrocklichē stands der munch / . . .' in Köhler *et al.*, F 208, #593

————— 'Ein Sendbriff Johannis Schwan. Darinne er anzeigt ausz der Bibel und Schryfft warūb er Barfusser orden des er etwan ym kloster zŭ Bassell gewest verlassen' in Köhler *et al.*, F 1186, #2980

Spelt, Heinrich, 'Ain ware Declaration oder Erklãrung der Profession /
Gelübten uñ leben / So die gemalten / falschen / Gaystlichenn / wider
alle Ewangelische freyhayt Und Christliche lyeb / thũn' in Köhler *et
al.*, F 47, #131

Stadtarchiv Ulm, *Ratsprotokollbände der Jahre 1517–1555*, vol. 7

———— *Ratsdekrete in Sachen der Reformation, 1522–1568*

———— *Rychard, Nr. 1–2: Briefwechsel Wolfgang Rychards*, (transcript by M. Georg Veesenmeyer, 1823)

———— *Brost, Nr. 6–8 and 16: Untersuchungen zum Briefwechsel
Wolfgang Rychards*

———— *Predigten und Schriften der Franziskanermönche Heinrich von
Kettenbach und Eberlin von Günzburg*

———— *Ulmische hauss Chronic, Worinnen enthalten ist Der Stadt
Ulm Anfang, Ursprung und Continuation, samt denkwürdigen
Sachen und Geschichten, Aemtern, auch andern schönen Mercken
und Gebauen. Die sich da selbst befinden, wie sie angefangen und in
das Merck gesetzt worden*

Valla, Lorenzo, 'The Profession of the Religious' in Olga Zorzi Pugliese
(ed. and trans.), *'The Profession of the Religious' and the principal
arguments from 'The Falsely-Believed and Forged Donation of
Constantine'* (Toronto: Centre for Reformation and Renaissance
Studies, 1985), pp. 17–61

Voyt, Joan, 'Eyn Sermon võ Newen Jare, durch Joan Voyt gepredigt zu
Weymar yn Parfusser Closter, Darumb er als ein ketzer von den
selben seinen Brudern geacht, und mit vil verfolgung veriagt' in
Köhler *et al.*, F 934, #2330

Wackernagel, Hans Georg (ed.), *Die Matrikel der Universität Basel.*
Vol. 1: *1460–1529* (Basel: Verlag der Universitätsbibliothek, 1951)

William of St Amour, 'De periculis Ecclesiae' in Ortwin Gratius,
Fasciculum rerum expetendarum, ed. Edward Brown (London, 1690;
reprint edn, Tucson, AZ: Audax Press, 1967), pp. 17–41

———— 'Sermo Magistri Wilhelmi de S. Amore, I' in *Fasciculum rerum
expetendarum*, pp. 43–7

Zwingli, Huldrych, *Huldreich Zwinglis Sämtliche Werke*, ed. Emil Egli,
Georg Finsler, Walter Köhler; vol. 7: *Zwinglis Briefwechsel*, vol. 1:
Die Briefe von 1510–1522 (Leipzig: Verlag von M. Heinsius
Nachfolger, 1911)

Secondary sources

Adamcyk, Roberta, *Die Flugschriften des Johann Eberlin von Günzburg*, Phil. Diss. (Universität Wien, 1981)

Ahrens, Hans-Herbert, *Die religiösen, nationalen und sozialen Gedanken Johann Eberlin von Günzburgs mit besonderer Berucksichtigung seiner anonymen Flugschriften*, Phil. Diss. (Universität Hamburg, 1939)

Ameln, Konrad, 'Psalmus In excitu Israel verdeutscht,' *Jahrbuch für Liturgik und Hymnologie*, 28 (1984), pp. 65–7

Arbesmann, Rudolph, *Der Augustinereremitenorden und der Beginn der humanistischen Bewegung* (Würzburg: Augustinus-Verlag, 1965)

Augustijn, Cornelis, 'Die Stellung der Humanisten zur Glaubensspaltung 1518–1530' in *Confessio Augustana und Confutatio. Der Augsburger Reichstag 1530 und die Einheit der Kirche*, ed. Erwin Iserloh (Münster: Aschendorffsche Verlagsbuchhandlung, 1980) pp. 36–48

Bagchi, David, ' "Eyn merklich underscheyd": Catholic Reactions to Luther's Doctrine of the Priesthood of All Believers' in *The Ministry: Clerical and Lay*. Studies in Church History, vol. 26, ed. W.J. Scheils and Diana Wood (Oxford: Basil Blackwell, 1989), pp. 155–65

———— *Luther's Earliest Opponents: Catholic Controversialists, 1518–1525* (Minneapolis: Fortress Press, 1991)

Baldini, A. Enzo, 'Uno Scritto di Johann Eberlin sull Educazione di un Principe all Indomani della Guerra dei Contadini' in *Studi Politici in Onore di Luigi Firpo*, ed. Sylvia Rota Ghibaudi and Franco Barcia (Milan: Franco Angeli, 1990), vol. 1, pp. 431–79

Barge, Hermann, 'Karlstadt, nicht Melanchthon der Verfasser der unter dem Namen des Bartholomäus Bernhardi von Feldkirch gehenden Schrift Apologia pro Bartholomeo Praeposito,' *ZKG*, 24 (1903), pp. 310–18

———— *Andreas Bodenstein von Karlstadt*, vol. 1: *Karlstadt und die Anfänge der Reformation* (2nd edn, Nieuwkoop: B. de Graaf, 1968)

Baron, Hans, 'Cicero and the Roman Civic Spirit in the Middle Ages and Early Renaissance,' *Bulletin of the John Rylands Library*, 22 (1938), pp. 73–97

———— 'Franciscan Poverty and Civic Wealth in Humanistic Thought,' *Speculum*, 13 (1938), pp. 1–37

Bartholemé, Annette, *La Réforme Dominicaine au XVe Siècle, en Alsace et dans l'Ensemble de la Province de Teutonie* (Strasbourg: Heitz & Co., 1931)

Bast, Robert J, '*Je geistlicher . . . je blinder*: Anticlericalism, the Law, and Social Ethics in Luther's Sermons on Matthew 22:34–41' in Dykema and Oberman, pp. 367–78

Baum, Johann Wilhelm, *Franz Lambert von Avignon* (Strasbourg and Paris: Treuttel und Würtz, 1840)

Baur, August, 'Rezension der Herausgabe von Eberlins Schriften (Bd. 1) durch Ludwig Enders,' *Göttingische Gelehrte Anzeigen*, 159 (1897), pp. 1–7

Bebermeyer, Gustav, 'Eberlin von Günzburg,' *Die Religion in Geschichte und Gegenwart*, vol. 2 (3rd edn, Tübingen: J.C.B. Mohr (Paul Siebeck), 1958), p. 297

Bell, Susan Groag, 'Johann Eberlin von Günzburg's Wolfaria: The First Protestant Utopia,' *Church History*, 36 (1967), pp. 122–39

Benz, Ernst, *Ecclesia Spiritualis: Kirchenidee und Geschichtstheologie der franziskanischer Reformation* (Darmstadt: Wissenschaftliche Buchgesellschaft, 1969)

Berg, Dieter (ed.), *Bettelorden und Stadt. Bettelorden und städtischer Leben in Mittelalter und in der Neuzeit* (Werl: Dietrich Coelde Verlag, 1992)

Berger, Arnold E., *Die Sturmtruppen der Reformation. Ausgewählte Schriften der Jahre 1520–1525* (Leipzig: Philipp Reclam jun. Verlag, 1931)

Blochwitz, Gottfried, 'Die antirömischen deutschen Flugschriften der frühen Reformationszeit (bis 1522) in ihrer religiössittlichen Eigenart,' *ARG*, 27 (1930), pp. 145–254

Brady, Thomas A. Jr, ' "You Hate Us Priests": Anticlericalism, Communalism and the Control of Women at Strasbourg in the Age of the Reformation' in Dykema and Oberman, pp. 167–207

Brändly, Willy, 'Johannes Lüthard der Mönch von Luzern,' *Zwingliana*, 8 (1946), pp. 305–41

Bräuer, Helmut, 'Zwickau zur Zeit Thomas Müntzers und des Bauernkrieges,' *Sächsische Heimatblätter*, 20 (5) (1974), pp. 193–223

Brecht, Martin, 'Die deutsche Ritterschaft und die Reformation,' *Ebenburg-Hefte*, 3 (1969), pp. 27–37

————— 'Johann Eberlin von Günzburg in Wittenberg 1522–1524,' *Wertheimer Jahrbuch*, 1983 (1985), pp. 47–54

————— (ed.), *Martin Luther und das Bischofsamt* (Stuttgart: Calwer Verlag, 1990)

————— 'Antiklerikalismus beim jungen Luther' in Dykema and Oberman, pp. 353–65

Breitenbruch, Bernd, *Predigt, Traktat und Flugschrift im Dienste der Ulmer Reformation*, Veroffentlichen der Statbibliothek Ulm, vol. 1 (Ulm: Anton H. Konrad Verlag, 1981)

Bubenheimer, Ulrich, 'Streit um das Bischofsamt in der Wittenberger Reformation 1521/22. Von der Auseinandersetzung mit den Bischofen um Priesterehen und den Ablaß in Halle zum Modell des evangelischen Gemeindebischofs. Teil 1,' *Zeitschrift der Savigny-Stiftung für Rechtsgeschichte*, Kan Abt. 73 (1987), pp. 155–209

Classen, Albrecht, 'Anticlericalism in Late Medieval German Verse' in Dykema and Oberman, pp. 91–114

Claus, Helmut, *Die Zwickauer Drucke des 16. Jahrhunderts* (Gotha: Forschungsbibliothek, 1985)

Clemen, Otto, 'Zwei Gutachten Franz Lamberts von Avignon,' *ZKG*, 22 (1901), pp. 129–43

————— 'Ein unbekannter Druck einer Schrift Eberlins von Günzburg,' *ZKG*, 28 (1907), pp. 41–4

Cohn, Henry J., 'Anticlericalism in the German Peasants' War 1525,' *Past and Present*, 83 (1979), pp. 3–31

Cole, Richard G., *Eberlin von Günzburg and the German Reformation*, PhD dissertation (Ohio State University, 1963)

————— 'The Pamphlet and Social Forces in the Reformation,' *Lutheran Quarterly*, 18 (1965), pp. 195–205

————— 'Law and Order in the Sixteenth Century: Eberlin von Günzburg and the Problem of Political Authority,' *Lutheran Quarterly* 23, (1971), pp. 251–6

————— 'The Dynamics of Printing in the Sixteenth Century' in *The Social History of the Reformation*, ed. Lawrence P. Buck and Jonathan W. Zophy (Columbus, Ohio: Ohio State University Press, 1972), pp. 93–105

————— 'The Reformation Pamphlet and Communication Processes' in *Flugschriften als Massenmedium der Reformationszeit. Beiträge zum Tübinger Symposion 1980*, ed. Hans-Joachim Köhler (Stuttgart: Ernst Klett Verlag, 1981), pp. 139–61

Coleman, Janet, 'FitzRalph's antimendicant "proposicio" and the Politics of the Papal Court at Avignon,' *Journal of Ecclesiastical History*, 35 (1984), pp. 376–90

Coulton, G.G., *Five Centuries of Religion*, vol. IV: *The Last Days of Medieval Monachism* (Cambridge: Cambridge University Press, 1950)

Davis, Kenneth, *Anabaptism and Asceticism: A Study in Intellectual Origins* (Scottdale, Pa. and Kitchener, Ont.: Herald Press, 1974)

Dawson, James Doyne, 'Richard FitzRalph and the Fourteenth-Century Poverty Controversies,' *Journal of Ecclesiastical History*, 34 (1983), pp. 315–44

Degler-Spengler, Brigitte, *Das Klarissenkloster Gnadenthal in Basel 1289–1529*, Quellen und Forschungen zur Basler Geschichte, vol. 3 (Basel: Kommissionsverlag Friedrich Reinhardt A G, 1969)

————— 'Observanten ausserhalb der Observanz. Die franziskanischen Reform sub ministris,' *ZKG*, 89 (1978), pp. 354–71

Deuerlein, Ernst, 'Johann Eberlin von Günzburg (um 1470 bis zum 1526)' in *Lebensbilder aus dem Bayerischen Schwaben*, ed. Götz

Freiherrn von Pölnitz (Munich: Max Hueber Verlag, 1956), vol. 5, pp. 70–92

———— 'Nachtrag zu Johann Eberlin von Günzburg' in *Lebensbilder zus dem Bayerischen Schwaben*, ed. Götz Freiherrn von Pölnitz (Munich: Max Hueber Verlag, 1958), vol. 6, p. 495

Dickens, A.G. and Tonkin, John, *The Reformation in Historical Thought* (Oxford: Basil Blackwell, 1985)

Dipple, Geoffrey, 'Johann Rot-Locher: Ein radikaler Reformator?', *Mennonitische Geschichtsblätter*, (1993), pp. 47–58

———— 'Humanists, Reformers and Anabaptists on Scholasticism and the Deterioration of the Church,' *Mennonite Quarterly Review*, 68 (1994), pp. 461–82

———— 'Uthred and the Friars: Apostolic Poverty and Clerical Dominion between FitzRalph and Wyclif,' *Traditio*, 49 (1994), pp. 235–58

———— 'Luther, Emser and the Development of Reformation Anticlericalism,' *ARG* (forthcoming, 1996)

———— 'Anti-Franciscanism in the Early Reformation: the Nature and Sources of Criticism,' *Franciscan Studies* (forthcoming, 1996)

Dohna, Lothar Graf zu, 'Von Ordensreform zur Reformation: Johann von Staupitz' in Elm (ed.) (1989), pp. 571–84

Döllinger, J., *Die Reformation, ihre innere Entwicklung und ihre Wirkungen*, vol. 1 (1846; reprint edn Frankfurt a.M.: Minerva, 1962)

Douie, Decima L., *The Nature and Effects of the Heresy of the Fraticelli* (Manchester: Manchester University Press, 1932; reprint edn, New York: AMS Press, 1978)

———— *The Conflict Between the Seculars and the Mendicants at the University of Paris in the Thirteenth Century* (London: The Aquin Press, 1954)

Drexhage-Leisebein, Susanne, 'Reformerisches Engagement städtischer Obrigkeit in der zweiten Hälfte des 15. Jahrhunderts. Die franziskanischen Reformbewegungen in der städtischen Kirchen- und Klosterpolitik am Beispiel ausgewählter Städte im Gebiet der Sächsischen Ordensprovinz' in Berg (ed.), *Bettelorden und Stadt*, pp. 209–34

Dufeil, M.M., *Guillaume de St Amour et la Polemique Universitaire, 1250–1259* (Paris: Editions A. et J. Picard, 1972)

Eckstein, Otto, *Die Reformschrift des sog. Oberrheinischen Revolutionärs. Versuch einer geschichtlichen und politischen Würdigung*, Phil. Diss. (Universität Leipzig, 1939)

Egli, E., 'Konrad Pellikan,' *Zwingliana*, 2 (1908), pp. 193–8

Ehmer, Hermann, 'Johann Eberlin von Günzburg in Wertheim,' *Wertheimer Jahrbuch*, 1983 (1985), pp. 55–71

Elm, Kaspar (ed.), *Stellung und Wirksamkeit der Bettelorden in der städtischen Gesellschaft*, Berliner historische Studien, vol. 3 (Berlin: Duncker und Humblot, 1981)

—————— (ed.), *Reformbemühungen und Observanzbestrebungen im spätmittelalterlichen Ordenswesen*, Berliner historische Studien, vol. 14 (Berlin: Duncker und Humblot, 1989)

—————— 'Reform- und Observanzbestrebungen im spätmittelalterlichen Ordenswesen. Ein Überblick' in Elm (ed.) (1989), pp. 3–19

—————— 'Die Franziskanerobservanz als Bildungsreform' in Hartmut Bookmann, Bernd Moeller and Karl Stackmann (eds), *Lebenslehren und Weltentwürfe im Übergang vom Mittelalter zur Neuzeit* (Göttingen: Vandenhoeck und Ruprecht, 1989), pp. 201–13

—————— 'Antiklerikalismus im deutschen Mittelalter' in Dykema and Oberman, pp. 3–18

Emery, Richard W., 'The Second Council of Lyons and the Mendicant Orders,' *The Catholic Historical Review*, 39 (1953), pp. 257–71

Fabian, Ernst, 'Die Einführung des Buchdrucks in Zwickau 1523,' *Mitteilungen des Altertumsvereins für Zwickau und Umgegend*, 6 (1899), pp. 41–128

Franck, J., 'Heinrich von Kettenbach,' *ADB*, vol. 15 (reprint edn, Berlin: Duncker und Humblot, 1969), pp. 676–8

Friedensburg, Walter, 'Beiträge zum Briefwechsel der Katholischen Gelehrten Deutschlands in Reformationszeitalter,' *ZKG*, 18 (1) (1897), pp. 106–31

Geiger, Gottfried, *Die Reichstadt Ulm vor der Reformation. Städtisches und kirchliches Leben am Ausgang des Mittelalters*, Forschungen zur Geschichte der Stadt Ulm, vol. 11 (Ulm, 1971)

—————— 'Die reformatorischen Initia Johann Eberlins von Günzburg nach seinem Flugschriften' in *Festgabe für Ernst Walter Zeeden zum 60. Gehurtstag am 14. Mai 1976*, ed. Horst Rabe, Hans-Georg Molitor and Hans-Christoph Rublach (Münster: Aschendorffssche Verlagsbuchhandlung, 1976), pp. 178–201

Genet, Jean Phillipe, 'The Dissemination of Manuscripts Relating to English Political Thought in the Fourteenth Century' in Michael Jones and Malcolm Vale, (eds), *England and Her Neighbours: Essays in Honour of Pierre Chaplais* (London: Hambledon Press, 1989), pp. 217–37

Goertz, Hans-Jürgen, *Pfaffenhass und gross Geschrei. Die reformatorischen Bewegungen in Deutschland 1517–1529* (Munich: C.H. Beck, 1987)

—————— ' "What a Tangled and Tenuous Mess the Clergy Is!" Clerical Anticlericalism in the Reformation Period' in Dykema and Oberman, pp. 499–519

———— *Antiklerikalismus und Reformation* (Göttingen: Vandenhoeck und Ruprecht, 1995)

Götze, Alfred, 'Ein Sendbrief Eberlins von Günzburg,' *Zeitschrift für deutsche Philologie*, 36 (1904), pp. 145–54

Graus, Frantisek, 'The Church and its Critics in Time of Crisis' in Dykema and Oberman, pp. 65–81

Gwynn, Aubrey, *The English Austin Friars in the Time of Wyclif* (London: Oxford University Press, 1940)

Hagen, Karl, *Deutschlands literarische und religiöse Verhältnisse im Reformationszeitalter*. Vol. 2: *Der Geist der Reformation und seine Gegensätze I* (Frankfurt a.M., 1868; reprint edn Aalen: Scientia Verlag, 1966)

Hamm, Berndt, 'Geistbegabte gegen Geistlose: Typen des pneumatalogischen Antiklerikalismus – zur Vielfalt der Luther-Rezeption in der frühen Reformationsbewegung' in Dykema and Oberman, pp 379–440

Hammer, G., 'Militia Franciscana seu militia Christi: Das neugefundene Protokoll einer Disputation der sächsischen Franziskaner mit Vertretern der Wittenberger theologischen Fakultät am 3. und 4. Oktober 1519,' *ARG*, 69 (1978), pp. 51–81 and 70 (1979), pp. 59–105

Hampe, Theodor, 'Archivalische Miszellen zur Nürnberger Literaturgeschichte,' *Mitteilungen des Vereins für Geschichte der Stadt Nürnberg*, 27 (1928), pp. 251–78

Hassencamp, F.W., *Franciscus Lambert von Avignon*, Leben und ausgewählte Schriften der Väter und Begründer der reformirten Kirche, part 9 (Elberfeld: R.L. Friderichs, 1860)

Hecker, Norbert, *Bettelorden und Bürgertum: Konflict und Kooperation in deutschen Städten des Spätmittelalters* (Frankfurt: Peter Lang, 1981)

Heger, Günther, *Johann Eberlin von Günzburg und seine Vortstellungen über eine Reform in Reich und Kirche*, Schriften zur Rechtsgeschichte, vol. 35 (Berlin: Duncker und Humblot, 1985)

Held, Paul, *Ulrich von Hutten. Seine religiös-geistige Auseinandersetzung mit Katholismus, Humanismus, Reformation* (Leipzig: W. Heinsius Nachfolger Eger & Sievers, 1928)

Hendrix, Scott H., 'Considering the Clergy's Side: A Multilateral View of Anticlericalism' in Dykema and Oberman, pp. 449–60

———— *Luther and the Papacy: Stages in a Reformation Conflict* (Philadelphia: Fortress Press, 1981)

Hillenbrand, Eugen, 'Die Observantenbewegung der deutschen Ordensprovinz der Dominikaner' in Elm (ed.) (1989), pp. 219–71

Hillerbrand, Hans J., 'The German Reformation and the Peasants' War' in *The Social History of the Reformation*, ed. Lawrence P. Buck and

Jonathan W. Zophy (Columbus, Ohio: Ohio State University Press, 1972), pp. 106–36

Hitchcock, William R., *The Background of the Knights' Revolt 1522–1523* (Berkeley and Los Angeles: University of California Press, 1958)

Holborn, Hajo, *Ulrich von Hutten and the German Reformation* (New Haven: Yale University Press; reprint edn, New York: Harper and Row, 1966)

Holzapfel, Heribert, *Handbuch der Geschichte des Franziskanerordens* (Freiburg i. Br.: Herdersche Verlagsbuchhandlung, 1909)

Hsia, R. Po-Chia, 'Anticlericalism in German Reformation Pamphlets: A Response' in Dykema and Oberman, pp. 491–8

Huber, Raphael M., *A Documented History of the Franciscan Order, 1182–1517* (Milwaukee: Nowiny Publishing Apostolate, Inc., 1944)

Huizinga, J., *The Waning of the Middle Ages* (New York: Doubleday, 1989)

Janssen, Johannes, *Geschichte des deutschen Volkes seit dem Ausgang des Mittelalters*, vol. 2: *Vom Beginn der politisch-kirchlichen Revolution bis zum Ausgang der sozialen Revolution von 1525* (Freiburg i. Br.: Herdersche Verlagsbuchhandlung, 1880); vol. 6: *Kunst und Volksliteratur bis zum Beginn des dreissigjährigen Krieges* (1888); vol. 8: *Volkswirtschafftliche, gesellschaftliche, und religios-sittliche Zustand. Herenwesen und Herenverfolgung bis zum Beginn des dreissigjährigen Krieges* (1894)

Jung, Wolfgang, 'Oekolampad an Hedio,' *Ebenburg-Hefte*, 5 (1971), pp. 87–94

Kalkoff, Paul, 'Die Prädikanten Rot-Locher, Eberlin und Kettenbach,' *ARG*, 25 (1928), pp. 128–50

Kaminsky, Howard, *A History of the Hussite Revolution* (Berkeley and Los Angeles: University of California Press, 1967)

Karant-Nunn, Susan, *Zwickau in Transition, 1500–1547: The Reformation as an Agent of Change* (Columbus, Ohio: Ohio State University Press, 1987)

——— 'Clerical Anticlericalism in the Early German Reformation: An Oxymoron?' in Dykema and Oberman, pp. 521–34

Kawerau, G., 'Heinrich von Kettenbach,' *Realencyklopädie für protestantische Theologie und Kirche*, vol. 10 (3rd edn Leipzig: J.C. Heinrichs'schen Buchhandlung 1901), pp. 265–8.

Keim, C. Th., *Die Reformation der Reichstadt Ulm. Ein Beitrag zur Schwäbischen und Deutschen Reformationsgeschichte* (Stuttgart: Chr. Belser'schen Buchhandlung, 1851)

Keller, Ludwig, 'Aus den Anfangsjahren der Reformation. Nachrichten über Hans Greifenbach, Hans Sacks, Hans Locher und Heinrich von

Kettenbach,' *Monatschefte der Comenius-Gesellschaft*, 8 (1899), pp. 176–85

Knowles, David, *Christian Monasticism* (Toronto: McGraw-Hill, 1969)
———— *The Religious Orders in England*, vol. 2: *The End of the Middle Ages* (Cambridge: Cambridge University Press, 1961); vol. 3: *The Tudor Age* (1961)

Köhler, Hans-Joachim, ' "Der Bauer wird witzig": Der Bauer in den Flugschriften der Reformationszeit' in *Zugänge zur bäuerlichen Reformation*, ed. Peter Blickle (Zurich: Chronos Verlag, 1987), pp. 187–218

Köhler, Walter E., *Die Quellen zu Luthers Schrift 'An den christlichen Adel deutscher Nation.' Ein Beitrag zum Verständnis dieser Schrift Luthers*, Phil. Diss. (Universität Heidelberg, 1895)

Kolde, Th., *Die deutsche Augustiner-Congregation und Johann von Staupitz* (Gotha: Friedrich Andreas Perthes, 1879)
———— 'Zur Geschichte Eberlins von Günzburg,' *BbKG*, 1 (1895), pp. 265–9
———— 'Eberlin von Günzburg,' *Realencyklopädie für protestantische Theologie und Kirche*, vol. 5 (3rd edn Leipzig: J.C. Heinrichs'sche Buchhandlung, 1898), pp. 122–5

Krodel, G. ' "Wider den Abgott zu Halle." Luthers Auseinandersetzung mit Albrecht von Mainz im Herbst 1521, das Luthermanuskript Add. C. 100, S. C. 28 660 der Bodleian Library, Oxford und Luthers Schrift "Wider den falsch genannten geistlichen Stand des Papstes und der Bischöfe" von Juli 1522. Ein Beitrag zur Lutherbiographie aus der Werkstatt der Amerikanischen Lutherausgabe,' *Lutherjahrbuch*, 33 (1966), pp. 9–87
———— 'Luther und das Bischofsamt nach seinem Buch "Wider den falsch genannten geistlichen Stand des Papstes und der Bischöfe" ' in Brecht (ed.) *Luther und das Bischofsamt*, pp. 27–65

Kunzelmann, Adalbero, *Geschichte der deutschen Augustiner-Eremiten*, vol. 5: *Die sächsische-thüringische Provinz und die sächsische Reformkongregation bis zum Untergang der Beiden* (Würzburg: Augustinus-Verlag, 1974)

Kurten, Edmund, *Franz Lambert von Avignon und Nikolaus Herborn in ihrer Stellung zum Ordensgedanken und zum Franziskanertum im Besonderen*, Reformationsgeschichtliche Studien und Texte, vol. 72 (Münster: Aschendorffsche Verlagsbuchhandlung, 1950)

Lambert, M.D., *Franciscan Poverty. The Doctrine of the Absolute Poverty of Christ and the Apostles in the Franciscan Order 1210– 1323* (London: SPCK, 1961)
———— 'The Franciscan Crisis under John XXII,' *Franciscan Studies*, 32 (1972), pp. 123–43

Langguth, Erich, 'Einmütig in der neuen Lehre: Dr Johann Eberlin – Graf Michael II. – Dr Andreas Hoffrichter. Der Wechsel im Wertheimer Pfarramt 1530,' *Wertheimer Jahrbuch*, 1983 (1985), pp. 73–102

Langguth, Otto, 'Eberlin von Günzburg. Kleine Beiträge aus dem Wertheimer Archiv,' *ARG*, 31 (1934), pp. 228–39 and 33 (1936), pp. 256–8

Laube, Adolf, 'Zur Rolle sozialökonomischer Fragen in frühreformatorischen Flugschriften' in *Flugschriften als Massenmedium der Reformationszeit. Beiträge zum Tübinger Symposion 1980*, ed. Hans-Joachim Köhler (Stuttgart: Ernst Klett Verlag, 1981), pp. 205–24

Leff, Gordon, 'The Apostolic Ideal in Later Medieval Ecclesiology,' *Journal of Theological Studies*, n.s. 18 (1967), pp. 58–82

Lippens, Hugolin, 'Le Doit Nouveau des Mendiants en Conflit avec le Doit Coutumier du Clergé Séculier, du Concile de Vienne à celui de Trente,' *Archivum Franciscanum Historicum*, 47 (1954), pp. 241–92

Leitzmann, A., 'Zu Eberlin von Günzburg,' *Beiträge zur Geschichte der deutschen Sprache und Literatur*, 43 (1918), pp. 275–8

Lohse, Bernhard, 'Die Kritik am Mönchtum bei Luther und Melanchthon' in *Luther und Melanchthon. Referate und Berichte des zweiten internationalen Kongresses für Lutherforschung Münster 8.–13. Aug. 1960*, ed. Vilmos Vajta (Göttingen: Vandenhoeck und Ruprecht, 1961), pp. 129–45

——— *Mönchtum und Reformation. Luthers Auseinandersetzung mit den Monchsideal des Mittelalters* (Göttingen: Vandenhoeck und Ruprecht, 1963)

Lucke, Wilhelm, *Die Entstehung der '15 Bundesgenossen' des Johann Eberlins von Günzburg*, Phil. Diss. (Universität Halle, 1902)

Lutz, Robert Hermann, *Wer war der gemeine Mann? Der dritte Stand in der Krise des Spätmittelalters* (Munich and Vienna: R. Oldenbourg Verlag, 1979)

Maeder, Kurt, *Die Via Media in der Schweizerischen Reformation: Studien zum Problem der Kontinuität im Zeitalter der Glaubenspaltung* (Zurich: Zwingli Verlag, 1970)

Mann, Jill, *Chaucer and Medieval Estates Satire: The Literature of Social Classes and the General Prologue to the Canterbury Tales* (Cambridge: Cambridge University Press, 1973)

Martin, Francis Xavier, 'The Augustinian Order on the Eve of the Reformation' in *Miscellanea Historiae Ecclesiasticae II* (Louvain: University of Louvain, 1967), pp. 71–104

——— 'The Augustinian Observant Movement' in Elm (ed.) (1989), pp. 325–45

Maurer, Justus, *Prediger im Bauernkrieg* (Stuttgart: Calwer Verlag, 1979)

Maurer, W., 'Lambert von Avignon und das Verfassungsideal der Reformatio ecclesiarum Hessiae von 1526,' *ZKG*, 48, n.s. 11. (1929), pp. 208–60

Maurer, Wilhelm, *Der junge Melanchthon zwischen Humanismus und Reformation*. Vol. 2: *Der Theologe* (Göttingen: Vandenhoeck und Ruprecht, 1969)

Moeller, Bernd, *Imperial Cities and the Reformation: Three Essays*, trans. H.C. Erik Midelfort and Mark U. Edwards, Jr (Philadelphia: Fortress Press, 1972; reprint edn, Durham, North Carolina: Labyrinth Press, 1982)

———— 'Klerus und Antiklerikalismus in Luthers Schrift *An den Christlichen Adel deutscher Nation von 1520*' in Dykema and Oberman, pp. 353–65

Moorman, John, *A History of the Franciscan Order From Its Origins To The Year 1517* (Oxford: Clarendon Press, 1968)

Moser, Andres, 'Franz Lamberts Reise durch die Schweiz im Jahre 1522,' *Zwingliana*, 10 (1957), pp. 467–71.

Müller, Karl, *Luther und Karlstadt; Stücke aus ihrem gegenseitigen Verhältnis* (Tübingen: J.C.B. Mohr, 1907)

Neidiger, Bernhard, *Mendikanten zwischen Ordensideal und städtischer Realität. Untersuchungen zum wirtschaftlichen Verhalten der Bettelorden in Basel* (Berlin: Duncker u. Humblot, 1981)

———— 'Liegenschaftsbesitz und Eigentumsrechte der Basler Bettelordenskonvente' in Elm (ed.) (1981), pp. 103–17

———— 'Stadtregiment und Klosterreform in Basel' in Elm (ed.) (1989), pp. 539–67

Nimmo, Duncan, 'Reform at the Council of Constance: The Franciscan Case.' *Studies in Church History*. Vol. 14: *Renaissance and Renewal in Christian History*, ed. Derek Baker (Oxford: Basil Blackwell, 1977), pp. 159–73

———— *Reform and Division in the Medieval Franciscan Order, From St Francis to the Foundation of the Capuchins* (Rome: Capuchin Historical Institute, 1987)

———— 'The Franciscan Regular Observance. The Culmination of Medieval Franciscan Reform' in Elm, (ed.) (1989), pp. 189–205

Nyhus, Paul 'The Observant Reform Movement in Southern Germany,' *Franciscan Studies*, 32 (10) (1972), pp. 154–67

———— 'Caspar Schatzgeyer and Conrad Pellican: The Triumph of Dissension in the Early Sixteenth Century,' *ARG*, 61 (1970), pp. 179–204

———— 'The Franciscans in South Germany, 1400–1530: Reform and

Revolution,' *Transactions of the American Philosophical Society*, n.s. 65 (8) (1975), pp. 1–43

———— 'The Franciscan Observant Reform in Germany' in Elm (ed.) (1989), pp. 207–17

Oberman, Heiko, 'The Gospel of Social Unrest' in *The German Peasants' War of 1525 – New Viewpoints*, ed. Bob Scribner and Gerhard Benecke (London: George Allen and Unwin, 1979), pp. 39–51

Oelschläger, Ulrich, 'Der Sendbrief Franz von Sickingens an seinen Verwandten Dieter von Handschuchsheim,' *Ebernburg-Hefte*, 4 (1970), pp. 71–85

Overfield, James, 'A New Look at the Reuchlin Affair,' *Studies in Medieval and Renaissance History*, 8 (1971), pp. 167–207

———— *Humanism and Scholasticism in Late Medieval Germany* (Princeton: Princeton University Press, 1984)

Owst, G.R., *Literature and Pulpit in Medieval England* (Oxford: Basil Blackwell, 1961)

Ozment, Steven, *The Reformation in the Cities. The Appeal of Protestantism to Sixteenth-Century Germany and Switzerland* (New Haven: Yale University Press, 1975)

———— 'The Social History of the Reformation: What can we learn from Pamphlets?' in *Flugschriften als Massenmedium der Reformationszeit. Beiträge zum Tübinger Symposion 1980*, ed. Hans Joachim Köhler (Stuttgart: Ernst Klett Verlag, 1981), pp. 171–203

Packull, Werner, 'The Image of the "Common Man" in the Early Pamphlets of the Reformation,' *Historical Reflections*, 12 (2) (1985), pp. 253–77

Pater, Calvin Augustine, *Karlstadt as the Father of the Baptist Movements: The Emergence of Lay Protestantism* (Toronto: University of Toronto Press, 1984)

Paulus, Nikolaus, *Die deutschen Dominikaner im Kampfe gegen Luther (1518–1563)*, Erläuterungen und Ergänzungen zu Janssens Geschichte des deutschen Volkes, vol. 4, books 1 and 2 (Freiburg: Herdersche Verlagsbuchhandlung, 1903)

———— *Kaspar Schatzgeyer, ein Vorkämpfer der katholischen Kirche gegen Luther in Süddeutschland*, Strassburger theologische Studien, vol. 3, book 1 (Strasbourg: Agentur von B. Herder, 1898)

Peters, Christian, *Johann Eberlin von Günzburg ca. 1465–1533. Franziskanischer Reformer, Humanist und konservativer Reformator* (Gütersloh: Gütersloher Verlagshaus, 1994)

Peuckert, Will-Erich, *Die Grosse Wende* (Hamburg, 1945; reprint edn Darmstadt: Wissenschaftliche Buchgesellschaft, 1966)

Press, Volker, 'Ein Ritter zwischen Rebellion und Reformation: Franz von Sickingen (1481–1523),' *Ebernburg-Hefte*, 17 (1983), pp. 151–77

Preus, James S., *Carlstadt's Ordinaciones and Luther's Liberty: A Study of the Wittenberg Movement 1521–1522*, Harvard Theological Studies, vol. 26 (Cambridge, Mass.: Harvard University Press, 1974)

Radlkofer, Max, *Johann Eberlin von Günzburg und sein Vetter Hans Jakob Wehe von Leipheim*. Nördlingen: Verlag der C.H. Beck'schen Buchhandlung, 1887

———— 'Die alteste Verdeutschung der Germania des Tacitus durch Johann Eberlin,' *Blätter für das Bayerische Gymnasial-schulwesen*, 23 (1887), pp. 1–16

Ranke, Leopold von, *History of the Reformation in Germany*, trans. Sarah Austin (London: George Routledge and Sons, 1905)

Rapp, Francis, 'Die Mendikanten und die Straßburger Gesellschaft am Ende des Mittelalters' in Elm (ed.) (1981), pp. 85–102

Riggenbach, Bernhard, *Johann Eberlin von Günzburg und sein Reformprogramm: Ein Beitrag zur Geschichte des sechszehnten Jahrhunderts* (Tübingen: Fr. Freus'sche Sortiments – Buchhandlung, 1874)

———— 'Eberlin von Günzburg' *ADB*, vol. 5 (Reprint edn, Berlin: Duncker und Humblot, 1968), pp. 575–6

Ritschl, Albrecht, *Geschichte des Pietismus*. Vol. 1: *Der Pietismus in der reformirten Kirche* (Bonn: Adolph Marcus, 1880)

———— 'Widertäufer und Franziskaner' *ZKG*, 6 (1884), pp. 499–502

Rosenfeld, Hellmut, 'Die Entwicklung der Ständesatire im Mittelalter' *Zeitschrift für Deutsche Philologie*, 71 (1951/52), pp. 196–207

Rublack, Hans-Christoph, 'Zur Rezeption von Luthers De Votis Monasticis Iudicium' in *Reformation and Revolution. Beiträge zum politischen Wandel und den sozialen Kräften am Beginn der Neuzeit. Festschrift für Rainer Wohlfeil zum 60. Geburtstag*, ed. Rainer Postel and Franklin Kopitzsch (Stuttgart: Franz Steiner Verlag, 1989), pp. 224–37

———— 'Anticlericalism in German Reformation Pamphlets' in Dykema and Oberman, pp. 461–89

Rummel, Erika, '*Et cum theologo bella poeta gerit*. The Conflict Between Humanists and Scholastics Revisited,' *Sixteenth Century Journal*, 23 (1992), pp. 713–26

Rupprich, Hans, *Das Zeitalter der Reformation* (Munich: C.H. Beck'sche Verlagsbuchhandlung, 1973)

Scase, Wendy, *'Piers Plowman' and the New Anticlericalism*, Cambridge Studies in Medieval Literature, vol. 4 (Cambridge: Cambridge University Press, 1989)

Schauder, Karlheinz, 'Martin Bucer und Franz von Sickingen,' *Ebernburg-Hefte*, 16 (1982), pp. 226–33

Scheible, Heinz, 'Reform, Reformation, Revolution. Grundsätze zur Beurteilung der Flugschriften,' *ARG*, 65 (1974), pp. 108–34

Schmidt, Johann Heinrich, *'Die 15 Bundesgenossen' des Johann Eberlin von Günzburg*, Phil. Diss. (Universität Leipzig, 1900)

Schnizlein, Aug., 'Zu Johann Eberlins Berufung nach Rothenburg,' *BbKG*, 22 (1916), pp. 88–90

Schornbaum, Karl, 'Leutershausen bei Beginn der Reformationszeit und das Ende Eberlins von Günzburg,' *BbKG*, 11 (1905), pp. 5–34, 78–92

Schottenloher, Karl, *Die Buchdruckertätigkeit Georg Erlingers in Bamberg von 1522 bis 1541 (1543). Ein Beitrag zur Geschichte der Reformationszeit* (Leipzig, 1907; reprint edn, Wiesbaden: Kraus Reprint – Otto Harrasowitz, 1969)

——— *Flugblatt und Zeitung* (Berlin: Richard Carl Schmidt and Co., 1922)

——— 'Buchdrucker und Buchführer in Kampf der Schwärmer und Wiedertäufer 1524–1568' in *Buch und Papier. Buchkundliche und Papiergeschichtliche Arbeiten* ed. Horst kunze (Leipzig: Otto Harrasowitz, 1949), pp. 90–113

——— 'Wer ist Johann Locher von München' in *Der Münchner Buchdrucker Hans Schobser 1500–1530* (Munich: Verlag der Münchner Drucke, 1925), pp. 109–42

Schulz, Hans, 'Die sogenannte Reformation Kaiser Sigismunds. Eine soziale Reformschrift des 15. Jahrhunderts,' *Monatshefte der Comenius-Gesellschaft*, 8 (1899), pp. 240–6

Schulze, Manfred, *'Onus ecclesiae*: Last der Kirche – Reformation der Kirche' in Dykema and Oberman, pp. 317–42

Scribner, Robert W., *For the Sake of Simple Folk: Popular Propaganda for the German Reformation* (Cambridge: Cambridge University Press, 1981)

——— 'Anticlericalism and the Reformation in Germany' in *Popular Culture and Popular Movements in Reformation Germany* (London: Hambledon Press, 1987), pp. 243–56

——— 'Anticlericalism and the Cities' in Dykema and Oberman, pp. 147–66

Seibt, Ferdinand, *Utopica: Modelle Totaler Sozialplanung* (Düsseldorf: Verlag L. Schwann, 1972)

Sessions, Kyle C., 'Christian Humanism and Freedom of a Christian: Johann Eberlin von Günzburg to the Peasants' in *The Social History of the Reformation*, ed. Lawrence P. Buck and Jonathan W. Zophy (Columbus, Ohio: Ohio State University Press, 1972), pp. 137–55

Sider, Ronald J., *Andreas Bodenstein von Karlstadt. The Development of his Thought 1517–1525*. Studies in Medieval and Reformation Thought, vol. 11 (Leiden: E.J. Brill, 1974)

Sikes, J.G., 'Jean de Pouilli and Peter de la Palu' *English Historical Review*, 49 (1934), pp. 219–40

Simon, Matthias, 'Zur Geschichte der Kirchenbücher. Das Konfitenten-register Eberlins von Günzburg 1531 als Kommunikantenbuch,' *ZbKG*, 36 (1967), pp. 99–105

Smahel, Frantisek, 'The Hussite Critique of the Clergy's Civil Dominion' in Dykema and Oberman, pp. 83–90

Smet, Joachim, 'Pre-Tridentine Reform in the Carmelite Order' in Elm (ed.) (1989), pp. 293–323

Specker, Hans Eugen and Weg, Gerhard (eds), *Die Einführung der Reformation in Ulm. Geschichte eines Bürgerentscheids*. Forschungen zur Geschichte der Stadt Ulm, vol.2 (Stuttgart: Kommissionsverlag W. Kohlhammer, 1981)

Stamm, Heinz-Meinolf, *Luthers Stellung zum Ordensleben* (Wiesbaden: Franz Steiner Verlag, 1980)

Steinmetz, David, *Luther and Staupitz: An Essay in the Intellectual Origins of the Protestant Reformation* (Durham, NC: Duke University Press, 1980)

Steinmetz, Max and Brendler, Gerhard (eds) *Weltwirkung der Reformation* (Berlin: VEB Deutscher Verlag der Wissenschaften, 1969)

Steitz, Heinrich, 'Franz von Sickingen und die reformatorische Bewegung,' *Ebernburg-Hefte*, 2 (1968), pp. 19–28

Stöckl, Kurt, *Untersuchungen zu Johann Eberlin von Günzburg*, Phil. Diss. (Universität München, 1952)

Strobel, G., 'Nachricht von Johann Eberlins von Günzburg Leben und Schriften,' *Literarisches Museum*, 1 (3) (Altdorf, 1778), pp. 363–85

Szittya, Penn, 'The Antifraternal Tradition in Middle English Literature,' *Speculum*, 52 (1977), pp. 287–313

———— *The Antifraternal Tradition in Medieval Literature* (Princeton: Princeton University Press, 1986)

Ulpts, Ingo, 'Zur Rolle der Mendikanten in städtischen Konflikten des Mittelalters. Ausgewählte Beispiele aus Bremen, Hamburg und Lübeck' in Berg (ed.) *Bettelorden und Stadt*, pp. 131–51

Van Engen, John, 'Late Medieval Anticlericalism: The Case of the New Devout' in Dykema and Oberman, pp. 19–52

———— 'Anticlericalism among the Lollards' in Dykema and Oberman, pp. 53–63

Veesenmeyer, Karl Gustav (ed.), 'Sebastian Fischers Chronik, besonders von Ulmischen Sachen,' *Mitteilungen des Vereins für Kunst und Alterthum in Ulm und Oberschwaben*, 5–8 (1896), pp. i–x, 1–278

Veesenmeyer, M. Georg., 'Nachricht vom Heinrich von Kettenbach, einem der ersten Ulmischen Reformatoren, und seinem Schriften' in *Beiträge zur Geschichte der Litteratur und Reformation*, ed. M. Georg Veesenmeyer (Ulm: Wohlerschen Buchhandlung, 1792), pp. 79–117

———— 'Verantwortung der Evangelischen Bürger zu Ulm gegen Peter Hutz, genannt Nestler' in *Beiträge zur Geschichte der Litteratur und Reformation*, pp. 117–126

———— 'Revocationsacte Martin Idelhausers von 1522, nebst einer Einleitung dazu, worinn die Nachrichten von diesem Kaplan am Münster zu Ulm gesammelt sind' in *Beiträge zur Geschichte der Litteratur und Reformation*, pp. 127–51

Vogler, Günter, 'Reformprogramm oder utopischer Entwurf? Gedanken zu Eberlin von Günzburgs "Wolfaria," ' *Jahrbuch für Geschichte des Feudalismus*, 3 (1979), pp. 219–32

———— Steinmetz, Max and Laube, Adolf, *Illustrierte Geschichte der deutschen frühbürgerlichen Revolution* (Berlin: Dietz Verlag, 1974)

Volz, Hans, 'Heinrich von Kettenbach' in *Die Religion in Geschichte und Gegenwart*, vol. 3 (3rd edn, Tübingen: J.C.B. Mohr (Paul Siebeck, 1959), p. 1256

———— 'Heinrich von Kettenbach,' *NDB*, vol. 8 (Berlin: Duncker und Humblot, 1969), pp. 412–13

Wackernagel, Rudolf, *Humanismus und Reformation in Basel* (Basel: Verlag von Helbing und Lichtenhahn, 1924)

Walsh, Katherine, 'Archbishop FitzRalph and the Friars at the Papal Curia in Avignon 1357–60,' *Traditio*, 31 (1975), pp. 233–75

———— *A Fourteenth-Century Scholar and Primate: Richard FitzRalph in Oxford, Avignon and Armagh* (Oxford: Clarendon Press, 1981)

Wehrli-Johns, Martina, 'Stellung und Wirksamkeit der Bettelorden in Zürich' in Elm (ed.) (1981), pp. 77–84

Weidhase, Helmut, *Kunst und Sprache im Spiegel der reformatorischen und humanistischen Schriften Johann Eberlins von Günzburg*, Phil. Diss. (Universität Tübingen, 1967)

Weiermann, Albrecht, *Nachrichten von Gelehrten, Künstlern und andern merkwürdigen Personen aus Ulm* (Ulm, 1798)

———— *Neue historisch-biographisch-artistische Nachrichten von Gelehrten und Künstlern auch alten und neuen adelichen und bürgerlichen Familien aus der vormaligen Reichstdt Ulm* (Ulm: Stettinischen Buchhandlung, 1829)

Werner, Julius, *Johann Eberlin von Günzburg. Ein reformatorisches Charakterbild aus Luthers Zeit* (2nd edn, Heidelberg: Carl Winter's Universitätsbuchhandlung, 1905)

Williams, Arnold, 'Chaucer and the Friars,' *Speculum*, 28 (1953), pp. 499–513

Winters, Roy Lutz, *Francis Lambert of Avignon: (1487–1530). A Study in Reformation Origins* (Philadelphia: The United Lutheran Publishing House, 1938)

Wolf, G., *Quellenkunde der deutschen Reformationsgeschichte*, vol. 2
(Reprint edn, Hildesheim: Georg Olms Verlagsbuchhandlung, 1965)
Wolff, Ernest, 'Eberlin von Günzburg,' *NDB*, vol. 4 (Berlin: Duncker
und Humblot, 1959), pp. 247–8
Wolfs, Servatius Petrus, 'Dominikanische Observanzbestrebungen: Die
Congregatio Hollandiae (1464–1517)' in Elm (ed.) (1989), pp. 273–92
Workman, Herbert, *John Wyclif: A Study of the English Medieval
Church* (Oxford: Clarendon Press, 1926; reprint edn, Hamden,
Conn.: Archon Books, 1966)
Wulkau, Curt, *Das kirchliche Ideal des Johann Eberlin von Günzburg*,
Phil. Diss. (Universität Halle-Wittenberg, 1922)
Ziegler, Walter, 'Reformation und Klosterauflösung. Ein ordens-
geschichtlicher Vergleich' in Elm (ed.) (1989), pp. 585–614.
Zoepfl, F., 'Eberlin von Günzburg,' *Lexikon für Theologie und Kirche*,
vol. 3 (Freiburg: Verlag Herder, 1959), col. 632
———— 'Heinrich von Kettenbach,' *Lexikon für Theologie und Kirche*,
vol. 5 (Freiburg: Herder Verlag, 1960), col. 193
Zöllner, Walter, 'Johann Locher – Ein Kämpfer der Bauernkriegsziet' in
Der deutsche Bauernkrieg und Thomas Müntzer, ed. Max Steinmetz,
Siegfried Hoyer and Hans Wermes (Leipzig: Karl-Marx-Universität,
1976), pp. 191–7

Index

HIEBERT LIBRARY

3 6877 00152 1516

BR
350
.E24
D57
1996

DATE DUE

Demco, Inc. 38-293